Perfect Wives, Other Women

Perfect Wives,

Other Women

ADULTERY AND INQUISITION IN EARLY MODERN SPAIN

Georgina Dopico Black

DUKE UNIVERSITY PRESS   Durham & London   2001

© 2001 Duke University Press   All rights reserved   Printed in the United States of America on acid-free paper ⊗   Designed by C. H. Westmoreland   Typeset in Monotype Fournier by Tseng Information Systems, Inc.   Library of Congress Cataloging-in-Publication Data appear on the last printed page of this book.

FOR JOSÉ AND LEONOR DOPICO

AND MARÍA PINTOS DEL VALLE

Contents

Acknowledgments

Perfect Wives' past life was as a Yale University dissertation, so it seems only fitting to first mark my debts to the two individuals who advised the text out of which this one grew and who have played no small part in its transformation into this book. Since the day I met him, more than a dozen years ago, Roberto González Echevarría has not stopped giving me books, both figuratively and literally. It is a privilege, then, to acknowledge the tremendous role he has played in the making of this one. Jacques Lezra, who first sent me in search of a definition in Covarrubias' *Tesoro* — of the word *murmullo*, as I recall it — deserves more thanks than I can possibly express for his always brilliant and generous advice. This project has benefited in countless ways from the *ruido manso* of his friendship for all these many years. James Fernández has not only read *Perfect Wives* in all its incarnations but has patiently nurtured each one. Like the Cervantine *amigo, gracioso y bien entendido,* he is always there when I need him most, asking the right questions and pointing me in the right directions, with extraordinary warmth and intelligence.

Having Reynolds Smith of Duke University Press as my editor has been a singular stroke of good fortune; I cannot thank him enough for his belief in this project and for all he has done in bringing it to its present form. I am grateful to my anonymous readers at Duke for their very helpful suggestions; to my copyeditor, Kim Hastings, for the elegance and rigor of her purple pencil; and to Sharon Parks Torian and Rebecca Johns-Danes for their fine work in preparing the manuscript.

This book could not have been completed without the intelligent and tireless help of John Charles, my research assistant in 1998–99, who proved not only a formidable sleuth of sources and translations but a superb translator and meticulous reader and indexer. To Colleen

Read and Abigail Pessin, my research assistants from 1997–98 and
1999–2000, respectively, my best thanks for their immense help on
this and other projects.

I owe a special debt of gratitude to María Rosa Menocal for her
support and her intellectual daring, and for the many lessons she has
taught me, many of which have cabalistically found their way into
these pages. The bright dialogue and friendship of Cristina Moreiras
buoyed my spirits through seemingly endless revisions and many a
gray New Haven afternoon. Josefina Ludmer and Giuseppe Mazzotta
were among the earliest readers of this manuscript; I am grateful
for their thoughtful responses and their warm support. The help and
encouragement offered at different stages of this project by Rolena
Adorno, Ramón and Felicitá Alba, Carlos Alonso, David Boruchoff,
María Mercedes Carrión, María Crocetti, Anne Cruz, Carlos Eire,
Jacinto Fombona, Sandra Guardo, Sylvia Molloy, Kathleen Ross, and
Alison Weber have contributed in untold ways to what follows. My
students and colleagues at Yale and NYU have helped me think through
and elaborate many of the ideas presented here.

I also wish to express my sincere gratitude to Samuel and Ronnie
Heyman, benefactors of the Heyman Prize, awarded to an earlier version of this manuscript in 1997. A Morse Fellowship from Yale University in 1998–99 allowed me to complete revisions. I am grateful
to the other fellows of the Whitney Humanities Center that same
year for their interest and collegiality. The A. Whitney Griswold Faculty Research Fund of Yale University provided generous research
grants.

My family, both Dopico and Black, deserve more thanks than I can
put into words for their unwavering support. I am especially grateful to my sister, Ana Dopico, for listening to inchoate paragraphs
at less than a moment's notice and responding with her intelligence
and impeccable style. Steve Black, who has lived with these perfect
and imperfect wives more intimately than anyone, makes possible the
various articulations of my life in more ways than he can ever imagine. Thanking him in this space seems both necessary and vastly insufficient. Christopher and Julia, who have grown up alongside this
demanding and capricious book-sibling, are a constant source of dis-

traction, joy, and wonder, and the very best reminders of what's really important.

Finally, let me mark my great debt to Hugo Rodríguez Vecchini. I am sorry he did not live to see the final version of a project that profited so much from his inimitable brilliance.

Preface

"Muger," writes Sebastián de Covarrubias in his 1611 *Tesoro de la lengua castellana o española*, "del nombre latino *mulier a mollitie (ut inquit Varro) immutata et detracta litera, quasi mollier, et proprie mulier dicitur quae virgo non est*. Muchas cosas se pudieran dezir en esta palabra; pero otros las dizen y con más libertad de lo que sería razón." [Woman. From the latin *mulier*, from *mollitie* (as Varro says) changing and taking away a letter, almost *mollier*, and properly *mulier* is said of (a woman) who is not a virgin. Many things could be said at this word; but others say them and with more liberty than is reasonable.] [1] In an unusual moment of verbal reticence, the prolix lexicographer-canon of Cuenca, adviser to the Inquisition and chaplain of the king, defines "woman" in only the scantest terms: as a word properly applied to nonvirgins and as a subject that might elicit so many words that he will leave the task of defining it to others, others destined, by definition, to overstep the bounds of reason and propriety. *Perfect Wives, Other Women* opens in the space of Covarrubias's uncomfortable silence. It seeks not to define *muger*—suggestively both "woman" and "wife" in Spanish— but to tell some of those "muchas cosas" that the term embodies, or that the bodies behind the term might somehow tell.

Throughout this book I argue that readings of the body—specifically, of the body of the wife in early modern Spain and America— are often entangled with questions of signification and interpretation and that these, in turn, are haunted by the body of an excluded Other that is an intrinsic part of the formation of a cultural Self. In Spain, as elsewhere in Europe, in the sixteenth and seventeenth centuries, the body and soul of the married woman became the site of an enormous amount of anxious inquiry, a site subject to the scrutiny of a remarkable array of gazes: inquisitors, theologians, religious reformers, confessors, poets, playwrights, and, not least among them, husbands. At one level, this book is about that inquiry, about the diverse readings that the bodies of perfect and imperfect wives (the "other women" of the book's title) elicited. But this book is also about the broader tensions that underwrite those readings. Throughout I suggest that the anxieties that attach to the body of the married woman in early modern Spain point beyond themselves: to larger cultural and political questions, to the difficulties and the dangers of reading, to the tenacious interconnectedness of gender, religion, race, nation, and interpretation.

The first chapter, "Visible Signs," concerns itself with the various tensions that animate readings of the wife's body and in a sense make possible its use as this sort of "transcoder" of other discourses and anxieties. In the pages that follow I trace a relation between the body of the married woman and two other bodies that were likewise sites of intense social, political, and religious debate and inquiry in sixteenth- and seventeenth-century Europe: the body of Christ in the eucharistic host, and the body—and soul—of the cultural Other. Each of these sites—these bodies—plays a central role in a particular sacrament of transformation: the marital sacrament that converts the body of the wife into "one flesh" with her husband's, the eucharistic sacrament that via transubstantiation converts bread and wine into the body and blood of Christ, and the baptismal sacrament that through the operation of words and water converts infidels—synonymous in early modern Spain with Muslims and Jews—or innocents—young children or Amerindians, to the extent that New World converts were considered "children in the faith"—into Christians, specifically Catholics. It is no coincidence that these three sacraments stood at the core of Counter Reformation debates (theologic, political, aesthetic) or that the violations associated with each of them fell under inquisitorial jurisdiction since all were, in one form or another, violations of Otherness: the adultery of the wife's body, the "real presence" of the body of Christ in the eucharistic host (the heart of the Protestant heresy), and false or ungenuine conversion—crypto-Judaism or crypto-Islam in the Old World, the "idolatrous" preservation of native beliefs and practices (idolatry being a biblical cognate for adultery) in the New.

I argue that the anxious inquiry that these bodies occasioned was largely the result of their status as sacramentally converted Others and of the fact that the transformations they ostensibly suffered were conceived as conversions in and of the flesh and thus subject to at times extreme literalization. What was at issue, precisely, was the efficacy of the sacrament; the mere suspicion (or worse, the realization) that these bodies might retain a vestigial trace—a lingering, inextirpable memory—of their former Otherness was potentially devastating. This, I suggest, helps explain the tremendous threat these traces represented: the irksome breadness of the consecrated host, the "tainted" blood of a *converso* or Morisco Other (at a moment when exclusion becomes overtly racialized through the institution of purity of blood statutes), or, finally, the will of the wife, manifested in the desires of her body. These remnants—all signed, moreover, by a problematic legibility—were deemed so threatening precisely because they could give the lie to the efficacy of the sacrament. Anxiety, however, is seldom far from desire: in this case, a kind of cultural desire to discover such traces of recidivism, insofar as the construction of a cultural or (proto) national identity is always dependent on the demarcation of Otherness. In some respects, then, this book is about the efficacy of different types of signs in early modern Spain, about the dangerous instabilities with which they are fraught, and about the relation between those signs vested with power and the disciplining and containment of different kinds of bodies, bodies that were marked by (or for) difference.

But if sacraments provide *Perfect Wives* a privileged point of entry into the relation between interpretation (the reading of signs) and authority (the control of bodies), there is, of course, quite a bit more to the story. Here we return to the question of the wife's will, to the thorny matter of her subjectivity. I argue that the extramarital anxieties that attach to the body of the married woman can also be explained in part by the particular form of the relation between "woman" and "wife" in the sixteenth and seventeenth centuries, by the ways in which the discursive category "wife" at once exceeds and is exceeded by that of "woman" (a geometry not so different perhaps from the overlap but noncoincidence between the two meanings of the Spanish term *muger*). I suggest that by and large—and there are important exceptions to be noted—marriage represented the most common means through which women were constituted as subjects in early modern Spain, so that it was often through the body of the "wife" (defined in legal, religious, and economic discourses) that "woman" (defined primarily in biological or anatomical terms) acquired a kind of subjectivity and, at the same time, became the object of a very specific kind of subjection. This passage, or this position — one that potentially places the wife alongside the husband — helps account for the inquisitorial hermeneutics deployed in the reading of her body (and by inquisitorial hermeneutics I refer not only to the specific reading practices of the Inquisition, practices that were very often exercised on bodies, but, more generally, to the strategies of surveillance and containment associated with the institutional presence of the Holy Office in early modern Spain).

If marriage, then, placed women's bodies at an uneasy juncture between subjectivity and surveillance, so too did two important textual phenomena of early modern Spain, each centrally preoccupied with reading and perfecting wives' bodies but never considered together: the explosion of conduct literature for married women in the sixteenth century (a phenomenon connected with the subjective possibility of "Renaissance self-fashioning") and of adultery–wife-murder plays in the seventeenth (dramas in which wives' bodies and desires become the subject of a kind of self-fulfilling inquisitorial surveillance). Beyond noting the complex web that entangles the perfect wives of the former with the imperfect ones of the latter (and the literary-historical-epistemological conditions within which these two types of works flourished), *Perfect Wives* proposes a relation between the "shift" in modes of perfecting wives that the transition from conduct literature to honor plays might suggest — a shift from what we might term a revisionist model that seeks to convert an imperfect wife into a perfect one through various forms of discipline to an exclusionary model that seeks to excise the imperfect wife's body from being a determinant of her husband's honor by the most radical means imaginable — and a similar (though by no means analogous) "shift" in modes of perfecting Others' bodies in relation to that of the nation (a shift punctuated by the 1609 Morisco expulsion).

In one sense (the most concrete, perhaps), this study endeavors to read these two textual traditions — these two wifely bodies — side by side. The central chapters of this book are, in fact, close readings of the two early modern Spanish texts consistently held up as paradigmatic examples of the conduct manual and adultery-honor drama "genre," respectively: Luis de León's *La perfecta casada* (1583) and Pedro Calderón de la Barca's *El médico de su honra* (1629). In the final chapter, I explore Sor Juana Inés de la Cruz's *Los empeños de una casa* (1683) as an Americanist rereading — or, better, rewriting — of the problems of marital and racial purity, of honor, of desire, and of the legibility or illegibility of the Other's body. Reading the anxieties produced by the wife's body in relation to broader interpretive and cultural questions allows entirely new readings of these three works. Works that have traditionally been considered marginal (*La perfecta casada*), complicitous with power (*El médico de su honra*), or derivative (*Los empeños de una casa*) emerge as far more important and more defiant works than has previously been imagined. Not only do these texts offer radical challenges to inquisitorial reading practices, but they do so, precisely, through or on the body of the wife.

Luis de León's *La perfecta casada* unquestionably forms part of the conduct manual genre that proliferated throughout Europe in the sixteenth century; to the extent that it prescribes appropriate behaviors and proscribes inappropriate desires for would-be perfect wives, the treatise is a remarkable index of early modern conceptions of the proper place of married women. But if *La perfecta casada* is, as some would argue, a textbook example of prescriptive literature for women, it is also much more: I argue here that it can also be read as a manual *about* interpretation (a text in the tradition of Augustine's *De doctrina christiana*) and, what is more, as a text of resistance that responds, almost point by point, to the accusations that kept Fray Luis imprisoned in the Inquisition's secret jails for five years. Fray Luis's diatribes against makeup (which he likens to adultery) and against woman's wandering (her noncontainment) are largely a function of the threats these pose to a reading strategy based on similitude. I am particularly interested in the troubled status of analogy throughout the text: a figure that *La perfecta casada* at once depends on and consistently compromises. I am intrigued too by the complex relation between categories of "seeming" and "being," between the accidental and the essential. If on one hand the treatise privileges the latter, condemning makeup in part because it is mere accident — because it clouds legibility — on the other, *La perfecta casada* advises women that they must seem to be perfect wives at least as much as they must actually be so. This is related to the prescriptive nature of the text and to the paradoxes inherent in conduct literature for women: the (subjective) possibilities for self-fashioning associated with texts like *La perfecta casada* are, in the hands of women, nonetheless condemned as a challenge to a divinely ordained telos.

Calderón de la Barca has traditionally been read by both his apologists and his detractors as a playwright fully aligned with Counter Reformation dogma and Philippine politics, a writer whose dense, metaphoric drama reinforced, in good baroque fashion, the dominant ideology of seventeenth-century Spain. Calderonian theater has been held up as a complex but solid example of the conservative, almost propagandistic function that José Antonio Maravall ascribed to early modern Spanish drama. My reading of *El médico de su honra* suggests otherwise; I argue that the drama represents a scathing indictment not only of the honor code per se (in both its sexual and its social dimensions) but of the sort of inquisitorial hermeneutics that was put at its service, particularly in the enforcement of *limpieʒa de sangre* (purity of blood) statutes. Calderón writes *El médico de su honra* at a moment in which limpieza statutes were the subject of fierce debates: between proponents of a softening or *relajamiento* (relaxation) of those statutes (a position linked to Olivarista politics and to the Crown's economic interests) on one hand, and those who (like Francisco de Quevedo) not only called for stricter application of the purity of blood statutes but argued for a second, more rigorous Jewish expulsion on the other. I suggest that by exposing the illegitimacy — and the ultimate tragedy — of inquisitorial reading strategies such as those practiced by Gutierre on Mencía's body (a body considered so impure that it must be bled in order to purge it of its suspected Otherness,) Calderón carries out a powerful critique of limpieza de sangre ideology and the institution charged with preserving it in early modern Spain.[2]

I turn to Sor Juana Inés de la Cruz's *Los empeños de una casa* in order to outline the form that an Americanist version of the intersection between the discourses of race, gender, power, and interpretation might assume. As a rewriting produced from the margins of empire and gender hierarchy—Sor Juana writes her play within the walls of a convent in the Vice Royalty of New Spain—*Empeños* effects a critical rereading of literary and social codes. I argue that the transvestite "passing" of the American *gracioso* Castaño (would-be perfect wife) radically destabilizes legibility, exposing the degree to which, for Sor Juana, gender, race, and class roles are performative in nature—little more than surface inscriptions that can be put on or taken off as easily as a change of clothes. But what is most original about *Los empeños de una casa* is the way in which the space of illegibility—a space occupied by the cross-dressed Castaño within the text, and his double Sor Juana outside the text—is emptied of its punitive inquisitorial charge and appropriated as a productive site of negotiation and resistance. Rather than closing *Perfect Wives*, this final chapter is intended to open up an American terrain for reading the bodies of wives and Others and the provocative ways in which they are wed.

A few words are perhaps in order here concerning my understanding of the discursive and material constitution of the early modern wives' bodies that inhabit the pages of this book. In reading the wife's body as a transcoder for interpretive anxieties, on one hand, and for cultural and political anxieties, on the other, I cast the body as somehow inseparable from its reading or, in Thomas Laqueur's apt phrase, from the "myriad discourses" that echo through it.[3] The bodies that I attend to throughout *Perfect Wives, Other Women*, then, cannot be divorced from their sociocultural context or from their own symbolic, material, and discursive constitution. If the wife's body (and this holds true for other bodies as well) is not merely a metaphor or discursive construction, neither is it some sort of essence or matter "in itself," which exists prior to or independent from the cultural mechanisms and discourses that produce, interpret, and even repress it. There is, in other words, no degree zero of materiality that grounds the body absolutely. I follow Judith Butler in understanding materiality itself to be "an effect of power," in turn understanding by this the peculiar and radically historical transcoding of discourse and "body" at work in the determining texts of early modern European culture.[4] The body I read throughout this book works, as Peter Stallybrass and Allon White contend, as "a privileged operator for the transcoding of other areas," other areas that can profitably be read, I would add, as transcoders of the body.[5] The knot of problems and questions that arise from reading the wife's body as this sort of privileged operator in three determining texts of early modern Spain and America is the subject of *Perfect Wives, Other Women.*

Visible Signs

Reading the Wife's Body in Early Modern Spain

Cuando Dios creó a nuestro primer padre en el Paraíso Terrenal, dice la Divina Escritura que infundió Dios sueño en Adán, y que, estando durmiendo, le sacó una costilla del lado siniestro, de la cual formó a nuestra madre Eva; y así como Adán despertó y la miró, dijo: "Esta es carne de mi carne y hueso de mis huesos." Y Dios dijo: "Por ésta dejará el hombre a su padre y a su madre, y serán dos en una carne misma." Y entonces fue instituido el divino sacramento del matrimonio, con tales lazos que sólo la muerte puede desatarlos. Y tiene tanta fuerza y virtud este milagroso sacramento que hace que dos diferentes personas sean una misma carne; y aún hace más en los buenos casados, que, aunque tienen dos almas, no tienen más de una voluntad. Y de aquí viene que, como la carne de la esposa sea una misma con la del esposo, las manchas que en ella caen, o los defectos que se procura, redundan en la carne del marido, aunque él no haya dado, como queda dicho, ocasión para aquel daño. Porque así como el dolor del pie, o de cualquier miembro del cuerpo humano, le siente todo el cuerpo, por ser todo de una carne misma, y la cabeza siente el daño del tobillo, sin que ella se le haya causado, así el marido es participante de la deshonra de la mujer por ser una misma cosa con ella.

[When God created our first father in the earthly paradise, Holy Scripture tells us that He caused a deep sleep to fall on him, and in his sleep took one of the ribs of his left side and created our mother Eve; and when Adam awoke and looked on her, he said: "This is now bone of my bones and flesh of my flesh." And God said: "Therefore shall a man leave his father and his mother, and they shall be one flesh." Then was instituted the divine sacrament of marriage, whose bonds are soluble only by death. This miraculous sacrament has such strength and virtue that it makes two different persons one single flesh; and with happily married couples it does more, for though they have two souls they have only a single will. Hence it arises that, as the flesh of the wife is one with the flesh of the husband, the blemishes which fall on her or the defects she incurs recoil upon the flesh of the husband, although, as I have said, he may be in no respect the cause of the trouble. For, just as the whole body feels the pain of the foot or of any other limb, since they are all one flesh; and the head feels the ankle's pain, although it is not the cause of it; so the husband shares his wife's dishonour, being one with her.]

—Miguel de Cervantes, *Don Quixote*, bk. 1, chap. 33

"Señales ocultas"

In the early months of 1632, Juan de Quiñones, an official in the court of Philip IV, addressed a memorandum to the king's confessor, Inquisitor General Fray Antonio de Sotomayor, citing what he presented as incontrovertible "means for knowing and persecuting the Jewish race":

> entre otras maldiciones que padece [la raza judía] corporeal y espiritualmente, dentro y fuera de su cuerpo, por aber perseguido el verdadero Mesías Christo nuestro redentor, hasta ponerlo en una cruz, que todos los meses muchos dellos padecen flujo de sangre por las partes posteriores, en señal perpetua de ignominia y oprobio. . . . Dicen pues muchos autores que todos aquellos judíos que cuando Pilatos dijo,

como refiere San Mateo, que estaba inocente de la sangre del Justo, clamaron y dijeron que la sangre dél fuese sobre ellos y sobre sus hijos, quedaron con esta mácula, plaga, y señal perpetua y todos sus descendientes afectos a ella que cada mes padeciessen flujo de sangre como las mujeres. . . . La señal no es otra cosa que poner algo para que aya diferencia entre las otras, que no se confunda con ellas . . . y quando el reconocimiento es difícil por el aspecto del rostro, se ha de recurrir a ver las señales ocultas que ay en el cuerpo.

[among other curses which they (the Jews) suffer, bodily and spiritually, inside and outside the body, for having persecuted the true Messiah, Christ our redeemer, to the point of placing him on a Cross, is that every month many of them suffer a flowing of blood from their posterior parts, as a perpetual sign of infamy and shame. . . . Many authors say therefore that when Pilate said, as Saint Matthew relates, that he was innocent of the Just One's blood, all those Jews who shouted and said let his blood be on them and their children, they and all their descendants remained with this blemish, plague, and perpetual sign so that every month they suffer a flow of blood like women. . . . The sign is nothing more than making a mark (on something) so that it is different from others, so that it is not confused with them . . . and when recognition is difficult from the look of the face, one should resort to the hidden signs that are on the body.][1]

Disturbing as it is, Quiñones's claim that the most effective sign for identifying Jewish men is a monthly bleeding—perhaps best described as a form of male menstruation—was not especially far-fetched in seventeenth-century Spain. The suggestion that crypto-Jews could be identified by any one of a series of "señales de oprobio" [signs of infamy] written in secret, if scarlet, letters on a bodily text was neither new nor particularly uncommon.[2] What is perhaps most striking, if not most problematic, about this type of reading is the strategy it invokes in order to make the body legible, specifically, legible as that of a culpable Other, by investing it with an explicitly female physiology.

Gutierre Alfonso Solís, the hypochondriac husband of Calderón's *El médico de su honra* (first performed in 1629 and published in 1637), who murders his innocent wife on the mere suspicion that she has stained

his honor by committing adultery, would almost certainly have con-
curred with Quiñones's method of inquiry. Albeit on a different register, his own diagnostic technique is not, after all, so far removed from
the courtier's symptomatologic approach. Whereas Quiñones feminizes the inquired body of the cultural Other, Gutierre reads his wife's
body as polluted by the radically Other. Although they approach the
honor question from different sides, as it were, both men take up issues
of contamination, containment, and an economy of blood purity. More
importantly, perhaps, in practicing a reading strategy that seeks to
connect meaning with truth as punishment, both are guilty of a profound misreading of bodies that inevitably participates in what I shall
call an inquisitorial hermeneutics.

The anxieties over somatic legibility shared by the historical Juan
de Quiñones and the fictional Gutierre Alfonso Solís are neither coincidental nor unimportant. Throughout this book I argue that in early
modern Spain the wife's body served as a kind of transcoder of and for
various types of cultural anxieties, a site on which concerns over the
interpretation and misinterpretation of signs and especially signs of
Otherness — racial, religious, cultural — were at different times projected, materialized, codified, negotiated, and even contested. On one
hand, it should perhaps not surprise us to find that the relation between husband and wife, more specifically, competing readings of the
wife's body — or of the wife *as* body — should have been used, deliberately or not, to address or even encode other areas. As Natalie Zemon
Davis has compellingly argued, sociopolitical concerns in early modern Europe — particularly the relation between groups constituted as
unequal — found ready symbolization within the domestic sphere.[3]
On the other hand, the specific historical context of Spain in the sixteenth and seventeenth centuries — its heavy-handed implementation
of Tridentine doctrine, the imperial enterprise, the institutional presence of the Inquisition, severe inflation and economic decline, monar-
chic centralization, and so on — helps account for the particular form
that the resonances between the wife's body and the racial or religious
Other's body assumed.

The wife's is not, of course, the only body in which such an intersection between various discourses of exclusion can be found. What
makes hers such a rich and at the same time economical one on which

to read the sorts of transcodifications I suspect are at work in the period is the way in which the category of "wife" marks a point of intersection between two sets of discursive attributes or positions: what we might provisionally set forth as a biologic or anatomic one that distinguishes — or purports to distinguish — male from female and that is generally used to define the category "woman," and one determined by a legal, religious-theologic, or economic discourse — or, more likely, some combination of the three — that under the rubric of "wife" invests "woman" with a subject position, albeit a secondary one, that she is not for the most part otherwise afforded.[4] I do not mean to imply by this that there is such a thing as an essential relation to anatomy in the case of "woman" or to the law/religion/economy in the case of "wife," but simply to note that the terms "woman" and "wife" function practically at different levels. A curious kind of geometry is at work here, one that suggests that the category "wife" is more than merely a particular instance of the category "woman." If, one might argue, all wives are perforce women (something about which Sor Juana Inés de la Cruz has a thing or two to say), one might also argue that in respect to the languages of the law, economics, and theology, most women are (potential if not actual) wives, or they are not (yet) women (about which Sor Juana also has something to say). That the Spanish term *mujer* translates as both woman and wife suggests not only the pervasiveness of this conception (in which being a woman all but implies being somebody's wife) but its naturalization within language.

One must be careful not to overstate the "wife" case here, for there are clear exceptions to be noted: the category "woman" intersected legal, religious, economic, and even medical discourses at a number of other sites or positions in early modern Spain, from the body of the prostitute to the queen's to that of the nun. But for many women, marriage represented the most accessible passage to a *kind* of subjectivity, if also to a kind of subjection markedly different from the form that generally preceded it, that of daughter to father. It was the moment when a woman became a subject in the eyes of church and state — acting for the first time as her (legal) self, giving a word (a word with specific legal, economic, and religious repercussions) to her husband before the presence of both civil and ecclesiastical authorities, and, in so doing, performatively constituting herself as an entity who could eventually own her husband's property, give birth to legitimate children and be held at least partly responsible for them, be subject to punishment for adultery or bigamy, and so forth. It was, for most women, the moment at which they entered a public discursive sphere, even as that entry signaled their enclosure within a private domestic space as their husbands' private property.

The "wife" represents, then, the primary (although not the only) site on which "woman" was legally and religiously constituted as a subject in early modern Spain, and, at the same time, immediately subjected to certain forms of control. If guilds, colleges, brotherhoods, municipalities, and other ensembles functioned — as George Mariscal, drawing on Antonio Domínguez Ortiz, argues — as sites on which subjectivities were constituted in the sixteenth century, women were, with rare exception, categorically excluded from these various groups.[5] My point here is not that marriage represented for women the equivalent of one of the groups that Domínguez Ortiz cites as bestowing on its members certain privileges (and imposing certain restraints) and that Mariscal implicates in the constitution of a male, aristocratic subject.[6] It is, rather, that for many women the position of "wife" — and the privileges and restraints that accompanied marriage — were to some degree the next closest thing.

The anxieties that attach to the legibility or illegibility of the wife's body can consequently be seen as at least partly the result of her body's attachment to (or its definition in terms of) categories that exceed anatomy, and that potentially class the "wife" — as subject — alongside the "husband." This is not to say that these anxieties can be subsumed in a sort of general early modern discovery that subjectivity and anatomy — or subjectivity and position — are not isomorphous. Rather, the wife's overdetermined subject position in emerging institutional discourses (vis-à-vis the more static — if less defined — position set for "woman") helps explain why a kind of inquisitorial hermeneutic is employed in the surveillance of her body. In other words, if there is some sort of collusion between an inquisitorial hermeneutic and the question of the legibility/illegibility of the wife's body, it is not irrelevant that the state, church, *and* Inquisition (a hybrid politico-religious institution) emerged at this time as central institutions for the production and regulation of anxieties in the various arenas to which the wife's body is connected.

In identifying and exploring this uneasy marriage between the anxieties generated by the wife's body and those provoked by the body of the cultural Other in early modern Spain, I attend to a triple displacement. The first of these involves a shift from bodily instabilities to interpretive ones. I argue that the threats posed by the excesses and desires of wives' bodies in a number of sixteenth- and seventeenth-century Spanish and Spanish American texts coincide with broader concerns over the excesses of interpretation and the threats of illegibility, that is, the difficulties of reading, the impossibility of knowing a body, a text, in itself. The stakes of this initial gesture seem clear: the body is used as a figure or screen for semiotic and epistemic questions at a historical moment (in the wake of Trent) when the status of the sign — more specifically, the status *as* sign of the eucharistic host, the body of Christ — was under heavy debate. But there is a second movement that in some sense mirrors — even as it distorts — the first. If anxieties concerning the wife's body and its pleasures betray anxieties over reading or knowing, quite often questions over the illegibility and indeterminacy of signs in turn remit back to the body, albeit on different terms. Concerns over the interpretation and misinterpretation might be seen as either symptoms or projections of the anxieties provoked by the body of the racial or religious Other, specifically, the insecurities generated by the interpretive depth of the converso's or Morisco's body: how to know what was concealed beneath the surface, or if an orthodox appearance might mask a crypto-Jew or a crypto-Muslim. If a kind of epistemology is prioritized (even as it is threatened) in the first displacement, then the body is reprioritized in the second, raising the stakes of reading and more radically historicizing the relation that obtains between the somatic and the semiotic. There is, finally, what can be imagined as a third movement already anticipated by the other two: a kind of fluidity (and, at times, a substitutability) between the wife's body and the converso's or Morisco's body. Not only does this third shift destabilize any sense of specular linearity or binarism that might be suggested by the other alignments, but it renders explicit the pervasive and provocative intersection (of which Quiñones's letter is such a good example) of the discourses of race and gender.

If in describing the relations between these various fields, I invoke a language of movement from a first moment (the shift from body to sign) to a second one (the shift from sign back to body) and the implicit inscription of a third (the intersections between the wife's body and the Other's body), I do not mean to imply that those relations are governed by either temporality or causality. On the contrary, what is so suggestive about them is precisely the absence of a causal narrative or temporal prioritization among what I have provisionally set forth as first, second, and third instances. One gesture does not necessarily follow on the other; the three fields they connect (somatic, semiotic, and politico-cultural) are, rather, much more ambiguously and even indiscernibly related than my rendering suggests. Neither is it my intention to propose that the connections between these fields are always explicit or even viable. There are instances where some, but not all, of these intersections may obtain, as well as those in which none do, in which the wife's body (or the sign's, or the Other's) may invoke other areas altogether, or none at all.

Perhaps what best accounts for the rich but problematic relation that links the respective bodies of wife, sign (condensed in the body of Christ in the Eucharist), and Other is the central role each of these bodies plays in three different sacraments of transformation, all heatedly (and at times bloodily) debated in early modern Europe and America and, given their importance to Counter Reformation theology, politics, and even aesthetics, the subject of long sessions at Trent: the one-flesh doctrine of matrimony (which putatively renders the wife of the same flesh as her husband), the transubstantial conversion of the *hoc est corpus meum* (that converts the bread of Communion to the body of Christ), and the baptismal conversion of the Jewish or Islamic or Amerindian Other into a Christian, specifically, a Catholic "self." Each of these sacraments was in turn associated with a particular transgression of Otherness, subject to inquisitorial surveillance and discipline; particularly threatening in each case were the doubts these violations cast on the efficacy of the sacrament. The wife's will, materialized in her adulterous agency, or the leftover breadlike properties of the Host used to deny "real presence", or the "impure" blood of a *cristiano nuevo* might be understood, then, as the vestigial traces of an Otherness that was thought to have been left behind, a mark of recidivism and contamination that was at once feared and desired. The argument to be made from these various alignments is not that the questions raised by early modern readings of wives' bodies are in some exclusive or indissoluble way (to borrow a Tridentine language on matrimony) about interpretation or cultural anxieties, however, but rather that race and gender discourses are often inextricably linked with questions of interpretation and signification, particularly when the body is invoked as cultural category or as object of reading.

Although this study clearly draws on recent work about the Inquisition, and the Holy Office is very much present at its discursive horizons, my purpose here is neither to trace a cohesive narrative of the Inquisition in sixteenth- and seventeenth-century Spain nor to survey in any systematic way the specific roles it played in the lives of early modern Spanish women.[7] The former has been amply done (particularly over the past two decades, which have seen renewed interest in inquisitorial scholarship both in and out of Spain), producing rich, polemical, and often contradictory results; the latter, undertaken only in part (less with respect to married women, for example, than to religious women), represents a valuable but very different approach to the question of reading wives' bodies in an inquisitorial context from the one I follow here. Nevertheless, because the institutional presence of the Inquisition—a presence that extends beyond the specific fields in and on which the Inquisition concretely acted—is crucial to the arguments I sustain throughout this book, it may be helpful to briefly lay out what I understand to be the primary functions fulfilled by the Inquisition in early modern Spain.

Perhaps the place to begin such an outline is not in Spain, as one might expect, but rather in Rome, shortly after the day in 1478 on which Pope Sixtus IV granted Ferdinand and Isabel the papal bull that allowed them to introduce the Inquisition to the territories and dioceses of their combined Crowns. (The Inquisition had existed nominally in the Crown of Aragon since the thirteenth century, but was, for all intents and purposes, a dormant institution.) The manifest purpose of the Holy Office was to maintain religious orthodoxy, defending the newly minted Catholic nation from the threats of heterodoxy in its many faces, especially its Jewish and Muslim ones. But the Inquisition's role in Spain was to be at least as much political — and, arguably, economic — as it was religious. Sixtus realized too late the tremendous power he had placed at the hands of the Spanish Crown by providing it with an institution whose proceedings were not only secret but that, because it was constituted as a royal and not a papal court, denied Rome any voice in appointments or appeals. In calling on this particular version or moment of an inquisitorial fable of origins, I do not mean to suggest that the Holy Office was exclusively or even principally a secular organ at the disposal of the Hapsburg monarchy, although that argument can be — and indeed has been — made. My point, rather, is that among other things (and, in some instances, primarily) the Spanish Inquisition served as an instrument of national centralization. It is no coincidence that the Supreme Council of the Inquisition (the Suprema), charged with the administration of the vast and complex bureaucratic machinery that the Inquisition would become in its Spanish incarnation, was the first — and, during the reign of the Catholic Monarchs, the only — formal institution with jurisdiction over all the kingdoms of Spain and, later, her New World possessions.

If the Holy Office's usefulness as an instrument of centralization was partly a function of its successful institutionalization, institutionalization did not imply immutability. Quite the contrary: not only was the Spanish Inquisition many things to many people, but its spheres of concern and activity fluctuated tremendously over the course of its 359-year history. This adaptability derives in part from its founding mandate, "Exigit sincerae devotionis affectus" [examines the dispositions of genuine religious observance],[8] which, by defining the mission of the Holy Office in Spain as the defense of the Catholic faith, allowed tremendous room for interpretation of where its jurisdiction began and ended, since offenses against the faith could easily accommodate a broad range of transgressions. As Jesús de Bujanda postulates, "The coercive power received by the Holy Office from the Church and the state varies according to how Catholic faith is understood. . . . The Inquisition, acting as an instrument of religious and social control throughout its entire existence, modifies the object of its activities and its field of action, adapting itself to changing circumstances."[9] By examining both the number and the nature of the crimes tried by the Inquisition at different moments and at different locations, scholarship undertaken in the last decade—by Solange Alberro, Bartolomé Bennassar, Jaime Contreras, Jean-Pierre Dedieu, Ricardo García Cárcel, Gustav Henningsen, Henry Kamen, Bernard Vincent, and many others—has gone a long way toward demythologizing the extents and limitations of the Inquisition's power in early modern Spain and her overseas empire. Among the many suggestive findings of these investigations, three are particularly relevant to the arguments posed in this book: (1) According to the classification system used by inquisitors, crimes of Otherness—those related to the categories of "Jews," "Moors," and "Lutherans"—were considered capital offenses and accounted for more than forty percent of all cases between 1540 and 1700. (The category of "Illuminati" also fits in this group but constitutes only 0.03 percent of the total.) (2) In the years following the closing of the Council of Trent, the Inquisition actively participated in campaigns to impose or enforce Tridentine dogma. The category "heresy" was broadened to explicitly include marital transgressions since crimes such as adultery and bigamy violated the indissolubility of holy matrimony that had been reaffirmed at Trent. Moreover, because Tridentine legislation covered everything from coital questions to the nakedness of the human body in religious paintings, sexuality itself became an area of inquiry for the Holy Office. (3) The Inquisition's activities declined markedly after the 1620s; by the mid to late seventeenth century, the Spanish Holy Office had lost much of its earlier power and prestige. (This will be of some importance for the argument I present in chapter three.)

But even taking into account the significant variations in both the intensity of prosecutions and the nature of offenses tried by the Inquisition, certain constants—more formal than material, in some cases—remain. These include a preoccupation with uncovering hidden truths, often achieved through the reading and/or disciplining of the body (two operations that become, at times, inseparable), the use of informants, secret proceedings, appeals to a rhetoric of contamination and cleansing (consonant with the operative politico-theological model of a corporate state, on one hand, with the implementation of limpieza de sangre statutes, on the other), a confessional imperative, and, above all, a compulsion toward surveillance as the most reliable means to a consistent end: the containment of Otherness, broadly and variously

defined. These last two in particular—surveillance and the containment of Otherness—and the anxieties they produce and reproduce,
at least as much as the direct impact that inquisitorial legislation on
sexuality may have had on the lives of early modern wives, I invoke
throughout this study when I link questions concerning the illegibility
of the wife's body to an inquisitorial hermeneutics. It is worth repeat-
ing that what I qualify as inquisitorial here and in the chapters ahead
is not necessarily identical with or limited to the specific actions or
mandates of the Inquisition, but is at once more and less than these.
A good example of this noncoincidence is the passage from Quiñones
that I cite at the opening of this chapter, which I take as an explicit
instance of an inquisitorial hermeneutic at work, despite the fact that
Quiñones himself was not affiliated with the Inquisition proper (although his addressee certainly is) and despite the further fact that his
letter dates from a period not only of relative inactivity on the part
of the Holy Office, but in which exposing crypto-Jews (the substance
of his recommendations) was not the main order of business. What I
refer to as an inquisitorial hermeneutic can be read as shorthand, then,
for the sorts of reading practices employed by the Inquisition but also,
more broadly, for the sorts of ideas (both *mentalités* and in a more
traditional sense), anxieties, and even epistemology either fostered or
reflected by its institutional presence in early modern Spain.[10]

Caminos de perfección:
Conduct Literature and Honor Plays

My choice of wives as a starting point for the sort of analysis I carry
out in the pages that follow has to do largely with two distinct and dis-
tinctly important textual phenomena of early modern Spain rarely, if
ever, considered alongside one another: the proliferation in fifteenth-
and particularly sixteenth-century Spain of conduct manuals pre-
scribing duties and proscribing desires for perfect wives, and the vast
popularity in sixteenth- and especially seventeenth-century Spain of
honor-vengeance dramas, plays in which wives, defined as radically
imperfect on the mere suspicion of adulterous desire, were routinely
and graphically murdered by their husbands onstage. One of the ob-

jectives of this study is to read these two traditions both with and against each other. Reading Luis de León's *La perfecta casada* and Calderón de la Barca's *El médico de su honra* side by side not only permits a different kind of historicizing than reading each alone might afford but also raises a number of questions concerning the relations between them: about the different inquisitorial strategies and counterstrategies that lurk at the horizons of each text, about how adultery as illegibility in Fray Luis in some sense anticipates the illegibility of adultery in Calderón, or, perhaps most interestingly, about how questions concerning wifely illegibility invariably become entangled with an inquisitorial hermeneutic and how, in this entanglement, the question of the wife's will either becomes or is made to seem a threat that must somehow be contained. But in order to get to these questions, it is first necessary to situate each text within its particular literary-historical context and then briefly explore some of the ways in which those contexts—those traditions—inscribe constructions of wives' bodies that at once complement and compete with one another.

Early modern conduct manuals for wives represent a provocative and largely ignored body of texts that, in the words of Nancy Armstrong and Leonard Tennenhouse, "strive to reproduce, if not always to revise, culturally approved forms of desire." [11] In so doing, these texts are integral not only to the history of desire and its circulation, but also to the study of the wife's body as both token of exchange and privileged site for reading, as well as to a continued questioning of the concepts of Renaissance and self-fashioning and their problematic applicability to the lives of early modern women. It is worthwhile to open a parenthesis here in order to briefly sketch out the relation between these two concepts, on one hand, and conduct manuals, on the other. Of the numerous definitions of the Renaissance proposed in the wake of Burckhardt, the most useful—and, arguably, the most problematic—for the sorts of readings I undertake here are those that link the period with the emergence of new cultural identities or with the constitution of a so-called premodern or early modern subject. [12] One of many possible ways to define this subject is as one capable or conscious of exercising agency in the process of signification, in controlling identity, one that no longer understands meaning or identity as a (generally divine) given, but rather as a product on which it acts and with which it conspires. This is not to say that meaning in thirteenth-century Spain, for instance, was consistently understood as something fixed or immutable (one need look no further than *El libro de buen amor* to radically challenge such a claim) or, alternately, that in the transition from the fifteenth to the sixteenth century individuals were afforded greater freedom or flexibility in determining social or cultural identities than they previously had been. (The question of where we situate the passage from a medieval to an early modern period is particularly knotted. For the moment, I follow convention and operate under the assumption that in Spain this transition occurs in the last years of the fifteenth century.) On the contrary, empirical evidence suggests that the opposite is true: the institutionalization of various mechanisms of cultural control—including, in Spain, the belated introduction of the Inquisition by the Catholic Monarchs—very often reduced the relative autonomy of early modern Spanish "subjects." This is particularly so in the case of women.[13] Perhaps a more accurate statement, then, would be that in the sixteenth century, a different understanding emerges of how meanings—and, with them, identities—are generated.

Whether understood in terms of Stephen Greenblatt's notion of "Renaissance self-fashioning" or of what Thomas Greene has termed "flexibility of the self," where self-representation is concerned, this difference can be seen as hinging, in large part, on the possibility of attributing or imposing meaning on the body as a site of reading.[14] That conduct literature of the sort that flourished throughout sixteenth-century Europe either helped prompt or was itself prompted by this possibility hardly seems debatable. But it draws attention to the central paradox of prescriptive literature specifically *for* women. On one hand, there is little question that the conduct manuals for wives form part of the broader prescriptive tradition associated with an early modern subjectivity, with the ability, in other words, to fashion and, more importantly, refashion the Self. On the other hand, however, the manuals for wives generally repudiate all forms of wifely mutability; the greatest threat of makeup, for example—something against which almost all the conduct books (and *La perfecta casada* in particular) rail—is precisely that it empowers women with the ability to remake themselves as something "other" than what they truly are, to effectively misrepresent themselves. The wife of the conduct manuals is, in this respect, walking a precariously fine line between subjectivity and surveillance: she is at once exhorted to perfect herself and immediately censured for the agency she displays in doing so. These paradoxes surrounding fashioning and self-fashioning that come to a head in conduct manuals written specifically for women points to a somewhat different — but in many ways related — problem that similarly turns on questions of will and illegibility. Alongside the possibilities for constructing meaning or fashioning the Self that is either partly the cause or partly the result of the sixteenth-century explosion of conduct literature arises the suspicion of the interpretive duplicity of the Other's body. The particular historical circumstances of early modern Spain almost guaranteed that this kind of suspicion would have a very specific target: the body of the converso or Morisco Other.

In contrast to the relative paucity of studies on the subject of conduct literature, the honor plays not only have elicited tremendous critical attention throughout the years but — because the question of honor was so often linked (especially in the mid- to late nineteenth century and into the early decades of the twentieth) with that of a Spanish national character — figure prominently in arguments concerning the very "essence" of Spanishness: "el honor convertido en nacionalidad" [honor transformed into nationality], in Hartzenbusch's formulation.[15] Because the bibliography is both vast and well known, I will not rehearse it here (I return to the secondary literature on honor in chapter 3); rather, let me briefly lay out the terms of the debate or, more appropriately, debates concerning honor and their particular relevance to the question of the wife's body. The complex meanings and different manifestations of honor in early modern Spain, along with the highly charged history of the concept, make it difficult to define. This difficulty — or, more precisely, this overdetermination — is one of honor's fundamental traits. Nevertheless, for the past hundred years or so, the most important critical discussions surrounding honor in the Golden Age have been largely concerned with only a handful of issues. These can perhaps be most concisely expressed as a series of at times opposing, at times overlapping positions: honor as virtue versus honor as reputation; honor as an innate quality (synonymous for some with a kind of *hombría* [manliness]) versus honor as a social construction; honor as a hierarchical force that reifies social difference versus honor as an equalizing (and potentially revolutionary) force (roughly alignable with what Gustavo Correa respectively terms vertical and horizontal honor);[16] honor as a dramatic convention versus honor as a historical reflection; honor as a private concern versus honor as belonging to the public domain; honor as issuing from birth or blood (aristocracy, limpieza de sangre) versus honor as a function of one's deeds; honor as a strict code that in favoring status over essence or vengeance over forgiveness violates Christian morality (honra negra in both Teresa de Avila's Vida and the Lazarillo de Tormes) versus honor as a redeeming value, somehow reconcilable with Christian beliefs (this last argument generally associated with notions of what is Spanish); and, finally, in nearly all of the honor plays, (male) honor as radically dependent on (female) chastity—honor, then, as the site, localizable on the wife's body, through which the husband's subjectivity is vulnerable to the wife's will. The question of whether a woman can possess or manifest honor or whether she is a mere receptacle for her husband's honor—or, if she is unmarried, her father's or her brother's—is quite salient. In the majority of the honor plays, mention of a woman's honra almost invariably remits to her chastity.

The honor plays in which I am most interested here are those more specifically referred to as adultery-vengeance or wife-murder plays: dramas in which a husband murders his wife—or arranges for her murder—on the mere suspicion of adultery. Very often these plays turn on secrecy: first a secret examination of the wife's motives and actions and, once she has failed this test (as she inevitably does despite rarely actually being adulterous), the meting out of punishment to restitute the damaged honor (honor as hombría), but in secret so that that same honor (now as reputation) will not undergo any further loss. A good number of these plays, although certainly not all, are variations on a recurring plot. First act: Reappearance of wife's ex-lover (generally after a long disappearance) and declaration of his intent to repossess the woman who, in his absence, has perforce married another man. Second act: Intensification of husband's suspicions of his wife's dishonor; wife's continued resistance against ex-lover's continued advances. Wife remains faithful in deed, if not entirely in thought. Third act: Convinced of his wife's guilt and in deference to the fickleness of

the *qué dirán* (literally, "what will people say?" synonymous with public opinion, reputation, even gossip), husband exacts his vengeance
(murder of his wife) in secret, in order to cleanse his polluted honor.
King or other father figure who discovers (but does not publicize) the
alleged "malady" and its bloody "cure" applauds wife's execution and,
in several of the plays, concerts widowed husband's remarriage, quite
literally over the dead body of his first wife. The specifics, of course,
are infinitely more complicated. What stands out, however, in nearly
all the wife-murders plays regardless of the particulars of plot or playwright is the extreme precariousness of honor and the almost defining
capriciousness of the qué dirán. More than anything else, perhaps, it
is this radical precariousness of honor that makes possible the sort of
reading of the wife-murder plays I propose in chapter 3: as a critique
of inquisitorial hermeneutics of all sorts, whether practiced on the
body of the wife onstage or on the bodies of conversos and Moriscos
offstage.

The sheer number of conduct manuals and adultery-honor plays
written in the period is staggering; even citing only the most canonical
examples of each renders a sizable corpus. Among the better-known
conduct manuals dedicated to wives, for instance (or, in some cases,
works that include something very much akin to a conduct manual in
the kind of advice dispensed to young, married or soon-to-be married women), one finds: Juan Luis Vives's *Manual de instrucción para
la mujer casada,* the most popular of the conduct manuals after *La perfecta casada* and part of the longer *De institutionae feminae christianae,*
which also includes instructions for virgins and widows; Fernán Pérez
de Guzmán's *Relación a las señoras e grandes dueñas de la doctrina que
dieron a Sarra;* Francisco de Osuna's *Norte de los estados;* Antonio de
Guevara's *Letra para recién casados;* Pedro Mexía's *Silva de varia lec-
ción;* Alonso Gutiérrez de la Vera Cruz's *Speculum coniugorum;* Alonso
de Herrera's *Espejo de la perfecta casada;* Pedro de Luján's *Coloquios
matrimoniales;* Fray Vicente Mexía's *Saludable instrucción del estado de
matrimonio;* Alfonso de Valdés's *Diálogo de Mercurio y Carón,* which,
although not a conduct manual per se, includes a dialogue between
the protagonists and the soul of a deceased wife on such matters as
conjugal relations, bringing up daughters, and managing household
servants; and Luisa de Sijea's *Diálogo de dos vírgenes sobre la vida en la*

corte y la vida retirada, if not the only, then certainly one of very few manuals for women authored by a woman, although its text, in Latin, for the most part repeats Vives's prescriptions.

In the role models it offered its female readers, Martín de Córdoba's *Jardín de las nobles donzellas* could be seen as forming part of the wifely conduct manual tradition, if somewhat more marginally, as could Alvaro de Luna's *Libro de las virtuosas e claras mujeres* and Juan de Espinosa's *Diálogo en laude de las mujeres.* To this list of related works, we might also append the numerous philogamous treatises written in sixteenth-century Spain, several of which included sections specifying the attributes of an ideal spouse. In an Erasmian line, these works generally privileged marriage over monastic celibacy or, alternately, defended the sacramentality of matrimony against Protestant attacks. Among the most widely circulated of these were Juan de Molina's *Sermón breve en loor del matrimonio para mayor alegría y consolación de todos los bien casados;* Basilio Ponce's *De sacramento matrimonii;* and Tomás Sánchez's *Disputationem de sancto matrimonii sacramento.* Finally, we might close our list with the marital works (theological treatises *and* conduct manuals) of Erasmus, Luther, and Alberti, several of which appeared on inquisitorial indices but were nonetheless fairly well known in early modern Spain: Erasmus's *Enconium matrimonii, Institutio christiani matrimonii, Vidua christiana,* and *Coniugium impar;* Luther's sermon on the state of marriage, *Ein sermon dem Elichen Standt vorendert und corrigiert durch D. Martinû Luther Augustiner ordens zu Wittenbergk;* and Alberti's *Liber secundus familiae: De re uxoria* and *Liber tertius familiae: Economicus.*

The list of wife-murder plays is no less extensive.[17] The obligatory place to begin would no doubt be Calderón's *El pintor de su deshonra* and *A secreto agravio, secreta venganza,* the two plays that together with *El médico de su honra* form the classic Calderonian honor trilogy. But Calderón wrote several other plays in which a husband kills his wife or has her killed, among them *El mayor monstruo, los celos, Celos aun del aire matan, Céfalo y Pocris,* and (with Juan de Zabaleta) *Troya abrasada.* Lope, whose "Arte nuevo de hacer comedias" records the tremendous popularity that *casos de la honra* (cases concerning honor) enjoyed with the paying *vulgo* (masses), had successfully tried his hand at (and, indeed, considerably reworked) the formula from years before, in such plays as *La bella Aurora, El buen vecino, El castigo del discreto, El castigo sin venganza, Los comendadores de Córdoba, La contienda de Diego García de Paredes con el capitán Juan de Urbina, La desdichada Estefanía, Las ferias de Madrid, La locura por la honra, El médico de su honra* (from which Calderón borrowed freely), *El sufrimiento de honor, El toledano vengado, La vitoria de la honra,* and the attributed *La prudencia en el castigo.* Though not an honor play in the strictest sense, Tirso's *Vida y muerte de Herodes* nonetheless satisfies the basic criteria of the wife-murder tradition, as do Lupercio Leonardo de Argensola's *Alejandra* and Cristóbal de Virués's *Atila furioso* and *La cruel Casandra.* More faithful interpretations include Gaspar de Aguilar's *La venganza honrosa,* Andrés Claramonte's *La infelice Dorotea,* Alvaro Cubillo de Aragón's *La mayor venganza de honor,* Antonio Enríquez Gómez's *A lo que obliga el honor,* Agustín Moreto's *La fuerza de la ley,* Francisco de Rojas Zorrilla's *Cada cual lo que le toca* and *Casarse por vengarse,* Agustín Salazar y Torres's *El amor más desgraciado,* Tirso's *El celoso prudente,* and Vélez de Guevara's *Los celos hasta los cielos.*

Although the very number of texts cited above makes a strong case for avoiding generalizations of any sort, it is nonetheless possible to tease out some common threads that could be used to compare the wives' bodies variously framed in these works. The impossibly perfect wife of the conduct manuals is constructed as an object of desire and masculine exchange whereas her counterpart in the honor dramas, the imperfect wife murdered by her husband as punishment for adultery from the waist up, or more precise still, from the neck up, is guilty primarily of being or becoming a desiring subject, of assuming agency (in her husband's eyes) in the circulation of her own body. In terms of the places they occupy, the wife idealized in the conduct literature is repeatedly confined to the interior of her (husband's) home; she is a perfect wife (*casada*) by virtue of being perfectly housed or encased (*casa-da*). In the adultery-murder plays, this encasement reaches a kind of macabre literalization as the wife's body is perfected in(to) the claustrophobic space of her own casket. Extreme measures, no doubt, but for what is billed as an extreme imperfection: manifesting or eliciting a desire that exceeds the domestic space, allowing a sacrosanct interior—the house's or the body's—to be penetrated, sullied, contaminated even, by an Other.

Perhaps more than anything else, it is this threat or suspicion of Otherness that renders signs so recklessly adulterous in the honor plays as if they, too, were somehow haunted by difference. If the conduct manuals, not just those for wives but as a broader early modern cultural phenomenon, depend on a kind of semiotic stability that renders them "practical" at some level (if someone can fashion him or herself into a perfect courtier or a perfect wife, for instance, it is because there are accepted codes for courtliness or wifeliness that can be rehearsed — cited — by and on the body), the honor plays, with their migrating signs and their consistently misread clues are, on the contrary, plagued by a semiotic instability that troubles the very notion of legibility or, indeed, of epistemologic certainty. But here, as everywhere else that the imperfect wife meets her perfect double, things are perhaps not as straightforward as they might appear. To the extent that conduct manuals rely on what we might term conjunctive codes of interpretation (on the belief, in other words, that a certain marker of being an exemplary courtier or wife, to stay with the examples at hand, will be correctly interpreted as such), they also work to unground the conjunctiveness of these very codes. In holding out the possibility that a subject who is *not* exemplary can, by heeding the advice prescribed in such a work, either become or, in a more Machiavellian spirit, pass for a model courtier or wife, the manuals effectively manipulate — or teach its readers to manipulate — norms of legibility, confounding categories of essence and accidence and calling into question the very notion of perfectibility on which conduct literature rests.

This brings us to what is no doubt the most crucial question that emerges from reading the wifely conduct manuals beside the wife-murder plays — to what is, in many respects, the most vexing question of all, one that weaves together the various narratives of desire, will, Otherness, and even legibility that we have been considering: Is there, for the wife, a possible *camino de perfección* (path to perfection)? Or, to put it in slightly different terms, how is the wife's body perfected in each of these discursive fields (if we assume that conduct manuals and honor plays occupy separate — if at times overlapping — discursive spaces) and by whom? There is a notable "shift" at work here. In the conduct manuals, the imperfect woman's body can ostensibly — and perhaps only so, for reasons we have seen — be fashioned, disciplined, corrected, and *converted* into that of a perfect wife. (Crucial questions remain, however, as to who authors that conversion and how genuine it is.) In the honor dramas, this revisionist possibility is categorically foreclosed to the wife. She is, as a rule, beyond redemption, not only imperfect but also imperfectible (except, possibly, in death). Her body must be excised, then, from being a determinant of her husband's honor by the most radical means imaginable: by an almost surgical excision (and in the case of *El médico de su honra*, quite literally so) that is, a priori, destined for failure.

But what is most provocative of this shift in strategies for perfecting the wife's body is that it gestures toward a similar (though not exactly analogous) shift in models of perfecting, indeed, of *defining* a national identity — a shift in the way the Other's body is imagined in relation to that of the nation: as one that can be disciplined, corrected, and converted to more or less conform to a prescribed standard of what is (or should be) "Spanish" in the first instance, to one that must be excised from being a determinant of a protonational identity, a body conceived as being so tainted by Otherness that it can only be perfected (and, in so doing, restore to perfect health the ailing national body) through a kind of civil death. That the timing of this second shift (from an inclusive to an exclusive national model) corresponds, roughly speaking, to that of the first (from conduct manuals to honor plays) and is in fact punctuated by the 1609 Moorish expulsion, is not coincidental, but speaks, rather, of other kinds of politico-cultural shifts taking place in Spain at the time, shifts that might be seen as the culmination of a program initiated more than a century earlier with the Jewish expulsion. As David Boruchoff compellingly argues, it was sometime in the mid-sixteenth century that "the theological understanding of Christian unity as an expectant (outwardly-directed) ideal" gave way to "the Inquisitorial proposition that unity may be brought about by prohibitions and other exclusionary (inwardly-directed) measures, so as to separate faithful Christians, and the Crown's loyal subjects, from those about them." [18]

In suggesting a possible relation between these two shifts in strategies for perfecting subjects that are somehow marked by difference (or — and the reason for my quotation marks around the word "shift" above — between the retrospective fiction of such shifts that the sort of reading I undertake here conjures), my intention is not to suggest a transparent analogy between the anxieties generated by the wife's body and those generated by the racial-religious Other's body or to argue that one shift is a reflection or, far less, a consequence, of the other. Such a move would be flawed for many reasons, not the least of which is that if there is any kind of narrative to be traced here, it is neither causal nor evolutionary. Although we can more or less locate the heyday of conduct literature in the mid-sixteenth century and that of honor plays in the early seventeenth, there are, clearly, numerous exceptions, not just temporal, but even in the sorts and degrees of control exercised on wives' bodies in these two types of works—in the measure to which they adopt the "perfecting" strategies outlined in the preceding paragraphs. What is more, if the willful possibilities that, albeit by accident or default, the conduct manual's generic ties to notions of self-fashioning may have provided wives posed a real or imagined threat that was somehow taken up by the wife-murder plays, this neither does nor should be taken to mean that the adultery-honor plays derived from or even responded to the prescriptive literature.

Not only must these same kinds of disclaimers be made for the historical shift in modes of perfecting the Other's body with respect to that of the nation's (since here, too, there are clear exceptions to be noted and one model does not simply cede the path to another), but also, and more importantly, for the relation between what we might term the wife model and the Other model. Simply put, the possibility of reading one of these shifts should in no way be adduced as evidence of the other. Both shifts correspond to broader changes, to the institutionalization and centralization of various mechanisms of control.

Neither is it my intention to claim that the texts I examine make this case in anything more than provisional terms or, conversely, that the sorts of readings of the wife's body I undertake here are viable only for these two texts or for the two traditions they represent. On the contrary, there are numerous early modern Spanish texts—neither conduct manuals nor wife-murder dramas—that inscribe wives' bodies or soon-to-be wives' bodies that could profitably be read in the terms I set forth: from *La Celestina*, in which Celestina's work as *reparadora de virgos* (hymen mender) casts significant doubts on hymeneal legibility, calling into question any prospect of interpretive stability;

to Teresa de Avila's *Vida,* in which the triangular relations between
God (as Holy Spouse), Teresa, and her confessors, or, alternately, between God, Teresa, and the Devil, might be mapped as an adulterous
geometry that makes of Teresa both a perfect and an imperfect wife
(and the very term "perfection" is, of course, extremely charged in
Teresa's rhetoric); or from Francisco Delicado's *La loçana andaluça,*
in which Aldonza's picaresque pilgrimage to Rome in some sense anticipates — and suggests alternate readings of — the peregrinations of
Fray Luis's perfectas casadas; to Lope's *El castigo sin vengança,* among
the very few honor plays that stage a case of real — and not just imagined — adultery; or even from the *autos sacramentales* — a large number of them by Calderón himself — that rewrite the traditional honor-
vengeance script by casting Christ as the husband who, instead of
punishing, forgives his adulterous bride, *la naturaleça humana* (human
nature); to what is perhaps the most brilliant response to the Spanish preoccupation with honor and wifely perfection, Cervantes's "El
curioso impertinente," in which the undetectability of adultery on
Camila's inquired body suggests a radical questioning of early modern
evidential paradigms.[19] The fourth chapter of this book, dedicated to
Sor Juana's *Los empeños de una casa,* seeks, in part, to explore the sorts
of tensions produced or deployed when a work that is neither a conduct manual nor an honor play is read in terms of the perfection of the
very unorthodox wives' bodies it inscribes. What particularly interests
me about the conduct manuals' perfect wives and the imperfect wives
of the adultery-honor plays, however, is that they mark the inner and
outer limits of desire. Fray Luis's nameless perfecta casada and Calderón's Mencía are both uncomfortably situated at the intersection of
surveillance and subjectivity: it is at this uncertain pass where perfect
wives meet — or become — other women.

Flesh of My Flesh: *Reading Adultery*

Although the relationship between textuality (in the broadest sense)
and corporeality that at some level grounds the conflation between
somatic and semiotic or epistemologic concerns ideally holds true
for all kinds of bodies, historically, it is a gendered, female (or femi-

nized) body that has most frequently been aestheticized and textualized. In contrast to representations of the male body, which is often (and problematically) rendered as neutral or invisible, the female body has regularly been appropriated as an object of reading, a site on which to project—and contest—interpretations. If the position of the female is symbolically characterized in terms of phallic lack, that perceived lack is overcompensated by an ascribed material, linguistic, and semiotic overdeterminacy—an overdeterminacy that strengthens its metaphoric bonds with a textual body that is similarly deemed excessive and uncontrollable. Both bodies seem to invite, and even require, hermeneutic work. The connection is further bolstered by the secondariness of the female with respect to the male; the ostensibly derivative nature of women's bodies (Eve's creation from Adam's rib being perhaps the best example) rivals that of all language, all text. It is precisely this sort of "feminization of the esthetic" that Howard Bloch has aptly identified as the founding topos of misogynist discourse, arguing that "misogyny in our culture consists of a series of specific associations between the esthetic and the feminine, which in essence turns woman into a text to be read, and thus appropriated."[20]

There is, of course, a tremendous irony that underwrites the imputed visibility of the female body; although traditionally cast as object of the gaze, its specularity invests it with a specific opacity. In other words, the very excess that renders the body so explicitly and even provocatively legible on one hand, tends, on the other, to destabilize it as an object of reading. In sixteenth- and seventeenth-century Spain, this instability becomes—or is made to seem—particularly disruptive in the case of the wife's body, so that if the female body is culturally and historically designated as a space for reading and, moreover, for projecting anxieties concerning illegibility, it is on the symbolic body of a wife that those anxieties are most suggestively and also most problematically engaged. This is true for a number of reasons that remit not only to the symbolic and epistemologic topography of early modern Spain, but to its specific political and sociocultural topography as well. One of the most compelling among them has to do with the very specific sort of illegibility with respect to illicit penetrations that the wife's body was thought to encode. The problem arises from the crucial distinction (from the point of view of the patriarchy) between the bodies of virgin and wife. If the (ostensibly) intact hymen of a virgin is made to serve as a univocal sign for chastity (obviating, for the moment, the duplicitous readings that hymeneal mendings of the sort practiced by a Celestina permit), then it is possible to "read" any violation of that virginity by the absence of blood on the wedding sheets.[21] The figure of the hymen is granted, in this sense, the status of an unequivocal sign, inasmuch as its "integrity" supports one reading (virginity) while its "fragmentation" supports another (penetration) with no perceptible middle ground for misinterpretation. Sebastián de Covarrubias's well-known emblem for virginity (see figure 1)[22] is a case in point, inscribing the sense or irreparability and absoluteness with which the concept—materialized in the hymen—is charged: "Nulla reparabilis arte".[23] As Mary Gossy has suggestively argued, however, "The emblem in place to define *virgen* indicates 'broken hymen' instead. Covarrubias's writing in the virgin space seeks certainty in the destruction of the object it tries to define and takes comfort in the authoritative affirmation that the hymen he has rent cannot be mended."[24] Gossy goes on to suggest that hymen menders, from Celestina to the spurious aunt in Cervantes's *La tía fingida*, challenge this sort of claim by confounding meaning, keeping what she refers to as "the untold story" provocatively untold.

But what is interesting for our purposes here is that, even without the ministrations of a Celestina, in the case of a married woman it becomes impossible to accurately read the signs of sexual transgression (specifically, marital infidelity) on her body—or her bed—since in order to legally fulfill the requirements of legitimate wife (and, not by coincidence, legitimate heir), the marriage must be already consummated. In other words, where her chastity is concerned, the wife's body is illegible in ways that are not only specific to but requisite of her legal status as wife. Illegibility, in this context, is a precarious condition: although it could be construed as liberating (inasmuch as it positions the body in a certain "beyond binarism"), it is, more often, cause for anxiety.

The legal and social implications of this form of illegibility that is specific to the wife's body are not, as we shall see, unimportant in a culture that institutionalizes exclusions based on blood and that symbollically charges the wife, as potential mother, with responsibility

Figure 1. Sebastián de Covarrubias, *Emblemas morales.* [The beauty and excellence of the virginal flower is so great among mortals that even celestial spirits honor and revere it. Precious jewel, unequaled bounty, virginal breasts must not lose it. For to repair it is a feat beyond heaven or earth, nature or art.]

for perpetuating the purity of that blood. One of the reasons for controlling the wife's sexuality had to do, precisely, with the possibility that through childbirth she could pass off as "Same" what was in fact "Other," since a child born of an adulterous affair could potentially be taken for legitimate, clouding not just questions of inheritance but also of limpieza de sangre. Anxieties concerning such passings might help account for the distinction in both ecclesiastical writing and in legal statutes of the period between *adulterio* and *fornicación* (that is, sex between an unmarried man and an unmarried woman — most often a prostitute), with the more serious punishment reserved for adulteresses.[25]

But the semiotic and epistemologic implications of the wife's illegibility vis-à-vis adultery are, for our purposes here, no less important. The virtual absence of a visible, bodily sign of transgression (penetration) tends to destabilize the referential contract (itself conceivable as a marriage). The wife's adultery becomes, in this sense, a kind of signified without a signifier or, at least, without the somatic signifier that, because of the premium placed on virginity (narrowly defined as hymeneal integrity), one might expect. There is, in other words, no somatic *signum visibile* of wifely adultery (and, by extension, no sign to disprove it); the "natural" signifier that ought to be there is missing as an index (or exists, rather, only as a kind of *blank* index) to guarantee legibility. In its absence, almost anything can — and usually does — take its place: makeup or noncontainment (as in Fray Luis), whispers in the dark or another man's dagger (as in Calderón). Signs of adultery can always potentially encode an adultery of signs. The proliferation of "incorrect" signifiers for the signified "adultery" is alignable, in this sense, with a disjunctive, baroque aesthetics.[26] The cultural desire (masked by anxiety) *for* the signified "adultery" (the need to know) together with the kind of magnetic force generated by the vacant signifier position (that results in this baroque proliferation) become particularly dangerous for the wife, however, since almost any sign can be read as confirmation of her sexual transgression and, consequently, as pretext for punishment. Paradoxically, the ungrounding of epistemologic certainty and the radically disjunctive (and, one might argue, catachrestic) semiosis that the illegibility of adultery on the wife's body instances become coterminous with an inquisitorial and punitive hermeneutic.

As it happens, the possibility of "improper" semiotic transfer that adultery mobilizes (and even naturalizes) is not, in some respects, unlike the equally improper semantic transfer of the term current in early modern Spain and recorded in Sebastián de Covarrubias's *Tesoro:*

> Adulterar. Es tener ayuntamiento carnal con persona que es casada, o siendo ambos los que se juntan casados, y haziendo trayción a sus consortes. Adulterio, el tal ayuntamiento ilícito; *adulterium, quasi ad alterum.* Adulterino, el hijo concebido desta cópula. Transfiérese a otras cosas, quando son sacadas de su propio ser y las falsifican y contrahazen. En la Sagrada Escritura, adulterar, vale idolatrar.

> [Adulterate. Is to have carnal relations with a person who is married or, both the parties who have intercourse being married, and betraying their consorts. Adultery, such illicit coupling; *adulterium,* as if *ad* (toward) *alterum* (the other). Illegitimate child, the child conceived from this joining. It is transferred to other things, when they are taken out of their proper context and are falsified and counterfeited. In Holy Scripture, adultery means idolatry.][27]

The misappropriation of the term (the move away from a strictly sexual or somatic register that Covarrubias points to) suggests reading a narrative of adultery inscribed in the use of the term "adultery," as if the lexical signifier were, in some sense, unfaithful to its literal (or at least more narrow) meaning of a specifically sexual transgression of the marital bond. The condition that Covarrubias stipulates for the lexical transfer ("quando son sacadas de su propio ser" [when they are taken out of their proper context]) is, of course, easily satisfied by the transfer itself, confirming not only the impropriety of the borrowing, but also its own adulterous quality. More important to my argument about early modern uses of the wife's body (and, quite often, of an "adulterous" wife's body) as a transcoder for other areas, however, is the way in which the *concept* of adultery was used in sixteenth- and seventeenth-century Spain not only to signify other things (that generally had nothing to do with violations of the marital contract) but, moreover, to expose their impropriety, their perceived Otherness.

The etymology of adultery, as Covarrubias suggests (*ad alterum*), implies, precisely, a movement toward the Other.[28] Among those "otras cosas" that adultery wrongly names, none is more suggestive for the sort of reading of wives' bodies that I propose here than its scriptural meaning of idolatry.[29]

But if the use of the wife's body as a figure for both interpretive and political anxieties is partly the result of the illegibility of adultery that derives from her status as nonvirgin and the disjunctive semiosis that this illegibility seems to harbor (both of which find haunting resonances in readings of the converso's body), it is also the result of the liminal position with respect to categories of Self (or Same) and Other—or, to put it in slightly different terms, of classic and grotesque—that her body is made to occupy.[30] It hardly seems necessary to rehearse the countless cultural mechanisms by means of which the position of the female has historically been constructed as an Other against which a male subject could define itself; it is precisely this sort of construction that has legitimated the textualization and aestheticization of the female body as an object of reading.[31] The dialectic of Self and Other that informed so much of the philosophical feminism of the late 1970s is, as Hélène Cixous exposed in her recovery of Medusa's laughter, a tenaciously gendered one.[32] The analogy Self : Other :: Male : Female that inscribes sexual difference as a fundamental binarism is firmly rooted in the founding discourses of both philosophy (in Aristotle's *Metaphysics*, for example) and religion (in the text of Genesis 2 that inscribes woman's ancillary creation). Albeit spurious, it is nonetheless the ubiquitousness of this dialectic that makes gender relations—and particularly marriage—such a useful and economic master trope for figuring relations of power and inequality in early modern Europe.[33] In the words of Natalie Zemon Davis,

> Sexual symbolism, of course, is always available to make statements about social experience and to reflect (or conceal) contradictions within it. At the end of the Middle Ages and in early modern Europe, the relation of the wife—of the potentially disorderly woman—to her husband was especially helpful for expressing the relation of all subordinates to their superiors. . . . In the little world of the family, with its conspicuous tension between intimacy and power,

the larger matters of political and social order could find ready symbolization.[34]

" 'Woman' becomes," in the words of James Fernández, "a handy,
internal, European 'other,' to be evoked and exported whenever necessary." [35] But such a move is at least partly dependent on the fact that she
is, as Fernández deftly exposes, "handy" and "internal." Anne Cruz
and Mary Elizabeth Perry, who cast the issue largely as a question of
gender control, also point to this sort of no-man's-land that women
inhabited in early modern Spain, neither insider nor outsider but both:
"Women posed different problems of control: crossing both class and
ethnic lines, women were perceived in the Counter-Reformation as
the most dangerous threat to Christian morality, yet they could not
be totally separated from the majority, and indeed, they were ever
present, whether as wives, daughters, sisters, or mothers." [36] This is
particularly so, I would argue, in the case of the wife; she represents
the Other who is, quite literally, closest to home (if not contained
within it) — so much so, in fact, that her body is sacramentally designated as being "of the same flesh" as her husband.[37] The very passage of Genesis 2 that inscribes woman's Otherness (by marking her
body's secondary and derivative creation) effectively sanctions her
matrimonial Sameness (not to be confused with equality, however).
Trent's institution at its Twenty-Fourth Session (11 November 1563)
of the indissolubility of marriage — authorized, precisely, by invoking
the Genesis text — confirms the centrality of the one-flesh doctrine
within Catholic dogma:

> The perpetual and indissoluble bond of matrimony was expressed by
> the first parent of the human race, when, under the influence of the
> divine Spirit, he said: *This now is bone of my bones and flesh of my flesh.*
> *Wherefore a man shall leave his father and mother and shall cleave to his*
> *wife, and they shall be two in one flesh.* But that by this bond two only
> are united and joined together, Christ the Lord taught more plainly
> when referring to those last words as having been spoken by God,
> He said: *Therefore now they are not two, but one flesh*, and immediately
> ratified the firmness of the bond so long ago proclaimed by Adam
> with these words: *What therefore God has joined together, let no man*
> *put asunder.*[38]

If the position of the Other is potentially dangerous for the wife to occupy, that of a sacramentally converted Same is not necessarily any less vulnerable. The immediate threat stems from the degree to which the one-flesh doctrine that inscribes the wife's carnal "Sameness" was subject to overliteralization.[39] In other words, by means of a too literal understanding of the transformation effected by the marital sacrament, adulterous penetration of the wife's body translates into penetration of the husband's body, since husband and wife are, effectively, two in one flesh. What is more, given the alignments between marriage and Sameness, and between adultery (*ad alterum*) and Otherness, the liminality between positions of Self or Same and Other that makes the wife's body such an attractive figure for projecting and reading both hermeneutic and political anxieties finds particularly rich resonances in the adulterous wife's body.[40]

If up to now I have laid out the mechanisms of appropriation of the wife's body as a privileged site through which semiotic, epistemologic, and political discourses resonate that derive either from her body specifically or from the ways in which marriage and adultery lend themselves to troping, I now turn to the means through which the conflation of somatic and nonsomatic fields of signification is specifically supported by the text of theology. I choose eucharistic transubstantiation (and Tridentine Counter Reformation, more generally) as a point of departure for my argument in the pages ahead not because I credit it with full responsibility for the uncertainty of signs in early modern Spain, but for a number of other reasons that may help account for the displacements among the body of the wife, the body of Christ (the Host), and the body of the cultural Other. First, the extreme sort of literalization that transubstantiation inscribes is perhaps not unlike the literalization of the marital sacrament's one-flesh doctrine. Second, the transubstantial debate explores the mechanics of conversion (in this case, of bread to body) in ways that are both provocative and problematic when considered alongside other sacraments of conversions in early modern Spain. And third, Tridentine eucharistic dogma expounds something akin to an early modern sign theory of crucial importance to the particular form of the baroque that develops in Spain and her American colonies.

"Accidente sin sujeto"

The literalization of the marital sacrament's one-flesh doctrine that renders extremely problematic (if not outright dangerous) the ambiguous position with respect to categories of Same and Other that the wife's body occupies, reenacts, in some senses, the literalness attributed by canon law to another sacrament of fleshly conversion. I refer, specifically, to the eucharistic sacrament's literalization of the hoc est corpus meum, an issue over which a good deal of ink—as well as blood—was spilled throughout the sixteenth century. The importance of eucharistic dogma to early modern theology—and, more broadly, to an early modern epistème—can hardly be overemphasized. In an incisive study that exposes Galileo's persecution for Copernicanism as a red herring used to divert attention from, while still punishing, the threat that his revived atomism represented to eucharistic transubstantiation, Pietro Redondi outlines the centrality of the transubstantial debate in the history of the conflict between faith and reason: "Transubstantiation was the only dogma to render flagrant the antinomy between the testimony of the senses and the affirmation of doctrinal faith. . . . It was not difficult to foresee that this would result in casualties among philosophers and scientists." [41]

It was a questioning of the literalness of transubstantiation, understood as the transformation through consecration of the communion offering into the actual blood and body of Christ, that was considered to be one of the central affronts of the protestant heresy. The eucharistic sacrament became, by extension, a central preoccupation and primary order of business for the Tridentine fathers, who understood their conciliar task as righting heretical wrongs, among which was Reform skepticism concerning the real presence of Christ's body in the Communion Host:

> The holy, ecumenical and general Council of Trent, lawfully assembled in the Holy Ghost, the same legate and nuncios of the Holy Apostolic See presiding, though convenes, not without the special guidance and direction of the Holy Ghost, for the purpose of setting forth the true and ancient doctrine concerning faith and the sacraments,

and of applying a remedy to all the heresies and the other most griev-
ous troubles by which the Church of God is now miserably disturbed
and rent into many and various parts, yet, even from the outset, has
especially desired that it might pull up by the roots the cockles of execrable errors and schisms which the enemy has in these our troubled
times disseminated regarding the doctrine, use and worship of the
Sacred Eucharist, which our Saviour left in His Church as a symbol
of that unity and charity with which He wished all Christians to be
mutually bound and united.[42]

The "execrable errors and schisms" disseminated by the Protestant "enemy" consisted primarily in positing a return to a simpler
(Augustinian) vision of the Eucharistic sacrament: eliding the complicated metaphysics by means of which the Church attempted to
rationalize the transubstantial mystery. The specifically Lutheran
"heresies" regarding eucharistic doctrine were reducible, at some
level, to the nominalist theory of consubstantiation that "admitted the
co-presence of the original substances [of bread and wine] with that of
the body and blood of Christ." [43] Protestants in the Reformed tradition
(who coined the term "consubstantiation" as a critique of what they
held to be too "papist" a stance on Luther's part) went even further
than Lutheran theologians, imagining a certain disjunction or "distinction" between the bread of Communion, as a kind of sign, and the
body of Christ (only virtually or spiritually present in the Host), as
its sacramental meaning.[44] The permanence of the bread's perceptible
phenomena, the cornerstone both of the Lutheran co-presence argument and of the Reformed position, provided the material evidence for
the ungrounding of a literal understanding of the conversion effected
by the pronouncement of the hoc est corpus meum. In other words,
insofar as the Host retained, even after consecration, all its breadlike
properties (color, odor, and taste), it could be conceived, according to
the Reformed reading, as a visible sign or figure for Christ's body, but
not as the literal body of Christ, as the Catholic Church affirmed. The
question became, in this sense, not just an isolated theological debate
but one ripe with semiotic and epistemologic implications as well. The
status of both signification and representation hung in the balance.
The Council of Trent devoted countless sessions to refining its

stance on the mechanics of eucharistic conversion, which was finally institutionalized as dogma during the Council's Thirteenth Session (11 October 1551). The first two "Canons on the Most Holy Sacrament of the Eucharist," which directly responded to the two most threatening aspects of Protestant eucharistic heresy, read as follows:

> Canon 1. If anyone denies that in the sacrament of the most Holy Eucharist are contained truly, really and substantially the body and blood together with the soul and divinity of our Lord Jesus Christ, and consequently the whole Christ, but says that He is in it only in a sign, or figure or force, let him be anathema.
>
> Canon 2. If anyone says that in the sacred and holy sacrament of the Eucharist the substance of the bread and wine remains conjointly with the body and blood of our Lord Jesus Christ, and denies that wonderful and singular change of the *whole* substance of the bread into the body and the *whole* substance of the wine into the blood, the *appearances* only of bread and wine remaining, which change the Catholic Church most aptly calls transubstantiation, let him be anathema.[45]

Trent resolved the question of the Eucharist's status as sign by effectively denying it any symbolic or representational value, arguing instead for the most conjunctive kind of semiosis imaginable: an absolute collapse of the distance between the literal and the figural, or, put another way, between the bread as sign and the body as meaning. The rationalization of this extreme literalness was provided in Canon 2, which definitively reinscribed as dogma the Thomist theory of "accidents without subject" as the most effective and logically frugal explanation for the transubstantial mystery.[46] By grounding his arguments on an Aristotelian hylomorphism that defined substance as the product of both matter (aligned with a body's extension) and form, St. Thomas had managed to rationalize transubstantiation by positing a single (and miraculous) separation of matter from extension.[47] The problem of perceptible phenomena was thus circumvented, since the accidents that derived from the Host's extension (the irksome color, odor, and taste) were, by this mechanism, completely divorced from the "*whole* substance" of the converted bread or wine. The troubling "appearances . . . of bread and wine" that remained even after consecration became quite beside the point, since they were now reduced to "appearances only": accidents suspended without subject ("accidentes sin sujeto").⁴⁸ The eucharistic mystery was institutionalized, then, not as a "formal conversion," but as a fully "substantial one" that inscribed the real—not just the virtual—presence of Christ's body in the consecrated Host. The incredible irony, of course, was that the only way to accomplish this kind of absolute conjunctiveness, on which real presence depended, was by the most radically disjunctive means imaginable: the separation of accidents from substance.

Foreseeably, the fallout of this ongoing debate was not insignificant for systems of representation and signification. Against a Reformation aesthetic posited on a disjunctive semiosis that established a (bridgeable) distance between sign and meaning, there emerged a Counter Reformation aesthetic that sought to deny that distance by arguing for a radical conjunctiveness, a kind of indissoluble marriage between signifier and signified. What is extraordinary about this semiotic code, however, is the way it betrays its own disjunctiveness at the very moment it aims to be most conjunctive, reenacting in this sense the separation of accidents from substance that in theory rationalized the literalness attributed to the transubstantial mystery. In other words, even (or particularly) in the presence of this type of literalization—which seeks to deny or discipline allegorical reading in the most absolute way imaginable by effectively eliminating the distance between interpretive levels—signs are adulterous, reinscribing that distance as an unbridgeable gap and leaving access only to the surface, to the illusion of the trompe l'oeil that is so characteristically baroque.

At a fundamental level, then, the status of the sign itself was at stake in the eucharistic dispute. This has suggestive implications for the argument I make here. If the literalization of the one-flesh doctrine can be seen, in part, as somehow related to the literalization of the transubstantial hoc est corpus meum, then the distance from the wife's body (via the Host) to the sign's body is perhaps not so far to go. In this sense, it is of considerable interest that the Incarnation of Christ, understood as a prefiguration of the transubstantial miracle, was metaphorically figured as a marriage—moreover, as a marriage in and of the flesh. In *De los nombres de Cristo* (1583), for example, Fray Luis explains the significance of the name "Esposo" by sustaining this very point:

Porque, demás de que tomó nuestra carne en la naturaleza de su humanidad, y la ayuntó con su persona divina con ayuntamiento tan firme que no será suelto jamás, el cual ayuntamiento es . . . *un matrimonio indisoluble*, celebrado entre nuestra carne y el Verbo, y el tálamo donde se celebró fue . . . el vientre purísimo, así también esta misma carne y cuerpo suyo, que tomó de nosotros, lo ayunta con el cuerpo de su Iglesia y con todos los miembros de ella, que debidamente la reciben en el Sacramento del altar, allegando su carne a la carne de ellos, y haciéndola, cuanto es posible, con la suya una misma.

[For God became flesh, made Himself human in such a way that the union has become an *indissoluble marriage*, one in which our flesh and the Word have become one, and the nuptial bed where this union took place was . . . the immaculate womb of Mary. Having entered human flesh, endowed with a human body, He then joined His body to the body of His Church, to all those who in His Church make use of the sacrament of holy communion.] [49]

Fray Luis's characterization of the bond between the Word and the flesh as a "matrimonio indisoluble" is not accidental and is perhaps best read as a sign of the times, an example not only of the intersection between these two discourses (marital and eucharistic) but of the way in which each of these two "indissoluble unions" was consistently invoked to confirm the perfection of the other.

Indeed, the exact language of indissolubility that Fray Luis incorporates had been adopted by the Council of Trent during its Twenty-Fourth Session, which explicitly addressed doctrinal controversies surrounding matrimony and, particularly, those raised by protestant arguments in favor of its desacramentalization. [50]

But the grace which was to perfect that natural love, and confirm that indissoluble union, and sanctify the persons married, Christ Himself, the instituter and perfecter of the venerable sacraments, merited for us by His passion, which Paul the Apostle intimates when he says: *Husbands love your wives, as Christ also loved the Church, and delivered himself up for it;* adding immediately, *This is a great sacrament, but I speak in Christ and in the Church.*

The Tridentine fathers authorized marital indissolubility by citing the Pauline analogy between Christ's union with his church (materialized in the eucharistic sacrifice) and the husband's union with his wife. Insofar as the indissolubility of marriage supported its sacramentality, and sacramentality served a fairly explicit political agenda (a papal voice in dynastic unions, for example), the mystery of the Incarnation, and by extension, that of transubstantiation (both of which were used to legitimize marital indissolubility), became, *in potentia,* politically charged.[51]

But even without taking into account the political implications of institutionalizing—or alternately, of deinstitutionalizing—Holy Matrimony as a sacrament, there is little question that both marriage and transubstantiation were issues of much more than theologic concern in early modern Spain. Doctrinal literature of the period confirms this; the late sixteenth and early seventeenth centuries constituted a golden age for both eucharistic and matrimonial treatises not only in Spain but throughout Europe. There is also little question that these two discourses (eucharistic and marital) were metaphorically related, as Fray Luis's gloss on "Esposo" and the Tridentine passage above already suggest. The grounding for this interrelation is provided, on one hand, by the literalness ascribed to both the one-flesh doctrine and the hoc est corpus meum (partly as a result of the corporeal subtext they share), and, on the other, by the indissolubility—and, in this sense, the absolute conjunctiveness—with which they are both charged by the Counter Reformation Church. No doubt the best proof of the alignment between these areas can be found in the autos sacramentales (particularly the Calderonian autos)—the Corpus Christi plays celebrating the transubstantial mystery that exploded during this period and that dramatized the relation between Christ and human nature or between Christ and the Communion Host as a marriage.

Perhaps the most compelling alignment between these various fields, however, returns to the question of conversion or transformation that both transubstantiation and the one-flesh doctrine of marriage presuppose. But if it is conversion that most suggestively links these two sacraments, it is virtually impossible to talk about conversion in sixteenth- and seventeenth-century Spain without invoking what is, undoubtedly, its fundamental cultural signification during this period: the conversion through baptism of the racial and religious Other—Jew, Moor, Amerindian. Indeed, the rendering of Other into Same that in some ways describes the effects of both marital and eucharistic consecration can easily be read as a description of the hegemonizing, protonationalist project of Christian conversion, initiated in the late fifteenth century by the *marriage* of the Catholic Monarchs and carried out by their heirs.

Although the relation between the one-flesh doctrine of marriage, transubstantiation, and baptismal conversion is by no means a perfect analogy, the possibility of a conflation between these three sacraments aligns well with the triple relation I have set forth between the anxieties generated by the wife's body, the sign's body (materialized in the eucharistic Host), and the body of the cultural Other. What is more, the fluidity of these discourses suggests that the anxieties and threats posed by—or against—any one of these areas could potentially be displaced on either one (or both) of the other two. Thus, for example, the literalization that proved so dangerous to the wife's body when transferred from a transubstantial to a marital register proves at least equally problematic when it is transposed to a racial-religious context. If, as a political program, conversion was intended to reduce or transform the non-Christian Other into a Christian Self, a literal reading of that supposed transformation gave rise to very real dangers. Any sign of suspected Otherness was deemed (just as adultery was seen as a sign of wifely deviance, or insistence on the substantial permanence of perceptible phenomena, as a sign of eucharistic heresy) subject to persecution and punishment by the Inquisition. The position of a sacramentally converted Same became, as I suggested earlier with respect to the wife's body, as precarious as that of Other, since, save for (and even in) the case of a miracle such as that which putatively rationalized the transubstantial conversion, any "remnant" of Otherness was inevitably read as a mark of contamination, a locus of disease that required extirpation.

The cultural anxiety to discover a vestigial remnant or trace of a supposedly discarded Other derives, largely, from the extent to which the symbolic construction of a cultural—and national—Self is dependent on the demarcation of Otherness. Definition of the subject seems to require, in other words, a marker of difference; a canon—national or otherwise—is as much the product of exclusion as it is of inclusion. "Differentiation," as Stallybrass and White maintain, "is dependent upon disgust." The argument they pose with respect to the formation of a bourgeois subject could easily apply to that of an early modern subject as well: "The bourgeois subject continuously defined and re-defined itself through the exclusion of what it has marked out as 'low'—as dirty, repulsive, noisy, contaminating. Yet that very act of exclusion was constitutive of its identity. The low was internalized under the sign of negation and disgust."[52] In early modern Spain, the move seems strikingly paradoxic, however, given the historical pretext of the late fifteenth century. If the expulsion and forced conversion program instituted by the Catholic Monarchs was intended to either banish or incorporate (through baptism) the semitic Other under the banner of a monolithic, Christian Spain, then once that program was successfully negotiated and the Jewish Other had been (at least symbolically) eradicated from the cultural landscape, the need arose for a *new* Other against which the Self could articulate itself. While this vacancy was partly filled by the body of the Morisco and, from across the ocean, by the body of an indigenous, American Other that conveniently appeared on the scene at this precise juncture, its pull was so forceful as to elicit the institutionalization of a secondary division within the category (Christian) that previously conferred sameness. The demarcation that emerged—between cristianos viejos and cristianos nuevos—formed the basis for what would become perhaps *the* central cultural obsession in Spain throughout the sixteenth and seventeenth centuries: the preoccupation over limpieza de sangre. Religious exclusion thus gave way to a kind of racial exclusion, as evidenced by the renewed fervor with which purity of blood statutes were applied. Albert Sicroff writes:

> Despite the sharp reduction in the number of Conversos convicted of relapsing into Judaism, the pure blood statutes were enforced with increasing severity in the latter part of the 16th century and during most of the 17th century. The implications of this increased preoccupation with blood purity in Spain, while the number of Judaizing New Christians decreased, must not be overlooked. By the middle of the

16th century, these statutes had taken on a new importance in Spain. Whereas in the 15th century they had been instituted by the Spanish Old Christians as an instrument for delivering Spain from the hands of the Conversos—as a sort of second Reconquest directed against an *internal* enemy—in the latter part of the 16th century the statutes were the instrument for keeping intact the *racial* honor of Spanish communities as 'pure Christian.'[53]

But if this new binarism between tainted and pure blood partly filled the vacancy left by the Jewish expulsion, it also resulted in (as much as it was the result of) fundamental semiotic and epistemologic problems, problems that are intimately tied not only to the institutional presence and function of the Inquisition in early modern Spain, but to a baroque ungrounding of certainty itself. To begin with, insofar as the new rift was posited on suspicions of pseudo-Christianity on behalf of conversos and Moriscos, it rendered entirely questionable the ascribed efficacy of the baptismal sacrament. Even more troubling, however, was the lack of visible signs for this new Otherness, specifically, for the crypto-Judaism and crypto-Islam of which cristianos nuevos were suspect. Historically, both Jews and Moors had been forced, by law, to explicitly display their difference on their bodies. The mid-thirteenth century legal codex of Alfonso el Sabio, *Las siete partidas*, includes instructions on "cómo los judíos deben andar señalados porque sean conoscidos" [how the Jews must be marked so that they be recognized]:

> Muchos yerros et cosas desaguisadas acaescen entre los cristianos et los judios et las cristianas et las judias, porque viven y moran de so uno en las villas, et andan vestidos los unos asi como los otros. Et por desviar los yerros et los males que podien acaescer por esta razon, tenemos por bien et mandamos que todos cuantos judios et judias vivieren en nuestro señorio, que trayan alguna *seña cierta* sobre las cabezas, que sea atal porque conoscan las gentes manifiestamente cual es judio o judia.

> [Many crimes and illicit things occur between Christians and Jews, both male and female, because they live and reside together in cities, and dress alike. And in order to avert the crimes and offenses which

could take place for this reason, we deem it proper, and we order that
all Jews male and female living in our realm shall bear some manifest
sign upon their heads, by which people may plainly recognize who is
a Jew or a Jewess.] [54]

Whether or not laws of this sort were observed or even enforced is not
perhaps as important as the fact that they recognized the need for an
institutionalized system for reading difference.

Once expulsion forced semitic difference underground in the late fifteenth century, there was no longer any reliable way to identify Otherness. By the seventeenth century, the interpretive anxieties provoked
by this epistemologic and semiotic ungrounding generated a kind of
nostalgia for the more secure legibility of bygone days. Traces of this
nostalgia can be gleaned, for example, from Covarrubias's entry for
the term *judío,* specifically, from his definition of *judíos de señal.*

Judío. . . . En España han habitado judíos de muchos siglos atrás, hasta
que en tiempo de nuestros abuelos, los Reyes Católicos, sin reparar
en lo que perdían de sus rentas, los echaron de España. . . . En tiempo
del rey don Enrique, cerca de los años de mil e trezientos e setenta,
en las Cortes que se tuvieron en Toro, se mandó que los judíos que
habitavan en el reyno, mezclados con los christianos, *truxessen cierta
señal con que fuessen conocidos y diferenciados de los demás. Estos se llamaron judíos de señal.* Y el año de mil quatrocientos y cinco se ordenó
y executó que los judíos truxessen por señal un pedaço de paño roxo,
en forma redonda, sobre el ombro derecho . . . y dende a tres años
mandaron traer a los moros otra señal de paño açul, en forma de luna
menguante con cuernos. . . . Traer el judío en el cuerpo, estar con
miedo.

[Jew. . . . Jews have lived in Spain from many centuries back, until
when, in our grandparents' time, the Catholic Monarchs drove them
out of Spain, without regard as to what they would lose in taxes. . . .
In the time of King Don Enrique, around the year 1370, in the Courts
that were held at Toro, it was ordered that all Jews who lived in the
kingdom, mixed with Christians, *should wear a certain sign by which
they would be known and differentiated from the rest. These were called
signed Jews.* And in the year 1405, it was ordered and executed that

Jews should bear as their sign a piece of red cloth, cut in a circle, over their right shoulder . . . and within three years, Moors were ordered to wear another sign made of blue cloth, in the shape of a waning moon with horns. . . . To carry the Jew in one's body means to be afraid.] [55]

In the absence of any natural or somatic sign of Otherness, the very fact of being a convert became sign enough, indicator of a potential atavism that might contaminate the emergent subject or, more broadly, the nascent body of the corporate state. It is no wonder, then, that "traer el judío en el cuerpo" was synonymous with being afraid.

On the margins between Same and Other, the converso's or Morisco's body could be conceived, in this sense, as analogous to the wife's body: always a potential source of "disease" and "impurity." [56] It is no coincidence that the honor code and limpieza statutes shared a rhetoric of maculacy and immaculacy (the former associated with adultery and semitic blood, the latter with marital chastity and cristiano viejo origins), or that both applied this rhetoric to a narrative of blood. Neither is it a coincidence that for both the (adulterous) wife and the (presumably false) converso or Morisco the threat of contamination was perceived as particularly serious because of its fundamental illegibility. If, as I have argued, the absence of a reliable, somatic sign of a wife's adultery suggests reading it as a kind of signified without a stable signifier, it is not difficult to imagine a similar dynamic at work with respect to impure blood.

The lack of an authoritative signum visibile of impure blood did not, however, deter somatic readings. On the contrary, in an effort to render legible the symptoms of Otherness, the bodies of conversos suspected of Judaizing were regularly submitted to rigorous examination, mined for incriminating evidence. Perhaps the last remaining somatic (and in this sense, presumably "reliable") sign of Jewish Otherness was circumcision. Strippings to discover the presence of this indelible mark constituted, in effect, one of the most common forms of investigation for male converts from Judaism. The case of Juan Xardim, a converso from Toledo suspected of Judaizing, is, in many respects, representative. On 22 October 1546 the Suprema of the Holy Office wrote to local inquisitors and suggested the following course of action: "se devía hazer alguna diligençia con todo rrecato y secreto para saver y ver si

los hijos del dicho Juan Xardim están circumçidados y . . . se ha ofre-
çido un medio en de que el maestro descuela donde andan a leer, con
alguna ocasión de açotarlos, lo mirase" [some steps should be taken
with all caution and secrecy to find out if the sons of the aforementioned Juan Xardim are circumcised and . . . a means has presented
itself by way of their schoolteacher, who, by finding some occasion to
administer lashes to them, might take a look].[57] The passage underscores, among other things, the conflation and almost double causality
in the relation between punishment and inquisitorial knowledge. Not
only is punishment the end term of the series, since the confirmation
of suspicion will presumably lead to further discipline, but it is also
its starting point; here bodily punishment (in the form of the boys'
undeserved lashing from their schoolteacher) is proposed as a kind of
surveillance technique that will ostensibly provide the sought-after
knowledge.

But what is perhaps most suggestive of the passage and, more
broadly, of the reading of male bodies for signs of circumcision is the
problematic legibility of that "sign" once difference is institutionally
defined as transgressive. On one hand, the physical evidence of circumcision on a converso did not necessarily prove nonorthodoxy so
much as point to a past life. If the baptismal sacrament were effica-
cious, after all, then circumcision could be conceived as a kind of accidente sin sujeto, the ungrounded remnant of a previous state, much
like the breadlike qualities of color, odor, and taste that remained in
the Communion Host after transubstantiation. On the other hand, a
crypto-Jew — or the male child of one — might not have been circumcised precisely in order to avoid indicting readings. The absence of a
somatic sign of Otherness, then, was not considered sufficient to prove
orthodoxy. But neither was the presence of a sign of orthodoxy, since
it was assumed — and not erroneously — that signs could be falsified.
Readings were particularly vexed in the case of the Muslims since the
Islamic principle of *taqiyya* (precaution) allowed them to feign acceptance of Christian beliefs without transgressing Islamic law. Shortly
after the expulsion, a Morisco exiled in Tunis wrote, "Apremiaron (los
cristianos) esta nación andaluça con prisiones, tormentos y muertes y
con todo (los nuestros) sustentaron la firmeça de la fe verdadera mos-
trándoles uno y teniendo en su coraçon otro. . . ." [The Christians

imposed prison, torture and death upon this Andalusian nation and even so (our brethren) sustained the firmness of true faith, manifesting one thing and holding in their hearts another. . .].[58] In fact it was a mistrust in signs — absent or present ones — and the duplicities they encoded that legitimated the institutional presence of the Inquisition in early modern Spain. The irony, of course, is the extent to which that very presence contributed to an uncontrollable proliferation of — and, consequently, a radical mistrust in — the very signs the Inquisition sought to regulate. The status of evidence — and even physical, bodily evidence — was always questionable at best.

I opened this chapter with an epigraph from Cervantes's "El curioso impertinente," a text that turns precisely on the complicated relation between the body of the wife and the body of evidence in early modern Spain. I would like to close by returning to that passage — the moment in which Lotario appeals to a literalized version of the one-flesh doctrine in what proves to be a futile effort to dissuade Anselmo from putting his wife's perfection to the test — specifically, to the word that in a sense determines and at the same time renders questionable the efficacy of the conversion on which the "two shall become one" logic depends: "voluntad" [will]. It is around the question of the wife's will that the various knots we have been raveling and unraveling throughout these pages become most suggestively entangled. If, as I argued above, the "wife" marks the point at which "woman" is constituted as a subject before the discourses of the law, religion, and economics, it is also the point at which that subject is — through a literal reading of the marital sacrament, not substantially different from the one Lotario cites — immediately subjected to her *husband's* will. But like the eucharistic conversion of bread to body, or the baptismal conversion of a circumcised Jew or Muslim, the marital conversion leaves a remnant that exceeds the supposed reduction (of two bodies to one flesh, or, in Lotario's account, two souls to one will) that the sacrament ostensibly effects. This excess — the trace that reveals that the wife is neither of one body nor of one soul with her husband — is starkly manifested in the *wife's* will, and specifically, in the expression of that will that is, on the surface, most radically at odds with the will of her husband — the adulterous agency of her body.

It is tempting to speculate what a Tridentine reading of the wife's will (in the form of this excess agency) might have consisted of. One alternative — exploiting the relation we have been articulating between the marital and eucharistic sacraments — would be to consider it a kind of accidente sin sujeto, not unlike the breadlike properties that fired the transubstantial debate. One might argue that in sixteenth- and seventeenth-century Spain, the wife's will could only appear, after all, under the aspect of the accident: performatively constituted the moment she gave her hand in marriage, but in theory purged or reduced to the category of mere accident almost simultaneously. This argument, like the Thomist hylomorphism it recites, is largely predicated on a scholastic understanding of the word "accident": as an inessential attribute that somehow grazes but does not alter the subject in its essence. This was, in fact, the prevailing signification of "accidente" in early modern Spain and it is in this sense that Covarrubias's *Tesoro* defines the term.

> Acidente. *Latine accidens.* Este término es muy usado de los dialécticos, y tómase por toda calidad que se quita y se pone en el sujeto sin corrupción suya. Dezimos comúnmente el accidente de la calentura y otra cualquiera indisposición que de repente sobreviene al hombre.
>
> [Accident. *Latine accidens.* This term is very common among those who practice dialectics, and is taken for any quality that can be removed or added to a subject, without corrupting it. We commonly say accident to refer to fever or any other indisposition that suddenly befalls man.][59]

But as Covarrubias's reference to sudden afflictions — those *calenturas de repente* — tidily exposes, the term "accident" also stood for, and increasingly so, something that occurs unexpectedly, that which "suddenly befalls man." This second meaning (partly grounded in the etymology of the Latin *accidens*) is of some consequence for the first: the unforeseen accident might be seen as that which in a sense reveals and secondarily determines the essence of the thing (the subject), precisely by threatening it with contingency. If this poses the (accidental) danger of somehow essentializing the accident, the seeming paradox should not surprise us, however. If the accident (in the second sense of chance occurrence) marks the outside, the aberration, that which escapes or exceeds the norm, it is also what constitutively marks the boundary, the exception that writes the rule.

It is perhaps not by accident, then (in either sense), that the three textual bodies that *Perfect Wives* reads all engage, to varying degrees, the category of the accidental in their respective readings of wives' bodies. A different version of this project might make this engagement its central concern, tracing, for example, the aesthetic and theologic dimensions of the accident in early modern Europe and in these works particularly, or plotting what we might term an "accidental genealogy" from Aristotle — or even Plato — to Aquinas, Augustine, Suárez, and Descartes, among others, and then reading that genealogy in relation to early modern notions of gender, or of matrimony, or of the body. (A variant of this last direction can be found in Jacques Lezra's stunning reading of history effects and body effects in an early modern genealogy of the event, where event is understood as both an occurrence that marks a history and a kind of accident.)[60] Although these questions remain only at the margins of this study, let me, if only in a cursory way, try to account for the presence of the accident in the three works that concern us.

In *La perfecta casada,* the accidental is that which threatens or obscures legibility: the colors of makeup, for example, or what Fray Luis refers to as "obrecillas menudas" [small matters]. One could say that the treatise stakes the wife's perfection on the distinction between the accidental and the essential, a distinction that proves, foreseeably, impossible to uphold within the text's discursive economy. *El médico de su honra* is everywhere riddled by the accident. Not only is the play doubly framed by accidental occurrences — it opens with the signature Calderonian fall from a horse that delivers Enrique at Mencía's doorstep and closes with the murder that Gutierre doctors to look like an accident — but its action moves through what might be seen as a chain of accidents that troubles the supposed antinomy between the causal and the casual, even as it points to the author's hand behind the curtain — or on the unruly horse's reins. In *Los empeños de una casa,* the category of the accidental appears almost as if by accident: Sor Juana fully incorporates the accident, but the gesture takes the form of a subtle baroque nod. The accident appears as a trace, an absent remnant, in the wordplay of the drama's title that slyly transforms *Empeños de un acaso* (the title of a contemporary play by Calderón) to *Empeños de una casa*. The accidental *un acaso* — "lo que sucede sin pensar ni estar prevenido" [what occurs without thinking or warning] in Covarrubias's formulation [61] — is feminized (through an accident at the material level of the letter) to *una casa*, the house of *empeños* — whims, desires, but also, suggestively, pawns, debts, and obligations. It is in this uncanny, domestic space haunted by accident where the bodies of the would-be casa-das of the drama are contained and bartered ("empeñadas") and where gender itself is shown to be little more than an accident, a superficial inscription that is not even skin-deep. [62]

We might say that in all three works, the accidental crops up to belie the possibility of reading the wife's will as a hylomorphic *accidente sin sujeto*. If, as I suggested above, the wife's will can appear only under the aspect of the accident in sixteenth- and seventeenth-century Spain, it nevertheless resists the possibility of being suspended without subject. It is precisely this resistance — the irreducibility of the wife's subjectivity, the inscrutability of her will — that requires surveillance. The accident can be said to occur at the meeting place of subjectivity and surveillance; it marks the limits of both, if not of legibility itself. It is no surprise, then, that the accident should play a central role in conduct manuals for married women and adultery-honor plays, textual sites where subjectivity and surveillance continuously overlap and do so, moreover, through or on the willful body of the wife.

"Pasos de un peregrino"

Luis de León Reads the Perfect Wife

Buscas en Roma a Roma, ¡oh, peregrino!

y en Roma misma a Roma no la hallas.

[You search in Rome for Rome, oh pilgrim,

and in Rome itself Rome you do not find.]

— Francisco de Quevedo

"A Roma sepultada en sus ruinas"

On 29 June 1492, as Columbus was making final arrangements for his westward sail to the East and thousands of Jews were preparing to flee Spain in compliance with the Edict of Expulsion that the Catholic Monarchs had signed into law only weeks after the fall of Granada, two converted Jews from the town of Quintanar were condemned to a diaspora of a different sort. That afternoon, the Holy Office of the Inquisition for the bishopric of Cuenca and Sigüenza ordered that the corpses of Fernán Sánchez de Villanueva Daviuelo and his wife, Elvira Sánchez, be exhumed from consecrated ground, their remains burned and scattered, and all their former possessions confiscated from their descendants.[1] Although neither as momentous nor as tragic as the other events that took place that fateful summer, the case of the Quintanar couple is both momentous and tragic on its own terms, a dramatic statement of the extent of the Inquisition's power in those years, from which not even the grave provided a reliable safe haven. The accusations of heresy and apostasy brought against the Sanchezes were largely corroborated by their daughter-in-law, one Juana de la Serna, remarried widow of Gonçalo de Quintanar, who recounted before two inquisitors, identified as Sancho Licenciado and el Bachiller del Castillo, how during the year and a half that she lived with her in-laws, she watched silently as her father-in-law "read books in Hebrew every day, especially Saturdays . . . making the gestures and actions that Jews make when they read" [todos los dias leer en unos libros de ebraico especialmente los sabados . . . haçiendo gestos e abtos que los judios azen cuando leen], and witnessed her mother-in-law not only rendering homage to the Torah but defending its authority over Christian Scripture.[2]

The incident is by no means extraordinary. Among the annals of the Holy Office countless cases can be found of individuals similarly condemned as heretics on evidence as tenuous and as paltry as that which resulted in the posthumous excommunication and disinterment of Fernán and Elvira Sánchez. Two of those cases, in fact, occurred in the same family, pointing to the perverse irony — or inquisitorial efficacy — by which the most tragic histories seem to repeat themselves. Twenty years later, in 1512, Leonor de Villanueva, granddaughter of Fernán and Elvira Sánchez, together with her sister, Juana Rodríguez, were condemned of Judaizing and were reconciled in a Cuencan auto-da-fé. And another sixty years after that, Leonor de Villanueva's great-grandson would be imprisoned by the Valladolid branch of the Inquisition on charges not unlike those leveled against his forebears in 1492: defending the authority of Hebrew Scriptures and reading literally, like a Jew.

"Al salir de la cárcel"

In March 1572, Fray Luis de León, Augustinian friar, chair of theology and later of scripture at the University of Salamanca, brilliant humanist, theologist, poet, prose writer, translator, philologist, Latinist, Hebraist, and great-great-great-grandson of Fernán Sánchez de Villanueva and Elvira Sánchez, was arrested and jailed by the Valladolid Inquisition. It was not Fray Luis's first encounter with the Holy Office. Since 1566, rumors about his unorthodox criticisms of the Vulgate translation had been circulating at Salamanca, raising inquisitors' ears and eyebrows; the year prior to his arrest, he had been denounced

—but not officially charged—for his teachings on marriage. This time, however, the charges against him were not only far more serious but also well substantiated: favoring the original Hebrew Scriptures over the Vulgate, questioning the accuracy of the LXX Interpreters, advocating pluralism in the interpretation of Holy Writ, and translating the *Song of Songs* into Spanish. Fray Luis's most vocal accusers were his own colleagues at Salamanca, where he had made a number of enemies over the years largely as a result of his irrepressible and at times contentious brilliance. Chief among them were the Dominican friars Bartolomé de Medina and León de Castro, who both envied Fray Luis's considerable talents and with both of whom Fray Luis had clashed loudly and regularly on matters of translation and interpretation.

Luis de León would spend nearly five years in the Inquisition's secret jails awaiting a verdict, the first several months of them without even knowing of what he was accused. The inquisitorial documents relating to his case and especially the heart-rending *auto-acusaciones* are a compelling testimony to the terroristic efficacy of the Inquisition's strategies for coercing confessions by means of its own silence. By purposely withholding from the accused the nature of the charges against them, while at the same time forcing detailed, written confessions, the Holy Office often obtained sufficient material to fuel new allegations; in attempting to clear their names of suspicion by second-guessing (in order to respond to) their alleged wrongdoings, detainees would often implicate themselves further. During those five years, Fray Luis was held in a small, poorly ventilated cell, with little food and less light. He was denied the sacraments, despite asking for them repeatedly, and suffered from depression and ill health. His medical condition was serious enough that his jailers were ordered to torture him with restraint so as not to further endanger his precarious state. In December 1576, the long-awaited verdict finally came: Fray Luis was absolved of all charges against him and resumed his faculty position at the university. Though no doubt an apocryphal story, popular lore has it that on his triumphant return to Salamanca, he entered his classroom, took up the book he had been forced to abandon five years earlier, and seemingly unshaken by the ordeal he had undergone, began his lesson with the words "Decíamos ayer" [as we were saying yesterday].

In 1583, more than ten years after his initial arrest and a year after yet another inquisitorial process against him was dropped, Fray Luis published his first work in Spanish: a double edition that contained the first part of *De los nombres de Cristo* together with *La perfecta casada*, a prescriptive instruction manual intended for the moral and practical edification of housewives. The conduct manual for wives, which was reprinted five times in as many years, would become, together with the thirty or so poems that canonized their author as perhaps the greatest lyric poet of Spanish literature, Fray Luis's most widely read work.[3] Despite its broad popularity, however, the treatise was not well received critically. Censured early on for treating a subject matter deemed inappropriate for a man of the cloth, the work was soon marginalized within Fray Luis's corpus as a book strictly "for women," not particularly worthy of critical attention, on one hand, or of its author, on the other.[4]

The critical reception bestowed on *La perfecta casada* throughout the four centuries since its publication, has tended, for the most part, to recast the terms of the early debate and, with them, the work's marginality. The criticism offered by Manuel Durán is representative: "Perhaps one of the reasons for the book's [popular] success is its 'single-mindedness.' The book has one purpose and one message, the purpose being to describe the perfect 'woman-about-the-house' and the message is that busy, cheerful, loving acceptance of everyday tasks is the one and sure passport to married bliss."[5] Aubrey F. G. Bell, whose 1925 *Luis de León: A Study of the Spanish Renaissance* remains the authoritative biography on Fray Luis, laments ("Alas") that the treatise was "read [presumably by women] without understanding, for a foreign observer at the end of the sixteenth century records that women painted their faces as much as ever: 'in Spagna tutte le donne fanno la faccia d'un colore' [in Spain, all women make-up their faces with color]."[6] Joaquín Antonio Peñalosa praises the treatise for its frivolity: "A lo largo de casi cuatro siglos, no deja de leerse este juguete delicioso y popularísimo que todavía hoy, como aseguraba Marañón, 'casi todas las novias españolas reciben entre sus regalos nupciales' " [Over the course of almost four centuries, this delightful and very popular toy does not cease to be read, so that even today, as Marañón asserted, 'almost all Spanish brides receive it among their wedding gifts'].[7] More recently, Colin Thompson's valuable book-length study of the workings of language and biblical hermeneutics in the writings of Luis de León devotes one mere sentence to the treatise: "The only other work which approaches [*De los nombres de Cristo*] in terms of bringing the Bible to the people is *La perfecta casada,* much more restricted in its intention and its scope."[8] Even J. A. Jones, who quite rightly contextualizes *La perfecta casada* within an early modern epistème that conceived of the universe as an Aristotelian Chain of Being discards "the political, social and religious implications" of Fray Luis's vision in order to attend to "the implications on the personal, individual level of the perfect wife."[9]

Although Fray Luis's work clearly responds to—and to some extent models itself on—a tradition of conduct literature intended to keep women in their "proper place," the casting of *La perfecta casada* in strict generic terms (and, as a result, its casting aside from canonical inclusion) glosses over the suggestive contradictions that underwrite the text: contradictions that remit to questions of interpretation in an inquisitorial setting and that are most often born of readings of a prostituted, adulterous female body. These questions are the focus of my reading of the wife's body inscribed in the treatise, a reading that seeks to recover the textual body of *La perfecta casada* from the fate to which it has apparently been condemned—that of a frivolous, minor work undeserving of any kind of canonical inclusion, or worse, a wedding shower gift. If I have inscribed Fray Luis's "juguete delicioso" within the somber context of his ancestors' inquisitorial trial, it is because I believe their disinterment speaks eloquently, if tragically, to a number of anxieties constitutive of early modern Spanish society, anxieties having to do with questions of reading and of Otherness, and anxieties that are legible throughout the pages of Fray Luis's "passport to married bliss." I propose, in fact, to read *La perfecta casada* not only as a conduct manual or even as exegesis (both of which it clearly is, Fray Luis being the first to say so),[10] but also, more provocatively, as a treatise *on* exegesis, a meditation *about* interpretation and its mirages, a text equally at home in the company of Augustine's *De doctrina christiana* as, for example, of Vives's *Manual de instrucción para la mujer cristiana,* and what is more, a reflection on interpretation vehemently grounded in a historical moment in which the stakes of reading were remarkably high. Before doing so, however, I want to very briefly outline some of the ways in which as a textual body, *La perfecta casada* can only be compared to the body of the most *imperfect* of wives, and situate this seeming paradox within debates over the treatise's pro- or antifeminism.

Perhaps the critical persistence in seeking first and foremost "la perfecta casada" in *La perfecta casada* is largely attributable to the treatise's purported goal: to serve as a model of imitation for all married women.[11] Dedicated to Fray Luis's niece, Doña María Varela Osorio, on the occasion of her wedding, the text is clothed in the traditional garb of conduct literature, declaring "las leyes y condiciones que tiene sobre sí la casada" (78) [the laws and conditions imposed upon a wife (5)]. The model on which Fray Luis fashions his textual bride is located in Scripture, conveniently enough, specifically in verses 10 through 31 of the last chapter of Proverbs, described in the treatise sometimes as mirror, sometimes as verbal painting of the inimitable, perfect wife.

> Pues entre otros muchos lugares de los divinos libros que tratan desta razón, el lugar más proprio y adonde está como recapitulado o todo o lo más que a este negocio en particular pertenece, es el último capítulo de los Proverbios, adonde Dios, por boca de Salomón, rey y profeta suyo, y como debajo de la persona de una mujer, madre del mismo Salomón, cuyas palabras él pone y refiere, con gran hermosura de razones *pinta* acabadamente una virtuosa casada, con todos sus colores y partes para las que lo pretenden ser, y débenlo todas las que se casan, se miren en ella como en un espejo clarísimo, y se avisen mirándose allí de aquello que les conviene para hacer lo que deben. (77–78, italics mine)

> [Among the many other places in Holy Scripture that treat this matter, the most proper place and the one in which all or that which is most relevant to this particular business is summed up is the last chapter of Proverbs, where God — through the mouth of Solomon, His King and Prophet and as in the person of a woman, Solomon's mother, whose words Solomon sets down and refers — with great beauty of expression, perfectly paints a virtuous wife, with all her colors and parts, so that those who aspire to be virtuous wives (and all those who marry should) may behold themselves in her as in the clearest mirror

and learn, by seeing themselves there, what it behooves them to do
in order to do as they should.]

The entire treatise is structured, in fact, as a gloss on this scriptural
"painting," a gloss on a gloss, it might be said, since Proverbs 31 is itself
an acrostic: the initial letter of each of its final twenty-two verses combine to form the twenty-two letters of the Hebrew alphabet.[12] There
is little question that the abecedarian cryptogram is part of what attracts Fray Luis to the passage in the first place, although, with good
reason, given his reputation as a Judaizer, he never makes explicit the
philological detail.

Each of the Solomonic verses, which Fray Luis translates into Spanish from the Hebrew (at times going so far as to carefully explicate his
translation), forms the basis for one of the chapters. These are for the
most part comprised of prescriptions and proscriptions for the house-
wife, derived, if somewhat circuitously on occasion, from the particular verse in question. The centerpiece of the treatise, and what has
most consistently sparked the imagination of its readers, is a long and
often virulent reprobation of cosmetic adornment that accounts for a
good third of the text and that freely incorporates Spanish translations
of patristic treatises against face painting.[13] But whether singing the
wife's praises or condemning her faults (two sides of the same coin,
after all), *La perfecta casada* returns time and again to the exemplarity
of the wife of Proverbs and, by extension, to its own status as textual
model, road map even, for domestic perfection:

> esta casada es el perfecto dechado de todas las casadas, y la medida
> con quien, así las mayores como las de menores estados, se han de
> ajustar cuanto a cada una le fuere posible; y es como el padrón desta
> virtud, al cual la que más se avecina es más perfecta. Y que esto sea así
> bastante prueba es que el Espíritu Santo la pinta desta manera. (101)

> [this wife is the perfect model of all wives; the standard by which
> women of all classes, the most exalted as well as the humblest, are
> to measure themselves, in so far as they find it possible; and the pat-
> tern of this virtue, diligence, to which she who comes closest is most
> perfect. And the sufficient proof of all this is that the Holy Spirit . . .
> portrays her after this fashion. (26–27)]

This exemplarity has several implications. To begin with, the notion of model, particularly of the painted model Fray Luis inscribes, clearly invokes the somatic register, suggesting, among other things, that as a model the treatise be read as a textual body. The practice of referring to books as bodies was common enough in early modern Spain: one need look no further than the frontispiece of any number of texts to find, in the inquisitorial censor's "aprobación y licencia," permission for printing a set number of "cuerpos de libros."[14] The "Escrutinio de la librería" chapter of the *Quixote* is no doubt the most stunning, if not the most satirical, meditation on such an alignment. Indeed, Fray Luis himself calls on the analogy between texts and bodies in a striking passage of *De los nombres de Cristo* in which Juliano praises Marcello's somatic exegetics as a particularly apt methodology for explaining the significance of each of the divine names.

> Estas cosas, Marcello, que agora dezís, no las sacáys de vos, ni menos soys el primero que las traéys a luz; porque todas ellas están como sembradas y esparzidas, assí en los libros divinos como en los doctores sagrados, unas en unos lugares y otras en otros; pero soys el primero de los que he visto y oydo yo que, juntando cada una cosa con su igual cuya es, y como pareándolas entre sí y poniéndolas en sus lugares, travándolas todas y dándoles ordén, avéys hecho *como un cuerpo* y como un texido de todas ellas. (bk. 1, 211, italics mine)

> [These things which you are now expressing, Marcelo, you are not drawing from yourself and you are not the first to express them. These are strewn and diffused in the divine books, and in the holy Fathers of the Church in divers places. But among those whom I saw and heard, you are the first to have united them with others that correspond to them, to have assembled them, given them their proper place, a structure, and an order, and to have made of them *one body* and one fabric. (129)]

In its textual composition that salvages and recycles passages "sembradas y esparzidas . . . unas en unos lugares y otras en otros" [strewn and diffused . . . in divers places] as well as in the hermeneutic impulse that forms the seams of the "remiendo," the text of *La perfecta casada* can easily be read as a body, in the very terms that Fray Luis describes.

From here, it is not difficult to imagine that the reflections on bodies contained in the treatise can themselves be read as referring not only to the wife's body, but also to the text's. The irony of such a reading resides in the fact that, as a body, *La perfecta casada* is guilty of almost all the same faults it imputes against the imperfect wife, particularly in her made-up excess. In other words, not only does the treatise lend itself to being read as a (textual) body that is gendered (or made-up as) female, but, moreover, as a female body that is monstrously assembled from fragmented and displaced parts, adulterous in its textual borrowings, and wantonly given to the seductions of color (rhetorical, if not cosmetic). What is even more ironic, it is precisely from these attributes of an abominated secondariness that *La perfecta casada* assigns itself value within the economy of textual and material recirculation that it generates. Part of the argument I make in the course of this chapter is that the reading of the body of the casada that *La perfecta casada* enacts is, in almost every sense, a self-implicating one, embracing at one level all that it claims to condemn at another: color, seduction, duplicity, secondariness.

One outcome of this paradox is the untenable position it accords the historical woman who must live by the manual's strictures. Within a social and textual economy that clearly privileges the notion of proper place, she is relegated to a place that is always necessarily improper. In this respect, the paradoxes and inconsistencies that plague Fray Luis's discourse can be seen as inconsistencies common to the discourse of misogyny that invariably produce the same effect. The point seems almost facile since the contradictions that render the body of *La perfecta casada* so imperfect as model are, in fact, at least partly inherited from the antifeminist writings that Fray Luis translates and cannibalizes. It may be argued, then, that in subscribing to an aesthetic moral economy that adjudicates value to the original and denounces as corrupt anything considered derivative, and in partaking of this culpable secondariness at a constitutive level, Fray Luis is merely inscribing himself within a long, fertile tradition of "cosmetic theology" dating back to the first centuries of Christianity, a tradition with clear misogynist leanings.

The contested issue of Fray Luis's pro- or antifeminism has been and will no doubt continue to be a commonplace of *Perfecta casada* studies (perhaps the only one, given the relative scarcity of critical work the treatise has elicited).[15] The debate's outcome, however, is almost entirely dependent on the definitions afforded its terms. If misogyny is narrowly but ambiguously defined, as it typically is, as hatred of women, then Fray Luis's text is not antifeminist; the treatise is, in fact, more generous in its tone and less repressive in the position it accords the wife than many of its contemporary generic counterparts, going so far as to suggest that the wife is *not* her husband's slave and that if she in fact owes him care and obedience, he must earn it by treating her with love and respect.[16] If, however, misogyny is much more suggestively, but problematically, defined, as it is by Howard Bloch, as "any essentialist definition of woman, whether negative or positive, whether made by a man or a woman," [17] then the manual incurs in misogyny. Without engaging the debate directly (which tends to naturalize its terms without sufficiently critiquing them), my reading of *La perfecta casada* represents, in part, an effort to unmask some of the text's "internal incoherences" (to borrow Bloch's term), incoherences that are standard currency in misogynist discourse, and that result from an ordering that not only assigns woman a secondary place but essentially aligns her with such secondariness.

There is no question that much of what is so provocative about Fray Luis's text are its sustained and sustaining aporias, many of which are imported. But two crucial distinctions need to be made. The first has to do with the treatise's mode of composition. If *La perfecta casada*'s textual borrowings (in the form of attributed and unattributed citations) are partly responsible for its incoherences, then it is Fray Luis's own exegetical labor with respect to the passages he appropriates — "poniéndolas en sus lugares, travándolas todas y dándoles ordén" [giving them their proper place, a structure, and an order] — that is primarily to blame, since the disordering and reordering mechanism that produces new readings inevitably produces new inconsistencies as well. The second qualification has to do with the tensions that motivate Fray Luis. If, as Bloch has further suggested, "the church fathers' relegation of woman to the realm of esthetics and their condemnation of the artificial are located in a metaphysical fear of the flesh," [18] in *La perfecta casada* the "fear" that pervades the text is not of the flesh in and of itself, but rather of a flesh so overdetermined as to become illegible. Founding obsessions with questions of cosmetic, on one hand, and noncontainment, on the other, the two wifely threats that are most visible — and most censured — throughout the treatise can also be read as preoccupations over issues of interpretation. Fray Luis's attention to "painted women" betrays his critical anxieties over reading and misreading; conversely, concerns over interpretive stability mask displaced anxieties over painted women. Charges of adultery, whorishness, and monstrosity imputed against the made-up, wandering casada — charges that can readily be applied to the text itself — are all reducible, at some level, to charges of illegibility.

But if in its attention to, and anxieties over, issues of reading, interpretation, and even ways of (not) knowing *La perfecta casada* seems to privilege interpretive or epistemological questions, its hermeneutic tensions extend beyond purely formal categories. My point, then, is not simply to mark the text's incoherences (often manifested as a rhetorical reenactment of thematic prohibitions) or to recast somatic concerns as purely semiotic ones but, rather, to read the interpretive anxieties that Fray Luis mobilizes on the body of his imperfect textual spouse in terms of broader cultural anxieties, particularly within an inquisitorial context. Here, finally, we come full circle, returning to the body, to the third movement, as it were, of the triangular interplay between the somatic and the semiotic. It is here that we return to the heretical gestures made by Fray Luis's great-great-great-grandfather, and to the problematic and even dangerous implications of reading like a Jew — that is, reading with and through the body ("haçiendo gestos e abtos que los judios azen cuando leen") and also reading bodies of both words and flesh.

It seems almost redundant by now to point out that in early modern Spain bodies — and bloodlines — were quite literally read for signs of Otherness. Fray Luis's five-year imprisonment over matters of translation and interpretation dramatizes the extent to which matters of reading were not only overtly politicized but, at given moments, visibly punishable on the body. The biographical anecdote with which I opened this chapter is not merely incidental to a reading of *La perfecta casada;* it is, I would argue, indispensable. There are more than subtle traces throughout Fray Luis's works of his encounter with the Inquisition; some of the poems — primarily those that explicitly address questions of prison and deliverance — have fruitfully been read in this light.[19] (The famous *décimas,* "Aquí la envidia y mentira / me tuvieron encerrado" [Here envy and lies / had me confined], thought to have been written — and thus titled — "al salir de la cárcel" [on leaving prison], is no doubt the canonical example.)[20] It is not, I hope, too improbable to consider that the same Fray Luis who prefaced all his publications after his release from prison with the Horatian motto "Ab ipso ferro" and an emblem of an ax chopping the branches of an oak tree (a fairly explicit reference to Horace's *Odes* 4.4, in which the Romans are compared to an evergreen oak that draws strength "from the very iron" that cuts it down) might conceivably respond to the charges of misreading that had kept him jailed for five years from the pages of a treatise — albeit for married women — that on more than one occasion takes up the issue of both textual and somatic interpretation.[21] I do not mean to suggest by this that Fray Luis deliberately encoded the conduct manual with cryptic responses to his inquisitorial adversaries or, taken to another extreme, that the text should be read in a humanist "Life and Works" tradition. My contention, rather, is that the interpretive and philological concerns that are so prevalent throughout Fray Luis's writings and that also remit to social and cultural anxieties *about* translation and interpretation in an inquisitorial setting (including those that resulted in his own imprisonment) are clearly legible on the body of *La perfecta casada,* a much more daring and complex text, in many respects, than has traditionally been imagined.

In order to outline the general form that such a reading might take, I would like to briefly review the principal charges brought against Fray Luis by the Valladolid Inquisition as they were originally formalized. In his "Acusación del fiscal a Fray Luis de León" of 5 May 1572, el liçenciado Diego de Haedo states the following:

1. — Primeramente que el susodicho, con animo dañado de quitar la verdad y autoridad a la Sancta Escriptura, ha dicho y afirmado que la edition Bulgata tiene muchas falsedades y que se puede hazer otra mejor.

2. — Yten que, estando en çierta junta de theologos . . . dixo que aunque fuese verdadero el sentido y declaracion de los evangelistas tambien podia ser veradadera la ynterpretacion de los judios y rabi-

nos, aunque fuese el sentido diferente, afirmando que se podian traer explicaciones de Escriptura nuebas. De lo qual dio grande escandalo.

3.—Yten que, abiendo leydo publicamente çierta persona que en el Viejo Testamento no habia promision de vida eterna, el dicho maestro Fray Luys de Leon disputo y sustento lo mismo contra quienes los que tenian lo contrario y la verdad.

4.—Yten que el susodicho . . . en las declaraciones de la Sancta Escriptura ha preferido a Batablo y a Pagnino y a los rabies y judios a la edition Bulgata y al sentido de los sanctos, espeçialmente en la declaracion de los Psalmos y letiones de Job.

5.—Yten que el susodicho ha hablado mal de los LXX ynterpretes, diziendo que no habian entendido bien la lengua hebrea y que traduxeron mal el hebreo en griego de que resulto escandalo. . . .

6.—Yten que el dicho Fray Luys de Leon, confirmando los dichos herrores, ha dicho y afirmado que los *Cantares de Salomón* eran *carmen amatorium ad suam uxorem* y profanando los dichos *Cantares* los traduxo en lengua bulgar, y estan y andan en poder de muchas personas, a quienes el los dio, y de otras en la dicha lengua de romançe.

[1.—First, that the above-mentioned, with the corrupted determination to wrest truth and authority from the Sacred Scripture, has said and affirmed that the Vulgate edition contains many falsehoods and that a better one can be made.

2.—Likewise, that, present at a certain meeting of theologians . . . he said that even though the meaning and explanation of the evangelists were true, the interpretation of the Jews and rabbis could also be true, although the meanings were different, affirming that new explanations of Scripture were possible. Because of this, he caused a great scandal.

3.—Likewise, that, after a certain person had read publicly that in the Old Testament there was no promise of eternal life, the aforementioned teacher Fray Luis de León argued and upheld the same view against those who maintained the contrary and the truth.

4.—Likewise, that the above-mentioned, . . . in declarations regarding Sacred Scripture, has preferred Batablo and Pagnino, and the rabbis and Jews to the Vulgate edition and the judgment of the Saints, especially in their explanation of the Psalms and lessons of Job.

5. — Likewise, that the above-mentioned has spoken ill of the LXX translators, saying that they had misunderstood the Hebrew language and that they translated the Hebrew into Greek poorly, and from this a scandal ensued. . . .

6. — Likewise, that the aforementioned Fray Luis de León, confirming the aforementioned errors, has said and affirmed that the Song of Solomon was *carmen amatorium ad suam uxorem* (a love song to his wife), and profaning the aforementioned Song, he translated it into vernacular language, and now it is in the possession of many people whom he gave it to, and of others in the aforementioned Romance language.][22]

With the exception of the "séptimo capítulo" (in which he is accused of advancing the Lutheran doctrine of justification by faith alone and which he outrightly refutes as a gross misinterpretation of his theological position), Fray Luis's point-by-point response to the charges against him generally takes the form not of a denial but of a defense. Fray Luis never recants (and this holds true throughout his imprisonment), offering instead what amount to careful but pointed recapitulations of the positions and readings against which the inquisitorial accusations are formulated. I cite, by way of example, an excerpt from an early "respuesta" to the first capítulo (which might, moreover, also apply to its virtual recasting in the fifth).

> Quanto al primer capitulo . . . Si llama falsedades dezir que el interprete [de la Vulgata] algunos lugares no los traduxo tan clara ny tam comodamente ny tam del todo conforme al original, esto en aquella lectura . . . lo digo.

> [With regard to the first reproof, . . . if it is deemed a falsehood to say that the translator (of the Vulgate) did not translate some parts so clearly or comfortably, or so in accordance with the original, this is precisely what I say in that reading.][23]

It is in this same tenor that those passages of *La perfecta casada* that return to the "controversies" for which Fray Luis was incarcerated and which, at the time of his release, he was explicitly warned to avoid — translation to the vernacular, (textual) Judaizing, plural interpretations—can perhaps best be understood. Clear traces of Fray Luis's problematic loyalty to the "original" Hebrew Scriptures and the questioning of the accuracy (and even adequacy) of the Vulgate translation that such loyalty was assumed to imply—the two charges that form the basis of capítulos 1 and 5 in the prosecutor's statement—can be gleaned from an early passage of *La perfecta casada* that addresses the difficulties of literal translation.

> Lo que aquí decimos mujer de valor; y pudiéramos decir mujer varonil, como Sócrates acerca de Jenofón, llama a las casadas perfectas, así que esto que decimos varonil o valor, *en el original es una palabra de grande significación y fuerza, y tal, que apenas con muchas muestras se alcanza todo lo que significa.* Quiere decir virtud de ánimo y fortaleza de corazón, industria y riqueza, y poder y aventajamiento y, finalmente, un ser perfecto y cabal en aquellas cosas a quien esta palabra se aplica. Y todo esto atesora en sí la que es buena mujer, y no lo es si no lo atesora. Y para que entendamos que es esto verdad, la nombró el Espíritu Sancto con este nombre que encierra en sí tanta variedad de tesoro. (86, italics mine)

> [I repeat the term "valiant woman," and might even speak of her as a manly woman, as Socrates (meaning Xenophon) calls a perfect wife. Because, indeed, what is termed virile, or valiant *in the original, is a word of deepest significance and force, so that even with numerous examples one can hardly capture its full meaning.*
>
> It betokens many things: virtue of mind, and fortitude of heart, resourcefulness, and wealth, power, prosperity, and, in fine, a being perfect and complete in all those qualities which are embraced within the meaning of the word; and all these the good woman treasures within herself, and she is not good, if she does not treasure them. And that we may comprehend the truth of this, the Holy Spirit applied this particular name to her because it holds within itself such a treasury of varied meanings. (13)][24]

The passage, suggestive for a number of reasons (including its characterization of the most "perfecta casada" as a "mujer varonil" [manly woman] and the poetics of containment as "atesoramiento" [treasuring] that it embraces), points to the difficulty, if not the impossibility, of suitably rendering the original word for "mujer de valor" in another language ("apenas con muchas muestras se alcanza" [even with numerous examples one can hardly capture its full meaning]). Fray Luis's strategy throughout the treatise can be seen, in fact, as an effort to supply those "muchas muestras"—to achieve through analogy and example what cannot be accomplished by translation alone. What is more, the impossibility of adequately translating that "palabra tan rica y significante como es la original" (88) [so rich and expressive a word as is the original] (14) is in great measure due to the relative richness of the original word (and, by extension, of the original language), which Fray Luis praises in the same economic terms ("rica," "significante," "de grande fuerza," "tesoro") that will be metonymically transferred onto the perfect wife's body ("industria," "riqueza," "poder," "aventajamiento"). He cautiously refrains, however, from making explicit that the original language he lauds, the language of the Holy Spirit ("la nombró el Espíritu Sancto con este nombre") is, of course, Hebrew.[25]

The charges of indulging in "explicaciones de Escriptura nueba" [new explanations of Scripture] or of preferring noncanonical (and even rabbinical) readings over those of "the Vulgate edition and the judgment of the Saints" (capítulos 2 and 4, respectively, in the "Acusación") are similarly countered in *La perfecta casada* in a long defense of plural interpretations.

> porque se ha de entender que la Sagrada Escriptura, que es habla de Dios, es como una imagen de la condición y naturaleza de Dios; y así como la divinidad es juntamente una perfection sola y muchas perfectiones diversas, una en sencillez, y muchas en valor y eminencia, *así la Sancta Escriptura por unas mismas palabras dice muchas y diferentes razones, y como lo enseñan los sanctos, en la sencillez de una misma sentencia encierra gran preñez de sentidos. Y como en Dios todo lo que hay es bueno, así en su Escriptura todos los sentidos que puso en ella el Espíritu Sancto son verdaderos.* Por manera que el seguir el un sentido, no es desechar el otro, ni menos el que, en estas sagradas letras, entre muchos y verdaderos entendimientos que tienen, descubre el uno dellos y le declara, no por eso ha de ser tenido por hombre que desecha los otros entendimientos. (84–85, italics mine)

[For it is to be understood that the Sacred Scriptures, which are the word of God, also reflect His nature and attributes. And as God is conjointly one single perfection and many diverse perfections, one in simplicity, yet many in value and pre-eminence, *so Holy Writ in one and the same words embraces many and varied meanings; and as saintly writers teach us, within the simplicity of a single sentence there lie hidden a great plurality of interpretations. And as God is entirely good, so in His word, all the manifold meanings enclosed therein are wholly trustworthy.* Wherefore, to adopt one rendering, is not to reject others, and even more, he who among many and varying interpretations discloses and explains one of them must not be thought to exclude all the rest. (12)]

The passage could easily be read as an elaboration of the defense of interpretive plurality that Fray Luis provided in his "Respuesta al interrogatorio de la primera audiencia" of 18 April 1572 and that he repeated numerous times throughout the course of his trial: "Si se diere otro sentido que no sea contrario, aunque sea differente, el qual sentido sea catholico y de sana dottrina, se puede el tal admitir" [If another meaning were given that is not opposed, even though it may be different, and such a meaning is Catholic and of sound doctrine, it can be allowed].[26] It is by no means insignificant to a reading of wives' bodies in the treatise that Fray Luis should refer to multiple meanings as a "preñez de sentidos" (literally, "pregnancy of meanings"). The alignment of plural meanings with a pregnant female body was neither new nor uncommon in early modern Spain (a variation of the phrase appears in the prologue to *La Celestina* and its use is colorfully documented by Covarrubias), but it is noteworthy that the word's body should be gendered female (and even endowed with a womb) precisely when its interpretive duplicity is at issue. Beyond making a case for the plurality inscribed in Holy Writ (and metaphorically figured on a wife's pregnant body), however, Fray Luis's repeated claims that "el seguir el un sentido no es desechar el otro" [to adopt one rendering is not to reject others] might be read as an acknowledgment on his behalf that the particular "sentido" he would be explicating was not the conventionally accepted one for Proverbs, but rather one in need of a prefacing apologia.

The potential transgressiveness of *La perfecta casada*'s reading of Proverbs 31 lies, primarily, in its privileging of literal over figural meaning. Fray Luis was right to be concerned. Literal reading — particularly of the Old Testament — was considered by some to be roughly the equivalent of "reading like a Jew." Fray Luis's seemingly obstinate tendency to explicate Scripture literally (which is addressed by the prosecutor's third and sixth charges, and which comes up at various moments throughout his trial) had already been a serious source of contention with respect to his translation and interpretation of the *Cantar de los cantares* [*Song of Songs*]. A large part of the criticism surrounding that text (which had provided his accusers with substantial ammunition against him) was grounded in this very question; those who opposed Fray Luis's exegesis argued that in opting for literal over figural levels of signification, he not only reduced the *Cantar* to a mere love song (*carmen amatorium*), but, moreover, that he read the scriptural passage *as if he were a Jew,* without submitting it to the interpretive sublimation that ostensibly purified its obvious erotic connotations.[27] In the prologue to the *Cantar,* Fray Luis had, in fact, set forth his critical agenda as a philological one that would attend, first and foremost, to the "corteza de la letra" [cortex of the letter], leaving for others the "secretos de gran misterio" [secrets of great mystery] that lay beneath the naked words:

> Solamente trabajaré en declarar la corteza de la letra así y llanamente, como si en este libro no hubiera otro mayor secreto del que muestran aquellas palabras desnudas y al parecer dichas y respondidas entre Solomón y su esposa, que será solamente declarar el sonido de ellas y aquello en que está la fuerça de la comparación y del requiebro, que aunque es trabajo de menos quilates que el primero, no por eso carece de grandes dificultades.

> [I will only work to expound, simply, the cortex of the letter, as if in this book there were no greater secret than that revealed by those naked words, seemingly exchanged between Solomon and his wife, which will only be to explain their sound and where the force of the comparison and of the amorous words dwells, which although it is a task of less value than the first, not for that reason is it want of great difficulty.][28]

Fray Luis's words here are not strikingly different from those that would appear in the opening paragraphs of *La perfecta casada* twenty-two years later, in which he again attempts to justify literal reading on its own terms:

Pero, antes que comencemos, nos conviene presuponer que, en este capítulo, el Espíritu Santo *así es verdad que pinta una buena casada declarando las obligaciones que tiene,* que también dice y significa, y como *encubre debajo desta pintura cosas mayores y de más alto sentido,* que pertenecen a toda la Iglesia. . . .

Pues, digo que en este capítulo Dios, por la boca de Salomón, por unas mismas palabras hace dos cosas. Lo uno *instruye y ordena* las costumbres, lo otro profetiza misterios secretos. Las costumbres que ordena son de la casada, los misterios que profetiza son el ingenio y condiciones que había de poner en su Iglesia, de quien habla como en figura de una mujer de su casa. En esto postrero da luz a lo que se ha de creer, en lo primero *enseña lo que se ha de obrar.* Y porque aquésto sólo es lo que hace agora a nuestro propósito, por eso hablaremos dello aquí solamente, y procuraremos, cuando nos fuere posible sacar a la luz y poner como delante de los ojos todo lo que hay en esta imagen de virtud que Dios aquí pinta. (85, italics mine)

[But, before we begin, we must of necessity take for granted that in this chapter, the Holy Spirit, *although in very truth He portrays a perfect wife, and indicates her obligations,* at the same time declares and signifies, and as it were, *hides beneath this portrait things far greater and of deeper import,* which apply to the whole Church. . . .

So I repeat that in this chapter, our Lord, through the mouth of Solomon, by means of the same words accomplishes two things. The first *teaches and prescribes* the manner of well-ordered conduct; the other foretells secret mysteries. The customs it sets forth are those which relate to a wife; the mysteries prophesied pertain to the nature and conditions which He meant to embody in the Church, which is spoken of under the similitude of a wife in her home. In the latter, light is shed upon matters of faith; in the former, the Holy Spirit *teaches how one must act.* And because this last alone belongs to our subject, we shall concern ourselves exclusively with it, and try, in so far as possible, to bring to light, and place before our very eyes whatever there is of excellence in this picture of virtue painted by God Himself. (11–12)]

By alluding to the practical and pedagogical value ("enseña lo que se ha de obrar" [it teaches how one must act]) of a literal level of interpretation, Fray Luis's defense of his hermeneutic desire for the body (as opposed to the spirit) of his textual bride subtly invokes the exegetical *auctoritas* that charges literality with precisely this function: "littera gesta docet." [29] But the painting metaphor that Fray Luis calls on in order to distinguish a literal (the "pintura" itself) from a figural level of meaning (what lies "debajo desta pintura" [beneath this portrait]) is problematic for many reasons, not the least of which is the surface-depth/exterior-interior binarisms it mobilizes, binarisms that will come back to haunt the text in its censures of feminine cosmetic. Simply put, the literal meaning that Fray Luis so avidly defends paradoxically becomes (in its alignment with painting, surface, exteriority) like the cosmetics he so fervently criticizes, reversing the already troubling alignment suggested by the prologue to the *Cantar* in which nakedness becomes a trope for literalness; clothing, presumably, for figurality.[30]

But if the controversies surrounding Fray Luis's edition of the *Cantar* (controversies that could well apply to *La perfecta casada*) were largely the result of his attention to literal meaning, at least as condemning in the eyes of the Holy Office was the fact that he had translated the text into the vernacular ("traduxo en lengua bulgar") and, in so doing, had made the verses widely accessible to an unlearned populace who might not understand them ("andan en poder de muchas personas"), as the sixth chapter of the prosecutor's statement alleges. It is suggestive, then, that *La perfecta casada* contains outright defenses (that smack, moreover, of Erasmianism) of the scriptural text as a sort of textual panacea, a "mercado público y general" [public market] where remedies against ills of all sorts could be found.[31] Translating the text of Proverbs 31 may have represented for Fray Luis a way of reopening this "tienda común," of putting the Bible in the hands of readers (especially women) who did not know Latin but who could putatively benefit from its practical advice (even if doing so was for the expressed purpose of removing from their hands the far more "dangerous" texts that *were* available in Spanish: "Porque muchos destos malos escriptos ordinariamente andan en las manos de mugeres donzellas y mozas" [Many of these evil writings are ordinarily found in the hands of young people (maidens and young girls)].[32] Even more suggestive is the fact that throughout his writings — and most forcibly in the introduction to the first and third books of *De los nombres de Cristo* — Fray Luis repeatedly defends the propriety of Spanish as a language suitable for treating any subject, from the most lofty to the most mundane.[33]

Despite Fray Luis's defiant outspokenness on the matter, the issue of vernacular translation of Holy Writ was no less controversial by the time *La perfecta casada* was published in 1583 than it had been at the time of Fray Luis's arrest eleven years earlier. Quite the contrary, the inquisitorial index that appeared that same year explicitly prohibits the publication not only of vernacular Bibles but of any portion of Scripture in the vernacular.[34] Fray Luis's incursion into the conduct genre and, specifically, into a subject that he himself confesses to be "ajena de mi profesión" [outside my profession] might conceivably be seen, then, as a way of getting around this type of prohibition, since the transgressive reading and translation of Proverbs 31 appears "disguised" as a wifely conduct manual. There is no better proof of the effectiveness of such a strategy (whether conscious or not on Fray Luis's part) than the fact that *La perfecta casada* was criticized neither for its translation nor for its literal reading of Proverbs (the two main charges brought against the *Cantar*) so much as for the impropriety implicit in its author's intrusion into the "oficio de la casada."

In outlining a reading of *La perfecta casada* as a text that has as much to do with questions of interpretation as it does with rules of wifely conduct and that responds, moreover, to the charges of misreading that kept Fray Luis imprisoned in the jails of the Holy Office for nearly five years, my intention has been not only to suggest the extent to which the treatise is more central to Fray Luis's corpus than has traditionally been imagined, but also to begin to explore the means by which *La perfecta casada* mobilizes the wife's body as a site on which to inscribe interpretive anxieties. It may be argued that Fray Luis does nothing new in this since the body, and the female body in particular, is always the purveyor of such a site; that texts that inscribe bodies and bodily concerns generally tend to inscribe questions of legibility as well. What is especially provocative about *La perfecta casada*, however, is not so much its appropriation of the wife's body as a site of and for reading, but the extent to which that site proves to be radically unstable in Fray Luis's hands.

Roads to Rome

The excesses and contradictions that beset (and even adorn) the textual body of *La perfecta casada* are perhaps most visible in Fray Luis's almost hysterical diatribes against the casada's use of cosmetic on one hand and her noncontainment on the other. The seemingly disproportionate force of Fray Luis's tirade against these two wifely transgressions (given their apparent levity) is largely the result of the significant threat they pose to a mode of reading based on semblances and proper places. "Semejanza" and "proprio lugar" (otherwise expressed as "proporción") are privileged terms in Fray Luis's critical discourse. They mark the satisfaction of the preconditions necessary for establishing meaning; similitudes in particular provide a logical way of ordering reality, of coming to terms with the hidden signatures that encode "the order of things." [35] As a textual commentary structured as a direct gloss on a previous text, *La perfecta casada* moves precisely by reading, by locating instances of sameness and, moreover, by incorporating those instances into their proper places, so to speak, within the new (critical) discourse — the exegesis — that this type of "reading" produces.

The rhetorical expression of a reading strategy founded on similitudes can be located in the numerous similes and analogies that mark Fray Luis's writing. There is no dearth of analogy in *La perfecta casada;* it is, unquestionably, its privileged discursive mode. [36] A good example of Fray Luis's recourse to analogic form occurs in a passage about woman's uncontrollability that, apparently contaminated by the sense of excess it describes, offers what amounts to a sixfold simile for woman's insatiable appetite:

La buena casada, de quien vamos tratando, cualquiera que ella sea, fea o hermosa, *no ha de querer parecer otra de lo que es,* como se dirá *en su lugar.* . . . [L]as mujeres, que nacieron para sujeción y humildad, . . . si comienzan a destemplarse, se destemplan sin término, y son *como* un pozo sin suelo, que nada les basta, y *como* una carcoma, que de continuo roe, y *como* una llama encubierta, que se enciende sin sentir por la casa y por la hacienda hasta que la consume. . . . Y *como* los caballos desbocados cuando toman el freno, cuanto más corren tanto van más desapoderados; y *como* la piedra que cae de lo alto, que cuanto más desciende tanto más se apresura, *así* la sed déstas crece en ellas con el beber, y un gran desatino y *exceso* que hacen les es principio de otro mayor. (95–96, italics mine)

[The perfect wife of whom we are treating, be she homely or handsome, *should not want to appear other than she is,* as will be explained *in its place.* . . . (W)omen, born as they are for submission and humility . . . let them once begin to be immoderate, and there is an end to moderation. They are *like* a bottomless well, never full, no matter how much is poured into it; or *like* a wood-borer perpetually boring; or *like* a hidden blaze which spreads silently throughout the house and property, until everything is consumed. . . . Even *as* runaway horses, once they get the bit in their mouths, become more ungovernable the harder they run, and *like* the stone which, dropped from a height, gains in velocity the lower it falls, *so* the thirst of such women increases with drinking, and some great piece of folly or an *excess* which they commit marks the beginning of one even greater. (21–22)]

The threat of feminine Otherness that haunts *La perfecta casada* is explicitly associated here with the threat of limitlessness; in some respects, Fray Luis's agenda throughout the treatise can be described as an unmitigating attempt to impose limits (of the perfecta casada's conduct, of her desire, of her geography, even of her anatomy), to contain, in some manner, the perfect wife he names. Ironically enough, the comparison partakes of the same scandalous and unbridled ineconomy that it censures. But if the voracity that Fray Luis seeks to curb in his perfect wife is unleashed by her desire to appear "otra de lo que es" [other than she is], it may be argued that the prodigality of the analogy indulges that very desire, repeatedly (if paradoxically) making her

seem "other" ("pozo," "carcoma," "llama," "caballo," "piedra") by
outfitting her in tropes of sameness. In other words, if woman is condemned *for* her otherness and her excess, then she is, all the same,
condemned *to* these very "faults."

The preponderance of "semejanzas" in Fray Luis's text responds, in
part, to a sixteenth-century epistème that still read the world as a Great
Chain of Being, as an analogically linked and harmoniously ordered
universal machine.[37] For Fray Luis, the hierarchical chain that at its
highest point is closest to God is organized as a function of each creature's grade of perfection, defined not absolutely, but rather by the
extent to which it contains (or is endowed with the capacity to contain)
all others. This conception is elaborated in the remarkable opening
section of *De los nombres de Cristo* that, although referring to a more
general sort of teleologic perfection, is not without implications for
wifely perfection.[38]

> Porque se ha de entender que la perfección de todas las cosas . . . con-
> siste en que cada una dellas tenga en sí a todas las otras, y en que siendo
> una, sea todas, cuanto le fuere possible; porque en esto se avecina a
> Dios, que en sí lo contiene todo. . . . Consiste pues la perfección en
> que cada uno de nosotros sea un mundo perfecto, para que por esta
> manera . . . se abrace y eslavone toda aquesta máquina del universo.
> (bk. 1, 27–28)

> [We must understand this: The perfection of all things . . . is that each
> bears in itself all the others and is in turn all the others because in this
> it has its affinity to God, who contains in Himself all. . . . The perfec-
> tion of all things is that each one of us strives to be a perfect world
> so that in this way . . . we all embrace and link this whole universal
> mechanism. (43–44)][39]

Beyond providing an effective reading strategy, then, the semblance
that serves as foundation for the analogic Chain of Being provides
the only possible access to God. Fray Luis goes on to suggest that in
this world, perfection (defined, ultimately, as a universal "eslavonamiento" [linkage] can be achieved only linguistically: "porque no era
posible que las cosas assí como son materiales y toscas, estuviessen
todas unas en otras, [la naturaleza] les dió a cada una dellas demás del

ser real que tienen en sí, otro ser del todo semejante a este mismo, pero más delicado que él, y que nace en cierta manera dél" (29) [Since it was impossible that coarse material things be in each other, [nature] gives to them, besides the real being that they have in themselves, another being similar to the first but more delicate and which is born from it (44)]. Words provide the only vehicle, then, for quite literally being like the Absolute ("avecinarse la criatura a Dios"); the Great Chain of Being becomes, in Fray Luis's version, a Great Chain of Words.

The notion of a divinely ordered semiosis forms part of what, with respect to Augustine (Fray Luis's model, no doubt), John Freccero has aptly termed a "theology of the Word" that conceives of God as the ultimate referent, the end term of all desire as well as of all signification.[40] Specifically, the name functions in Fray Luis's system as the spiritual counterpart ("ser espiritual") of a material being ("ser material"). Unrestrained by the burdens of corporeality, words substitute for things, effectively providing the means for the totalizing synthesis that is the hallmark of divinity.[41] The basis for that substitution is also rooted in semblance—in the phonic, figural, or etymological proximity that presumably binds a name with that which it designates.

> si el nombre, como hemos dicho, sustituye por lo nombrado, y si su fin es hacer que lo ausente que significa, en él nos sea presente, y cercano, y junto lo que nos es alejado, mucho conviene que en el sonido, en la figura, o verdaderamente en el origen y significación de aquello de donde nace, se avecine y asemeje a cuyo es. (bk. 1, 33)

> [if the name, as we have said, is given for what is named and if its purpose is to make what is absent and what is designated become present to our mind, and close and near what is distant, it is fitting that in the sound, in the form or truly in the origin and significance from which it is born, it should approach and become similar to what it is. (46)]

There is a subtle sleight of hand on Fray Luis's part here, an incoherence that, on a broader level, haunts the relation between the Great Chain of Being and the Cratylism of the linguistic theories that generally endorse it. If, on one hand, the analogic relations that structure the ontological chain are logically based on the same principle of similitude by virtue of which, in a Cratylist system, names substitute for things, rhetorically, analogies imply a conscious recognition of the imperfection of language in representing directly. In other words, analogy manifests itself as a necessary mediation that violates the illusion of a perfect reciprocity between a name and the thing named. It is not exactly a question of the naturalness versus the arbitrariness of the linguistic sign, but rather of the sign's problematic claim to an authority based on any sort of primary or direct resemblance, given its recourse to resemblance of a second (analogical) order. Simply put, the issue arises from the existence of two different species of linguistic similitude. Fray Luis's "duplicity," if we can call it that, consists in resorting to both means of similitude (analogy and, albeit to a lesser extent, a kind of Cratylism) in order to achieve ultimate perfection: semblance to the Divinity. Part of the difficulty (or indeed the difference between these two forms) may reside in the degraded status of language after Babel, a possibility that Fray Luis explicitly addresses by remitting to "la primera lengua" and, more specifically, to Hebrew Scripture, as the prime source of "semejanza y conformidad."[42] Perhaps the paradox is best understood, however, as inherent to the structure of analogy itself that, by inscribing Otherness within Sameness (or alternately, by affirming identity through difference), problematizes the alleged transparency of similitude as an epistemologic tool.[43]

Fray Luis is by no means oblivious to the hermeneutic dangers with which semblance is fraught; on the contrary, there are various passages throughout *La perfecta casada* that record a certain apprehension on his part with the instability that inheres in a reading method based on similitudes. This instability is made to seem particularly disruptive when it lays claim to an adjudicative register, as in the following example.

Porque así como hay algunos vicios que tienen *apariencia* y gran *semejanza* con algunas virtudes, así hay virtudes también que están como ocasionadas a algunos vicios. . . . Y puede tanto este parentesco y disimulación que no solamente los que miran de lejos y ven sólo lo que se parece, engañándose, nombran por virtud lo que es vicio, mas también esos mesmos que ponen las manos en ello y lo obran, muchas veces no se entienden a sí, y se persuaden que les nace de raíz de virtud lo que les viene de inclinación dañada y viciosa. *Por donde todo lo semejante pide gran advertencia* para que el mal, disimulado con el bien, no pueda engañarnos. (119–20, italics mine)

[For as there are some vices which have the *appearance,* and take on the *semblance* of virtues, so likewise there are virtues which are, as it were, exposed to the danger of becoming certain vices. . . . So potent, indeed, is this relationship and this dissimulation that not merely those who look from afar, and regard resemblances only, are deceived, and apply the name virtue to what is really vice, but also those who put hands to an undertaking and accomplish it, very frequently have no understanding of themselves, and are persuaded that the action, which is due to a vicious and perverse inclination, springs up in them from some root of virtue. *So it comes about that things which appear similar call for great alertness* in order that the evil concealed under the semblance of good may not lead us astray. (43–44)]

Far from providing certainty, then, the similitude that is putatively aligned with legibility becomes the stuff of illegibility. The passage anticipates the often profound mistrust in semblance routinely ascribed to a seventeenth-century baroque epistème.[44]

If semejanzas are clearly privileged in Fray Luis's text, their status is far from unproblematic. Quite the opposite, the destabilization of analogic semblance obtains not only through what could be considered its thematic inscription in the treatise (Fray Luis's cautionary remarks about "todo lo semejante" [things which appear similar]), but also through its purchase on the text's discursive practice. In other words, inasmuch as Fray Luis recognizes the inherent threat to legibility posed by similitudes due to the interpretive excess they house, it is, nonetheless, an excess of which his own writing fully partakes. The analogic principle of identity that subtends *La perfecta casada* is, more often than not, troubled by this very excess, which can paradoxically manifest itself as insufficiency or lack. This holds true at a logical, rhetorical, and even grammatical level. Analogies — and especially those in the form of a four-term proportion, "a is to b as c is to d" — are often haunted by a fifth term, or in fact triangular in structure, or logically inconsistent in light of their semantic charge.

Similitude is burdened to such a degree in the text that not even what might be considered its ground zero (ontological equivalence) is exempted; the reflexive property that ostensibly informs the verbal copula is violated on more than one occasion. Thus, for example, in order to comply with the definition of goodness, a woman must actually exceed it, overcompensating, as it were, for her own deficient subjectivity: "la mujer buena es más que buena . . . ni es buena la que no es muy buena" (88) [a good woman is more than good. . . . One who is not much more than good, is not good at all (14–15)]. This particular instance of transgressed similitude occurs in a provocative, and in many ways seminal, passage of *La perfecta casada:*

> El Espíritu Sancto a la mujer buena no la llamó como quiera buena . . . sino llamóla *mujer de valor* y usó en ello una palabra *tan rica y tan significante como es la original* que dijimos, para decirnos que *la mujer buena es más que buena,* y que esto que nombramos bueno es una medianía de hablar, que no abraza ni allega a aquello excelente que ha de tener y tiene en sí la buena mujer; y que, *para que un hombre sea bueno le basta un bien mediano, mas en la mujer ha de ser negocio de muchos y subidos quilates.* (88, italics mine)

> [The Holy Spirit did not call a virtuous woman merely virtuous . . . but He called her a *woman* of value, and to convey this meaning made use, as we have pointed out, of *so rich and expressive a word as is the original.* And this by way of telling us that *a good woman is more than good,* and that this which we call goodness, is a temperate mode of speech which does not reach the supreme worth which a good woman has, and is bound to have within herself. Of course, *for a man to be good, an average degree of goodness suffices; but for a woman, goodness is a matter of very many and very costly degrees of goodness.* (14)]

The problem, at first, seems primarily one of translation; the "original" text cannot be rendered into a second language without resorting to a kind of semantic violence (in this case, the asymmetry between "buena" and "más que buena").

But beyond the linguistic excess (the Hebrew word's virtual untranslatability), the difficulty seems to reside in a question of sexual difference: woman's essence, it appears, cannot be defined in unmediated language. In fact, where woman's representation is concerned, Fray Luis relies on analogy to such an extent that he cannot even mention her attributes without the tempering effects of the word "como" [like]: "El ser honesta una mujer . . . es *como* el subjeto sobre el cual todo este edificio se funda, y es *como* el ser y la substancia de la casada" (90) [Fidelity in a wife . . . is *like* the foundation on which the entire superstructure is upbuilded. In a word, faithfulness is *like* the very being and substance of a perfect wife (16)]. The casada becomes, in this sense (and quite ironically so), like the Divinity whose textual representation requires recourse to either metaphor (as in Augustine) or analogy (as in Aquinas). It is in response to this feminine excess that Fray Luis turns to a rhetoric that not only is steeped in troubled (and troubling) analogies, but that explicitly draws on economic terms. I cite the passage at length:

> Y este es el primer loor que le da el Espíritu Sancto, y con éste viene *como* nacido el segundo, que es compararla a las piedras preciosas. En lo cual, *como* en una palabra, acaba de decir cabalmente todo lo que en esto de que vamos hablando se encierra. . . . Porque *así como* el valor de la piedra preciosa es de subido y extraordinario valor, *así* el bien de una buena tiene subidos quilates de virtud; y *como* la piedra preciosa en sí es poca cosa, y por la grandeza de la virtud secreta cobra precio, *así* lo que en el sujeto flaco de la mujer pone estima de bien, es grande y raro bien; y *como* en las piedras preciosas la que no es muy fina no es buena, *así* en las mujeres no hay medianía, ni es buena la que no es muy buena; y *de la misma manera* que es rico un hombre que tiene una preciosa esmeralda o un rico diamante, aunque no tenga otra cosa, y el poseer estas piedras no es poseer una piedra, sino poseer en ella un tesoro abreviado, *así* una buena mujer no es una mujer, sino un montón de riquezas y quien la posee es rico con ella sola, y sola ella le puede hacer bienaventurado y dichoso, y *del modo que* la piedra preciosa se trae en los dedos y se pone delante de los ojos, y se asienta sobre la cabeza para hermosura y honra della, y el dueño tiene allí juntamente arreo en la alegría y socorro en la necesidad, *ni más ni menos* a la buena mujer el marido la ha de querer más que a sus ojos, y la ha de traer sobre su cabeza, y el mejor lugar del corazón dél ha de ser suyo, o, por mejor decir, todo su corazón y su alma, y ha de entender que en tenerla tiene un *tesoro general* para todas las diferencias de tiempos. (88, italics mine)

[This is the first tribute of praise accorded to a steadfast woman by the Holy Spirit, and *as if* springing to birth from the first, comes the second: she is compared to priceless jewels. In this, *as* in a single word is said completely everything implied in what we have been asserting. For *as* the worth of a precious stone is very great and out of the ordinary, *so* the perfection of a good woman comprises ever greater heights of unalloyed virtue. And *as* the gem is in itself a small object, but by the splendour of its inherent quality brings a high price, *so* what is infused into the frail being of a woman by her appreciation of goodness becomes a rare and exceptional excellence.

And also, *as* in precious stones one which is not wholly genuine is worthless, *so* as regards women there is no half and half: one who is not much more than good, is not good at all. *In the same fashion* that a man is wealthy because a precious emerald or a flawless diamond is his, even though he own nothing else, and to possess either of these jewels is not to possess one alone but a considerable treasure in miniature, *so* a good wife is not solely a wife, but a mountain of riches, and he who possesses her is rich with her alone, and in herself alone she has the power to make him blissfully happy. And *as* a precious gem is worn on the finger, and kept before the eyes, and with it the head is crowned for honour and beauty, and in possessing it the owner has at one and the same time ornaments for his joyousness and assistance in his necessities, so, *in no less degree*, a husband is bound to cherish a good wife more than his eyes, to uplift her high above his head, and to safeguard for her the innermost sanctuary of his heart, indeed his whole heart and soul. Likewise, he comes to realize that in her he possesses a *manifold treasure*, ready to hand for all variations of circumstance. (14–15)]

The excess of Fray Luis's fivefold simile betrays the insufficiency of the Holy Spirit's original comparación; if the "loor" [praise] were as "cabal" [precise] as Fray Luis claims it to be (and his use of the term is not unimportant, particularly given its clear cabalistic echoes), an exegesis of the sort in which the passage indulges would be quite unnecessary. The most glaring violation of similitude the passage inscribes, however, is a virtual recasting of the buena/más que buena equation: "en las mujeres no hay medianía, ni es buena la que no es muy buena" [as regards women there is no half and half: one who is not much more than good, is not good at all]. But if, owing to the deficiency of woman's nature, medianía is disallowed from the attributes of perfection, it is precisely on a kind of medianía that her wifely value depends. The elusive, highly prized (and high-priced) "mujer de valor" is, after all, a "mujer varonil." Although Fray Luis clearly intends the "varonil" epithet as a compliment, it is, at best, a paradoxical one insofar as it extolls femininity by tempering it with virility.[45] It is almost as if to be a good woman, a woman must not only be more than good, but she must somehow be less womanly. The same sort of logic reappears later in the treatise, in a provocative passage that warns wives against the dangers of becoming "dos veces mujeres" (118) [women twice over (42)].

The troubled status of semblance in *La perfecta casada* becomes even more so when analogy is invoked (as it frequently is) to impose legibility on the wife's body by forcing an equivalence between "ser" [being] and "parecer" [seeming]. At one level, the relation between seeming and being is already implicated in the very structure of analogy that, by rhetorically exploiting semblances, tries to arrive at the latter by means of the former (hence the comparison not of things directly but of the relations between them). Analogy becomes especially problematic as an analytic and discursive tool when the notion of similitude that forms the basis of its internal logic assumes the status of an (external) analogic term. In other words, analogy is, implicitly, always and already about semejanzas; it involves a precarious crossing (that is normalized — and indeed made to seem perfectly rational — through analogic form) of the tenuous line that separates essence from appearance. When those terms are explicitly made to form a part of a particular analogic instance, problems of the type that plague *La perfecta casada* ensue.

One of the most suggestive instances of this interplay occurs in an early passage that addresses precisely the question of legibility (of the wife's chastity, no less) in terms of the distinction between "ser" and "parecer":

Ni tampoco ha de ser esto, como algunos lo piensan, que con guardar el *cuerpo entero* al marido, para lo que toca a las pláticas y a otros

ademanes y obrecillas menudas, se tienen por libres. Porque no es
honesta la que no lo *es y parece*. Y cuanto está lejos del mal, tanto de
la *imagen o semeja* dél ha de estar apartada. . . . Y cierto, como al que
se pone en camino de Sanctiago, *aunque no llegue,* ya le llamamos allá
romero, así sin duda es principiada *ramera* la que se tome licencia para
tratar destas cosas que son el camino. (91, italics mine)

[And women are not to think either that because they keep their body
whole for their husbands, they may consider themselves free in regard to their conversation, postures, and small matters of behaviour.
Because a woman is not truly good, unless she *is* good and *seems* to
be so. And as distant as she is from wrong-doing, must she also be
distant from the very *image or semblance* of wrong. . . . Certain is it
that as one who sets out for Santiago is called by us a *pilgrim, although
he may not reach his journey's end,* so, without shadow of doubt, is she
a *harlot* in the making who permits herself to treat such matters, for
these are the way. (17)] [46]

On the surface, Fray Luis seems to be arguing for a conjunctive semiosis; for legibility to obtain, a correspondence must exist between appearance (sign) and essence (meaning). As far as the casada is concerned, a faithful wife must not only be faithful, her body must also
manifest all the proper signs (symptoms, even) of faithfulness: "no es
honesta la que no lo es y parece" [a woman is not truly good, unless she
is good and seems to be so]. But if the inclusion of "parecer" within
the domain of "ser" is intended to facilitate legibility, the conflation
of the two terms may instead mask a prioritization of appearance (or
even accident) over essence that could be extremely disruptive for the
treatise as a whole.

It is in the logical and rhetorical structuring of the romero-ramera
analogy that this possibility becomes most clearly discernible. To begin with, the romero side of the equation contains an obvious catachresis. Covarrubias is instructive on this point; he defines *romero* as
"el peregrino que va a visitar los cuerpos santos de San Pedro y San
Pablo y los demás sanctuarios y a besar el pie al Papa; y de aquí se
llamaron romeros no sólo los que van a Roma por devoción, pero también los que van de romería o peregrinación a otras casas sanctas y
santuarios. Estos llevan vestido propio, por el qual son conocidos, y

se les haze caridad y hospitalidad" [the pilgrim who goes to visit the holy bodies of St. Peter and St. Paul, and the other sanctuaries, and to kiss the foot of the Pope; thus, not only those who go to Rome for devout purposes were called *romeros,* but also those who go on a *romería* or pilgrimage to other holy places and sanctuaries. They wear proper clothing, by which they are recognized, and they are given alms and shown hospitality] (913).[47] Covarrubias's insistence on the applicability of the term "romero" to all those on "romería" regardless of their destination ("no sólo los que van a Roma") points, precisely, to the catachresis inscribed in the term, given its almost transparent etymology. By locating his romero "en camino de Sanctiago," Fray Luis denaturalizes the metaphoric transfer, making explicit the semantic violation involved. Insofar as the analogy can also be conceived as a dramatization of the structure of synecdoche, the part-whole relation is disclosed as a monstrous one. The part, in this case ("en camino de Sanctiago"), leads, at best, to an "improper" whole (Roma), as if the pilgrim erred in his already wandering steps. But the analogy turns, precisely, on the notion of errancy; not only will Fray Luis's romero never arrive in Rome, he will most likely not even reach Santiago. The pilgrim's pre-scribed failure, however — "aunque nunca llegue" [although he may not reach his journey's end] — in no way diminishes (and may even contribute to) his essential pilgrimness, suggesting the extent to which appearance (Covarrubias's "vestido propio, por el qual son conocidos") or accident (finding oneself "en camino de Sanctiago") determines essence ("romero") and not the other way round.

This point is not to be taken lightly in a treatise bedeviled by anxieties about somatic legibility and that defines that legibility in terms of a perfect correspondence between categories of seeming and being. It may be argued that it is the very attempt to guarantee correspondence by investing the sign with an almost coercive causality over meaning (a form of seeming that determines being) that backfires, creating (or exposing) in the process a third level between a conjunctive and a disjunctive semiosis. To the extent that the force that animates the causal relation exceeds the desired binary equivalence, the legibility that is perforce produced by this mechanism only denounces its inherent illegibility. Perhaps the best way to grasp the disjunctiveness of the analogy is to imagine the pilgrim's process here as a kind of meta-phoric reenactment of the Augustinian drama of signification, of the sort of "theology of the Word" that generally informs Fray Luis's con-ception not only of the workings of language but, more broadly, of the "máquina del universo." A romero's journey to a holy site is not so dif-ferent after all from the pilgrimage the linguistic signifier (the word) embarks on in order to reach the signified (at a secular level, meaning [Santiago]; at a divine level, the Absolute [Rome]). In his efforts to secure interpretive transparency, however, Fray Luis effectively pro-vides the material condition ("nunca llegar" [never arriving]) for an infinite deferment of meaning.

The possibilities this third position raises become extremely prob-lematic when regrafted on the body of the wife. At face value, the ramera side of the analogy seems to imply that the mere appearance of dishonor constitutes dishonor, opening the door for the punitive, hypostatized readings practiced by Calderonian honor husbands. But the forced conjunctiveness between seeming and being inscribes the potential threat of a radical misreading, since "el ser honesta" (or by extension, perfecta) seems to have at least as much (if not more) to do with appearances (or with the manifestation of the "proper" signs of honesty) as it does with honesty (or perfection) as such, suggesting, among other things, the possibility of what could be seen as a nominal-ist reading of the passage. In other words, if merely seeming unfaith-ful without actually being so suffices to render an otherwise faithful wife (of "cuerpo entero" [whole body]) a "principiada ramera" [harlot in the making], then to what extent does the outward appearance of faithfulness in the absence of a "cuerpo entero" (a wife not given to the condemning "obrecillas" but whose body is *not* preserved integral for her husband) suffice to render her honesta? Insofar as Fray Luis presents his text as a handbook for becoming *like* a perfecta casada (it paints a model — "un dechado" — which is to be imitated, but which can never be attained), one might argue that the manual is providing instructions for succeeding at just this type of deception.

If the romero side of the equation is haunted (and even animated) by the possibility of never arriving, the ghost in the machine of the ramera side is the preservation of corporeal integrity. Insofar as the body of the casada is concerned, the privileging of appearance can be understood in part as a yielding to the facile legibility of "obrecillas menudas" (applying makeup, gossiping with her neighbors, stepping beyond the prescribed sphere of her house's interior, etc.) in comparison to the radical illegibility of any kind of signs of adultery on a body that is, by virtue of the marital contract, already not whole. And yet, a ramera of "cuerpo entero" represents an aporia, a logical impasse not unlike that which inscribes the pilgrim's perpetual errancy, but one that "errs," as it were, in the opposite direction. In other words, if Rome — or Santiago — represents the pilgrim's final but ultimately unreachable destination, then "cuerpo entero" (or even "cuerpo entero al marido") represents a point of origin to which (save for the needlework of a Celestina) the prostitute or, indeed, the casada can never return. The relation between the romero and the ramera is worth considering here, particularly since the "causa final" of the romero's romería are the ostensibly incorruptible fragments of an ideal cuerpo entero, canonized precisely for its wholeness.

The importance of corporeal integrity to legibility as Fray Luis understands it cannot be overstated; the question is especially critical for a passage that sermonizes about the insufficiency of monogamy as a criterion for determining wifely honesty yet does not even honor such a code, but plays, precisely, on the violation of another type of corporeal integrity — on the material corruptibility of the letters *o* and *a*. The verbal conceit that in many ways motivates the analogy, the paronomasia that transforms "romero" to "ramera," is neither innocent nor unimportant in this context, particularly in light of Fray Luis's discussion concerning the (trans)gendering of letters that is contained in the opening sections of *De los nombres de Cristo:*

> En algunos nombres se añaden letras, para significar acrecentamiento de buena dicha en aquello que significan; y en otros se quitan algunas de las debidas para hacer demostración de calamidad y pobreza. Algunos, si lo que significan, por algún accidente, siendo varón, se ha afeminado y enmollecido, ellos también toman letras de las que en aquella lengua son, como si dijésemos, afeminadas y mujeriles. Otros, al revés, significando cosas femeninas de suyo, para dar a entender algún accidente viril, toman letras viriles. En otros mudan las letras su propia figura, y las abiertas se cierran y las cerradas se abren

y mudan el sitio, y se trasponen y disfrazan con visaje y gestos diferentes, y, como dicen del camaleón, se hacen a todos los accidentes de
aquellos cuyos son los nombres que constituyen. (bk. 1, 39–40)

[In some names letters are added to signify an increase in good fortune and the removal of certain others shows poverty and calamity.
Certain names, if what they designate is male, undergo some accident which makes them feminine and soft and borrow letters from
those which in this language are of feminine softness. Others, on the
other hand, which signify feminine things for themselves, borrow
virile letters to make comprehensible a virile accident. Among others
the letters modify their own form, the open ones close and the closed
ones open, and they change places, they are transposed and disguised
with different faces and gestures like the chameleon. They adapt to
all the accidents of the (things) whose names they constitute. (49)]

The passage elucidates a stunning, problematic relation between categories of accidence, essence, and legibility.[48] Letters' ability to alter
their "propia figura" [own form] in order to conform to the accidents
that befall the things they name betrays a certain *im*propriety, a sort of
noncorrespondence between a letter's figure and its attributed meaning, an impropriety that is, moreover, "essential" to the letter's signifying function. Essence, where the letter is concerned, seems to be
predicated on accidence, in much the same way as it is in the reading
of the romero's and ramera's bodies.

The language of accident that Fray Luis invokes in the passage from
Nombres in describing the transformation of words via letters suggests viewing the process detailed by Fray Luis as a linguistic and even
graphic (per)version of the "accidents without subject" tenet that was
institutionalized as eucharistic dogma. But if such an alignment is possible at the level of the letter's figure, it is not so at that of the word's.
It may be argued, in fact, that a Cratylism of the kind that Fray Luis
documents (and not unlike the marriage between forms of seeming
and being that he prescribes) points to anything *but* a disassociation
between "accidents" and "subject."

Applying the Cratylist and cabalist ideas expressed in *Nombres* directly to the romero-romera wordplay confirms the suspicion of this
noncorrespondence between the letter's figure and its signifying func-

tion, since, one might argue, the semantic emasculation of a masculine "romero" to a feminine "ramera" is reversed at the level of the letter's figure: it is the *a*'s of "ramera" that are typographically castrated, as it were, to become the *o*'s of "romero."[49] But even obviating the discrepancy between appearance (the figures of the letters *a* and *o*) and a kind of essence (*a* as feminine, *o* as masculine) by approaching the conversion from the other direction, and imagining the figure of the *a* as an *o* with something more — a (nonphallic) excess that feminizes in the same way that makeup ostensibly feminizes — does little to render the analogy trouble-free, since regardless of whether the (figural) operation in question involves a castration or its opposite, the accident that results in the letter's transgendering is not accounted for by the alleged transparency of the copula at the center of the analogy. An analogy of proper proportionality (a:b=c:d) need not be based on any kind of transparency, of course, since the equal sign attests only to the equivalence of relations and not of terms. But the fact that the analogy inscribes a pun complicates things, insofar as the economy of the wordplay (the recycling of the letters *r_mer_*) suggests a reading of "romero" and "ramera" not as independent analogic terms, but as a kind of before and after in the terms set forth in *Nombres*.

The romero/ramera pun points, moreover, to a second wordplay that is only implicit in the passage, but that further elucidates the relation between pilgrim and prostitute. I refer, specifically, to the false palindrome of Roma/Amor that derives from the romero's unambiguous etymology. Like the Ave/Eva doublet, which had been adduced as linguistic evidence of the Virgin Mary's redemptory role, the Roma/Amor pair could be used to confirm the distinction between *buen amor* and *loco amor:* the sublime love whose institutional seat was Rome and that was ascribed to the pilgrim, the good wife, and Mary, versus the concupiscent love that characterized the whore, the imperfect wife, and their moral predecessor, Eve.[50] But as the Arcipreste de Hita had brilliantly intuited centuries before, the binarism proves radically false. The two terms are not merely two sides of the same coin but, quite literally, mirror images of one another, lexically distinguishable, in the end, only by the reader's position. This mirroring has potentially devastating implications for a text like *La perfecta casada* that presents itself precisely as an "espejo clarísimo" [clearest mirror]. One might argue, for instance, that as a mirror, it is the treatise itself—not the indictingly legible *obrecillas menudas*—that effects the reversal that reads Roma as Amor; that it is, in other words, *La perfecta casada* that reflects the *cuerpo entero* of an exemplary *perfecta casada* and returns, in its stead, the grotesque but much more marketable body of a *principiada ramera* who seduces errant pilgrims on roads that never lead to Rome.

From Pilgrim to Prostitute:
Threats of the Uncontained Wife

It is no accident that Fray Luis should turn to the figures of pilgrim and prostitute at a crucial moment in the elaboration of criteria of legibility in the text. On one hand, the two figures, who appear repeatedly throughout the treatise, respectively embody the wifely threats of wandering and cosmetic. It is possible, in fact, to imagine a reading of the entire text of *La perfecta casada* posited on the promiscuous intercourse between the two.[51] On the other hand, the errant figures of the pilgrim and the prostitute form part of what might best be described as a metaphorics of metaphor, figures consistently invoked in tropological descriptions of figurality itself. The association between the errancy of the pilgrim and that of figural language is made painstakingly clear in the very term used by sixteenth- and seventeenth-century rhetorical treatises—and notably in López Pinciano's 1596 *Philosophía antigüa poética*—to describe tropological discourse: "lenguaje peregrino" [pilgrim language].[52]

The figural topography inscribed in the prologue of *La perfecta casada* easily lends itself to this sort of reading. The treatise opens to discover the (not yet) perfecta casada setting foot on the *camino real* of marriage with all its "dificultades y malos pasos" [difficulties and rough places]:

El entrañable amor que le tengo y el deseo de su bien que arde en mí, me despiertan para que le provea de algún aviso, y para que le busque y encienda alguna luz que, sin engaño ni error, alumbre y *enderece* sus pasos por todos los *malos pasos* deste camino y por todas las *vueltas*

y rodeos dél. Y como suelen los que han hecho alguna larga navega-
ción o los que han *peregrinado* por lugares *extraños,* . . . así yo, en esta
jornada que tiene vuestra merced comenzada, le enseñaré no lo que
me enseñó a mí la experiencia pasada, que es ajena a mi profesión,
sino lo que he aprendido en las sagradas letras, que es enseñanza del
Espíritu Sancto. (76, italics mine)

[The profound affection I have for you, and the desire for your wel-
fare which burns within me, move me to counsel you, and to seek to
enkindle a light which, without deception or error, may illume and
straighten your steps through all the *difficulties* of this way, and also
through all its *windings and turnings.* In the same fashion as those who
have undertaken some long voyage, or gone on *pilgrimage* through
strange places, . . . so, likewise, will I impart to you for this journey
which you have undertaken, not what past experience has taught me,
since marriage is foreign to my profession, but what I have learned
from Holy Writ, which is the teaching of the Holy Spirit. (3)][53]

Fray Luis's metaphor for marriage (a road besieged by "windings and
turnings," in short, a troped path) can easily be read as a metaphor for
figural language, for metaphor itself. It is perhaps not terribly surprising that Fray Luis should resort to metaphor at the very moment he
promises to straighten the perfecta casada's steps, to untrope the road,
as it were. The imperfectibility of the promise is already prescribed in
the figurality of the language used to express it; the "enderezamiento"
[straightening] that presumably returns the figural to the literal can be
described only metaphorically.[54]

And yet, despite their alignment with figural language and indi-
rection, the romero and ramera are figures whose bodies are putatively marked by their manifest legibility. Covarrubias's definition of
"romero" is a case in point: "llevan vestido propio, por el qual son
conocidos" [they wear proper clothing, on account of which they are
recognized]. The same holds true for the whore; ostensibly marked by
wanton ornament and provocative dress, her body should lend itself to
unambiguous identification. It is precisely as a function of this alleged
lack of ambiguity that her body becomes marketable. It is also in this
capacity that Fray Luis repeatedly invokes her as antimodel for his textual bride. A good example of this can be found in his use of a citation

from St. Clement in which the ramera once again occupies the fourth-term position in an analogy that turns on the question of corporeal legibility:

> Porque sin duda, como el hierro en la cara del esclavo muestra que es fugitivo, así las floridas pinturas del rostro son señal y pregón de ramera. (139)
>
> [Because, undoubtedly, as the brand on the face of a slave betokens that he is a fugitive, so this gaudy painting of the countenance signifies and heralds the prostitute. (63)]

The passage registers a number of internal contradictions, not unlike those that plague the romero-ramera passage. To begin with, the legibility of iron on the slave's face is guaranteed by its indelibility. But the makeup ("floridas pinturas") that is the hierro's analogue is censured throughout the treatise for its impermanence, among other things. The colors of cosmetic eventually run: "Descúbrese por entre lo blanco un escuro y verdinegro, y un entre azul y morado; y matízase el rostro todo, y señaladamente las cuencas de los bellísimos ojos, con una variedad de colores feísimos; y aún corren a las veces derretidas las gotas, y aran con sus arroyos la cara" (128–29) [Here and there, amid the face-bleach, one detects darkness, a sort of greenish-blackness, something between purple and indigo: the whole face and particularly the sockets of the splendid eyes are tinged with a variety of livid colours and sometimes the drops melt and run down, and stream over the face in furrows (53)]. In an earlier (and by no means unrelated) reproach of woman's frivolous spending, Fray Luis had in fact already highlighted this (feminine) tendency toward the fleeting and the ephemeral as a marker of sexual difference: "Los hombres, si les acontece ser gastadores, las más veces son en cosas, aunque no necesarias, pero duraderas o honrosas, o que tienen alguna parte de utilidad o provecho . . . mas el gasto de las mujeres es todo en el aire" (96) [Whenever men turn out to be spendthrifts, in the majority of cases they spend, possibly not on necessary things, but on things which are at least lasting or estimable, or which to some degree, are somewhat useful or profitable . . . but the expenditures of women are all a puff of wind (22)].

But even without taking into account the threat to legibility that this "feminine" impermanence poses (an impermanence that applies equally well to the romero and the romera), the legibility that Fray Luis ascribes to the pilgrim and especially the prostitute is questionable at best. Perhaps the best proof of just how questionable is provided by the legal ordinances in effect in early modern Spain that required prostitutes to visually mark themselves by wearing yellow headdresses. The need for this type of ordinance suggests that rameras' bodies were far less "marked" than Fray Luis alleges. The sociohistorical counterpart to Fray Luis's anxieties over the sort of illegibility that makeup and noncontainment produce on the wife's body can be located in contemporary cultural anxieties over the illegibility of the prostitute's body, anxieties materialized in the very laws that sought to secure differentiation between "good" and "bad" women. More disturbingly, these ordinances find a clear parallel in the laws (already recorded in the *Siete partidas* of the mid-thirteenth century) requiring Moors and Jews to wear certain colors and head ornaments in order to unmistakably mark their bodies as "other."

Beneath her reputed legibility, then, the ramera is haunted by a fundamental illegibility that renders her body unsafe as a site of reading. It is not surprising that repeated attempts throughout the fifteenth and sixteenth centuries to institutionalize control over the somatic self-representation of prostitutes generally failed. More interesting than the failure itself, however, is the primary reason behind it, which brings us back from the body of the prostitute to the body of the not so perfect wife. As Mary Elizabeth Perry notes: "Laws requiring prostitutes to wear a yellow headdress did not clearly distinguish them from respectable women because, according to a royal ordinance, '*many women who are good, married, honorable, and honest*' were wearing the yellow head-coverings prescribed for prostitutes." [55] It is compelling to imagine reasons for this wifely trespass, particularly if the donning of yellow headdress is conceived as a subtle act of resistance by the casada, as an illicit gesture of transgressive self-fashioning. But regardless of her motives, it is precisely this sort of misdemeanor on the wife's part (like the indicting "obrecillas menudas" that radically trouble the distinction between "honest" and "dishonest" women) that mobilizes Fray Luis's interpretive anxieties. In a textual borrowing from Tertullian, for example, he rails against makeup precisely for the confusion of categories it provokes:

> '¡Cuánto será más digno de blasfemia si las que sois llamadas sacerdotes de honestidad *salís* vestidas y pintadas como las deshonestas se visten y afeitan; o qué más hacen aquellas miserables que se sacrifican al público deleite y al vicio, a las cuales, si antigüamente las leyes las apartaron de las matronas y de los trajes que las matronas usaban, ya la maldad de este siglo, que siempre crece, las ha igualado en esto con las honestas mujeres, *de manera que no se pueden reconocer sin error.*'
> (147)

> ['Yet, how much more conducive to blasphemy is it if you who are called the priestesses of modesty *go around* dressed and painted like those who are immodest! In fact, to what extent could one consider those poor, unhappy victims of organized lust to be beneath you? Even though in the past some laws used to forbid them to adorn themselves as married women or as matrons, now, surely, the corruption of our times which is daily growing worse *makes it very difficult to distinguish them* from the most honorable women.'][56]

Tertullian's words, which Fray Luis ventriloquizes, are almost identical to those of Juan de Quiñones in his Jew-hunting treatise ("el reconocimiento es difícil" [recognition is difficult]). Through the ministrations of cosmetic, honest women become indistinguishable from whores.

If the confusion between casadas and rameras that Fray Luis indicts is largely the result of transgressive self-representation on the part of married women, however, it is also the result of the improper place the wife's body occupies in wandering beyond the safe space of the house: "*salís* vestidas y pintadas como las deshonestas." Outside the interior space to which it is relegated, the body of the casa-da is taken for that of a whore.[57] The unlikely (or perhaps inevitable) couple of pilgrim and prostitute is curiously reworked in this context since a female pilgrim, a romera, cannot exist in Fray Luis's text without wandering (both morally and orthographically) toward the place (or the initial *a*) of ramera. The threat to the wife of wandering beyond the limits of her circumscribed sphere is materialized, then, in the body of the Other woman she becomes. Repeatedly and in no uncertain terms, the text delimits a space whose boundaries must not be breached by the per-fecta casada: "Y dice lo demás desto también porque, diciéndole a la mujer que rodee su casa, le quiere enseñar el espacio por donde ha de menear los pies la mujer, y los lugares por donde ha de andar, y como si dijésemos, el campo de su carrera, que es su casa propria, y no las calles, ni las plazas, ni las huertas, ni las casas ajenas" (157) [But there is another reason for this repetition: by telling a wife that she is to look into all the corners of her house, he means to point out to her the space within which her feet are to carry her, and the places where she must walk; in so many words, the field of her activities. Such is her home, no less; not the streets, nor the public squares, nor other people's houses or gardens (72–73)]. At least as important as keeping the outside out of the house (and body) is keeping what belongs inside of it in, pro-tecting that most private of the husband's properties, his wife's body. The textual relegation of the wife's body (and more broadly, of the woman's body) to a private enclosure ("Como son los hombres para lo público, así las mujeres para el encerramiento" [158] [As men were meant to mix in public, so women were made for seclusion (73–74)]) is justified as necessary in order to prevent its being misread as that of a whore, a *public* woman.[58]

Perhaps the most disturbing illustration of the fatal consequences of a woman's wandering beyond her prescribed sphere is found in a passage that perversely engages in bodily mutilation and deformity:

> Y como los peces, en cuanto están dentro del agua, discurren por ella y andan y vuelan ligeros, mas si acaso los sacan de allí, quedan sin se poder menear; así la buena mujer, cuanto para de sus puertas adentro, ha de ser presta y ligera, tanto, para fuera dellas, se ha de tener por *coja y torpe*. . . . Los chinos en nasciendo, les *tuercen* a las niñas los pies, por que cuando sean mujeres no los tengan para salir fuera, y porque, para andar en su casa, aquellos *torcidos* les bastan. (158, italics mine)

> [Fish, so long as they are in water, can pass swiftly through it, and speed, and move about lightly within it, but once out of it, they are unable to stir. So it is with the perfect wife: from her front door in,

she is to be quick and light of foot; from her front door out, she is to be *lame and clumsy*. . . . The Chinese *twist* the feet of girl-babies as soon as they are born, so that when grown, they may not use them for leaving the house, and because those *stunted feet* suffice for them to move around indoors. (73)]

The implicit stipulation against one type of troping (the casada's transgressive pilgrimage from inside to outside) is ironically subverted by the prescription offered against it—a much more dangerous troping of the body itself.[59] The double mutilation the passage registers presents a logical bind: the first wife who (like the fish out of water) is rendered "coja y torpe" [lame and clumsy] when she steps outside her house is no different in her deformity from the second (Chinese) wife also rendered "coja y torpe" when (and in order that) she remains inside it.[60]

The relegation of the female body to the interior of the house, like the injunction that prohibits the exterior's penetration of that sacrosanct interiority, is anatomically grounded in the relation of identity—both metonymic and metaphoric—that the text repeatedly endorses between the house and body of the perfecta casada. Not only in Fray Luis, but throughout the conduct literature, the female body is assigned to the interior space of the house because of the perceived violability of another interior space housed within it.[61] Like the house to which she is spatially confined, the woman's body—especially the body of the wife as definitive icon of her husband's private property—must be protected against (sexual) traffic between interior and exterior.

In *La perfecta casada,* images of sexual penetration and infection that suffuse textual warnings against pilgrim entrances to the domestic sphere readily lend themselves to readings of this sort, suggesting an easy substitutability between "cuerpo" and "casa" in the treatise. While Fray Luis designates as unthinkable—and clearly unmentionable—that a (perfecta) casada could be anything but honesta (read monogamous), the contiguity house-body challenges to some extent the impossibility he ascribes to that premise.[62] The textual namelessness of the wife's carnal dishonesty is thus sidestepped. An overtly sexual language that is repressed by Fray Luis (where penetration of the wife's body is concerned) returns with a vengeance in discussions of the house's permeability.

> Y, como dice Cristo en el Evangelio, que mientras el padre de la fa-milia duerme, siembra el enemigo la cizaña, así ella, con su descuido y sueño, meterá la libertad y la deshonestidad por su casa, que *abrirá las puertas y falseará las llaves y quebrantará los candados, y penetrará hasta los postreros secretos, corrompiendo* a las criadas, y no parando hasta poner su *infición* en las hijas. (110–11, italics mine)

> [Our Lord tells us in the Gospel that while the father of the family slumbered, the enemy came and sowed tares among the wheat. In the same fashion, the wife, with her slackness and sloth, will make room in her house for license and dishonesty. These *will open doors, falsify keys, break padlocks, and pierce the uttermost secrets, corrupt-ing* the maids, and pausing not until even the daughters have been *infected.* (35)][63]

It would seem, then, more than mere coincidence that the passage immediately preceding this one contains the most explicit statement in the text concerning the relation of identity that exists between a casada's house and her body: "Porque ha de entender que *su casa es su cuerpo*" (110, italics mine) [She must realize that *her home is (her) body* (35)].

The conflation between the "rape" of the house and the "rape" of the female body that is already inscribed in a rhetoric of violation is corroborated, moreover, by the frequency of textual images depicting either boundaries (doors, windows) or mechanisms (keys, padlocks, latches) that attempt to keep separate inside from outside. The threat here is one of liminality that renders such spaces especially vulnerable as sites of seduction. In a citation from Euripides (that in its intertextu-ality already transgresses its own prohibition against things foreign), Fray Luis instructs husbands on ways to fortify such liminal spaces: "conviénele al marido guarnecer muy bien con aldabas y con cerro-jos las puertas de su casa" (123) [guard ye well / With bolts and bars the portals of your halls (47)]. An anatomical reading of the house's architecture or, alternately, an architectural reading of the casada's anatomy suggests, among other things, that the doors and windows that must be safeguarded from penetration correspond to the openings on the wife's body that must likewise be "guarnecidas" against foreign entrances or temptations. These openings include not only the locus of sexual contamination but the spaces of sensual contamination as well. It is not just the wife's chastity that must be protected from adultery, then, but her ears that must be guarded against gossip, her eyes against visual seduction, and even her nose against the corrupting vapors of cosmetic ("madre de muy mal olor" [mother of very unpleasant odours]).

Perhaps the most critical anatomic boundary between inside and outside, however, is the wife's mouth, which, in accordance with the Pauline dictum condemning woman to silence, must remain closed. Noting the inescapable homology between the closed female mouth and genitals, on one hand, and the closed confines of the house, on the other, Peter Stallybrass writes: "Silence, the closed mouth, is made a sign of chastity. And silence and chastity are, in turn, homologous to woman's enclosure within the house." [64] In Fray Luis, the relation between closure (of the casada's mouth as stand-in for her sexuality) and enclosure (of the casada's body within the interior space) is rationalized via a naturalist argument:[65]

Porque, así como la naturaleza, como dijimos y diremos, hizo a las mujeres para que encerradas guardassen la casa, así las obligó a que cerrasen la boca. . . . Porque el hablar nace del entender, y las palabras no son sino como imágenes o señales de lo que el ánimo concibe en sí mismo; por donde así como a la mujer buena y honesta la naturaleza no la hizo para el estudio de las ciencias ni para los negocios de dificultades, sino para un solo oficio simple y doméstico, así les limitó el entender, y por consiguiente, les tasó las palabras y las razones. (155)

[Nature, indeed, as we have said already, and intend to say again, constituted women to stay in closely, and to be the guardians of their homes. So likewise has it laid upon them the obligation to keep their lips closed. . . . It is obvious that speech comes as the result of knowing, and words are but images or signs of what the mind conceives within itself. Wherefore, as a good and honest woman was not endowed by nature for the study of the various branches of knowledge, nor for the difficulties of business affairs, but was created for one single duty, simple and domestic, so was her understanding circumscribed, and, in consequence, her words and arguments limited. (70)]

This passage, among the most misogynist of the entire treatise rehearses a contradiction that is familiar enough within the history of antifeminist discourse. It lies in the fact that Fray Luis has, to some degree, himself adopted the (improper) place of woman: not only through the textual mediation that ostensibly legitimizes his writing about a subject that is, by his own confession, "ajeno" to him, but, moreover, through the very association of the feminine and the aesthetic that equates being a writer with being a woman.[66] In precluding woman from speech, Fray Luis is advocating his own (textual) silence. Even more troubling, however, is the fact that Fray Luis recommends the woman's silence precisely for the deceptive covering that it makes possible: "Mas como quiera que sea, es justo que se precien de callar todas, así aquellas a quien *les conviene encubrir* su poco saber, como aquellas que pueden sin vergüenza descubrir lo que saben" (154, italics mine) [Be this as it may, it is a rightful thing for all women to pride themselves on keeping silence, those who *have reason to cover over* their own ignorance, as well as those who need not be at all ashamed of their learning (70)]. Silence, then, ultimately renders woman as illegible as the excesses of speech. The homology between closure of anatomical openings and enclosure within the house, on one hand, and between the sensual and the sexual openings of woman's body, on the other, suggest that female garrulity (the open mouth) in *La perfecta casada* can be equated with harlotry (the open sex). Like the casada who transgresses the physical confines of her house, the woman who transgresses rhetorical boundaries is textually deemed a whore.

Made-up Adulteries and the Seductions of Color

Not until the eleventh chapter of *La perfecta casada*, after countless "vueltas y rodeos," does Fray Luis arrive, finally, like a pilgrim to Santiago, at that elusive "proprio lugar" from which to address the dangerous and alluring subject of cosmetic excess. The topos of makeup, the (common) place to which all textual roads lead, registers, not by accident, the treatise's most sustained reading of the relation between forms of seeming and being as well as of the wife's body as a site of and for interpretation.

> Y porque en esto, y señaladamente en las posturas del rostro, hay grande exceso, aun en las mujeres que en lo demás son honestas; *y porque es aqueste su proprio lugar,* bien será que digamos algo dellos aquí. Aunque, si va a decir la verdad, *yo confieso a vuestra merced que lo que me convida a tratar desto, que es el exceso, eso mismo me pone miedo.* (127, italics mine)

> [And whereas in all this, and particularly in the matter of cosmetics there is the greatest excess even among women who are honest in everything else, *and because this is its proper place,* it will be fitting for me to treat here of this subject. But if I am to confess the truth, *I must tell you that what invites me to consider this matter, namely, excess, is the very thing which fills me with foreboding.* (52)]

The almost climactic sense of fulfillment that colors the arrival at an issue that has haunted the narrative since its opening is neither trivial nor merely hyperbolic. At least twice before, Fray Luis found it necessary to repress the question of makeup, explicitly postponing the subject that perversely intimidates ("me pone miedo") even as it incites him ("me convida").[67]

Here, at this strange, disproportionate center of *La perfecta casada* (accounting for nearly one third of the treatise's length and located at its exact midpoint), Fray Luis surrenders, in a torrent of hysteria, to the inevitable seductions of color:

> ¿Por qué ¿pregunto, ¿por qué la casada quiere ser más hermosa de lo que su marido quiere que sea? ¿Qué pretende afeitándose a su pesar? ¿Qué ardor es aquel que le menea las manos para acicalar el cuero como arnés, y poner en arco las cejar? ¿Adónde amenaza aquel acro, y aquel resplandor a quién ha de cegas? El colorado y el blanco, y el rubio y el dorado y aquella artillería toda ¿qué pide? ¿qué desea? ¿qué vocea? No pregunta sin causa el cantarcillo común, ni es más castellano que verdadero: "¿Para qué se afeita la mujer casada?" Y torna a la pregunta, y repite la tercera vez, preguntando: "¿Para qué se afeita?"

Porque si va a dezir la verdad, la respuesta de aquel "para qué" es amor propio desordenadísimo, apetito insaciable de vana excelencia, codicia fea, deshonestidad arraigada en el corazón, adulterio, ramería, delicto que jamás cesa.

    ¿Qué pensáis las mujeres que es afeitaros? Traer pintado en el rostro vuestro deseo feo. (131–32)

[Tell me, if you can, why does a married woman desire to be more attractive than her husband wishes her to be? What is she after when, in spite of her husband, she puts on paint? What ardour is that which moves her hands to polish her skin as if it were a piece of harness, and pencil her eyebrows into the form of a bow? In what direction is this bow threatening, and whom does this splendour dazzle? Rosy, pale, blonde, golden — all that artillery! What is it asking, what does it want, what is it shouting for? Not without reason does the popular song ask, not once but three times (and this is as true as it is characteristically Castilian): "Why does the married woman paint herself?" And the song returns to the question, and repeats it a third time, asking "Why does the married woman paint herself?" Well, if one is to tell the truth, the answer to this "Why?" is the most disordered self-love, an unappeasable craving for empty excellence, an ugly covetousness, dishonesty deeply rooted in the heart: adultery, harlotry, a never-ceasing wrongdoing.

    What do you women think is the meaning of your makeup? It is to carry around your improper desires painted on your faces. (56–57)]

The threat of makeup, then, is that it makes visible the wife's excessive and disproportionate desire, a desire that adulterously exceeds her husband's.[68]

In this sense, it is hardly coincidental that Fray Luis's reproach of makeup's illegitimate pleasures is couched in a language of adultery, prostitution, and an insatiable feminine (sexual) appetite:[69] the discourse of adultery registers the intrusion of the Other, the exterior, the stranger within the realm of the Self-Same, the interior, the household. Both adultery and cosmetic are, in some sense, aligned with Otherness and substitution, and closer, as a result, to metaphor and allegory than to the alleged Sameness of analogy. In other words, through substitution (of one body or of one face for another) marital infidelity and makeup both violate the analogic contract on which legibility, as Fray Luis understands it, ostensibly depends. It is around the very question of legibility (or rather illegibility) that makeup—and the woman who recurs to it—are indicted as adulterous in *La perfecta casada;* this is so on at least two separate counts, both related to categories of the accidental and the secondary.

First, the application of makeup by a married woman is charged as adulterous for the deception it involves, a sort of ontologic infidelity grounded on a disjunction between forms of seeming and being. This sort of adultery is by no means limited to cases of cosmetic deception; it looms large throughout the treatise, as we have seen in the romero-ramera analogy, for example. And yet it is primarily with respect to makeup and its disconcerting effects that the question is most compellingly posed in *La perfecta casada*. Second, cosmetic is aligned with adulterous transgression in what could almost be considered teleologic terms, inasmuch as it makes the woman who uses it guilty of a secondary and rival re-creation of God's design and finished work. Adultery is explicitly conceived, in this case, as adulteration, corruption, mixture. It is not so much a question of "ser" as opposed to (or distinct from) "parecer" that makes reading precarious here, but rather the possibility of infinite rewritings (not unlike, one may argue, the kind of gloss that Fray Luis performs) that makes the original text of the wife's body illegible. The infidelity involved in this type of cosmetic re-creation (the wife's alleged unfaithfulness to the way that God created her) is explicitly associated, moreover, with the question of permissible subjectivities. The possibilities for self-fashioning that conduct literature gives rise to are, in the hands of women, nonetheless condemned as a challenge to a divinely ordained telos.

In general, an adulterous transgression requires the complicity of at least three bodies, two of which are bound by contract (presumably marital), and a third that disrupts and destabilizes the binary symmetry between the other two—an interloper who puts things (bodies, words, texts) out of place. The first kind of cosmetic adultery condemned in *La perfecta casada* is based on the existence of only two bodies—those of husband and wife. The third position is occupied by the wife herself, who in her cosmetic imposture becomes the "other woman" with whom her husband consummates an illicit passion. Citing Ambrose, Fray Luis outlines the dangers of this type of adulterous triangle, in a language that bespeaks the Otherness of the made-up wife:

> las mujeres, temiendo desagradar a los hombres, se pintan las caras con colores ajenos, y en el *adulterio* que hacen de su cara, se ensayan para el *adulterio* que desean hacer de su persona. Mas qué locura aquesta tan grande. . . . Porque el otro, en ti afeitada, no ama a ti sino a *otra*, y tú no quieres como otras ser amada. Enséñasle en ti a ser *adúltero*, y si pone en otra su amor, recibes pena y enojo. Mala maestra eres contra ti misma. Más tolerable en parte es ser adúltera, que andar afeitada, porque allí se corrompe la castidad, y aquí la misma naturaleza. (134, italics mine)

> [you women paint your faces with unnatural colours, because you are fearful of displeasing men: by adulterating your faces, you practise yourselves in that adultery which you desire for your persons. But what extraordinary folly this is. . . . A man will not love you, made up as you are, but some *other* person in you, yet you do not want to be loved as someone else! You teach your husband to be adulterous with you and then you are grieved and angry if he loves some other woman. A very poor teacher you are, to your own detriment. Adultery itself is preferable to going about with a painted face, for in the former chastity is ruined, but in the latter, nature itself. (59)]

On one hand, cosmetic adultery ("adulterio de la cara") is censured in the passage precisely for serving as a preface, a rehearsal to a more explicit sexual adultery ("adulterio de la persona"). On the other, and somewhat ironically, this preface to transgression becomes more incriminating than the transgression itself: actual adultery is dismissed as a lesser evil ("más tolerable") in comparison to the ontologic adultery that makeup engenders. The illegibility that in many ways defines cosmetic adultery is here materialized on a female body that acquires a monstrously doubled shape: the (wifely) Self becomes, via makeup, a duplicitous Other (woman). While the treatise attaches greater value to the former, the axiology fails to hold up; the husband—final arbiter, after all, of wifely desirability and the object toward whom the wife's desire is ostensibly directed—inevitably chooses the "otra" painted on his wife's skin over the genuine casada who hides beneath the makeup.[70]

Not just the husband is deceived by makeup, but also the wife, who naively puts her faith in its beautifying powers. In a passage that in its confessional tone differs significantly from the critical distancing that typically characterizes the discourse of cosmetic theology, Fray Luis assures his reader-wives that his indictment of makeup will not broach the topic of sinfulness, but will limit itself instead to unmasking afeite as a hypocrite, condemning it for its deception, for promising one thing and delivering another.

> Porque ¿quién no temerá de oponerse contra una cosa tan recibida? O ¿quién tendrá ánimo para osar persuadirles a las mujeres a que quie-ran parecer lo que son? . . . Y no sólo es dificultoso este tratado, pero es peligroso también, porque luego aborrecen a quien esto les quita. . . . Y si aman a aquellos que . . . las dejan asquerosas y feas, muy más justo es que siquiera no me aborrezcan a mí, sino que me oigan con igualdad y atención, que cuanto agora en esto les quiero decir, será solamente enseñarles que sean hermosas, que es lo que princi-palmente desean. Porque *yo no les quiero tratar del pecado* que algunos hallan y ponen en el afeite, sino solamente quiero dárselo a conocer, *demostrándoles que es un fullero engañoso, que les da al revés de aquello que les promete.* . . . (127–28, italics mine)

> [Who, indeed, would not be afraid to set himself in opposition to what is so generally accepted? Who has the necessary courage, or dares to persuade women to be willing to appear as they really are? . . . And not only is this attempt difficult, but it is perilous as well, because women will immediately detest him who takes away their powders and paints. . . . If they are so fond of those who . . . allow them to be loathsome and ugly, how much more just it is that at least they should not regard me with abhorrence, but listen to me with equanimity and attention, since all that I desire is what they themselves crave above everything: to show them how to be beautiful.

I do not mean to consider at all the sin which some are led into, and commit in the matter of their facial makeup, but only to reveal makeup for what it is and *prove to them that cosmetics are deceitful tricksters, giving the very opposite of what they promise.* . . . (52–53)]

The passage is compelling for a number of reasons, not the least of which is its almost hysterical manifestation of Fray Luis's authorial insecurity vis-à-vis the women (readers) whose cosmetics he would confiscate; the fear of incurring their disfavor makes writing the treatise not only difficult, he contends, but outright dangerous. Undoubtedly the most striking element of the passage is its inscription of an authorial promise (Fray Luis's guarantee that his reprobation of afeite will be grounded on questions of aesthetics and not ethics) in the midst of a sharp criticism of makeup's broken promises. What follows should perhaps come as no surprise:

Y esto es muy digno de considerar, y más lo que se sigue tras esto, que es el daño de la consciencia y la ofensa de Dios, que aunque *prometí* no tratarlo, pero al fin la conciencia me obliga a *quebrantar* lo que puse. (131, italics mine)

[All this is well worthy of consideration, and the consequences which follow, even more so, because these consequences are harmful to one's conscience, and an offence against God.

And now, although I *promised* to leave sin out of consideration, my conscience drives me to *break my promise*. (56)]

Seemingly spurred on by the contagious deception of color, Fray Luis fails to keep his promise, breaking his word to his readers and participating in the dangerous game of substitutions that invests cosmetic ("fullero engañoso" [deceitful trickster]) with its adulterous power.

If the adultery I have characterized as ontologic deception implicates both husband and wife (making him adulterous with the other woman his wife impersonates, and her with her painted mirror image), the second charge of adultery brought against the made-up wife in *La perfecta casada* is based on a transgression of an altogether different sort. It is not the marital contract between spouses that cosmetic violates in this case, but rather an implicit contract between creature and Creator. The wife who wears makeup is deemed adulterous for her defiant subjectivity, for the rival re-creation to God's original plasticity that her secondary cosmetic artifice represents.

Y si todavía les parezco muy bravo, oigan ya, no a mí, sino a Sant Cipriano . . . "en ninguna manera conviene ni es lícito *adulterar* la obra de Dios y su hechura, añadiéndole o color rojo, o alcohol negro, o arrebol colorado, o cualquier otra compostura que *mude o corrompa* las figuras naturales. . . . Las manos ponen en el mismo Dios cuando lo que Él formó lo procuran ellas reformar y desfigurar. Como si no supiesen que es obra de Dios todo lo que nace, y del demonio todo lo que se muda de su natural. Si algún grande pintor retratase con colores que llegasen a lo verdadero las facciones y rostro de alguno, con toda la demás disposición de su cuerpo, y acabado ya y perficionado el retrato, otro quisiese poner las manos en él, presumiendo de más maestro, para reformar lo que ya estaba formado y pintado, ¿paréceos que tendría el primero justa y grave causa para indignarse? Pues ¿piensas tú no ser castigada por una osadía de tan malvada locura, por la ofensa que haces al divino Artífice? Porque, *dado caso que por la alcahuetería de los afeites no vengas a ser con los hombres deshonesta y adúltera, habiendo corrompido y violado lo que hizo en ti Dios, convencida quedas de peor adulterio.*" (132–33, italics mine)

[But if I still appear to you to be in a rage, listen not to me but to St. Cyprian. . . . "in no manner whatever is it fitting or licit for them *to adulterate* the work of God and His workmanship by adding either red paint, or stibium, or rouge, or any other admixture which may *change or corrupt* their natural features. . . . Such as these lay hands on God Himself when they try to make over, and disfigure what He has formed. As if they were unaware that every living thing is God's handiwork, and that everything which deviates from its own nature comes from the Devil!

Suppose a superb artist were to paint in colours the features and countenance of some one, and, indeed, the whole figure to the life, and having completed and perfected the portrait, another person should wish to touch it up (presuming to be an even greater master) in order to amend what was already perfectly formed and painted, would it seem to you (and rightly) that the first had grave and just cause for indignation? Therefore, can you imagine that you will go unpunished for a boldness so perverted and insane, and for the offense which you yourself commit towards the Divine artificer?

Because *granted that through the seduction of your paints and make-ups you do not actually become dishonest and adulterous, nevertheless, having corrupted and violated God's workmanship in yourself, you stand convicted of a worse adultery."* (57–58)] [71]

Fray Luis's tactic of displacing his own hysteria ("si todavía les parezco muy bravo" [if I still appear to you to be in a rage]) by remitting to a citational mode is fairly common to the discourse of misogyny. Even more common is the argument he appropriates from Cyprian that aligns an original act of creation with God and characterizes as the work of the devil any superfluous additions.[72] Fray Luis incorporates, in fact, a number of patristic borrowings (not only Cyprian, but also Tertullian, Ambrose, and Clement) that basically repeat the same indictment, defining cosmetic adultery as teleologic adulteration.[73]

The irony of course is that, in its very composition, *La perfecta casada* is guilty of the identical transgression. Fray Luis's authorial project consists, precisely, of textual adulterations and manipulations ("poner las manos en él"), of reforming, by means of gloss, not only "what was already perfectly formed and painted" (or in this case, written), but, specifically, the text of Proverbs that had been "formed and painted" presumably by God (through the authorial intervention of the Holy Spirit). This is especially true in the chapter on makeup, which is overwhelmingly comprised of citations. It is not coincidental that the majority of passages that rail against the adulterous recycling of original creations (such as Cyprian's criticism of any "admixture which may change or corrupt their natural features") appear in cited auctoritas — texts that are themselves recycled, "moved and corrupted," by virtue of their inclusion in the very admixture we read them. But even without taking into account the contradictions that besiege the treatise at a formal level, the argument against teleologic adultery is plagued by incoherences. To begin with, the move from a human to a divine level of adultery makes it possible to imagine an adulterous triangle between husband, wife, and God, in which it remains unclear who (husband or God) occupies the position of legiti-

mate spouse. Tertullian's admonition, cited by Fray Luis, that the wife
should adorn herself with the cosmetics of the apostles and the colors
of chastity in order to seduce Christ is suggestive in this context;[74] so
too is the other adulterous triangle that cosmetic re-creation facili-
tates, the one between God, the made-up casada, and the demon lover
who inspires her handiwork ("es obra del demonio").

Even more suggestive are the questions about female subjectivity
that makeup raises, particularly in being deemed an adultery against
God. It may be argued that cosmetic's greatest threat lies precisely
in its empowering of a subordinate, repressed body (the wife's) with
the possibility not only of representing itself, but, moreover, of doing
so duplicitously—that is, of assuming agency (and even transgressive agency) in the process of signification. With men, this type of
agency is, as we have seen, considered part and parcel of the concept of Renaissance self-fashioning. In the case of women, however,
such agency (which is as a rule excluded from the mere realm of possibility for the objectified body) is conceived as a challenge—a sign
of unruliness—and is immediately remitted not only to human but,
more indictingly, to divine authority. God is represented as Divine
Craftsman; the woman who would reform His work is judged guilty
of insolence (and even aligned with demonic forces) for deeming herself greater than her maker: " 'Dice Dios: "Hagamos al hombre a la
imagen y semejanza nuestra," ¿y osa alguna mudar en otra figura lo
que Dios hizo?' " (132) ['God has said, "Let us make man in our image,
after our likeness," and does any woman make so bold as to alter the
semblance of what God has made, into something different?' (57)].
It is more than a little ironic that Cyprian (and Fray Luis by quoting
him) should here cite the very passage that was consistently invoked
to prove not woman's equal (creaturely) footing with respect to her
husband-mate, but, on the contrary, her secondariness, the argument
being that only the male of the species was created in God's likeness
whereas woman, an afterthought, was laterally created from Adam's
rib.

And yet, for all its vehemence, Fray Luis's reprimand throughout
the eleventh chapter of the made-up wife's aesthetic artifice stands in
sharp contrast to his praise, earlier in the treatise, of a not dissimilar

artifice (and, arguably, subjective agency) to which a good wife must recur in order to mold her body (composed of base, corruptible material) into something resembling that of the exemplary perfect wife.

> Y como cuando en una materia dura y que no se rinde al hierro ni al arte, vemos una figura perfectamente esculpida, decimos y conocemos que era perfecto y extremado en su oficio el artífice que la hizo, y que con la ventaja de su artificio venció la dureza no domable del sujeto duro; así y por la misma manera, el mostrarse una mujer la que debe entre tantas ocasiones y dificultades de vida, siendo de suyo tan flaca, es señal clara de un caudal de virtud rarísima y casi heroica. (87)

> [A similar case is that of some material, hard as adamant, which yields neither to the hammer nor to any artifice whatever. If, out of this unyielding matter, we see a figure perfectly sculptured, we acknowledge, and we say, that the artist who wrought it was expert and extraordinarily skillful in his profession, and that it was with the advantage of his resourcefulness that he conquered the indomitable hardness of his medium. In the same fashion, then, for a woman to prove herself what she should be amid such varying circumstances and perplexities of life, when she is so weak by nature, offers the clearest evidence of a treasury of most rare and almost heroic virtue. (14)]

The wife is here likened to both the "materia dura" [hard material] and the "artifice" [artist] who renders it pliable. The implications of this double position (another instance of analogy—or simile in this case—gone haywire) are radically at odds with the treatise's censure of teleologic adulteration.[75] They are, in a sense, the same as those that derive from the very existence of an instruction manual for married women: first, that the would-be perfect wife *should* exert agency in refashioning herself (ideally into a perfect wife) and second, that there *is* room for improvement ("siendo de suyo tan flaca" [when she is so weak by nature]), for refinishing a being (or arguably, a text) that was left in an imperfect state of creation. Not just formally, then, but at a constitutive, logical level, the text of *La perfecta casada* indulges in and even sanctions the same type of subjective self-fashioning that it so vehemently censures on the face of the made-up wife.

Judith's Crown, Holofernes' Head

Since *La perfecta casada* opens by invoking as model the Solomonic bride of Proverbs 31, it is, in many respects, only fitting that the treatise closes with the inscription of another biblical *casada*, a figure in whom all the attributes of wifely perfection are condensed and lauded.

Porque . . . ningún bien se viene tanto a los ojos humanos, ni causa en los pechos de los hombres tan grande satisfacción como una mujer perfecta, ni hay otra cosa en que ni con tanta alegría ni con tan encarecidas palabras abran los hombres la boca, o cuando tratan consigo a solas, o cuando conversan con otros, o dentro de sus casas, o en las plazas en público. Porque unos loan lo casero, otros encarecen la discreción, otros suben al cielo la modestia, la pureza, la piedad, la suavidad dulce y honesta. Dicen del rostro limpio, del vestido aseado, de las labores y de las velas . . . y *como a la Sanct Judit*, la nombran gloria de su linaje y corona de todo su pueblo; y por mucho que digan, hallan siempre más que decir. Los vecinos dicen esto a los ajenos, y los padres an con ella doctrina a sus hijos, y de los hijos pasa a los nietos, y extendiéndose la fama por todas las partes creciendo . . . y así no es posible que descaezca, ni menos puede ser que con la edad caiga el edificio que está fundado en el cielo. (173–74, italics mine)

[We know that . . . no other good appears so patent to the eyes of the beholders, nor arouses in the hearts of men such deep content as does a perfect wife. Nothing else is there concerning which men speak with such gladness or with such exalted expressions; either alone, in their intimate communings with themselves, or in conversation with others; either within their homes, or openly and in public.

For some will extol her housewifely capacities; others will laud her discretion; still others will exalt to the heavens her modesty, her purity, her sympathy, her sweet and sincere gentleness. They will comment on her shining countenance, the neatness of her dress, the labours of her hands, her watchings by night. . . . *And like holy Judith*, she is called the glory of her race, the crown of her people. And for all that they say, they will find still more to say. Her fellow townsfolk sound her praises to the stranger within their gates. Pointing to her, parents take her as an example for their children, and the children for their children, and so her fame extends everywhere, and ever more and more . . . so that in her there will be no decay. Nor will age suffer her house, founded in the heavens, to fall. (88–89)]

Glory of her lineage and crown of her people, Judith appears in the final sentences of Fray Luis's text as the epitome of the perfecta casada. But if the reference to "la Sanct Judit" marks the text's culminating analogy, it is also, in many respects, its most problematic. There is no little irony in the fact that the best wife in the treatise is a widow. On one hand, the logic is irrefutable; having no husband to judge her, any wife can be perfect. On the other, and from a more historical perspective, widowhood offered women in early modern Spain a degree of independence (both social and financial) unavailable to them in any other civil state.[76]

What is more, the abundance of "perfecciones" embodied in Judith as paradigm of the perfect wife (housewifely, discrete, modest, pure, etc.) gives rise to a boundless verborrhetic excess ("for all that they say, they will find still more to say") that clearly recalls the threatening limitlessness Fray Luis ascribes to (and rhetorically appropriates from) his most imperfect wives ("like a bottomless well"). This verbal excess that Judith's perfection demands explicitly violates the text's injunction for linguistic containment. But perhaps the supreme irony of the simile derives from the very acts that dub Judith "glory of her race": her seduction, deception, and decapitation of Holofernes. The biblical record is unambiguous in its account. Both romera and ramera, Judith ornaments her body, wanders beyond the walls not only of her house but also of the city gates, adulterously seduces a man to whom she is not married, deceives him by purposefully presenting herself as "otra de lo que es," and, in a final gesture of heroism and betrayal, beheads him with his own sword. One could argue that the analogy could not have been more precise; the apocryphal story of Judith seems almost a catalog of the gravest faults that Fray Luis imputes against the casada throughout the treatise. She is a woman who transgresses boundaries of both place and propriety, who empowers herself by recurring to aesthetic artifice, who manipulates categories of somatic illegibility, and, moreover, who clearly subscribes to a philosophy of ends justifying the means (problematic in a treatise where even "obrecillas menudas" are invested with condemning causality). As if all of this were not enough, Judith is not only explicitly Jewish, but also — and particularly during the Counter Reformation — an allegory of makeup, rhetoric, and color.[77]

Perhaps the only quality of wifely perfection (as defined in the treatise) that the Jewish heroine does embody is the paradoxical attribute of mujer varonil. But if, with Freud, we equate decapitation with castration, it becomes obvious that Judith's virility issues precisely from her bloody deed; if she is in fact "varonil," she is only so by virtue of Holofernes' head and sword (the removable phallus), which she holds as trophies in each hand. Confirming, in a sense, both Freud's and Fray Luis's worst suspicions, Judith wrests virility from the man who would desire her. La perfecta casada becomes, in the end, none other than la perfecta castradora.[78] The image of a virile, castrating Judith is provocative, however, not only for the way it returns to the manly mujer de valor who provokes masculine desire as well as anxiety, but, more suggestively, because her cross-gendering serves as a perfect complement to what might be seen as Fray Luis's hystericization throughout the text. Like Judith, and like the perfect wife he dresses and undresses in the treatise, Fray Luis's own authorial position is strangely divided between what could be construed as masculinized and feminized positions. If Fray Luis surveils — and, in a sense, penetrates — the wife's body as object of reading, his own body (and his text's body) lend themselves to similar penetration, not only because they are — or have been, by the time he writes La perfecta casada — feminized as sites of inquisitorial reading, but also because of the way they read themselves through the body of the imperfect wife. Perhaps this divided subject position best accounts for the contradictions that at once beset and adorn the text.

I have argued throughout this chapter that La perfecta casada is, in some senses, a defiant text in its advocacy of interpretive plurality and in its challenge to inquisitorial norms of reading. At the same time, the treatise can be read as an orthodox and even reactionary text in its adherence, where the wife's body is concerned, to what appears to be a fairly conjunctive semiotic code that attempts to close interpretive gaps between sign and meaning—or between categories of seeming and being—in order to guarantee a certain measure of interpretive certainty. I have also pointed to the centrality of analogy in Fray Luis's critical discourse. The preponderance of—and reliance on—analogic semblance in the text seems to respond to a particular early modern epistème that conceives of the universe as an analogically ordered Great Chain of Being. But the status of analogy is not secure in *La perfecta casada;* if on one hand the treatise depends on semejanzas, on the other it repeatedly surrenders to the excesses and confusions they allow. (Of course, analogy is already inherently troubled at a rhetorical level, inasmuch as it relies on Otherness in order to instance Sameness. But it is this very reliance that makes analogy so attractive—and also so problematic—for Fray Luis.) It may be argued that insofar as analogy is plagued by inconsistencies, so too is an analogic, hierarchical ordering of the universe (and of society), such as that which conceives of the female as an imperfect version of the male. In other words, if the status of analogy is problematized in—and by—Fray Luis's text, then the secondary status of woman on the analogically structured Great Chain of Being is called into question. I do not wish to suggest by this that *La perfecta casada* is a nascent or even cryptofeminist text that radically departs from the proscriptive misogyny of conduct literature for wives. Rather, in its seductive excesses and contradictions, the text offers a (most likely unconscious) resistance to the more repressive norms that it prescribes for perfect wives.

3

The Perfected Wife

Signs of Adultery and the Adultery of Signs in

Calderón's *El médico de su honra*

> The woman is perfected
> Her dead
> Body wears the smile of accomplishment
> —Sylvia Plath, "Edge"

Gutierre
Mencía a quien adoré
con la vida y con el alma
anoche a un grave accidente
vio su perfección postrada,
por desmentirla divina
este accidente de humana.
(ll. 2830–35)

. . . .

Rey
Cubrid ese horror que asombra,
ese prodigio que espanta,
espectáculo que admira,
símbolo de la desgracia.
(ll. 2876–79)

[*Gutierre*

Mencía, whom I adored with life and soul,

Had her perfections levelled and prostrated

By a most frightful accident, by which

It's contradicted that she was divine

Since such an accident proves she was human.

. . . .

King

Now cover up this horror-striking sight,

This prodigy of sorrow and affright,

This spectacle of wonder and despair,

This symbol of misfortune.]

—Calderón de la Barca, *El médico de su honra*

Blood Weddings

If the crowning model for the perfect wife in Luis de León's *La perfecta casada* is the widowed Judith, it seems almost perversely fitting
that Calderón's antimodel, the imperfect, adulterous wife typecast in
the honor dramas, should suffer the reverse fate, leaving a widowed
husband to grieve even as he celebrates his dead wife's "perfección
postrada" [prostrated perfection].[1] But unlike Plath's smiling corpse
and unlike the triumphant Judith, Calderón's perfected casada bears no
trace of authorial accomplishment, no crown to proclaim her lineage
of glory. Instead, in drama after drama, she is routinely murdered by
her husband in the name of honor: her body enclosed, examined, and
finally textualized into an eloquent "símbolo de la desgracia" [symbol
of misfortune] that must be covered, even as it is staged.

In this chapter I attend to the construction of the body of this
farthest-from-perfecta casada who is examined and ritually punished
in Calderón de la Barca's honor-vengeance tragedies. The wife's body
as a site for reading and interpretation is at once narrowly and diversely

figured in these plays; always a husband's private property that houses his honor (and is thus itself aptly housed), the body of the casada appears, at different moments, as an object that demands and yet resists representation; as a token of homosocial, if not homoerotic, exchange; as an eroticized but paradoxically pure and even mystified corpse; and, in what is perhaps the most compelling "use" of that body for a reading that seeks to connect the implicit Otherness of adultery with the Otherness ascribed to the non-Christian in early modern Spain, as a locus of disease and contaminated desire.[2]

It is in what is quite possibly Calderón's most unsettling play, *El médico de su honra,* that these various takes on the wife's body best come together. The play stages a radical misreading that results in an innocent woman's gruesome murder. Its plot conforms, in many respects, to what could be construed as model for the wife-murder tragedies. *El médico de su honra* opens with a signature Calderonian event: a fall from an impetuous horse.[3] Its rider, Prince Enrique, was en route to Seville (where the play is set), accompanying his half brother, King Pedro el Cruel (or Pedro el Justiciero, as he is also known), who would be holding court in the city. Unconscious from the accident, Enrique is led by his men to a nearby estate, while the king proceeds on his journey. The house where the prince is given refuge, however, belongs to none other than his old flame, Doña Mencía. But while Enrique is rejoicing over having rediscovered his long-lost love, Mencía reveals to him that during his long absence she was forced to marry Don Gutierre Alfonso Solís. Not dissuaded, Enrique embarks on a tenacious campaign to win Mencía back, a campaign that will have the expected tragic consequences. Mencía and Enrique are not the only ones with an amorous history, however; before the play begins, a jealous Gutierre had abandoned his former fiancée, Leonor, on a false suspicion of dishonor after having discovered another man in her house. That man, whose identity Gutierre ignores until Leonor herself reveals it at the end of act 1, was Don Arias, Prince Enrique's companion, who was in the house to visit his fiancée, who had been staying with Leonor. (During the course of the play, Leonor will seek juridic reparation from the king for her ex-lover's broken word.) Gutierre's jealousy comes back to haunt him, of course, as he begins to suspect his wife of adultery. The plot thickens with Enrique's continued advances against Mencía's continued resistance and the intensification of Gutierre's suspicions of his own dishonor at the hands of his wife. Adopting the metaphoric role of "médico de su honra" [surgeon of his honor], Gutierre mounts a series of examinations of his wife's body in order to diagnose the condition of his honor. Predictably, Mencía fails his tests and is misdiagnosed by her physician-husband as an adulteress who has polluted his honor and whose blood must be shed in order to cleanse it. The murder scene is particularly graphic; Gutierre hires a surgeon at knifepoint to bleed his wife to death, making it look like an accident so as to leave no evidence of the murder or, more importantly, of the dishonor that occasioned it. The king, aware that Gutierre has murdered an innocent woman, nonetheless approves of his methods and "sentences" him to marry his former betrothed, Leonor. The terms of the marriage, which close the play and suggest a repetition of the honor-vengeance cycle, are quite literally negotiated over Mencía's dead body.

Within the paradigm of the honor-vengeance plot, what is extraordinary about *El médico de su honra* is not only that it dramatizes an inquisitorial hermeneutics with fairly clear allusions to the sociopolitical situation of seventeenth-century Spain but, moreover, that the somatic and semiotic "examination" performed by Gutierre that results in Mencía's bloodbath is revealed as a perverse misreading that confirms only the questionable truth of its own assumptions. The implications of exposing Gutierre's misreading are significant, particularly given the context in which the play was written and publicly represented. That context has rightly suggested a reconsideration of honra by positing a relation between stage honor as a function of sexual purity and social honor as a function of racial purity.

This type of historicized reading of the wife-murder dramas first emerged on the critical field during the 1960s.[4] In 1960, Albert Sicroff pointed to a fundamental connection between honor and limpieza de sangre. Américo Castro reaffirmed the relation the following year; "los dramas de honra," he writes, "tenían como invisible trasfondo el drama vivo de los estatutos de limpieza de sangre" [Honor plays had as an invisible background the living drama of the statutes regarding purity of blood].[5] More recently, Melveena McKendrick has suggested that the parallels between the honor dramas and the limpieza statutes do not represent a case of deliberate or subversive substitution on the playwright's part, but rather one of mimetic transference of a sixteenth- and seventeenth-century national psychopathology. She concurs, however, with the basic premise that identifies "the real-life noble, condemned by the obsession with *limpieza de sangre*, with the stage *caballero*, also living his life in a state of permanent vigilance over something that may at any moment be snatched away from him, through no fault of his own. . . . Social insecurity is articulated as sexual insecurity, the real-life caballero hostage to his heredity becomes the stage gallant hostage to his wife's or his daughter's or his sister's virtue."[6]

I would like to map out my own reading of the honor-vengeance tragedies, specifically, of *El médico de su honra*, in this line that historicizes honor within an inquisitorial framework. First, however, it is necessary to rethink the terms of the relation between the honor obsession on stage and the limpieza de sangre obsession offstage as it has been critically articulated. That relation has generally taken the form of a four-term analogy between the husband's insecurity with regard to his wife's sexual honor and the cristiano nuevo's insecurity with regard to his Jewish or Muslim ancestry. Another, perhaps more compelling way to imagine that relation is to consider the wife's body (and not—or at least not only—the husband's) as occupying the position of the inquired, non-Christian body. In other words, if the suspicious husband, haunted by honor's qué dirán, can be considered as somehow analogous to a converso under the Inquisition's surveillance (ostensibly because both are persecuted for a transgression over which they have no direct control, whether a wife's infidelity or a semitic heritage), it seems at least equally, if not more, plausible to consider the honor-drama wife as occupying the dangerous position of the converso/a accused (and often punished) for a perceived violation over which she has no control (because of the stubborn persistence of both her ex-lover's advances and her husband's inquisitorial tactics) and, of which she is innocent (the adultery is never consummated). The husband, with his hermeneutics of suspicion, would be cast, instead, in the role of overzealous inquisitor who reads (and more often writes, as a result of his inevitable misreadings) an illicit text on an innocent body. At a fundamental level, what makes a reading of this sort possible is the radical illegibility with respect to transgression that the wife's body and the converso's body share (hymeneal in one case, almost genetic in the other).

Critical attention to the predicament of the wives in these plays has tended, for the most part, toward debates about the facticity of wife murder as punishment for adultery. There is no question that sixteenth- and seventeenth-century civil law afforded husbands ample freedom in the disposal of adulterous wives. Title XVII, Law XIII of the *Auténticas* added to Alfonso X's *Siete Partidas* reverses the treatise's earlier prohibition of wife murder, providing the legal vehicle by which husbands could lawfully execute unfaithful wives and their lovers. The 1569 *Recopilación de las leyes destos reynos hecha por mandado de la Magestad Cathólica del Rey Don Philippe segundo, nuestro Señor* explicitly states: "si muger casada ficiere adulterio, ella, i el adulterador ambos sean en poder de el marido, i faga dellos lo que quisiere" [If a married woman commits adultery, she and the adulterer both shall be at the mercy of the husband, and he may do with them as he wishes].[7] At issue, rather, is whether such punishments were consistently—or even more than sporadically—applied. As early as 1958, C. A. Jones suggested that the murder of adulterous wives on the Golden Age Spanish stage was a mere dramatic convention, closely concerned with neither "reality nor morality."[8] McKendrick, following Jones at least in part, has argued that there is little evidence indicating that the laws that permitted such punishments were more than very rarely invoked. Elena Sánchez Ortega, in contrast, argues that the historical record does not differ substantially from the dramatic one; she points to documents in the Simancas Archives suggesting that at different moments throughout the sixteenth and seventeenth centuries a wide number of husbands sought—and were granted—royal pardons for killing adulterous wives.[9]

Regardless of how the question is ultimately answered (which is not to say the question is irrelevant; clearly, it is not), the very institutionalization of legal control over the body of the not so *perfecta casada* supports the contention that hers is the scrutinized body. What is more, the fact that the Inquisition directly concerned itself with matters of wifely fidelity suggests a closer relation than has been supposed between limpieza de sangre and the preoccupation with female sexual immaculacy, a relation in many respects grounded on the invisible (and hence all the more dangerous) threat that a wife's adultery posed to a "pure" bloodline.[10] Like those suspected of racial or religious Otherness, women on the whole, and particularly married women suspected of assuming agency in their desire, were deemed susceptible to—or worse, carriers of—contamination.

By suggesting a shift in the analogy that has traditionally aligned the insecurity of the honor-drama husband with that of someone under inquisitorial surveillance and focusing instead on the wife's body as the penetrated, inquired body, I do not mean to imply that the husband, now in the role of examiner, is relieved of his sexual or cultural insecurities. Rather, I argue that these very anxieties motivate his heavy-handed examination tactics. If wifely adultery is the stuff of honor dramas, it is because in the presence of a literalized marital sacrament by means of which husband and wife ostensibly become one flesh, adultery provides an avenue for the surrogate penetration of the husband's body. It is the fear of this vicarious penetration—and of the consequent hystericization of the male body—that gives way to the inquisitorial-styled examination and persecution of the supposedly dishonored casada. We should not be surprised, however, if this fear masks desire or, to put it differently, if the rigors of Gutierre's medical surveillance of his wife's body encode a voyeuristic desire to read the signs of his own penetration at the hands of another. At different moments Gutierre occupies what could be conceived as a hystericized—and perhaps homoerotic—position of desire, a position explicitly reserved, in seventeenth-century Spain, for the marginalized Other. Simply put, the honor-play husband penetrates and inquires his wife's body in order that his own body not be perceived as being either subject to or desirous of penetration. The position of the angst-ridden honor husband comes disturbingly close in this to that of the inquisitor with doubts about his own limpieza; persecuting others represented an efficient and economic means of dispelling suspicion away from himself by establishing—through his fervent attack on Otherness—a legible sign of his own orthodoxy.

The recasting of the honor drama's never perfect wife in the role of inquired body-text with her husband as inquisitorial reader invites a recasting of the question of honor as a question of reading, of the interpretation of signs, and of the instability that inheres in any system that takes itself for authoritative, whether one that prescribes meaning or one that prescribes objects of desire and rules of conduct. This kind of instability represents a threat, then, not only to Renaissance signifying practices but also to the stable positions of masculine and feminine in which honra is invested.[11] What Calderón is challenging in *El médico de su honra* — and the same argument could be made for many of the honor-vengeance tragedies — is the rigidity inscribed in codes of reading and mechanisms of judgment that seek to monogamize meaning. The adultery these plays lay bare is never consummated, after all, on the body of the ostensibly "guilty" wife; Mencía dies an innocent death.[12] If there is an "adultery" to speak of, it is an adulterous representation that takes its cues from a radically disjunctive conception of allegory, posited on an unbridgeable distance between sign and meaning. What Gutierre, as epitome of the Calderonian honor husband, inevitably misreads as signs of adultery is actually an adultery of signs, unfaithful to the meanings with which they are conventionally wed.

The honor problem as it is presented in these dramas very often translates into a problem of reading that engages the provocative and problematic interrelations between the somatic, semiotic, and political registers in early modern Spain. My argument proceeds along two lines. The first of these, which both rearticulates and revises earlier critical work on the honor tragedies, is relatively straightforward: the play's hermeneutics of suspicion and examination and its specific attention to bodies that are figured as diseased encodes an inquisitorial script in which the husband enacts the role of inquisitor reading for limpieza de sangre and the wife's body is enclosed, scrutinized, and finally textualized. I accompany the wife's body through this three-stage trajectory (containment, inquisition, textualization) in the pages that follow. My second point, which I address throughout the chapter, takes on more directly the question of legibility and illegibility. I suggest that in attempting to impose a punitive stasis on meaning (by, for example, literalizing the metaphor), the inquisitor-husband inadvertently reveals the adultery inscribed in any semiotic code or representational contract that takes itself for absolute. Moreover, by ignoring the ambiguities of the signs he reads, he underscores the illegitimacy of his own (or any other, for that matter) inquisitorial enterprise. The question then becomes in what measure the "examinations" so meticulously carried out by the Gutierres of these works can be read as radical misreadings that only perform (and hence render questionable) the very evidence (of Otherness as guilt) they claim to uncover.

By exposing not only the illegitimacy of readings that seek to assign culpability for Otherness but also the extent to which they are motivated by the reader's anxieties over his own penetrability, Calderón criticizes the limpieza de sangre ideology and the institution charged with preserving it much more radically than has been previously suggested. I would argue, partly against Maravall, that seventeenth-century Spanish theater was not (or at least not only) a mechanism of reinforcing and reinscribing the dominant ideology of the ruling elites, but also a powerful and useful tool for questioning and dismantling that same ideological system, if for no other reason than its tremendous popularity and the ambivalences it exploited.[13] Theater was potentially both propagandistic and contestatory, sometimes both at once. It will not, I hope, seem too extravagant to suggest that the decline of certain kinds of inquisitorial power in Spain and the calling into question of limpieza statutes starting in the early seventeenth century not only provided the ideological conditions in which Calderón could carry out a critique of inquisitorial practices but may have been conditioned by the repeated exposure of the illegitimacy of that power and of those statutes on the honor-drama stage. In other words, Calderonian drama can be seen not only as a response to a political and ideological matrix (in this case, the loss of legitimacy of limpieza de sangre statutes and of the inquisitorial tactics deployed in their service) but also as an agent in the formation of that very matrix.

Strategies of Containment and Their Failures

The masculine effort to contain and reify the female body — specifically, the body of the (would-be) perfect wife — is perhaps nowhere so succinctly expressed in *El médico de su honra* as in the short passage from the end of the third act that I have adopted as epigraph for this chapter: "Mencía a quien adoré / con la vida y con el alma," laments Gutierre, standing over his wife's corpse, "anoche a un grave accidente / vio su perfección postrada" (209, ll. 2830–32) [Mencía, whom I adored with life and soul, / Had her perfections levelled and prostrated / By a most frightful accident (79)]. This almost macabre instance of irony, which inscribes the casada's perfection within the absolute stillness and total containment of death, is the culminating moment of an escalating process throughout the play that seeks to en-close—and even encorpse—the female body as a means to control her erotic agency and the male anxiety it provokes.[14] "Perfección" is here modified by Gutierre to reflect the only way it can be safely read by him on Mencía's body, that is, "postrada." But if death represents the most radical way to enclose the wife's body and its attendant threats, it is by no means the only mechanism available. Indeed, the play mobilizes a variety of tactics all directed toward the common goal of imposing both corporeal and interpretive stasis.

It should perhaps come as no surprise to discover a proliferation of strategies of containment at work in the honor dramas. If honor, as Hegel understood it, represents the extreme embodiment of vio-lability, the tacit conflation of enclosure and *in*violability, predicated on the militarist ideal of the fortress, makes the presence of reify-ing tactics in these works seem almost a natural, if not a necessary, precaution.[15] Neither is it surprising to discover that this prolifera-tion operates at various levels that supplement and at times collapse into one another. The analogy between "the enclosed body, the closed mouth, [and] the locked house" that Peter Stallybrass advances as cen-tral not only to techniques of surveillance over early modern women but also to "the production of a normative 'Woman' within the dis-cursive practices of the ruling elite" is suggestive in this context; the analogy inscribes two of the three levels at which strategies of con-tainment are enforced in the play.[16] The enclosure of the body within the locked house gives way in the drama to the containment of the word (the closed mouth) in order to prevent its adulterous dissemi-nation. But Calderón goes even further; the linguistic containment that supplements enclosure at a material or spatial level is in turn re-inforced by the imposition of what could be called a logical or even epistemological stasis that addresses and problematizes the assertion of inviolability inscribed in the *soy quien soy* (I am who I am).

On the surface, at least, the spatial containment of the wife's body is carried out as a means to protect—or reify—her chastity: the uncontained body, specifically, the open sex, deemed susceptible to penetration by an invasive Other, must be secured within the safety of the fortress-house. Transgressive entries into the domestic space are considered (by means of the house-body analogy) an attempt against chastity, hence Mencía's justifiable alarm over Enrique's entry into her house:

> ¿Pues, señor, vos . . .
>
> .   .   .   .   .   .
>
> . . . desta suerte . . .
>
> .   .   .   .   .   .
>
> . . . entrasteis . . .
>
> .   .   .   .   .
>
> . . . en mi casa, sin temer
> que así a una mujer destruye
> y que así ofende a un vasallo
> tan generoso y ilustre? (125–26, ll. 1084–90)
>
> [Then it is you, my lord—
>
> .   .   .   .
>
> In such a way have dared—
>
> .   .   .   .
>
> To enter here—
>
> .   .   .   .   .   .
>
> Here into my own house without a care
> Whether you ruin and destroy a woman,
> Or to a loyal vassal, one so noble
> And generous, bring insult worse than death—. (31)][17]

The reverse side of the coin, however, suggests that the wife's body is contained not so much because it is threatened, but rather because it is itself deemed a threat, a source of potential contamination that must be quarantined.

This threat is a dual one; it consists, first of all, of an improperly channeled erotic agency. Indeed, the honor plays gesture toward the possibility that the casada's body may harbor desires that are radically independent from those of the patriarchy, specifically her husband.

Mencía's longing reminiscence of her past love for Enrique—"Aquí fue amor" (81, l. 131) [This, once, was Love (7)]—speaks to this possibility, as does her resigned acknowledgment that even the space of her innermost feelings has been colonized and appropriated by Gutierre: "ya . . . ni para sentir soy mía" (82, ll. 137–38) [I have no right / To my own feelings].[18] Because this sort of feminine erotic agency is deemed extremely subversive when it exceeds the marital institution (itself invoked as an effective form of containment of female eroticism), however, it requires being disciplined through the most absolute means available: the (desiring) body's death. Second, the threat that contaminates the (unenclosed) casada's body is that of illegibility: outside its sentenced enclosure it becomes impossible, within the patriarchal interpretive economy that governs the play, to accurately read the signs encoded on the wife's body and thus determine its status. This impossibility is largely the result of the wife's nonvirginal status, which renders her illegible with respect to sexual transgression. After the wedding night, penetration—licit or illicit—has no sign of its own on the wife's body; anything can take the place of adultery's "missing" somatic signifier. It is thus that containment becomes a mark of chastity, noncontainment of sexual agency. Even cursory ventures to the outside are deemed problematic and demand that the body be subjected to further scrutiny.

> Bueno he hallado mi honor, hacer no quiero
> por ahora otra cura,
> pues la salud en él está segura.
> Pero ¿ni una criada
> la acompaña? ¿Si acaso retirada
> aguarda? . . . —¡Oh pensamiento
> injusto, oh vil temor, oh infame aliento!
> Ya con esta sospecha
> no he de volverme. (163, ll. 1900–1908)

> [having found my Honour
> Well and in health, needing no further physic.
> But—not a servant in her company?
> What if, perhaps, she waits, sequestered here,
> For somebody? Oh what an unjust thought!

What a vile fear and infamous suspicion!
I must not go back in the company
Of such a foul suspicion. (51)]

It is Gutierre's discovery of his wife alone and outside (he finds her
asleep in the garden) that reawakens his suspicions of her deshonra
and prompts him to recur to the whispered examination that will be
her undoing. Illegibility, then, calls for policing.

At a strictly tactical level, efforts at somatic enclosure move in the
drama from the seemingly benign containment within the domestic
space of the house to progressively more sinister degrees of reification
that eventually seal Mencía (and her polluted desire) within the absolute stillness of the casket. And yet even the benign home can assume,
in its Calderonian manifestation, a frightening sense of the *unheim-
lich*. For Mencía the house becomes, in the third act, a literal prison
that encages her with the shadow of her own death.

Mas ¡ay de mí! la puerta está cerrada. . . .
Destas ventanas son los hierros rejas,
y en vano a nadie diré mis quejas,
que caen a unos jardines, donde apenas
habrá quien oiga repetidas penas.
¿Dónde iré desta suerte,
tropezando en la sombra de mi muerte? (194, ll. 2499–2507)

[Alas for me! The door is locked. The windows
Are barred with iron, and my cries for help
Can only fall among some lonely gardens
In vain, for there are few or none to hear,
And what could they avail? For I already
Go stumbling in the shadow of my death. (70)]

The house's closure is here associated by Mencía with the virtual impossibility of disseminating the "quejas" [cries for help] that might
save her life. At some level, it is the problematic analogy between the
wife's house and her body (specifically, between the house's openings
and the orifices of the female body) that grounds what for Mencía will
prove to be a fatal relation between the closed door and the closed
mouth.

Mencía's designation of her house as a virtual jail cell contrasts strikingly, moreover, with the mobility that her husband is permitted in his "real" prison, from which he comes and goes almost at will. It also recalls the metaphoric jail that Gutierre invokes in describing his marriage during his temporary reprieve:

> pues si vivía
> yo sin alma en la prisión
> por estar en ti, mi bien,
> darme libertad fue bien,
> para que en esta ocasión
> alma y vida con razón
> otra vez se viese unida;
> porque estaba dividida,
> teniendo prolija calma,
> en una prisión el alma
> y en otra prisión la vida. (132, ll. 1200–1210)

> [for I lived
> Without my soul in prison, my beloved,
> Since it was here in you. To grant this brief
> Liberty, was to join my soul and body,
> For they were both divided until now
> Wearing out listless hours in separate cells —
> The one imprisoned there, the other here. (34)]

The ascetic figuration of the body as the soul's prison is here transferred by Gutierre onto an erotic register, transforming Mencía's body into the vessel that houses his soul. The construction of Mencía's body as container is troubling for a number of reasons, not the least of which is its anticipation of the fatal transformation of her body into the diseased vessel that houses her husband's corporealized honor.[19] What is more, insofar as Gutierre's projection (of his soul into Mencía's body) turn to one-flesh doctrine, his depends, in part, on a literal understanding of the rhetoric of symbolic incarceration in the depiction of his conjugal relation strikes a suggestive contrast with the literal incarceration that marriage represents for his wife.

But the disciplining of Mencía's body is not strictly literal in nature;

rather, her body is submitted to what might be considered metaphoric forms of containment as well. There is no question that the dangers associated with figural reification strategies can be as lethal to the wife's body as literal tactics of enclosure and encorpsement. Perhaps the clearest example of this kind of figurally imposed stasis is Gutierre's diagnosis of his fainted wife in terms that prefigure her final monumentalization into a cold and statuesque corpse: "Estatua viva se quedó de hielo" (192, l. 2461) [She is a living statue made of ice (68)]. The series of events leading up to this moment suggest that it is the threat of feminine erotic agency that provokes the containment of the female body, whether literal or metaphoric; the one time in the play in which Mencía attempts to assume authorial agency in the circulation of her desire, by writing Enrique a letter, she is reduced by her husband to a frozen statue. The male reading of Mencía's fainted body as a monument seems almost a perfect instance of what, with reference to Shakespearean theater, Abbe Blum has termed the "monumentalizing" of woman and which Valerie Traub defines as "the strategy by which female erotic energy is disciplined and denied." [20]

But perhaps the most dangerous form of somatic containment negotiated in the play is not the enclosure of Mencía's body but, rather, the representation of Mencía's body *as* enclosure, specifically, as the receptacle that holds—and presumably safeguards—her husband's honor.[21] If earlier Mencía's wifely prison-body was a jail for Gutierre's soul, here her maternal crypt-body becomes a tomb for his honor.

> A peligro estáis, honor,
> no hay hora en vos que no sea
> crítica, en vuestro sepulcro
> vivís, puesto que os alienta
> la mujer, en ella estáis
> pisando siempre la huesa. (155, ll. 1659–64)

> [You are in peril,
> Honour! Each hour you live's so critical
> That you're already living in your tomb,
> Because a woman guards your life. In woman
> Your safety lives—and walks on skulls and bones. (46)]

The inseparability of male honor and (a localized) female sexuality, on one hand, and the containment of honor's body within a feminine "huesa" [grave], on the other, suggests reading this passage in terms of its tacit inscription of the provocative womb-tomb equation. Gutierre's honor, explicitly somaticized in the apostrophe and gendered male even at the level of linguistic signifier (despite being médico de su honra, Gutierre here addresses his grammatically masculine "honor"), is at its paradoxically perpetual critical hour; if it is to survive, it must be quite literally delivered from Mencía's diseased uterus-tomb. Given the indissolubility of the marital sacrament after Trent and the over-investment in marriage that informs the honor plays, the delivery of Gutierre's honor from the sepulchre that houses it can only take the form of a bloody matricide. If the absence of mother figures in early modern Spanish theater (and honor theater in particular) denotes an elision of maternity, here maternity reappears in a disturbing incarnation that aligns fecundity with disease and infection. The cure of honor's body, once situated within the maternal womb-tomb, can be achieved only at the expense of the wife's body that encloses it: one's survival is wholly antithetical to the other's.

But if the long-term cure for Gutierre's ailing honor is the murder of his wife, the immediate prescription to avoid further contagion is a quarantine of the word. Spatial containment gives way to linguistic containment.

> Yo os he de curar, honor,
> y pues al principio muestra
> este primero accidente
> tan grave peligro, sea
> la primera medicina
> cerrar al daño las puertas,
> atajar al mal los pasos.
> Y así os receta y ordena
> *El médico de su honra*
> primeramente la dieta
> del silencio. (155–56, ll. 1665–75)
>
> [I have to cure you, Honour, since the first
> Incidents in your case portend great danger

And the chief remedy of all, in this,
Is first to close the doors against the evil
And intercept the danger in its stride.
So this is what the Surgeon of his Honour
Prescribes for his sick patient. For your diet —
Silence. (46)]

This moment that instances the literalization of the médico de su honra metaphor explicitly calls on a rhetoric of bodily pollution as a means to justify the play's commitment to closure; the language of dis-ease that Gutierre adopts in his apostrophe to honor recalls that which was applied to the racial Other in early modern Spain, reaffirming, in this way, the work's inquisitorial subtext. It is also the clearest example in the drama of the imposition of containment strategies at a linguistic level.

There is little question that tactics of linguistic containment are mobilized throughout *El médico de su honra* as a means to control the dissemination of excessive or illegitimate desire. Mencía is first to articulate such a strategy, engaging a self-surveillance of the desirous word that complements and even rivals her husband's efforts to enclose her desirous body.

Mas ¿qué digo?
¿Qué es esto, cielos, qué es esto?
Yo soy quien soy. Vuelva el aire
los repetidos acentos
que llevó; porque aun perdidos,
no es bien que publiquen ellos
lo que yo debo callar. (81–82, ll. 131–37)

[But what is this I've said? I am myself.
Then let the wind return my words, though lost
In it, for it would not be well to publish
What silence must conceal. (7)]

Linguistic containment, however, is almost always reactionary in form and gestures toward the very antecedent it intends to suppress. Here, for example, Mencía's attempt to curb her words immediately follows—and draws attention to—a clear articulation of illicit desire on her part. Strikingly, that desire is not so much sexual in nature as it is linguistic, manifested in a need to speak the burning word of passion:

> ¡Oh quién pudiera, cielos,
> con licencia de su honor
> hacer aquí sentimientos!
> ¡Oh quién pudiera dar voces,
> y romper con el silencio
> cárceles de nieve, donde
> está aprisionado el fuego! (81, ll. 122–28)

> [Heavens! Could I but give way
> To my great grief, and yet respect my honour!
> Could I but cry out my sorrow, jointly breaking
> The silence and this prison, here, of snow,
> Which is my breast! Its prisoner was once
> A fire. (7)]

Mencía expresses the containment of her verbal appetite by recurring to a prison metaphor, reaffirming yet again the association between closure and enclosure, not only of the wife's body, but also, now, of the word's.[22] Rhetorically, Mencía's repeated "¡Oh quién pudiera!" [Could I!] may be seen as a kind of *paralepsis* or *occupatio* that by pronouncing the unspeakability of her "sentimientos" [grief] (grammatically sealed by the contrary-to-fact subjunctive of the Spanish text) effectively grants the unspeakable a speaking voice. Put somewhat differently, the enunciation of the (illicit) desire to speak (an illicit) desire is transgression enough, as if once words were performed in language, they acquired a materiality that defied containment.[23] It might be argued that this sort of overliteralization is what motivates the final tragedy.[24] For Mencía, giving desire a word implies endowing it with a body that Gutierre can read for symptoms of adulterous disease.

For Gutierre, too, the linguistic inscription of dishonor is at least as damaging to his reputation as the material reality that ostensibly engendered it; hence, the premium on secrecy.

Mas ¿para qué lo repite
la lengua, cuando mi agravio
con mi desdicha se mide? (184, ll. 2300–2302)

[But why should I repeat it
Aloud, when my affront and my misfortune
Measure the same. (64)]

Although it is perhaps risky to associate this sort of materialization of the spoken word with notions of the performative, it is nonetheless useful to do so not only because of the provocative implications of reading linguistic performativity in a context of theatrical representation but also because it suggests imagining the irretractability of Mencía's (and later also Leonor's and Gutierre's) words as the triumph, as it were, of speech performance over and against linguistic containment. Utterances in the play that are intended by their speakers to be *not even* constative in nature (such as Gutierre's suspicions of Mencía's dishonor) assume performative force. Performativity opposes, in this sense, efforts to repress the word, tending instead toward its adulterous dissemination or pointing premonitorily to its inevitable return.[25]

Mencía's attempt to take back from the air the "acentos" [accents] of words best left unspoken ("lo que yo debo callar" [what I must keep silent]) is thus too little, too late; it serves only to mark the site of her linguistic transgression, the verbalization of extramarital desire ("¡Aquí fue amor!"). It is worth noting that her (failed) plea for containment is explicitly phrased as a command ("Vuelva el aire" [Then let the wind return]); it is almost as if the performative force of the linguistic utterance took precedence over the containment it prescribes — form contaminating content, as it were. It is also noteworthy that the "acentos" she would reappropriate are already "repetidos" as is Gutierre's verbal inscription of his "affront": "¿para qué lo repite la lengua?" [Why should I repeat it?]. On one hand, the gesture points to the derivativeness of words — specifically, words of dishonor — which are revealed as hollow repetitions, unoriginal imitations of a preexisting narrative. But if the acentos the wind steals are, in fact, copied, the repetition they record is not mimetic but, like all good gossip, riddled with difference. On the other hand, it is no accident in this context that the words that immediately precede the command are quite literally repetitive, not only the doubled "qué es esto" of "¿Qué es esto, cielos, qué es esto?" [What is this? Heavens, what is this?] but also the reificatory "soy" of the soy quien soy.

Perhaps what is most suggestive of Mencía's command is the fact that it is addressed to the wind ("vuelva el aire") as agent of linguistic (re)circulation. If the air tends toward a paradoxic sort of dissemination that reifies as it disperses the word, however, it is also invoked as an agent of linguistic containment that fragments the semantic message.

> Y yo ahora,
> por si acaso llevó el viento
> cabal alguna razón,
> sin que en partidos acentos
> la troncase, responder
> a tantos agravios quiero,
> porque donde fueron quejas,
> vayan con el mismo aliento
> desengaños. (88–89, ll. 281–89)

> [Now
> If there is any grain of sense in what
> You've scattered to the wind, in such disjointed
> Accents, I'll try to answer your complaints
> And accusations. (10–11)]

Effective linguistic containment seems to require, in this case, the wind's producing sufficient violence on the material body of the word: dismembering the "razón cabal" [(precise) sense] into the "partidos (but not *repetidos*) acentos" [disjointed (but not *repeated*) accents] that would render it unrecognizable and hence emptied of its fatal charge. But the strategy seemingly fails and Mencía must look to other means. Paradoxically, her prescription to counteract the devastating results of insufficient fragmentation of the linguistic signifier consists of further dissemination: "donde fueron quejas . . . vayan desengaños" [where there went complaints . . . let there go disillusion].[26] Perhaps not as well versed as her physician husband in contemporary medical wisdom and, specifically, in the practice of *cura por contrarios* (cure by contrary measures), she administers words as antidotes to other words, violating in the process her professed commitment to linguistic containment. That the instrument of dissemination is the breath ("aliento") — a kind of internalized wind — is not incidental but suggests the extent to which the epidemic spread of the (diseased) word is made to seem in the play as inevitable and indeed almost as natural as breathing.[27]

The image that Mencía conjures of a guilty (albeit linguistic) body cut up as a precaution against deshonra seems almost too clear a prefiguration of the eventual fate of her own body to go unnoticed.[28] But if it suggests a certain alignment between the wife's body and the word's, the terms of the relation are not altogether clear. Indeed, here the integrity of one (the wife's body) seems to depend on the fragmentation of the other (the word's body), in much the same way as the health of honor's body often requires, in these plays, the extirpation of the female body that symbolically contains it.

The drama's imperative to secure linguistic containment (materialized in Gutierre's and Leonor's custody of words) clearly responds to the public/private binarism so central to the concept (and maintenance) of honra in the Golden Age plays. There are a number of paradoxes inscribed in the mechanics of honor not the least of which is its problematic relation to the qué dirán. Honora, as manifested in these plays, is a social construction that depends, almost exclusively, on public opinion; deshonras, accordingly, must be kept secret. But the cleansing of a stained honor requires that the perceived offenses be washed with blood. For the "cure" to be effective, it must be publicly inscribed and acknowledged, if not by society in general, then by a worthy representative of the patriarchy (king or other father figure).[29] And yet that requisite act of acknowledgment, that subtle (or not so subtle) nod, violates the logic of containment. These incongruities pose significant dilemmas for the honor-play husbands (who usually devote at least one soliloquy to the subject), in deciding what the best method for murdering their wives will be.

> Arranquemos de una vez
> de tanto mal las raíces.
> Muera Mencía, su sangre

bañe el pecho donde asiste;

.   .   .   .

Mas no es bien que lo publique;
porque si sé que el secreto
altas victorias consigue,
y que agravio que es oculto
oculta venganza pide,
muera Mencía de suerte
que ninguno lo imagine. (284–85, ll. 2303–16)

[We must pull up the roots of so much evil.
Let Mencía die and wash with her own blood
The breast that it inhabits!

.   .   .   .

But it must not be known to anyone.
Secrecy can achieve great victories.
When an affront is secret, it demands
A secret vengeance. Let Mencía die
in such a way as no one would imagine. (64)]

It is not coincidental, in this context, that Mencía's initial plea for linguistic enclosure similarly inscribes a form of the word "public" ("no es bien que publiquen ellos / lo que yo debo callar" [it would not be well to publish / What silence must conceal]); both hers and Gutierre's meditations remit, on one hand, to the precarious line dividing the public from the private where honor is concerned and, on the other, to the physical "público" (the audience) to whom even their most private words are ultimately addressed.[30] One may argue that the resistance to containment associated with the performative (in its materialization of the word) and deemed so deadly to honor acquires particular vehemence in the case of theatrical representation, since all words uttered on the stage are bound, by their very context, to assume a kind of extraneous performative force. The problem acquires an even greater degree of complexity in the case of the numerous soliloquies and asides that advance the play's action and that are so prevalent in Calderón's honor dramas in particular. By giving an ostensibly private (at the level of plot) voice to secret thoughts on a space of public representation, the asides effectively collapse the distance between the two poles, rendering the private public, the unspeakable, plainly audible.[31]

Containment proves to be an impossible project, however; the re-pressed word always returns and quite often with a vengeance. Keep-ing the word enclosed—especially enclosed within the body where it can fester and become contaminated—has potentially devastating side effects. It is Gutierre who has perhaps the clearest notion of the dangers of containment, dangers that derive precisely from an in-terior/exterior binarism.

> ¿Celos dije?
> ¡Qué mal hice! Vuelva, vuelva
> al pecho la voz. Mas no,
> que si es ponzoña que engendra
> mi pecho, si no me dio
> la muerte (¡ay de mí!) al verterla
> al volverla a mí podrá;
> que de la víbora cuentan,
> que la mata su ponzoña,
> si fuera de sí la encuentra. (156–57, ll. 1697–1706)
>
> ["Jealousy," did I say? Then I spoke wrongly.
> Come back, come back, my voice, into my breast!
> But no! since, if it's venom that is bred
> within my breast, and if it did not kill me
> When thus I spat it from me, well it might,
> If it returned to me. They say the viper
> Is killed by its own poison if encountered
> From outside of its body. (46–47)]

If the word's movement from interior to exterior ("verterla") is dan-gerous, the move in the opposite direction ("volverla") is no less so. Words, like almost everything else in the honor plays, are irretractible. They are, in this sense, like virginity is fantasized to be.[32] But Gu-tierre's initial desire to contain the ill-spoken word by drawing it back into its original source is especially troubling; not only because he fig-ures his breast as an engendering womb that gives birth to a poisonous word, inscribing yet another grotesque figuration of maternity, but also because the desire is expressed as a command ("Vuelva, vuelva al pecho la voz" [Come back, come back, my voice, into my breast]). As such it inscribes the same paradox as Mencía's earlier "Vuelva el aire" command: the call to containment is somehow undermined by the performative force of the speech act. The analogy to the snake is also suggestive. Not only does it align Gutierre with the "víbora," but it hints at the presence in the word of the same sort of *reme-dio/veneno* (remedy/venom) duplicity as was commonly attributed to snake's venom. Given all of this, it is by no means incidental that the specific word that Gutierre struggles but ultimately fails to contain is "celos" [jealousy]; in the honor plays jealousy is invested with exactly this kind of irrepressible performative force.

If containment strategies in the honor dramas tend to register anxieties concerning violability, it is at the level of what may be termed logical or even epistemological containment that these anxieties are most economically but also most problematically engaged. I refer, specifically, to the recurrent use in these plays (and *El médico de su honra* is no exception) of the soy quien soy formulation as a defense mechanism to ward against the dangers that threaten to invade the precarious territory of the self. On the surface, soy quien soy is invoked as a technique to reify the subject in the face of destabilizing forces, through a neatly packaged formula of both semantic and logical containment. But the soy quien soy formula is not all it appears to be. Its status is inherently troubled, even at a grammatical level. On one hand, it is doubly (if implicitly) framed by the deictic "yo" (I), which, as a wholly transferrable subject position that may be appropriated by any speaking voice, points to the precariousness (and even flexibility) of the identity whose rigidity the formula presumably imposes. On the other, it is not the copula but the relative pronoun "quien" (who) that functions, positionally, as the mirror term in which the others are reflected; the grammatical function of the relative pronoun as shifter reaffirms the emptiness of the subject position. Indeed, here the ontological force of the verbal copula is in some sense diminished by its doubling, since what stands at the other side of the allegedly transparent "soy" is not an affirmation of self-identity, but a mere tautology, another "soy." It is a tautology that corresponds, moreover, to a radically atheistic hermeneutic (not unlike that which characterizes the performative), since it becomes impossible, by virtue of the formula's circular logic, to assign conventional criteria of truth or falsity to the statement. Put somewhat differently, as a kind of ontologic performative, soy quien soy is so reductive as to be always true. The almost complete grammatical and even logical accessibility of the soy quien soy formula discloses, then, the very emptiness—and vulnerability to penetration—that it so anxiously seeks to mask. For all its seeming conjunctiveness, the soy quien soy equation ultimately functions as a radically disjunctive and relativized performative.

But if as a strategy of containment the soy quien soy formula is already troubled by its inherent tautology, it becomes even more problematic when it is contextualized within the honor drama. Not surprisingly, perhaps, in *El médico de su honra* it is Mencía who first resorts to the protection against the violability of identity that soy quien soy ostensibly offers, calling on its reificatory capacity in the same passage (quoted above) in which she struggles to contain the illicit word: "¿Qué es esto, cielos, qué es esto? / Yo soy quien soy. Vuelva el aire." That the perceived threat to which the soy quien soy responds here is none other than Mencía's own articulation of illicit desire only a few verses earlier suggests the extent to which the invading Other (for Mencía, erotic agency) is always already contained within the Self. Even more suggestive is the fact that her ritual pronouncement of "soy quien soy" is almost immediately followed by the indicting "ya ni para sentir soy mía." Insofar as her queja points to the displaced sense of ownership over her body and its desires that (within the patriarchy) ideally characterizes the perfecta casada, it also suggests a rather thorny relation between the reification of self-identity that the soy quien soy formula allegedly inscribes and the excessive conjunctiveness of husband's and wife's identity that results from the literalization of the marital sacrament's one-flesh doctrine. In other words, if the "two shall become one flesh" injunction is imagined as being literally (or even figuratively) true, it renders the reflexive property that ostensibly grounds the soy quien soy equation if not overtly false then, in the very least, questionable.

The various instances throughout the play that metaphorically impose the conjunctiveness of the one-flesh doctrine become particularly troubling to (and troubled by) the notion of Self that is already so problematically inscribed in the soy quien soy. Perhaps the most explicit statement of this sort of excessive marital interpenetration can be found on Mencía's lips almost immediately following her husband's unexpected arrival, on the night that Enrique has penetrated the sacrosanct space of the house.

> Dicen que dos instrumentos
> conformemente templados,
> por los ecos dilatados
> comunican los acentos:
> tocan el uno, y los vientos
> hiere el otro, sin que allí
> nadie le toque; y en mí
> esta experiencia se viera;
> pues si el golpe allá te hiriera,
> muriera yo desde aquí. (132–33, ll. 1211–20)

> [They say two instruments in tune
> Are able to communicate
> Quite perfectly through every sound
> They make; for when the one is played,
> The sound is carried on the wind
> And wounds the other, which then will play
> In sympathy. My own experience now
> Bears witness to the truth of this,
> For as you, husband, suffered there,
> So correspondingly I suffered here.] [33]

The interplay between one and two that informs the passage (as well as numerous others in the play) is, in many respects, characteristic of the overliteralization of the one-flesh doctrine. That Mencía again invokes the wind as agent of transmission is, by now, hardly surprising; what *is* striking is that here the wind that was earlier aligned with dissemination (and, ostensibly, disjunction) is what makes the conjunctiveness between the two instruments (husband and wife) possible. Even more striking is that, despite the benign instrumental metaphor, the passage associates marital containment (of two into one) with images of pain and even death. Not only are Mencía's words clearly prophetic in this sense, but they gesture toward the kind of vicarious penetrability that marriage affords. In other words, it is as a result of the overliteralization of the marital sacrament's one-flesh bond that the wife's adulterous transgression (the actual or virtual penetration of her body by another man) is felt by her husband ("tocan el uno . . . hiere el otro" [one is played . . . wounds the other]), not only as an affront to some metaphysical sense of honor, but as carnal penetration.

Significantly, the only instance in the play in which Gutierre calls on the soy quien soy in its unadulterated form, as it were, is preceded by an assertion of his wife's inviolability.

> Y así acortemos discursos
> pues todos juntos se cierran
> en que Mencía es quien es,
> y soy quien soy. No hay quien pueda
> borrar de tanto esplendor
> la hermosura y la pureza. (155, ll. 1647–52)

> [But now
> Our arguments must be cut shorter since
> They all concur in this — that she's Mencía
> And I am who I am. No one alive
> Can cast a slur upon the bright effulgence
> Of so much beauty and such purity. (45)]

His effort to bolster his first-person soy quien soy with a third-person version — specifically, with the "third" person of his wife — discloses not only the extent to which his desire for ontologic containment is displaced onto her body, but also the extent to which his own affirmation of identity is dependent on that very displacement. The positioning of the two formulas side by side (as they appear here) suggests the possibility of reading them as somehow obeying the rhetorical structure of chiasmus, which would explain, in part, the kind of crossover that occurs between husband's and wife's identities. But perhaps the crucial word in the passage is the conjunction "y" [and] that joins the soy quien soy with the es quien es. That "y" can be read as a marker of excess that betrays the failure, as it were, of the one-flesh doctrine's conjunctiveness. In other words, if the one-flesh doctrine is imagined as being literally true, then the two statements tend toward redundancy. What is more, although Gutierre invokes the soy quien soy as a last word that would lay to rest any doubts he may harbor about the status of his wife's (and by implication, his own) honor, he seems particularly attuned to the violability that the formula attempts to disguise. Indeed, he almost immediately dismisses the sense of closure and logical containment that he provisionally ascribes to its pronouncement, in favor of the (self-)doubt and suspicion that are his trademarks: "*Pero sí puede,* mal digo" (155, l. 1653) [*And yet—yes! it can be,* I speak wrongly (45)].

But if the alleged reifying capacity of the soy quien soy is somehow diminished by an overinvestment in the marital contract (and vice versa), its efficacy as a defensive strategy of containment is rendered even more questionable by the metaphoric literalization in which the play repeatedly indulges and, particularly, by the overarching metaphor of médico de su honra. Gutierre's crucial (and literal) adoption of the role of physician (a mere fifteen verses after having uttered his defensive soy quien soy) explicitly violates the stasis of being that the formula would seem to guarantee. Simply put, in order to become the titular médico de su honra, Gutierre must cease being who he is (husband, nobleman, whatever) and reinvent himself as someone else.[34] The conversion is not perhaps as abrupt as it may appear. Even before assuming his defining role as honor's physician, Gutierre expresses a willingness to "dejar de ser quien es" [cease being who he is] in deference to a political hierarchy that accords the king ontological priority over his subjects: "Señor, señor, no juréis; / que mucho menos importa / que yo deje aquí de ser / quien soy, que veros airado" (116, ll. 900–903) [Forbear, my lord. I'd sooner cease to be who I am / Than see you angry].[35] The relative ease with which Gutierre abandons the rigidity putatively inscribed in the soy quien soy in obeisance to royal authority not only uncovers the temporal impermanence of being that, in its present-tense articulation, the formula masks, but suggests also the extent to which even ontology can be and is disciplined in the play.

The purposefulness and almost perverse pleasure that marks Gutierre's self-fashioning into el médico de su honra point to a metatheatrical consciousness on his part: his recognition of a certain need or desire to role-play, to perform. This tendency toward theatricalization is at least partly attributable in the play to the exigencies of honor, which calls on mechanisms of epistemic containment as a safeguard against dissemination. Hence Gutierre's strategy to cover his suspicions of his wife's betrayal with "finezas, agrados, gustos, amores, lisonjas" (156, ll. 1678–79) [kindnesses, favours, / Pleasures, endearments, flatteries, and caresses (46)]:

> Esta noche iré a mi casa,
> de secreto entraré en ella
> por ver qué malicia tiene
> el mal; y hasta apurar ésta,
> *disimularé*, si puedo,
> esta desdicha, esta pena,
> este rigor, este agravio,
> este dolor, esta ofensa,
> este asombro, este delirio,
> este cuidado, esta afrenta,
> estos *celos*. (156, ll. 1687–97, italics mine)

> [Tonight I'll go back to my house in secret,
> To prosecute a further diagnosis.
> And, till I find how far the ill's progressed,
> *I shall dissimulate*, if I am able,
> This terrible disaster, this deep grief,
> This injury, this cruelty, this anguish,
> This horror, this delirium, this disease,
> This mortal insult, and this *jealousy*—(46)]

In keeping with the strictures of the honor code, however, Gutierre's "disimulo" [dissimulation] exceeds the soy quien soy; it implies a pretense of being that clouds the ontological transparency the formula pretends to inscribe. The irony, then, is the extent to which this simulation that violates the formula is motivated by the public demands of (or on) the soy quien soy, by the imperative of maintaining "proper" appearances for the sake of the qué dirán. As Maravall compellingly argues, "resulta claro que 'soy quien soy' no es un principio que obligue ser fiel a sí mismo. . . . Es, por el contrario, un principio que se enuncia siempre en relación al comportamiento social, como una obligación de obrar de cierta manera—que es la propia, en atención a su calidad es-tamental" [it is clear that 'soy quien soy' is not a principle that obliges one to be true to oneself. . . . It is, on the contrary, a principle that is always enunciated in relation to social behavior, as an obligation to act a certain way—the proper one with respect to qualities of estate].[36] All of this suggests rewriting the equation as "soy quien disimulo que soy" [I am who I pretend to be] or "quien pretendo ser" [who I claim to be], disclosing, in the rewriting, the same type of problematic inter-play between categories of seeming and being as Fray Luis negotiates in *La perfecta casada* and positing a provocative connection between this sort of honor-driven disimulo and the notion of "passing" (for Old Christian, for example) in an inquisitorial setting. The implica-tion is that it is the inquisitor Gutierre (and not so much the inquired Mencía) who has something to hide.

Gutierre's disimulo is, moreover, a pretense of ignorance that rela-tivizes (but does not elide) the traditional conflation of knowledge and power. If the honor dramas—and *El médico de su honra* in particular—place a premium on knowledge (generally obtained through direct empirical examination), it is quite clearly on knowledge of a secret sort. The problematization of epistemological levels that is so char-acteristically Calderonian (and of which the paradigmatic instance is undoubtedly Segismundo's "porque no sepas que sé / que sabes fla-quezas mías" [so you won't know that I know / you already know my weaknesses] in *La vida es sueño*)[37] is expressed here in terms of doublings:

> *Gutierre* (Aparte)
> (Encendidas en mi fuego,
> si aquí estoy escondido,
> han de verme, y de todos *conocido,*
> podrá saber Mencía
> que he llegado a entender la pena mía,
> y porque no lo entienda
> y *dos veces ofenda,*
> una con tal intento,
> y otra *pensando que lo sé y consiento,*
> dilatando su muerte,

he de hacer la deshecha desta suerte.)
(168, ll. 1969–78, italics mine)

[*Gutierre* (Aside)
Yes, bring them lit and burning with the fire
That so consumes me. If they see me here,
Mencía will find out that I have *learned*
My sorry plight. So that she does not know it
And so that she will not *offend me twice* —
(The first time — as she means to, and the second —
By thinking that I tamely bear my wrong
Because I've spared her forfeit life so long) —
This is the ruse that I propose to try. (53–54)]

Strictly speaking, it is not knowledge per se but a baroque knowledge about knowledge that must be contained through performance as a defensive measure to protect the Self. The paradox of invoking performance as a strategy of containment seems, by now, fairly clear. That Gutierre describes his plans as "hacer la deshecha" [the ruse that I propose] is suggestive in this context. Covarrubias defines *desecha* as "la dissimulación para encubrir lo hecho" [dissimulation in order to cover up what's done],[38] echoing Gutierre's earlier call on "disimulo." The word's etymological inscription of "des-hacer" — which allows translating the verse as "I shall do the undoing" — might also remit to the sort of deconstruction of identity that Gutierre undergoes in becoming something other than what he is (to avoid being "de todos conocido" [known by all]) as well as to the eventual fate of Mencía's perfected body.

Compulsory Inquisitions
and the Adultery of Visible Signs

In the failure of containment strategies, and in the presence of haunting suspicions of adulterous Otherness, an inquisitorial imperative imposes itself in *El médico de su honra* with such force that examination and surveillance become almost compulsory in the drama. Without a doubt, the most obvious case of this sort of compulsion in the play can be located in Gutierre's detailed examination of his wife's body for symptoms of contaminating disease, of infectious Otherness. But if Gutierre can be conceived as a sort of inquisitor general in *El médico de su honra,* he is not alone. Virtually no one is exempted from the play's obsession with examining as a means to secure knowledge and power. Paradoxically, it is Mencía herself who first articulates what could be seen as an inquisitorial imperative in the drama; if her honor is to be deemed perfect, she contends, almost echoing the ill-fated curiosity of Cervantes's Anselmo, it must be submitted to trial by fire, or rather, trial by desire.

> solamente me huelgo
> de tener hoy que sentir,
> por tener en mis deseos
> que vencer, pues no hay virtud
> sin experiencia. . . .
>
> . . . .
>
> y así mi honor en sí mismo
> se acrisola, cuando llego
> a vencerme; pues no fuera
> sin experiencias perfecto.
> (82, ll. 140–44, 149–52)
>
> [I pride myself
> Today, that I have conquered my desires,
> Since virtue only can be proved by trial.
>
> . . . .
>
> And thus my honour, too, is thrice-refined
> And purified, when in the fire of passion
> I subjugate myself, because perfection
> Is only proved by putting to the test. (7)]

Mencía's testing is particularly dangerous, however, because it fails to establish a mediating distance between the inquiring subject and the object of inquiry; both are materialized on her body, which, as a female body, is allied with neither truth nor certainty. To make matters worse, her need for proving herself (specifically, her sexual restraint) could be considered in a more problematic and even heretical light as participating in a casuistry of erotic temptation—"potuit transgredi

et non est transgressus" [(one who) could transgress but did not] —
explicitly associated with the *alumbrado* sect.[39]

Almost as ruinous as Mencía's "pruebas de honor" [trials of hon-
our] — which she will qualify, too late, as "peligrosas pruebas" [peril-
ous trials] [40] — are the sorts of inquiries carried out by the king. Like
Gutierre, Pedro is an avid examiner, a physician not of his honor but of
the corporate body of the state. His nocturnal jaunts through Seville
are an attempt to diagnose that social body in order to consolidate his
political power.

> Toda la noche rondé
> de aquesta ciudad las calles,
> que quiero saber así
> sucesos y novedades
>
> .   .   .   .   .   .
>
> . . . y deseo
> desta manera informarme
> de todo, para saber
> lo que convenga. (143, ll. 1405–13, italics mine)

> [All evening I've been walking round the streets.
> That's how I get to know the news, affairs,
> And business. . . .
>
> .   .   .   .   .
>
> It's thus I get the information
> Which tells me how it's best to act as King. (40)]

The king's desire for panoptic knowledge ("quiero saber" [I want to
know], "deseo informarme" [I wish to find out]) is not surprising.
What makes his epistemic desire particularly threatening, however, is
its inscription within an economy of punishment and hypervigilance.
Don Diego's comment that the king must be a watchful Argos, "el
emblema de aquel cetro / con dos ojos lo declare" (144, l. 1417) [The
emblem of two eyes upon your sceptre / Declares the fact (40)] is suggestive in this context, not only because the scepter is a clearly phallic
token of empowerment that serves as instrument of state penetrations
(visual or otherwise), but also because of the excess of vigilance and of
a disciplinary voyeuristic desire that Pedro's two-eyed scepter repre-

sents (the emblem, according to Covarrubias, usually consists of a "cetro, sobre el cual está *un* ojo" [scepter, upon which is *one* eye], not two).[41]

Pedro's possession of this overdetermined scepter ultimately underwrites his readerly authority and invests it with specific legal powers: "como rey, supremo juez" (207, l. 2781) [As judge supreme, and King of all the realm (78)]. It is hardly surprising, then, that the judgments he pronounces as *juez* are premised on a phallogocentric inquisitorial logic that invariably results in or condones bloodshed.[42] The king's peculiar conflation of examination with punishment—specifically, of a bloody sort—is made explicit in a seemingly unimportant exchange between Pedro and Don Diego in which the king narrates his adventures during one of his diagnostic rounds.

> *Rey*
> Vi valientes infinitos,
> y no hay cosa que me canse
> tanto como ver valientes . . .
>
> .   .   .   .
>
> Mas porque no se me alaben
> que no doy *examen* yo
> a *oficio* tan importante,
> a una tropa de valientes
> *probé* solo en una calle.
>
> *Don Diego*
> Mal hizo tu majestad.
>
> *Rey*
> Antes bien, pues con su *sangre*
> llevaron *iluminada* . . .
>
> *Don Diego*
>   ¿Qué?
>
> *Rey*
> La *carta* del *examen.*
> (144–45, ll. 1427–40, italics mine)
>
> [*King*
> I saw a whole infinity of gallants

(and there is nothing that tires me
so much as seeing gallants).

.   .   .   .

So I felt I must
Examine a *profession* so important
And so I put the gallantry to *proof*
Of a whole troop of them, in a back alley.

Diego
You should not do such things your Majesty.

King
Why not? They carried off from their examination
Certificates *illuminated* with—

Diego
With what?

King
With their own *blood*. (40)]

Not only does the king's response highlight the inevitable marriage
of "examen" [examination], "oficio" [profession, with its resonances
of Santo Oficio] and "sangre" [blood] in the play, but the allusion to
a bloody text (the illuminated "carta") no doubt anticipates the final
textualization of Mencía's blood on Gutierre's doors, which is, as we
shall see, largely the result of another carta iluminada. At that moment too, the king will resort to a formula that equates knowledge with
bloodshed in order to provide a last ditch "remedio" to an otherwise
intolerable misreading. The imperative force of Pedro's "Sangrarla"
[Bleed her] at the play's end effectively sanctions what he knows to be
the murder of an innocent woman in order to preserve the illusion of
heuristic certainty.

If politically the king commands tremendous authority as a reader
figure, however, there is no question that the foremost inquisitor of *El
médico de su honra* is Gutierre. From his first appearance in the drama
when he comments on the impropriety of testing Enrique's motives
and then proceeds to do so ("a vos, señor, no es bien hecho exami-
naros el pecho" [92, ll. 376–77] [It's not my place to delve into your
motives (12)]), to his final attempt to secure interpretive closure by

imposing a narrative of honor on the bloody handprints that decorate his door, Gutierre repeatedly appears on stage reading or examining. The very literalization of the médico de su honra metaphor and the specific application he gives it ("curar a costa de sangre" [200, l. 2633] [to cure at the expense of blood])[43] confirm his privileged inquisitor status. At least initially, Gutierre seems to be trying to get at some sort of ultimate truth. The prevailing obsession in El médico de su honra with uncovering truths corresponds to a constative and even theologic hermeneutics.[44] Covarrubias's entries for examen — "la diligencia particular que se haze para averiguar la verdad de alguna cosa" [the particular diligence that is undertaken in order to find out the truth about something] — and prueva — "averiguar con testigos y escrituras y otros medios, ser verdad lo que dize o lo que pretende" [to verify what is said or claimed to be true through witnesses and writings and other means] — two expressions that frequent Gutierre's (as well as Pedro's and even Mencía's) lips — both remit to a teleology of truth. It comes as no surprise that the entry for inquirir is almost identical — "buscar, pesquisar, preguntar, hazer diligencia para saber la verdad de algún hecho" [to look for, to investigate, to question, to take steps to know the truth about some fact], except of course for its obligatory salute to the "Santo Oficio del tribunal de la Fe" [Holy Office of the Tribunal of the Faith] and its "integérrimos juezes" [judges of the highest integrity].[45]

The perversity of Gutierre's misreading, however, lies in his prior knowledge that the diagnosis he makes of Mencía's body is *not* constative, but radically performative, completely divorced from notions of truth or falsity. The only "truth" such a reading can confirm is the questionable truth of its own assumptions, which once uttered cannot be revoked:

> no porque sepa, señor,
> que el poder mi honor contrasta;
> pero imaginarlo basta
> quien sabe que tiene honor.
>
> . . . .
>
> . . . hombres como yo
> no ven; basta que imaginen,

que sospechen, que prevengan,
que recelen, que adivinen,
que . . . No sé cómo lo diga;
que no hay voz que signifique
una cosa, que aún no sea
un átomo indivisible.
(174–76, ll. 2085–88, 2127–34)

[Not that I know for certain that his power
Has overthrown my honour; but that the least
Cause to suspect, or even to imagine,
In one who lives for honour, will suffice
For such a resolution.

  .   .   .   .   .   .

. . . men like me
Do not require to see: it is enough
That to imagine, to suspect, to fancy,
To have an inkling, entertain a doubt,
Or even to perceive a — I can't say it,
Since there is neither word nor tone so small
As could express the atom of an atom
Infinitesimally indivisible! (58–59)]

More so even than Pedro, Gutierre practices a reading strategy
grounded in a preoperative (and even self-fulfilling) suspicion of guilt
that seeks to connect meaning with truth as punishment. His inquisition of his wife's body ends up being radically performative.

It is precisely within this economy of suspicion and surveillance that
the Leonor subplot functions in the play, establishing the clinical history of Gutierre's paranoia about wifely infidelity. Beyond serving as a
pretext of and for Gutierre's anxieties with respect to feminine desire,
his romantic history with Leonor may also suggest that the terms of
his relationship with his *wife* can themselves be imagined as somehow
"adulterous." In other words, Gutierre's misreading of Mencía's innocence as guilt could be a reflection of his own repressed guilt, imagining his marriage as unfaithful to his earlier liaison with Leonor. This
possibility underscores the fact that geometries of desire are never
simple in Calderón, but are more often double and even triple in struc-

ture. If it is possible to view Gutierre as enacting the same (cuckolded husband/inquisitorial reader) role in the Gutierre–Leonor–Don Arias triangle as he does in the Gutierre-Mencía-Enrique triangle (albeit with the important difference of being promised to Leonor but married to Mencía), it is also possible to conceive of him as occupying a radically different position in a Leonor-Gutierre-Mencía triangle.[46]

Mencía's voiced suspicions of her husband's desire for his former lover ("¿Quién duda que haya causado / algún deseo Leonor?" (98, ll. 514–15) [Why, who can doubt that Leonor has roused / Your passion once again?" (16)]) supports the case for the existence of this third triangle, as does Leonor's complaint to the king about Gutierre's abandon ("Diome palabra que sería mi esposo" [105, l. 649] [He gave his word that he would be my husband (20)]). Far more incriminating, however, is Gutierre's own response to Mencía's surprise over his "fineza de amante" [favour of a lover] — deserting his prison in order to visit her — whereby he explicitly inscribes his double role as husband *and* lover.

> No dejo de ser amante
> yo, mi bien, por ser marido. (131, ll. 1179–80)
>
> [I do not cease to be your lover still,
> Although I am your husband, my dear love. (33)]

Taking Gutierre strictly at his word (i.e., that he *is* husband and lover, but both things to Mencía) does little to improve the situation since it raises the possibility of yet another triangle of desire, this time between a doubled Gutierre — a Gutierre-esposo and a Gutierre-amante — and Mencía, not unlike, one might argue, Lorca's Don Perlimplín.

What is perhaps most compelling of this sort of adulterous geometry is the shifting of readerly subject and object positions (inquiring mind and inquired body) that it unveils.[47] If nothing else, the interchangeability of the positions suggests that Gutierre's conviction of his wife has at least as much to do with his own sense of guilt as it does with her alleged crime. The implication, of course, is that his slate (or, alternately, his bloodline) is no cleaner or purer than hers, but that by indicting her he can avert suspicion from himself in much the same way that converso inquisitors sought to do.[48] Moreover, if it is possible to view Gutierre as the desiring agent (and object of reading) in this third triangle, it is also possible to consider him as occupying the identical position in the other two. The fact that the play ends with the royal reinstatement of the Leonor-Gutierre bond explicitly predicated on Leonor's acceptance of Gutierre's radical honor cure suggests a return to the "original" triangle in which the *bulto* (as materialization of Gutierre's paranoid hysteria) occupied the third position. It may also suggest that Gutierre's murder of Mencía is, in his eyes, the most expedient recourse for extricating himself from the (always already guilty) object position and reinscribing his subject role as inquisitorial reader.[49]

Throughout the play there are numerous instances in which Gutierre deploys what we might term an inquisitorial rhetoric while examining the status of his wife's body. I turn now to two particular moments in which he quite purposefully assumes the role of reader-examiner. What is most arresting about these scenes of reading is not so much the reification of Gutierre as inquisitor, but the way in which the visual "texts" he reads as signs of infidelity are expressly made to seem uncertain, their legibility threatened by a semiotic adultery that troubles the very possibility of assigning them stable meaning. The first of these, the dagger left by Enrique behind Mencía's bed, marks the arousal of Gutierre's suspicions of his wife and becomes the most damning physical evidence against her. Its discovery is narrated in one of the many asides that punctuate Gutierre's dialogues:

> *Don Gutierre*
> (*Aparte* Mas engañóme, ¡ay de mí!,
> que esta daga que hallé, ¡cielos!
> con sospechas y recelos
> previene mi muerte en sí.
> Mas no es esto para aquí.) (141, ll. 1361–65)
>
> [*Gutierre*
> (*aside*) But to my woe
> I am deceived. This dagger which I found,
> With dire suspicions, shame, and dread, forebodes
> Worse than my death — but that is not for now. (38)]

For Gutierre, the other man's dagger having penetrated the space of the bedchamber is, at first glance, an unequivocal sign of his wife's deceit (predicated on the analogy other man's dagger : Mencía's bedroom :: other man's phallus : Mencía's body) and, consequently, of his own death by dishonor. But Gutierre temporarily suspends judgment on the dagger's significance ("no es esto para aquí" [that is not for now]), if only for the sake of the qué dirán; that suspension anticipates the suspension of meaning that results from the dagger's adulterous migration throughout the play—both literal (the dagger's physical movement as prop) and figurative (the various shifts of the dagger's meaning according to its different "readers").

The dagger's second reader is Mencía, who, without realizing that it has been left behind by Enrique, discovers it unsheathed in her husband's hands and assumes that he means to end her life with it.

> *Doña Mencía*
> ¡Tente, señor!
> ¿Tú la daga para mí?
> En mi vida te ofendí,
> detén la mano al rigor,
> detén . . .
>
> .   .   .   .
>
> Al verte así, presumía
> que ya en mi sangre bañada
> hoy moría desangrada. (141–42, ll. 1377–81, 1383–85)
>
> [*Mencía*
> Hold back, my lord! For me! a dagger?
> If I offend you in life—Oh, spare me!
>
> .   .   .   .
>
> To see you coming with that dagger thus,
> I thought you were about to take my life
> And that today I was to bleed to death
> And bathe in my own blood. (39)]

Ironically, it is Mencía's misreading of the dagger that is perhaps the most accurate; she prophesies not only the author, instrument, and manner of her death ("desangrada" [bled to death]), but also alludes to the ostensibly purificatory cure that (in Gutierre's eyes, at least) her bloodbath is meant to effect ("en mi sangre bañada" [bathed in my blood]). The dagger's trajectory does not end here, however. It is reread by Gutierre, who goes so far as to question the object of his inquisitorial gaze when he notes the similarities between the craftsmanship of the lost dagger and that of Enrique's sword: "*Coteja la daga que se halló con la espada del infante. (Aparte)* ¿Qué es esto que miro? ¡Ay Dios!" (151, l. 1532) [*He catches sight of Prince Henry's sword and compares it with the make and pattern of the dagger which he found—which are identical. (aside)* Ah God! Ah God! what do my eyes behold? (43)]. Gutierre somewhat tepidly attempts to convince himself of Mencía's innocence by systematically dismissing the evidence against her — chief among which is the dagger that he now knows to be Enrique's:

> En cuanto a que hallé esta daga
> hay criados de quien pueda
> ser. En cuanto (¡ay dolor mío!)
> que con la espada convenga
> del infante, puede ser
> otra espada como ella;
> que no es labor tan extraña,
> que no hay mil que la parezcan.
> (154, l. 1627–34)
>
> [As for the dagger that I found, it might be
> That of some servant. That it matched the sword
> Of Prince Don Henry is not final proof,
> For there may be a twin sword for his own
> With its attendant dagger matching this.
> There's nothing in its workmanship so strange
> But there may be a thousand others like it. (45)]

The attempt fails, however, as Gutierre persists in wedding the dagger as sign to a narrative of adultery: "A peligro estáis, honor" (155, l. 1659) [You are in peril, / Honour! (46)].

That marriage is, at best, an uneasy one. Perhaps the best indicator of just how uneasy can be found in the long exchange between Gutierre, Pedro, and Enrique that opens the third act and that explicitly concerns itself with the dagger's physical and semiotic transience. Gutierre here exploits the same type of disjunctive semiosis that will undermine the certainty of his final judgment. After complaining to the king about Enrique's improper advances toward his wife and against his honor, he obliquely invokes the dagger as material evidence corroborating his claims. The invocation (and the threat that inhabits it) is only implicit, however, encoded within a radically different script in which the dagger's tongue of steel testifies to the prince's safety at Gutierre's hands.

> No os turbéis: con sangre digo
> solamente de mi pecho;
> que Enrique estad satisfecho,
> está seguro conmigo
> Y para esto hable un testigo:
> esta daga, esta brillante
> lengua de acero elegante,
> suya fue; ved este día
> si está seguro, pues fía
> de mí su daga el infante. (175, ll. 2099–2108)

> [No, do not start, your Majesty! I mean
> The blood of my own flesh: not yours, not yours!
> That Henry's royal blood is safe with me
> Rest well assured: and let this dagger speak
> With its fine, white, effulgent tongue of steel
> As witness to his safety, for it was
> The Prince's, and confided to my care
> By no one less than he, in my own house,
> Although it was unwittingly he lost it. (59)]

For Gutierre the ambiguity in the dagger's meaning (as proof of either his wife's adultery or Enrique's safety) is strictly a function of protecting his public honor by maintaining allegations against it unspoken — or else spoken only by silent, steely tongues. For the king and Enrique, however, the dagger's semiotic instability will have very different, if equally ruinous, implications.

The analogy between the tongue and the phallus is, of course, classic, as is the dagger-phallus analogy that Gutierre overliteralizes. But what is extraordinary in the case of *El médico de su honra* is the extent to which the dagger-tongue-phallus is detachable from the body to which it is "naturally" assigned. It is almost as if the dagger's migration from hand to hand (and from reader to reader) dramatized the reassignability of the phallus as a kind of free-floating signifier that resists reification.

In referring to the dagger as a hieroglyph that bespeaks his brother's transgression, Pedro makes explicit the need for "reading" the dagger as a sign:

> *Rey*
> ¿Veis este puñal dorado?
> Jeroglífico es que dice
> vuestro delito: a quejarse
> viene de vos, y he de oírle.
> Tomad su acero, y en él
> os mirad; veréis, Enrique,
> vuestros defectos. (182, ll. 2257–63)
>
> [*King*
> You see this gilded dagger?
> It is the hieroglyph that spells your guilt.
> It comes to plead against you with its tongue.
> And I must hear it. Take your dagger, Henry.
> Look at yourself in it: you'll see your soul
> With its defects, reflected on the blade. (62–63)]

But if qualifying the dagger as hieroglyph establishes an interpretive imperative by emphasizing its signness, it also suggests that as a sign, the dagger's legibility is questionable at best. A hieroglyph is, after all, an uneasily deciphered "text"; the truth value of any reading (such as that which affirms Enrique's guilt, for example) must, necessarily, remain unconfirmed. From talking hieroglyph, the dagger is immediately transformed by the king into a kind of mirror that visually reflects the prince's defects. Here, too, the metaphor is somewhat slippery. If the figuration of the dagger as mirror suggests the possibility of a mimetic responsiveness that would seem to correspond to a conjunc-

tive reading code ("El espejo consultado responde a cada uno pun-
tualmente y con verdad" [The consulted mirror responds to everyone
promptly and truthfully], writes Covarrubias),[50] the reflexive quality
of the dagger as mirror can also be distorting, tending instead toward
a disjunctive code of representation.[51]

At least as revealing as the metaphoric shifts that Pedro mobilizes
in reading the dagger as a sign of his brother's offenses against a loyal
subject is the much more dramatic transformation of the dagger's
meaning that occurs at the precise moment when it physically changes
hands.

> *Rey*
> Tomad la daga—(*Dale la daga,*
> *y al tomarla, turbado el infante*
> *corta al rey en la mano*) ¿Qué hiciste
> traidor?
>
> *Don Enrique*
>   ¿Yo?
>
> *Rey*
>   ¿Desta manera
> tu acero en mi sangre tiñes?
> ¿Tú la daga que te di,
> hoy contra mi pecho esgrimes?
> ¿Tú me quieres dar la muerte?
> (182–83, ll. 2266–71)
>
> [*King*
>   Here, take
> Your dagger—What's this you've done?—
>
> *Henry takes the dagger in a dazed, shaken way and,*
> *in doing so, accidentally cuts the King's hand.*
>
>   —you traitor?
>
> *Prince*
> I, traitor?
>
> *King*
> Yes: for you have stained your steel

In my own blood. You turn against your King
The dagger that I gave you? Do you wish
My death? (63)]

It is at this instant of literal migration that the dagger's semiotic mutability becomes most politically threatening; it is no longer merely a sign of adultery or dishonor but also of future regicide.[52] The king's ostensibly inviolable body becomes, by virtue of the dagger, alignable with Mencía's inquired body. Both are revealed as being subject to penetration, bodies that bleed. A somewhat different alignment might envision the crown (or, for that matter, the cetro) as the "wife" that two men (in this case Pedro and Enrique) cannot share, calling attention to the curious interplay between Self and Other to which the drama seems to return time and again. It is not irrelevant in this context (particularly given the inquisitorial narrative that subtends the text) that the king's earlier reprimand of his brother's illicit advances should be couched not only in a language of blood, but, moreover, in words that mar the dividing line between the pure blood of an innocent Self and the contaminated blood of a guilty Other.

> *Rey*
> Si a la enmienda
> vuestro amor no se apercibe,
> dejando vanos intentos
> de bellezas imposibles,
> donde el alma de un vasallo
> con ley soberana vive,
> podrá ser de mi justicia
> que aun mi sangre no se libre.
> (179, ll. 2199–2206, italics mine)

> [*King*
> If your love does not undergo correction,
> Abandoning the fruitless quest of beauty
> Impossible to you because thereover
> Another's soul, although he is a vassal,
> Rules with right absolute, and sovereign sway —
> Then you will find that your blood, though my own,
> Is in no way exempted from my justice. (61)]

Although the king clearly means to imply Enrique as the object of his "justicia," the synecdochical "*mi* sangre" by which he refers to his brother makes possible another reading, in which Pedro himself is both "justiciero" [executor] and "ajusticiado" [executed]. The ambiguity might be associated with the type of shift in inquisitorial subject and object positions (he who penetrates/he who is penetrated) generated by the plurality of adulterous triangles that the work inscribes from early on. In other words, the inquiring body is once again exposed as being susceptible to — if not desirous of — penetration. The blood of the inquirer, in this case, not only is of the same genealogic descent as that of the penetrated body (which is not without consequences for a reading of limpieza de sangre), but, moreover, is apt to become "mixta" — or confused with it — at the very moment the blade cuts.[53]

More than simply a sign, then, the dagger can be conceived as a sort of instrument that writes texts in blood: the text of Mencía's various penetrations (the virtual penetration of Enrique's unconsummated advances and, inasmuch as it helps confirm Gutierre's suspicions of her infidelity, the real penetration of his prescribed bloodletting) as well as the text of Pedro's future demise at his brother's hands. But if the dagger writes a bloody narrative, it is a narrative that continuously points to its own weak spots — to the instability that inheres in the very letters that determine it. As an object of reading, the dagger seems, at times, more of a double-edged sword: imbued with double meanings and itself contaminated by an adulterous semiotic code that undermines the authority of the punitive text of bloodshed it pens.

If the dagger functions as a phallic writing instrument employed in the production of a male-authored text that is nonetheless rendered uncertain, there is another, more blatant text inscribed in the play that similarly calls attention to its problematic legibility and that can be considered (initially at least) a sort of female-authored text. The interpretation of that text — Mencía's letter, intended for Enrique but intercepted by Gutierre — marks the moment in which Gutierre most literally assumes the role of reader in the play, no longer attending to bodies or hieroglyphic signs, but to written words on a physical page. What is perhaps most noteworthy of this second scene of (nonsomatic) reading is the fact that the text Gutierre reads is explicitly defective, making conspicuous the inevitability of the misreading. As with the dagger, the letter — which will constitute Gutierre's final piece of evidence against his wife — is revealed to be a radically unstable sign, not (as one might expect in the case of a letter) because of its migration, but, ironically, because of its stasis. Mencía is caught in flagrante not in the arms of her lover, but rather with a pen in her hand, writing what her inquisitor-husband will read as a "guilty" text.

It is not unimportant that Gutierre's examination of the letter is expressly theatricalized as a gloss, a reading that is quite literally between the lines, already questioning the text's integrity and, moreover, its resistance to penetration.

> *Don Gutierre*
> *(Lee) Vuestra Alteza, señor . . .* ¡Que por Alteza
> vino mi honor a dar a tal bajeza!
> *No se ausente . . .* Deténte,
> voz, pues le ruega aquí que no se ausente,
> a tanto mal me ofrezco,
> que casi las desdichas me agradezco. (192, ll. 2462–67)
>
> [*Gutierre*
> *(reads).* "Your Highness" — It is from that very Highness
> The lowness comes, to which has stooped my Honour —
> "Your Highness, do not go away" — My voice,
> Stop short. That she should beg him to remain
> Would sacrifice me to such vaster evils
> As make my past misfortunes seem like pleasures. (68–69)]

What Gutierre reads as the final proof of his wife's adultery is proof only of the impossibility of reading authorial intent. (Mencía's purpose in writing Enrique begging him to stay was to dispel rumors that his departure was on her account.) The incompleteness of the letter's intended message points to the relativity of the diagnosis and the contingent nature of its assignment. The fact that Gutierre completes the incriminating text suggests the extent to which he is author of the guilt he reads: "*El amor te adora, el honor te aborrece; así el uno te mata y el otro te avisa. Dos horas tienes de vida; cristiana eres, salva el alma, que la vida es imposible*" (193, n.l.) [Though Love adores you, Honour must abhor you. / Though Honour slays you, Love would give you warning / and counsel. You have two more hours of life. / You are a Christian: save your soul, since, now, / It is impossible to save your life (69–70)].

Perhaps the greatest danger of the inquisitorial compulsion that drives *El médico de su honra* is precisely this self-reifying capacity; once the mechanism has been set in motion, there is no stopping it, its performative force is irrepressible. The body — particularly the feminized body — as sign has most to lose.

Writing on the Wall:
The Textualization of the Inquired Body

The inquisitorial imperative that generally informs *El médico de su honra* and that in many respects is condensed in the figure of Gutierre demands a text — specifically, a somatic text — on which to perform its readings. There is little question that Mencía's body, vessel of her husband's diseased honor, occupies this position in the drama. From the very moment in which Gutierre adopts the title and role of médico de su honra, her imperfect wife's body becomes the scrutinized object of his medical and critical gaze. But if Mencía's textualization can be seen as a continuous process throughout the play, it is, unquestionably, in the final scenes of the third act that it comes to a head in the most gruesomely literal way imaginable: her body and blood write a text that is not only read, but widely circulated and diversely manipulated. While Gutierre seems to have the upper hand in controlling that text, almost everyone else in the play appears to have a hand in it as well (and quite literally so). Yet despite its blatant visibility, it should perhaps not prove surprising if, in the end, Mencía's body resists legibility, as earlier it resisted strategies of containment, or, to put it in other words, if, in the end, her nonadulterous body becomes a radically adulterous sign.

Notably, it is the "real" physician in the play, Ludovico, who discloses the relative impossibility of accurately reading Mencía's body. He responds to Gutierre's anxious "¿Qué ves?" (198, l. 2574) [What can you see? (72)] with

Una imagen
de la muerte, un bulto veo
que sobre una cama yace:
dos velas tiene a los lados,
y un crucifijo delante. (198, ll. 2575–79)

[I seem to see an effigy of death,
A body lying on a bed, with two
Candles that burn on either side of it,
And, straight in front of it, a crucifix. (72)]

No doubt a trained diagnostician, he can describe the spectacle before him only by noting the ambiguity of the visual referent ("un bulto veo" [I see a body]). Covarrubias's entry for *bulto* as "todo aquello que hace cuerpo y no se distingue lo que es, como lo que uno lleva debaxo de la capa . . . cosa embuelta y confusa" [all that which takes the shape of a body without being able to tell what it is, like what one carries beneath a cloak . . . a covered and bewildering thing] supports this contention.[54] Ludovico is also quick to point out the scene's morbid iconography, positing a reading of it in terms of the strategies of symbolic containment it invokes. Indeed, the portrayal of Mencía's body — quite literally prostrated on her bed, with candles at either side and a crucifix above her — suggests imagining her monumentalization here as a kind of symbolic enclosure within the religious image of sacrificial lamb, awaiting slaughter on the altar. But if her body is textualized into a visual metaphor that remits to the crucifixion of Christ (and which extends even to the spatial crossing of her body), the allusion renders flagrant Gutierre's misreading.

It is, in fact, Ludovico's doubts about the moral propriety of Gutierre's lethal cure that prompt him to write an accusatory text with Mencía's blood. He paints the doors of the house with his handprints in order to mark what he assumes to be the scene of a crime:

saqué *bañadas*
las *manos* en roja sangre,
y que fui por las paredes,
como que quise arrimarme,
manchando todas las puertas,

por si pueden las *señales*
descubrir la casa.
(203, ll. 2698–2704, italics mine)

[my *hands* being *covered* with her blood,
I, feigning to support myself against
The doors, kept *daubing* them with crimson hand-prints
So as to *mark* the house for recognition. (75–76)]

Ludovico's characterization of his handprints as "señales" [signs] suggests the extent to which Mencía's body and blood are, like the Eucharist or the wedding sheets, invested with a semiotic charge. What is more, the painting of a door with blood as a means of encoding a legible sign seems a fairly clear allusion to the Jewish Passover rite, positing an analogy that is both compelling and potentially devastating not only in light of the play's inquisitorial rhetoric of contamination and purgation but in a context in which not just the doors but the bodies of Jews ("las partes posteriores" [the posterior parts]) were either literally or figuratively marked with—and read for—bloodied signs of accusatory difference.[55]

The next reading of Mencía's textualized corpse is offered by Gutierre, who perfects his wife's body, rewriting (and, in a sense, containing) her execution-styled murder as a tragic accident:

de la mayor desdicha,
de la tragedia más rara,
escucha la admiración
que eleva, admira y espanta.
(209, ll. 2822–25)

[Of the most terrible misfortune,
A (most rare) tragedy that cannot but
Demand for those who hear of it
Profoundest pity, greatest admiration.][56]

Gutierre's reading, punctuated with allusions to monstrosity ("rara," "admira," "espanta"), ends with the spectacularization of Mencía's bloody corpse, as called for in the stage direction "Descúbrese a Doña Mencía en la cama" [Doña Mencía is discovered lying in her bed]. The exhibitionism of the dead wife's body on the stage—a generic requirement of the honor-drama closure—was, no doubt, intended largely for dramatic effect. (Calderón perhaps intuited what Poe explicitly stated two centuries later: "there is nothing so poetic as the death of a beautiful woman.") [57] But beyond the sensationalism it may have produced (qualified perhaps by the frequency with which dead women's bodies appear in these plays), the spectacularization onstage of the imperfect wife's corpse cannot be understood separate from the honor question. Specifically, Mencía's textualized body stages the public/private paradox inscribed in the code of honor. Gutierre's act of cleansing his polluted honor (an act that requires, in his perception, the murder of his wife) is effective only if it is made legible through the exhibition of the (punished) female corpse that once housed—or encrypted—it. But if the efficacy of the *remedio* depends on its public display, vengeance must nonetheless be carried out in secret, leaving no traces so as not to further publicize the dishonor involved: "a secreto agravio, secreta venganza" [secret vengeance for secret insult]. Honor, in this sense, might be conceived as irreparable—nulla reparabilis arte; attempts to cure it only worsen its prognosis. [58]

The reading of the textualized body is next taken up by the king, who attempts to suppress the text, bowdlerizing it of its most disturbing implications.

> Que hagáis borrar
> las puertas de vuestra casa;
> que hay mano sangrienta en ellas.
> (213, ll. 2930–32, italics mine)
>
> [That you should wipe your doors
> Because there is a bloodstained hand on them. (81)]

His command that Gutierre erase the bloody handprints that mark his door might be read as a metonymic displacement of his desire to erase the narrative of (future) regicide encoded in his own bloody hand, earlier penetrated (like Gutierre's honor) by Enrique's migrating dagger. Pedro's call for cleansing the blood responds to what is perhaps the central preoccupation throughout the final scenes of the third act—washing, specifically, washing hands of blood—a concern that is highly charged given the cultural preoccupation with limpieza de sangre. It is not coincidental, in this context, that Ludovico earlier qualified his bloodstained hands as "bañadas en roja sangre" [bathed in red blood], reversing the usual semantic investment of "bañar." Bathing, generally associated with immaculacy — and, moreover, with limpieza — is used, instead, to signify maculation.

The subtext of pollution and purification is perhaps nowhere stronger than in Gutierre's reading of the handprints at his door.

> Los que de un oficio tratan,
> ponen, señor, a la puerta
> un escudo de sus armas;
> trato en honor y así pongo
> *mi mano en sangre bañada*
> a la puerta; que *el honor*
> *con sangre, señor, se lava.*
> (213, ll. 2933–39, italics mine)

> [Those who deal in a certain kind of business
> Are wont to put the sign upon their doors
> Of what they deal in. I who deal in Honour
> So place *a bloodstained hand* upon my door
> For *Honour can be only washed in blood.* (81–82)]

That Gutierre describes his dealings in honor as an "oficio" is suggestive for a historicized reading of the honor plays, particularly given the ubiquitousness of the Santo Oficio (Holy Office) in the seventeenth century. Equally suggestive is the double meaning of "escudo," which can be understood not only a coat of arms (a reified sign) but also a pretext or justification. Covarrubias writes: "Por alusíon llamamos escudo la *escusa* con que nos defendemos" [By allusion we call *escudo* (shield) the *escusa* (excuse) with which we defend ourselves].[59] This secondary meaning might hint at a certain sense of guilt on Gutierre's part, the acknowledgment of a wrongdoing that would require an *escusa*. Even more indicting, in this sense, is the semantic ambivalence provoked by the image of a hand bathed *in* blood side by side with an embodied honor bathed *by* blood. If bloodbaths — baños de sangre, or, alternately, limpiezas de sangre — effectively stain the hands, their capacity to purify honor seems questionable, at best. It is an ambivalence

Gutierre cannot afford. The honor physician claims authorship over Ludovico's handprint, appropriating the bloody text ("*mi* mano") as his personal emblem, in a last ditch effort to hypostatize — and hence render safe — its inherently unstable meaning.

But it is an effort destined for failure. The very possibility of repeated attempts to reify the meaning of Mencía's body-text betrays the uncertainty — the semiotic adultery — that it encodes. It is this very uncertainty — this tenuous legibility — that is deemed threatening to an authoritative reading code, more so even than the confirmation of suspicion. The historical relation between the female body and the Other's body is predicated on exactly this: "el reconocimiento es difícil." This holds especially true, as we have seen, for the married woman. In an important essay on Calderón, Bruce Wardropper has suggested that what ultimately separates comedy and tragedy in early modern Spanish theater is the marital status of their respective characters: "In the comedies, the characters are unmarried; in the tragedies they are married." [60] The notion of marriage as a clear, dividing line (that ultimately renders a work either a comedy or a tragedy) can also be elaborated in terms of the somatic legibility of a woman's chastity as a function of her marital — specifically, her hymeneal — status. In the comedies, women's — would-be wives' bodies are legible with respect to transgression; in the tragedies, they are not. Illegibility paradoxically becomes incentive for punishment. The wife's body becomes alignable, in this sense, with the grotesque body (one that is always already penetrated) and hence a space especially suited to further inquiries and penetrations.

It is precisely this type of logic that resolves, if problematically, the seeming paradox of Gutierre's cure. The murder he concocts ("una sangría pretendo darle" [a bloodletting I intend to give her]) makes Mencía's already grotesque body (debased, maternal, marked by openings and orifices) even more so by subjecting it to additional penetrations: Ludovico effectively opens her veins. His ultimate goal, however, is to transform that grotesque body that bleeds (the menstruating woman or the menstruating Jew) into a disturbingly perfect (or, rather, perfected) model of the classical body — elevated, static, and monumental. [61] Mencía's blood on her wedding sheets effectively returns her to a grotesquely virginal state, to the unrecoverable site — or moment — of original penetration. The irony, of course, is that the very blood that redeems her, reinstating her chastity and thus curing Gutierre's diseased honor also writes — in a luridly literal way — the text of her penetration; her "breve herida" (brief cut) bleeds anew. Even perfected, her textualized body is revealed as grotesquely human.

One might argue that the most troubling aspect of the final act is not — or at least not only — the murder in itself, but the fact that it is sanctioned by the king, who commands, as both a pardon and a sentence, that Gutierre wed his former betrothed. The disturbing terms of Gutierre's and Leonor's nuptials — which suggest a rescripting of the containment, inquisition, and textualization cycle to which the wife's body has been submitted throughout the course of the drama — are arranged quite literally over Mencía's dead body:

> *Gutierre*
> Mira que médico he sido
> de mi honra: no está olvidada
> la ciencia
>
> *Leonor*
>   Cura con ella
> mi vida, en estando mala. (214, ll. 2946–49)
>
> [*Gutierre*
> You see I am the Surgeon of my Honour.
> It's a science I do not forget,
> An art I have not lost.
>
> *Leonor*
> Then cure my own (life)
> When it's in need of it. (82)]

The marriage of Leonor and Gutierre seems an ambivalent and troubling resolution to the play. The marriage closure symbolically reintroduces the logic of an institutionally controlled, reproductive sexuality as a means of whitewashing the adulterous excesses (both sexual and semiotic) that have run rampant throughout the play. Yet Leonor's acceptance of Gutierre's mano in — and on — the conditions he offers it (that is, bloodied and willing to make bleed again) not only makes her a belated accomplice of sorts to the punitive, inquisitorial science he has practiced on Mencía, but also inscribes her consent that the ritual punishment be reenacted on her own wifely body.

And yet, Leonor's submissive "cura" is not given the last word in the play. Something else destabilizes the problematic endorsement of the honor code that the second marriage closure seems to inscribe. The play's final words—the formulaic *excusatio* directly addressed to the audience—are found not on the gracioso's lips, as one might expect, but rather on Gutierre's:

> Con esto acaba
> *El médico de su honra.*
> Perdonad sus muchas faltas. (214, ll. 2951–53)
>
> [Pardon its many errors, my good friends,
> For here *The Surgeon of His Honour* ends. (82)] [62]

The pertinent question becomes, then, to whom or to what does Gutierre refer by *El médico de su honra* of the play's penultimate verse? The obvious answer—and perhaps Calderón's, in this case—is the text, the play titled *El médico de su honra*. The closing lines of almost all Golden Age dramas were usually reserved for just this sort of belated *captatio benevolentiae*.

Things get slightly more interesting if we read the final inscription of the play's literalized metaphor as also referring to the embodied médico de su honra, Don Gutierre Alfonso Solís. The play's final verse might then be read as an admission of authorial guilt on Gutierre's part, a self-accusation of his own reading as one riddled with errors. It is an accusation that inscribes, moreover, our own complicity as spectators, somehow implicated for witnessing the extent of Gutierre's faults, the perversity of his misdiagnosis.[63] Perhaps Calderón's greatest subversion of the honor code consists in precisely this: letting us, as spectators, walk away with the knowledge that *any* reading, like Gutierre's inquisition of his wife's body, that seeks to wed Truth with punishment can only either confirm its own assumptions or betray the adultery of the signs on which it has relied. It is, after all, only *with* that knowledge that a critique of inquisitorial practices such as I have suggested is at stake in *El médico de su honra* could have been legible.

If the play questions absolute readings, it does so precisely by dramatizing the misreadings on which they are inevitably founded. In the
end, not only for Gutierre, but also for his spectators and his apologists, the only certainty the process yielded, the only truth uncovered,
is an innocent woman's corpse.

But it is a corpse that perversely resists being laid to final rest. The
wife's spectacularized body and blood can be aligned, finally, with
neither somatic nor semiotic closure; they defy classification, monstrously attracting and repelling the gaze.

> Cubrid
> ese horror que asombra,
> ese prodigio que espanta,
> espectáculo que admira,
> símbolo de la desgracia. (210, ll. 2876–80)

> [Now cover up this horror-striking sight,
> This prodigy of sorrow and affright,
> This spectacle of wonder and despair,
> This symbol of misfortune. (80)]

Even in the seemingly absolute containment of death, Mencía's textualized corpse resists strategies to contain it. Once "descubierto"
[uncovered] on the stage, it can no longer be closeted, even by royal
authority. Her wifely body exceeds the casket that would enclose it,
contests the reading that would render it safe. Perhaps only in the light
of that resistance, or in the horror of that "espanto" [fright], might we
begin to glimpse the traces of a smile of accomplishment on Mencía's
perfected body.

Sor Juana's *Empeños*

The Imperfect Wife

Las damas no desdigan de su nombre,
y si, mudaran traje, sea de modo
que pueda perdonarse, porque suele
el disfraz varonil agradar mucho.

[Let not ladies disregard their character,
and if they change costumes,
let it be in such wise that it may be excused;
for male disguise usually is very pleasing.]
—Lope de Vega,
Arte nuevo de hacer comedias

¿Qué más podré decir ni ponderar?, que hasta el hacer esta forma de letra algo razonable me costó una prolija y pesada persecución no por más de porque dicen que parecía letra de hombre, y que no era decente, con que me obligaron a malearla adrede y de esto toda esta comunidad es testigo; en fin ésta no será materia para una carta sino para muchos volúmenes muy copiosos. Pues ¿qué dichos son estos tan culpables?

[What else can I say or instance? —for even having a reasonably good handwriting has caused me worrisome and lengthy persecution, for no reason other than they said it looked like a man's writing, and that it was not proper, whereupon they forced me to deform it purposely, and of this the entire community is witness; all of which should not be the subject for a letter but for many copious volumes. Then again, what things have I said that are so blameworthy?]

— Sor Juana Inés de la Cruz, "Autodefensa"

In the early morning of 24 February 1669, the city of Mexico was undergoing final preparations for the wedding that promised to be among the most prestigious and memorable social events of the decade. Inside the Church of St. Jerome, where the ceremony would take place, almost every candle was lit and the altar adorned with its richest ornaments and its finest flowered curtains, not only to mark the splendor and solemnity of the occasion, but in honor of the distinguished company whose presence would grace the church pews. The long guest list included the aristocracy of both church and state, the highest court officials as well as the city's religious elite; it was even rumored that the viceroys themselves would attend the festivities. Outside the church, too, final arrangements were being made; the last details of the reception were negotiated, no expense spared for the gala to commemorate such a momentous event. The bride, after all, was the favorite of the viceregal court, the prodigiously bright and hauntingly beautiful young criolla who had turned away so many suitors that some had doubted whether she would ever wed.

As the last church candles were being lit, the bride-to-be was escorted, as was the custom of the day, on her *paseo* (stroll) through the streets of Mexico City by a godmother especially chosen for the occasion. Dressed in finery and adorned with lavish jewelry, she was paraded about town, in a token farewell to unmarried life. After this final, ceremonial exhibition as a single woman, the future casada was led to the church where she would make her lifelong vows. Stripped of her courtly taffeta gown, she was dressed by her attendants in her bridal whites: a simple, but elegant, long wedding gown with a high neckline and stylish double sleeves. She stared almost impassively as silver scissors cut her long, dark braids of hair: a final wedding gift for her future husband. Finally, with nothing else left to do, she donned her bridal veil and, waiting for her groom's arrival, imagined a poem she might one day write.

¡Vengan a la fiesta, vengan, señores,
que hoy se casa una Niña, y es por amores!

De hermosura está ella llena,
y Él de bellezas colmado;
Él es un Clavel rosado,
ella en su amor hoy se estrena,
y Él la colma de favores.
¡Vengan a la fiesta, vengan, señores!

Hoy una Niña que abrasa
un amoroso volcán,
sin mirar el qué dirán,
por el Vicario se casa.

Su recato comedido
paró en empeño amoroso,
porque dice que su Esposo
entre puertas la ha cogido.

Hoy logra su fino intento
que ha sido tan deseado,
que ha un año ya, que le ha dado
palabra de casamiento.

No digo yo que ésta es cosa
con que su virtud se impida,
que antes pasará una vida
como de una Religiosa:

porque es Él con quien se casa
de condición tan precisa,
que ni aun para que oiga Misa
la deja salir de casa.

Pero causa novedad,
aunque es tan santo el intento,
ver que pare en Casamiento
su Voto de Castidad.

De su Esposo los primores
su corazón abrasaron,

y por más que la encerraron
se nos casa por amores.

[Come to the celebration, come, everyone,
for today a girl marries, and it's for love!
Of loveliness she is full,
and He with beauties overflowing;
He is a pink carnation,
in whose love today she debuts,
and He showers her with favors.
Come to the celebration, come, everyone!

Today a girl, whom
an amorous volcano burns,
ignoring what others may say,
is to be married by the Vicar.

Her modest reserve
ended in amorous trial,
for she says that her Husband
has caught her indoors.

Today she fulfills her fine intention
that has been so desired,
for it's a year now, since she gave him
her word of marriage.

I hardly suggest this is something
that impedes her virtue,
for she will spend her life
as a cloistered nun:
because He whom she marries
is of conditions so precise
that not even to hear Mass
does He let her leave the house.

But it comes as a surprise,
although the intention is so holy,
to see that her vow of chastity
ends in marriage.

The beauties of her Husband
have inflamed her heart,
and however much they enclose her,
she marries for love.] [1]

Stranded at the Altar:
Sor Juana's Marriage of Convenience

The groom, of course, never arrived, at least not in person. Even so, the nuptials went on as planned. The "wedding" that took place in the Church of St. Jerome on 24 February 1669 and that was so central to the social and religious calendar of mid-seventeenth-century Mexico was not a marriage in the conventional sense, but the profession of a novice, Juana Ramírez de Asbaje, the future Sor Juana Inés de la Cruz. If my depiction of Sor Juana as a bride and of her profession ceremony as a matrimony is misleading, it merely exploits the suggestive metaphor that from at least as early as the fourth century has consistently been applied to nuns: "brides of Christ." [2] Indeed, except for the corporeal absence of the groom, the ceremony, with its exchange of vows and rings, bears striking resemblance to that of Christian marriage on which it is modeled. [3] Nuns themselves — Teresa de Jesús a striking example — often made use of the bride of Christ metaphor as a way of legitimizing not only the immediacy of their relation with God but, more pertinently, their authorial voice.

This, however, is not the case with Sor Juana. It is, for a number of reasons, highly problematic to consider her writing against a backdrop of either perfect or imperfect wives. To begin with, although Sor Juana's text does not exactly conform to the typical conventual genre (the confessional autobiography addressed to a priestly "vuestra merced" [your mercy] and destined for his eyes only), she nonetheless wrote as a nun. There is little question that the convent represented for many women a space of subtle but active resistance against the institution of marriage: a "catalyst for autonomy," as Electa Arenal suggests. [4] For Sor Juana, this is explicitly so. Of the two options available to "decent" young women in the seventeenth century — marriage

or the convent—she quite purposefully chose the latter; she herself
wrote (in what has become one of the most cited—and most controversial—passages of the *Respuesta*) that her religious profession was
largely fueled by her strong aversion to matrimony.

> Entréme religiosa porque, aunque conocía que tenía el estado cosas
> (de las accesorias hablo, no de las formales) muchas repugnantes a
> mi genio, con todo, para la total negación que tenía al matrimonio,
> era lo menos desproporcionado y lo más decente que podía elegir en
> materia de la seguridad que deseaba de mi salvación; a cuyo primer
> respeto (como al fin más importante) cedieron y sujetaron la cerviz
> todas las impertinencillas de mi genio, que eran de querer vivir sola;
> de no tener ocupación obligatoria que embarazase la libertad de mi
> estudio, ni rumor de comunidad que impediese el sosegado silencio
> de mis libros.
>
> [I became a nun because, although I knew that that way of life in-
> volved much that was repellent to my nature—I refer to its incidental,
> not its central aspects—nevertheless, given my total disinclination
> to marriage, it was the least unreasonable and most becoming choice
> I could make to assure my ardently desired salvation. To which first
> consideration, as most important, all the other small frivolities of my
> nature yielded and gave way, such as my wish to live alone, to have
> no fixed occupation which might curtail my freedom to study, nor
> the noise of a community to interfere with the tranquil stillness of
> my books.][5]

But not only did Sor Juana eschew literal marriage, she only rarely
invoked its figural application of *sponsa Christi* (bride of Christ) to
describe her own status as nun, and never charged it with the intensity or the eroticism that made the metaphor of spiritual matrimony
so rich for the Spanish mystics. (The four "Letras sagradas en la so-
lemnidad de la profesión de una religiosa"—the second of which I
cited above—are perhaps the best examples of the infrequent occa-
sions when she actually enlists the bride of Christ metaphor, and even
there its use is topical.) Sor Juana was not—and never intended to
be—a *perfecta casada* to any husband, Christ included; she describes

her spiritual nuptials, in fact, as a marriage of convenience, the "least unreasonable" alternative to the inconvenience of a conventional marriage.

And yet, despite all of this, it is particularly tempting to read Sor Juana's texts in search of wives' bodies that might somehow fit within the framework I have been elaborating throughout this book. Hers would be, after all, a text in which the fictional constitution of the wife's voice was carried out by a woman author—moreover, a woman who not only had very clear thoughts on the position of the wife in early modern culture, but who had carefully considered the issue with respect to the position of her own body. Of Sor Juana's works, it is probably *Los empeños de una casa*, her finest play and the one in which she most closely approaches Calderón, that best lends itself to such a reading: the drama explores both the status and legibility of the (future) wife's body in terms that suggest a provocative rewriting of the honor script. Marriage is, of course, the fate Sor Juana chose for Leonor, the protagonist of *Empeños* (perhaps the only one she could choose, given the generic constraints of comedia closure), who is typically—and, I would argue, problematically—considered Sor Juana's fictional alter ego.[6] But if part of the interest in reading *Empeños* derives from the fact that its author is a woman, an American, and a nun, it is also true that a certain reading of these "facts" could easily result in the essentializing of Sor Juana's body and authorial voice.

This is a pitfall we should avoid. Neither Sor Juana's biology nor her biography obviates the need for examining the construction and constructedness of the wife's body within her play (or indeed of the female author persona who ostensibly forges it). On the contrary, notions of constructedness are crucial to the drama's baroque aesthetics, so much so, in fact, that they are grafted even onto categories of gender and, to a certain extent, race. This transfer, materialized in the transvestism of the gracioso Castaño, is without question what is most arresting of Sor Juana's play. In this concluding chapter, I turn to a reading of wives' bodies in *Los empeños de una casa*, specifically, to the body of the cross-dressed Castaño—aspiring perfecta casada and, arguably, Sor Juana's best double—as a kind of epilogue to the reading of wives' bodies in Fray Luis and Calderón. The displacements I have set forth throughout this book between the wife's body, the status of the sign, and the Other's body find striking resonances in Castaño's transvestism and in the marriage proposal it elicits.

"Común de dos": *Sor Juana's Gender Fictions*

If Castaño's transvestism is, as he would have us believe, a standard "paso de la comedia" [part of the play], we should not, however, dismiss it as an isolated or unimportant incident, particularly given Sor Juana's propensity for challenging notions of gender stability and crafting gender fictions throughout her work. For better or for worse, it is this propensity that has largely colored her critical reception and her problematic canonization as "Tenth Muse" or even as "a woman of genius." [7] Sor Juana's express resistance to marriage, for example, has consistently been viewed within a certain line of criticism as evidence of a kind of androgyny on her part, an androgyny that is in turn linked to her brilliance. Perhaps the worst example of this type of reading is the 1946 psychoanalytic biography of Sor Juana by Ludwig Pfandl, who attributes her formidable intellectual capacity to what he describes as biological and psychological abnormalities. Pfandl describes Sor Juana as an "intersexual" being: "una personalidad neurótica en la que predominan fuertes tendencias masculinas" [a neurotic personality in which strong masculine tendencies predominate].[8] As Emilie Bergmann notes, "Not surprisingly, among the first major studies on Sor Juana's work were those by men like Ludwig Pfandl, who explained her unique intellectual accomplishments as resulting from a biological aberration combined with a narcissistic fixation on her father: if she could not be denied her intellectual accomplishments, she must be denied her identity as a woman." [9] A more benign, but no less problematic, example is Octavio Paz's reading of Sor Juana's decision to enter the convent in order to avoid marriage:

> puesto que no quiere casarse, el convento es lo menos desproporcionado y lo más decente para asegurar su salvación. Lo proporcionado hubiera sido el matrimonio; lo indecente, la soltería en el mundo, que la hubiera expuesto, como dice Calleja, a ser pared blanca borroneada

por los hombres.... ¿Por qué esa negación al matrimonio? Pensar que ella sentía una clara aversión a los hombres y una igualmente clara afición a las mujeres es descabellado. Por una parte, en caso de que esa suposición fuese cierta, en esos años de extrema juventud no es fácil que ella tuviese conciencia de sus verdaderas inclinaciones; por la otra, salvo atribuyéndole un libertinaje mental más propio de una heroína de Diderot que de una muchacha novohispana de su edad y de su clase, podía ella fríamente escoger como refugio un establecimiento habitado exclusivamente por personas del sexo que, supuestamente la atraía. No.... Aparte de esta repugnancia a la vida hogareña ... es vano tratar de saber sus verdaderos sentimientos sexuales. Ella tampoco lo sabía.

[since she does not want to marry, the convent is the least unsuitable and most honorable way to ensure her salvation. The suitable way would have been marriage; the dishonorable, to live unmarried in the world, which, as Calleja says, would have exposed her to being the white wall fouled by men. . . . Why this antipathy to marriage? To think that she felt a clear aversion to men and an equally clear attraction to women is absurd. In the first place, because even if that supposition were true, it is not likely that while she was still so young she knew her true inclinations, in the second, because only by attributing to her an intellectual and sexual license more appropriate to a Diderot heroine than to a girl of Juana Inés's age and social class in New Spain could she cold-bloodedly have chosen as refuge an institution inhabited exclusively by persons of the sex that supposedly attracted her. No. . . . Apart from this distaste for a life of hearth and home . . . it is futile to try to learn what her true sexual feelings were. She herself did not know.] [10]

The passage is extraordinary not only for the way it reductively fills the provocative silence that Sor Juana inscribes in her *Respuesta* when she characterizes the convent as "lo menos desproporcionado" [the least unsuitable], or for the striking and disturbing metaphor of "white wall" it borrows from Calleja's autobiography of Sor Juana, but, moreover, for the anxiety with which it categorically precludes ("es descabellado" [it is absurd]) the possibility of reading a lesbian subtext in Sor Juana's "negación al matrimonio" [antipathy to marriage].

Although we should be careful to avoid reading the *Respuesta* strictly at face value, without taking into account its rhetoricity and questioning its value as "autobiographical" source,[11] the letter documents Sor Juana's early cross-dressing as a means of access to a world of masculine learning that would otherwise have remained inaccessible to her: "Empecé a matar a mi madre con instantes e inorportunos ruegos sobre que mudándome el traje, me enviase a Méjico, en casa de unos deudos que tenía, para estudiar y cursar la Universidad" [I began to deluge my mother with urgent and insistent pleas to change my manner of dress and send me to stay with relatives in the City of Mexico so that I might study and take courses at the university].[12] Sor Juana's cross-dressing might be understood as a refusal not so much to be gendered feminine as to be intellectually constrained as a result of the predominant reading of that gendering. She enlists gender illegibility as a powerful strategy of resistance. Paz reads Sor Juana's profession in similar terms, almost as a kind of transvestism that might provide the means for satisfying, or at least abating, her desire for knowledge, a desire that was deemed incommensurate with being a woman.[13]

Beyond her own real or spurious early cross-dressing as a means of gaining entry into otherwise prohibited intellectual spheres, however, there are repeated instances of gender crossings throughout Sor Juana's writing, moments that question strict gender binarisms and that are perhaps best seen as a striking appropriation of and contestation to the concept of mujer varonil that was so often applied to her authorial figuration. Her poetic masterpiece, *Primero sueño*, for example, manages to avoid, throughout 975 verses, any grammatical indication of the gender of the body whose soul undergoes the quasi-mystic flight to knowledge; not until the poem's very last word—its very last letter, even ("despierta" [awake])—is the female gender of that body revealed. It is almost as if Sor Juana quite purposely lets slip the feminine grammatical marker—the final *a*—when it can no longer curtail her intellectual flight.[14] A somewhat different version of a textual gender performance can be located in the passage of the "Autodefensa" [Self-Defense] I take as epigraph. Sor Juana records the way in which she was forced to disguise—and cross-dress, at the level of the letter's form—her "masculine" handwriting in order to make it conform to expectations of women's handwriting.

Perhaps the best poetic example of Sor Juana's penchant for questioning the stability of gender assignments can be found in the reading of her own body that she inscribes in "Romance 48: Respondiendo a un caballero del Perú, que le envío unos barros diciéndole que se volviese hombre" [In Reply to a Gentleman from Peru, Who Sent Her Clay Vessels While Suggesting She Would Better Be a Man]:

> Y en el consejo que dais,
> yo os prometo recibirle
> y hacerme fuerza, aunque juzgo
> que no hay fuerzas que entarquinen:
>
> porque acá Sálmacis falta,
> en cuyos cristales dicen
> que hay no sé qué virtud de
> dar alientos varoniles.
>
> Yo no entiendo de esas cosas;
> sólo sé que aquí me vine
> porque, si es que soy mujer,
> ninguno lo verifique.
>
> Y también sé que, en latín,
> sólo a las casadas dicen
> *uxor,* o mujer, y que
> es común de dos lo Virgen.
>
> Con que a mí no es bien mirado
> que como a mujer me miren,
> pues no soy mujer que a alguno
> de mujer pueda servirle;
>
> y sólo sé que mi cuerpo,
> sin que a uno u otro se incline,
> es neutro, o abstracto, cuanto
> sólo el Alma deposite.
>
> [As for the counsel that you offer,
> I promise you, I will attend

with all my strength, although I judge
no strength on earth can en-Tarquin:

for here we have no Salmacis,
whose crystal water, so they tell,
to nurture masculinity
possesses powers unexcelled.

I have no knowledge of these things,
except that I came to this place
so that, if true that I am female,
none substantiate that state.

I know, too, that they were wont
to call wife, or woman, in the Latin
uxor, only those who wed,
and that the Virgin is common to both.

So in my case, it is not seemly
that I be viewed as feminine,
as I will never be a woman
who may as wife serve a man.

I know only that my body,
not to either state inclined,
is neuter, abstract, guardian
of only what my Soul consigns.][15]

The poem is remarkable for the sexual ambiguity it exploits. Sor Juana dismisses her interlocutor's advice that she become a man not only by remitting to a New World landscape ("acá Sálmacis falta" [here we have no Salmacis]) that is powerless to effect Ovidian transformations, but also by arguing that her body is neither male nor female ("sin que a uno u otro se incline" [not to either state inclined]) but already somehow neutral: "mi cuerpo . . . es neutro, o abstracto" [my body . . . is neuter, abstract].[16]

That neutrality, she claims, is a function of her virginal state ("es común de dos lo Virgen" [the Virgin is common to both]), which operates in the poem as a kind of shifter, casting doubts on Sor Juana's very gender. Paz writes:

En el tercer verso atenúa y casi pone en duda su condición femenina ("si es que soy mujer") y en los finales la niega: siendo virgen, es doble. Estos versos muestran que no sólo se daba cuenta de su conflicto sino que para ella había cesado de serlo, resuelto por su profesión religiosa y por su platonismo. Tomó las órdenes para que ninguno "verificase" que era mujer; al no haberse casado y ser virgen, es "común de dos." Declara así que espiritualmente es andrógino. . . . La profesión religiosa ha neutralizado a su sexualidad y su cuerpo no se inclina ni a lo masculino ni a lo femenino.

In the third verse she diminishes and almost places in doubt her feminine condition ("if true that I am female") and in the final lines negates it: being virgin, she is of both genders. These verses show not only that she was aware of her conflict but that, resolved by her religious vows and her Platonism, it had ceased to be a conflict. She joined the order so that no one should "substantiate" that she was a woman; because she had not married and was virgin, her nature was still dual. She thus declares that spiritually she is an androgyne. . . . Her religious state has neutralized her sexuality, and her body is inclined toward neither the masculine nor the feminine.[17]

While Paz accurately reads the relation the poem expounds between virginity and a kind of spiritual androgyny, his insistent characterization of Juana's religious state as a "neutralization" of her sexuality is problematic, altogether eliding the affective life the convent offered many early modern women.

Beyond its ties to androgyny, however, what is most suggestive of the conception of virginity that informs the poem is its marked difference from the prevalent one in seventeenth-century Spain and America. Virginity is not, as in Covarrubias's emblem, that which once rent cannot be mended and, as a result, an infallibly legible sign but, on the contrary, that which categorically precludes reading: "es común de dos." Sor Juana turns the tables on the alignments we have been exploring — on the legibility of the virgin body and the illegibility of the wife's body. Here, the wife's body is clearly legible as a woman's body whereas the virgin's body fosters duplicity. Sor Juana turns to Latin lexicography to support her contention, arguing that in Latin the term *uxor* (woman) is reserved for *casadas*. Indeed, she represents her body (assuming the poetic I is hers) as a failed or unsuitable wife's body ("no soy mujer que a alguno de mujer pueda servirle" [I will never be a woman who may as wife serve a man]); the specific nature of this un-suitability, however, remains provocatively unstated. The convent — the "aquí" [this place] of the third quartet — is presented as a safe space that not only shelters the ambiguity of that body with respect to a binary sex code, but preserves its strategic illegibility ("porque . . . ninguno lo verifique" [so that . . . none substantiate that state]). A kind of self-imposed somatic illegibility, then, becomes a mode of resis-tance against readings that would make Sor Juana's body into that of a man, or even a perfect wife.

The Cross-Dressed Wife

Of all the gender fictions inscribed in Sor Juana's work, the most ex-plicit instance of cross-dressing is, without question, that performed by Castaño in the third act of *Los empeños de una casa*, a performance that invites reading his body as that of a would-be wife. Castaño's transvestite "passing" can be conceived not only in terms of its desta-bilization of notions of legibility and codes of interpretation but also as a rubric for the performativeness of gender, race, and class cate-gories. The particular terms of this destabilization point, moreover, to an intersection of somatic, interpretive, and cultural anxieties not unlike those I have traced throughout previous chapters. But if Sor Juana's play posits an interplay between the wife's body, the status of the sign, and the Other's body that raises some of the same questions posed by the Calderonian honor dramas, it is worth noting that the slippages between these areas are by no means identical. One impor-tant difference is that the Other's body behind the curtain of *Empeños* is not that of an illegible converso or Morisco, but, rather, of a New World Other, an American converso.

It is also worth noting that *Empeños* is not an honor drama in the strictest sense. The play does not satisfy the basic requirement of honor tragedies as stipulated by Wardropper: that the characters (and espe-cially the woman whose honor is in question throughout the course of

the play) already be married.[18] Had the real or imagined shared masculine desire for the two women protagonists been postnuptials, there
is little doubt that they would have been murdered by their respective husbands. Rather than end in the bloody death scene of the wife-
murder dramas, however, Sor Juana's play ends in multiple marriages,
conforming, in this sense, with the comedia's generic requirement for
the restoration of order. In the previous chapter, I argued for a reconsideration of the workings of honor in the wife-murder plays as a question of interpretation, and proposed a rethinking of the unstable signs
of adultery in these works as an adultery of signs. If, as I suggested,
the dangers of and for honor-drama wives derive in great measure
from their hymeneal illegibility with respect to sexual transgression,
the potential wives of *Empeños* should in theory be less of an enigma
to the men who guard their chastity. Although not an honor drama
per se, the question of honor remains a central concern throughout
Sor Juana's play, as does the possibility of accurately reading bodies.
If there are no actual wives' bodies to read in *Los empeños de una casa*
until the final scene of the play, at least four *potential* wives' bodies are
variously textualized throughout: Ana's, Leonor's, Celia's, and Castaño's. Similarly, if there is no husband-reader, each of the men in the
drama takes up the reader position with respect to the body of his
future bride.

It may be helpful at this point to briefly review the rather baroque
plot of Sor Juana's *comedia de enredos* (comedy of errors). The play
opens to discover Doña Ana waiting up for her brother, Don Pedro,
and gossiping with her servant Celia about her latest infatuation. After
having been courted for several years by Don Juan (and, moreover,
having responded to his attentions), she has decided, almost on a whim
("no sé si es gusto o capricho" [I don't know if this is whim or plea-
sure]), to make the handsome and gallant Don Carlos de Olmedo the
new object of her affections. She also recounts to Celia her brother's
escapades that evening. It seems, on that very night, the beautiful,
gifted, and noble Doña Leonor de Castro had planned to elope from
her house with her lover (whose identity Ana ignores) in order to force
Leonor's father to accept their marriage. But Pedro, who wants Leonor
for himself, having caught wind of the lovers' plot, has recruited a
group of men to pose as police officers in order to kidnap Leonor away

from her fiancé and secretly deposit her at his own house, in the hopes of eventually winning her heart and marrying her. Ana's narration is interrupted by the arrival at the house of one of Pedro's hired men, still masked, who, in accordance with Pedro's secret instructions, surrenders Leonor over to the custody and care of this allegedly unknown lady. Leonor, grateful for the mercy she credits Doña Ana with having shown her by taking her in from the street and thus salvaging what is left of her honor, discloses her identity and tells her unfortunate story. When, in the midst of her autobiographical narration, Leonor reveals that her fiancé is none other than Carlos de Olmedo, Ana finds her interest in the young man piqued by Leonor's praises. Carlos, in the meantime, has run into hiding after the scuffle, fearing he has killed one of Leonor's cousins who tried to impede the elopement in order to protect the family's honor. Assuming he is being followed by the police or by Leonor's family, Carlos knocks on the first door he comes to, seeking refuge for himself and his servant Castaño. That house, of course, is Doña Ana's, who is all too pleased to give Carlos shelter in the hopes of winning his affections, while keeping him out of sight of both her brother and Leonor. The situation is further complicated by the presence of Don Juan, who has bribed Celia to hide him in the house, in the hopes of rekindling his cooling romance with Ana.

What follows is enredo upon enredo, as triangles of amorous desire are figured and disfigured inside the walls of the house that becomes (for Leonor and Carlos, at least) a *prisión-encanto* (enchanted prison). Pedro tries to woo Leonor while his sister tries to woo Carlos. Juan, who inadvertently discovers Ana's infatuation for Carlos, comes dangerously close to playing the role of jealous husband and, mistaking Leonor for Ana, goes so far as to threaten her for her scorn. Despite Castaño's best advice, Carlos remains true to Leonor. His efforts to defend Ana's honor (which his presence in her house has endangered), however, incur Leonor's jealousy. Leonor's father, meanwhile, is told by Pedro's men that his daughter's fiancé and kidnapper on the night of the attempted elopement was Pedro, not Carlos; he offers to forgive all, suspending the death threat he has issued against his own daughter—if Leonor and Pedro wed. Although Leonor suspects Carlos of being unfaithful to her with Ana, she nevertheless refuses to accept

Pedro's repeated advances, vowing instead to enter a convent before marrying a man she does not love.

This, roughly, is the state of things when the cross-dressing scene occurs. In an attempt to make amends with Leonor's father by explaining what really took place on the night of the foiled elopement, Carlos asks Castaño to deliver the old man a note, asking for Leonor's hand in marriage. Suspecting that warrants are out for both his and his master's arrests and that he will be apprehended the moment he sets foot outside the house, Castaño decides his best bet is to disguise himself in the clothing that, on the night of her flight, Leonor had entrusted to him for safekeeping. Pedro, alerted by Celia that Leonor is trying to escape her confinement, mistakes a transvestite Castaño for Leonor and reiterates his marriage proposal. Castaño (as Leonor) accepts the proposal, unknowingly buying enough time for the real Leonor to escape the house, at least temporarily, and for the rest of the plot to unravel. In the end, Carlos and Leonor are reunited, as are, almost by default, Ana and Juan. Pedro, thinking he has secured a promise of marriage from Leonor, discovers that his future bride is really Castaño in drag. Having promised Castaño/Leonor not to punish "her" in any way if he, Pedro, and not "she," should call off the wedding, Pedro not only is left without a wife, but is unable to exact revenge. To tie things up, a picaresque marriage is negotiated (but not exactly contracted) between Celia and Castaño.

The "gender trouble" that Castaño's cross-dressing provokes is, quite clearly, central to the plot resolution; it is the turning point of the play. But if Castaño's transvestism is the most important instance of blurred gender boundaries in *Empeños*, it is by no means the only one. The title of Sor Juana's play can already be read as a kind of transvestism of the title of Calderón's 1650 comedia, *Empeños de un acaso*, with which it shares several plot features (though not, significantly, the transvestite performance). The wordplay Sor Juana mobilizes is suggestive, not only because of the feminization it presupposes, but also because the seemingly insignificant linguistic shift from the letter *o* to the letter *a* has, as I suggested in chapter 1, far-reaching semantic implications, pointing to the important role that the architectural and political space of the house will be accorded in her rewritten *Empeños* and suggesting the extent to which the category of the accidental is the ghost in the machine of the drama. The accident in Calderón ("un acaso" [a chance]) gives way to a domestic topography in Sor Juana ("una casa" [a house]). It may be argued that Sor Juana's *Empeños* most resembles in this another Calderonian play that similarly exploits the dramatic possibilities of the early modern analogy between the female body and the house that contains her: Calderón's 1629 *La dama duende*.[19]

A more explicit instance of blurred gender boundaries in the play can be found in Leonor's early description to Ana of Carlos's beauty in terms that hint at a potential androgyny in the *galán* (suitor):

> Era su rostro un enigma
> compuesto de dos contrarios
> que eran valor y hermosura,
> tan felizmente hermanados,
> que faltándole a lo hermoso
> la parte de afeminado,
> hallaba lo más perfecto
> en lo que estaba más falto. (ll. 407–14)

> [His face was an enigma,
> composed of two contradictions —
> valor and beauty —
> so fortuitously harmonized,
> that his beauty,
> lacking the effeminate part,
> found the greatest perfection
> in what it lacked the most.][20]

Leonor locates "lo más perfecto" [the greatest perfection] of Carlos's enigmatic face in an effeminate beauty that is, however, lacking. The confession not only reveals the sexually ambiguous quality of Carlos's gallantry but points also to a possible homoeroticism on Leonor's behalf: albeit absent, it is her lover's femininity that she finds most attractive. One might argue, in this same vein, that Ana and Leonor's shared desire for Carlos mediates a certain attraction between the two women.

If at this point in the play the question of homoeroticism is only latent, it will not remain so for long. Before turning to the scene of Castaño's transvestism, it is worth recalling that theatrical cross-dressing not only was nothing new to Golden Age drama by the time Sor Juana wrote her *Empeños* but was, in fact, a favorite dramatic device: "suele el disfraz varonil agradar mucho" [male disguise is usually very pleasing], according to Lope.[21] There are literally hundreds of early modern Spanish plays in which women dressed as men elicited same-sex desire from other women; Lope (particularly in his later dramas) and Tirso had already pushed the cross-dressing plot and the sexual confusions it provoked quite far in plays such as *El anzuelo de Fenisa* or *Don Gil de las calzas verdes*. But if the woman in man's clothing was a relatively frequent occurrence on the early modern Spanish stage, the counter-instance of a cross-dressed man was a much rarer and potentially much more transgressive gesture.[22] Offstage, transvestism, particularly male to female, was a dangerous enterprise in both Spain and its American colonies. As Mary Elizabeth Perry argues, "men who dressed or appeared too much like women were likely to be suspected of homosexual sodomy, a crime legally punishable by burning alive."[23] Perry cites as an example the homilectics of Father Francisco de León, who "preached with vigor against 'men converted into women' and 'effeminate soldiers, full of airs, long locks, and plumes.'"[24]

That there was considerable anxiety about the effeminacy—and hystericization—of male bodies and that this anxiety was in turn associated with theatrical representation can easily be adduced from sixteenth- and seventeenth-century reprobations of theater, censured not only for its lasciviousness but for the dangerous feminization it was said to effect on its male spectators, even when cross-dressing was not involved.[25] It can also be corroborated from the very presence of actresses on the early modern Spanish and Spanish-American stage, justified as the lesser of two evils, in order to prevent the feminization of boy actors that would ostensibly ensue from their playing women's roles, specifically, from their wearing women's attire. (The same edict that allowed female actresses stipulated, however, and in no uncertain terms, that these actresses must be *married* women.[26] Although for the most part ignored, this sort of legislation reinscribes, in a strikingly literal way, the notion of the wife's body as an apt space for staging certain types of conflicts.) The representation of cross-dressing onstage was not significantly less risky than cross-dressing offstage; at least insofar as the antitheatricalists were concerned, *any* form of transvestism—real or feigned—was deemed unnatural and constituted grounds for discipline. These, then, were the stakes with which Sor Juana contended.

The actual scene of Castaño's cross-dressing is framed, suggestively, by an invocation to Garatuza ("Martín de Villavicencio y Salazar, a quien unos llamaron Martín Lutero, fue el famoso *Garatuza*, pícaro célebre nacido hacia el 1600 en Puebla de los Angeles; recorrió muchas poblaciones de la Nueva España fingiéndose sacerdote para hacer fraudes, trampas y raterías" [Martín de Villavicencio y Salazar, whom some called Martin Luther, was the famous *Garatuza*, the celebrated rogue born around 1600 in Puebla de los Angeles; he traveled through many towns of New Spain, pretending to be a priest in order to swindle, cheat, and steal]).[27]

> ¡Quién fuera aquí Garatuza,
> de quien las Indias cuentan
> que hacía muchos prodigios!
> Que yo, como nací en ellas,
> le he sido siempre devoto
> como a santo de mi tierra.
> ¡Oh tú, cualquiera que has sido;
> oh tú, cualquiera que seas,
> bien esgrimas abanico,
> o bien arrastres contera,
> inspírame alguna traza
> que de Calderón parezca,
> con que salir de este empeño! (ll. 2384–96)

> [Would that I were Garatuza,
> who, it is said in the Indies,
> performed many miracles!
> And I, since I was born there,
> have always worshipped him
> as the saint of my homeland.
> Oh Garatuza, whoever you have been;

whoever you may be,
whether you wield a fan
or drag the tip of your sword,
inspire me to find a scheme
worthy of Calderón
to escape these trials!]

The description of the New World pícaro Garatuza, whose own gender markings were in a state of flux ("bien esgrimas abanico o bien
arrastres contera" [whether you wield a fan or drag the tip of your
sword]), as a "saint" not only of Castaño's devotion but, more importantly, of his "homeland" is not incidental. On one hand, it openly
inscribes Castaño's Americanness (not entirely clear until this moment
given that the action of the play occurs in Toledo). The fact that the
servant Castaño was born in the Indies and that his name quite likely
refers to his dark skin color posits a compelling reading of the fluidi-
ties between the discourses of race and gender in the play, particularly
since the gracioso's status as racial Other is made explicit at the very
moment he decides to cross-dress. Among the suggestive questions
this raises is whether the actor who played Castaño in the play's earliest performances was either visually marked as or in reality "moreno"
[dark-skinned].

On the other hand, the *traȝa* (scheme) Sor Juana's gracioso prays for
is not just any, but, specifically, a metatheatrical one "que de Calderón parezca" [worthy of Calderón]. Castaño's longing to imitate "the
master" (within a play whose title quite clearly remits to Calderón) indelibly marks him as a Calderonian reader or, more likely, spectator—
a theatrical, American version of Alonso Quijano, perhaps, a playgoer
who has seen one too many comedias. It also corroborates the suspicion that the cross-dressed American gracioso who can't quite pass
off as "perfect wife" is Sor Juana's best double: both playwright and
character model themselves on Calderón. If Leonor is, in a sense, Sor
Juana's alter ego (where "Sor Juana" is a version of, but not necessarily identical to, Sor Juana) and Castaño in drag is a theatricalized
Leonor, then Castaño becomes, through the workings of the transi-
tive property, another "Sor Juana." The fact that the real Garatuza was
eventually condemned by the Inquisition for self-fashioning himself

through his disguises into something other than what he really was and, more specifically, for cross-dressing as a man of the cloth is by no means insignificant, particularly if Sor Juana's own "habit" (what makes her body legible as that of a nun) is conceived as a kind of transvestite disguise, along the lines of what Paz suggests. Albeit on a very different register from Garatuza, Sor Juana, too, would be persecuted by representatives of the church for self-fashioning herself into something (a woman writer and an intellectual) other than what she was supposed to be, according to the patriarchal reading: a perfect bride of Christ.

Beyond its metatheatrical resonances, however, what is perhaps most remarkable about Castaño's cross-dressing is the absolute explicitness with which it is rendered; the transformation from gracioso servant to would-be wife not only occurs on the space of representation, but is narrated in detail by the subject-object of transformation *as* it is enacted onstage. The conversion takes place in and through language and performance. The gesture, which reveals, quite literally, the seams of Castaño's transvestite disguise, is paradigmatically baroque. I cite the passage at length:

> Lo primero, aprisionar
> me conviene la melena,
> porque quitará mil vidas
> si le doy tantica suelta.
> Con este paño pretendo
> abrigarme la mollera;
> si como quiero la pongo,
> será gloria ver mi pena.
> Ahora entran las basquiñas.
> ¡Jesús, y qué rica tela!
> No hay duda que me esté bien,
> porque como soy *morena*
> me está del cielo lo azul.
> ¿Y esto qué es? Joyas son éstas;
> no me las quiero poner,
> que ahora voy de revuelta.
> Un serenero he topado

en aquesta faltriquera;
también me le he de plantar
¿Cabráme esta pechuguera?
El solimán me hace falta;
pluguiese a Dios y le hubiera,
que una manica de gato
sin duda me la pusiera;
pero no, que es un ingrato,
y luego en cara me diera.
La color no me hace al caso,
que en este empeño de fuerza
me han de salir mil colores
por ser dama de vergüenza. (ll. 2410–39, italics mine)

[First, I'll have to
tie up my long hair,
because a thousand lives will be lost
if I leave it a bit undone.
With this cloth I intend
to wrap up the top of my head;
if I put it on the way I want,
the delight will be worth the effort.
Now for the skirts.
Good heavens, what a fine cloth!
There's no doubt it looks good on me,
because, since I'm *dark-skinned*,
I look heavenly in blue.
And what's this? They're jewels;
I don't want to put them on
because now I'm off to scuffle.
I've found a scarf
in this sack;
I'll have to put it on too.
Will this bra fit me?
I need makeup;
Lord let there be some,
for just one brush of the hand

would no doubt put it on;
but no, that would be disagreeable,
for soon enough my face would blush.
There's no need for color,
for in this trial,
I'll be forced to blush plenty,
being a woman with a sense of shame.]

The direct relation between Castaño's transformation into an imperfect version of Leonor and the women's garments s/he dons suggests the extent to which the gender code is exposed not just as an abstract, cultural construct but as a material one as well: it is, after all, the assembled pieces of Castaño's dress that will be read by Pedro as signs of "woman." Materiality here does not imply, however, any kind of grounding or depth. Quite the contrary, it betrays the superficiality of the assignment of gender — it's all in the packaging, in the performance — disarming, in this way, one of the most basic binarisms that bolster codes of signification. The same, of course, applies to the linguistic markers of gender: Castaño easily becomes a moren*a* perpetrating a shift at the material level of the sign and specifically the letter (almost along the lines of what Fray Luis describes in *De los nombres de Cristo*) in order to reflect an accident in the referent to which the mutable sign corresponds. But like the shift from *o* to *a*, the accident at the level of the referent (in this case gender) is purely superficial, not because some deeper essence remains untouched but, rather, because gender itself — and its reading — proves to be an accidental and not an essential quality. All is in check here: male and female are revealed as surface inscriptions that can be put on and off as easily as an article of clothing or a final letter *a*.

Castaño goes so far in his travesty as to directly address the women in the audience, breaking yet another boundary, this time the one that establishes a distance between the action onstage and the spectators offstage and that is a basic postulate of almost any contract of dramatic representation.

¿Qué les parece, señoras,
este encaje de ballena?
Ni puesta con sacristanes

pudiera estar más bien puesta.
Es cierto que *estoy hermosa*.
¡Dios me guarde, que *estoy bella!*
Cualquier cosa me está bien
porque el molde es rara pieza.
Quiero acabar de aliñarme,
que aún no *estoy dama perfecta*. (ll. 2440–49, italics mine)

[What do you think, ladies,
of this whalebone corset?
Not even with petticoats
could it fit any better.
It's true that *I'm lovely*.
Lord help me, *I'm beautiful!*
Anything looks good on me,
because the model is a rare kind.
I want to finish tidying up
because *I'm* not *a perfect lady* yet.]

Castaño's incursion points to his consciousness as character of the double sense of performativeness with which his transvestism is charged· it is not just a drag performance, or a performance onstage, but the (theatrical) performance of a (gender) performance and vice versa. The continued use of the feminine adjective ("hermosa," "bella," "dama perfecta") together with the use of the locative "estar" instead of the copula "ser" reinforce the gracioso's conception of gender as a changeable, impermanent condition. It points also to the radical relativism of perfection, insofar as being a dama is concerned.

But the address to the "real" damas in the audience does not end here; Castaño calls on them a few verses later in an attempt to excuse himself for the transgressiveness that his public, cross-dressed performance represents.

Dama habrá en el auditorio
que diga a su compañera:
"Mariquita, aqueste bobo
al Tapado representa."
Pues atención, mis señoras,

que es paso de la comedia;
no piensen que son embustes
fraguados acá en mi idea,
que yo no quiero engañarlas,
ni menos a Vuexcelencia.
(ll. 2468–77)

[A lady in the audience
will say to her friend:
"Mariquita, this fool
is playing *el Tapado*."
But remember, ladies,
that it's part of the comedy;
don't think that concocting
tricks is my intention here,
for I don't wish to deceive you,
especially not Your Excellency.]

The allusion to "el Tapado" refers to the criminal trial that sharply divided Mexico City in 1683. Another New World pícaro, Don Antonio de Benavides, Marqués de Vicente, alias el Tapado, arrived in New Spain shortly after the sacking of Vera Cruz, allegedly as a royal *visitador* (inspector). Irving Leonard summarizes his case as follows:

The judges of the Audiencia and other viceregal officials, possibly fearing that they would be held responsible for the recent disaster [the sacking] and profiting by the emotional tensions prevailing, chose to regard the newcomer as an imposter. When the latter came to Puebla he was arrested and brought in custody to the capital. Public opinion was sharply divided, some condemning the apparently highhanded imprisonment of the king's representative, and others defending the viceroy's action. The trial of *el Tapado* . . . began on June 10, and the population followed its proceedings with eager interest. The effort to wring a confession by judicial torture brought attempted suicide, and feeling ran high during the remainder of 1683. Conservative elements, fearing a threat to their property, believed that the Hooded Man was an agent of the pirates, or that he was bent on inciting revolution in the realm; the more liberal minded espoused his cause and eloquently pleaded for his release.[28]

Among those who called for his acquittal was Sor Juana herself, in a poem dedicated to the viceroy's son on the occasion of his first birthday, but really addressed to his father.

> Y pues es el fausto día
> que se cumple el año vuestro,
> de dar perdón al convicto
> y dar libertad al preso,
>
> dad la vida a Benavides,
> que aunque sus delitos veo,
> tiene parces vuestro día
> para mayores excesos.
>
> A no haber qué perdonar,
> la piedad que ostenta el Cielo
> ocioso atributo fuera,
> o impracticable a lo menos.
>
> [And since it is the happy day,
> to celebrate your first birthday,
> to pardon the convict
> and free the captive,
>
> give Benavides his life
> because, although I see his crimes,
> your day has mercies
> for even greater excesses.
>
> If there were nothing to forgive,
> the mercy that Heaven bestows
> would be a superfluous attribute
> or, in the least, impracticable.][29]

Sor Juana's entreaties, however, like those of other public figures and intellectuals, proved futile; Benavides was hanged in 1684, only months after *Empeños* was staged.

By inscribing in the drama a second nonfictional figure who had allegedly pretended to be something he was not by means of forgeries and disguises, the allusion to el Tapado betrays the tenuousness of the line between transvestism (in the broadest sense of the word) on- and offstage. But invoking Benavides's case sets a dangerous precedent of (punishable) engaño from which Castaño feels compelled to distance himself. He renounces any admission of authorial guilt by immediately remitting to a cross-dressing tradition in the theater ("es paso de la comedia" [it's part of the comedy]), exposing, in the process, his own status as fictional character. Given that the excusatio is also addressed to the external authority figure ("Vuexcelencia") in whose honor the drama was staged (the new archbishop, Francisco de Aguiar y Seijas, who would play a leading role in the controversies leading to Sor Juana's eventual silence), one wonders whether Sor Juana (who can easily be aligned, as I have argued, with Castaño) may have been encoding in her gracioso's words a kind of apologia for her own authorial transgressiveness in having one of her characters openly cross-dress on stage.

It is important to note that if Castaño's drag performance is potentially transgressive (as both he and Sor Juana seem to have understood it to be), there is neither a necessary nor a direct relation between cross-dressing and the subversion of traditional gender binarisms. Rather, as Judith Butler has argued, "drag may well be used in the service of *both* the denaturalization and reidealization of hyperbolic heterosexual gender norms." [30] But if through this sort of reidealization transvestism can be construed as a potentially misogynist gesture (the argument being that a man usurps a woman's place in order to act out a degrading masculine construction of her), the gender bending that Castaño mobilizes tends, instead, toward the kind of denaturalization of gender norms that Butler records.

> Ya estoy armado, y ¿quién duda
> que en el punto que me vean
> me sigan cuatro mil lindos
> de aquestos que galantean
> a salga lo que saliere,
> y que a bulto se amartelan,
> *no de la belleza que es,*

sino de la que ellos piensan?
(ll. 2478–85, italics mine)

[Now I'm armed, and who doubts
that the moment they see me,
four thousand handsomes,
of the kind that court
come what may,
fall in love straight away,
not with the beauty that exists,
but with that which they imagine?]

The substitution of "vestido" [dressed] for "armado" [armed, as-
sembled] not only points to the extreme constructedness of Castaño's
gender performance but hints at a militarist undertone. ("Armar,"
writes Covarrubias, "vale apercibir las armas necesarias para no ser
ofendido de los enemigos y poderles acometer y hazer rostro" [*Armar*
("to arm") means to furnish the necessary weapons in order to not be
hurt by enemies and to be able to attack them and put up a fight].) [31] If
the play in fact draws some sort of gender battlelines, the gracioso's
allegiance seems to be squarely with the women whose clothes he borrows. Very much in the spirit of Sor Juana's "Hombres necios," Castaño
parodies the stereotypical, masculine version of what feminine beauty
should be, exposing the economy of desire that underwrites it as an
arbitrary construct, shakily founded not even on appearances themselves ("la belleza que es" [the beauty that exists]), but on the baroque
appearance of an appearance ("la que ellos piensan" [that which they
imagine]).

Tellingly, the only discrepancy Pedro perceives between the real
Leonor and Castaño in drag is neither gender driven (the visual signs
of masculinity beneath the feminine disguise) nor racially driven (Castaño is a morena, Leonor presumably not) but, rather, a function of
her/his "palabras necias" [foolish words].

¿Qué palabras son éstas,
y qué estilo tan ajeno
del ingenio y la belleza
de doña Leonor?

.   .   .   .   .   .

¿Posible es, Cielos, que aquéstas
son palabras de Leonor?
¡Vive Dios, que pienso que ella
se finge necia por ver
si con esto me despecha
y me dejo de casar!
¡Cielos, que así me aborrezca;
y que conociendo aquesto
esté mi pasión tan ciega
que no pueda reducirse!
(ll. 2559–62, 2593–2602)

[What words are these,
and what manner so unlike
the talent and beauty
of Doña Leonor?

.   .   .   .   .   .

Good heavens, is it possible
that these are Leonor's words?
My Lord, I think she's
playing the fool to see
if this will anger me enough
so I decide not to marry!
Heavens, how she loathes me;
and knowing that,
might my passion be so blind
that it cannot be diminished!]

Perhaps Pedro is not such a misreader in the end. He concurs with
Sor Juana, after all, in according an unsexed intellect precedence over
other qualities in the determination of identity.

The exchange between Castaño (as Leonor) and Pedro contains
what are unquestionably the most humorous and suggestive moments
in the entire play.

Castaño
Don Pedro, yo soy mujer

que sé bien dónde me aprieta
el zapato, y pues ya he visto
que dura vuestra fineza
a pesar de mis desaires,
yo quiero dar una vuelta
y mudarme al otro lado,
siendo aquesta noche mesma
vuestra esposa.

Don Pedro
        ¿Qué decís,
señora?

Castaño
        Que seré vuestra
como dos y dos son cuatro.

.   .   .   .

Don Pedro
mas, señora, ¿habláis de veras
o me entretenéis la vida?

Castaño
¿Pues soy yo farandulera?
Palabra os doy de casarme,
si ya no es que por vos queda.
(ll. 2614–24, 2637–41)

[*Castaño*
Don Pedro, I'm a woman
who knows where the shoe
pinches; and since I've seen
that your wooing will bear
the weight of my insults,
I want to turn about
and switch sides.
This very night, I
will be your wife.

Don Pedro
What did you say, Señora?

Castaño
That I'll be yours
as sure as two and two are four.

. . . .

Don Pedro
But, Señora, are you telling the truth
or toying with my life?

Castaño
Do you think I'm a comedienne?
You have my word that I'll marry you,
unless you don't want it.]

We should not be too hasty, however, to dismiss Pedro's same-sex desire for a cross-dressed Castaño as mere levity. Although the interchange is clearly meant to evoke laughter and even ridicule, it is also one of the most transgressive moments in the play.

Questions raised by the formalist-historicist debate over cross-dressing on the Shakespearean stage (specifically, about whether the theatrical convention of boys' playing women's parts was so widely accepted and even naturalized that boys were viewed by playgoers as women, therefore making discussions of same-sex desire beside the point, as the formalist camp contends, or whether, as the materialist-historicists argue, the gender of the boys in drag did have significance to the text represented) become irrelevant in the case of Castaño's cross-dressing.[32] This is not only because anxieties over effeminacy barred boys from playing the roles of women in early modern Spanish and, by extension, Spanish-American theater, as we have seen, but, more pertinently, because the cross-dressing in *Los empeños de una casa* is explicitly staged within the time and space of the dramatic representation (and not in a dressing room before the play begins or off-stage, between acts.) My point, then, is that it is almost impossible to overlook the same-sex desire that colors the exchange between Pedro and Castaño.[33] A marriage is negotiated, after all, between two "men." As I argued in the case of Calderón's Gutierre, I do not mean to suggest by this that Pedro is a closeted homosexual but, rather, that he temporarily occupies what could be conceived as a homoerotic position of desire, a position no longer mediated (as it is in the honor plays)

by a voyeuristic desire on the part of the husband to see himself penetrated through his wife's body but, rather, that renders visible and audible his desire for another male body (Castaño's). If, as Valerie Traub
contends, "the boy actor works in specific Shakespearean comedies
as a basis upon which homoeroticism can be safely explored — work-
ing for both actors and audiences as an expression of non-hegemonic
desire within the confines of conventional comedic restraints," the absence of boy actors playing women's roles on the early modern Spanish and Spanish-American stage makes the dramatic exploration of
homoerotic desire a much more dangerous undertaking.[34]

If it becomes impossible, then, *not* to read Castaño's gender bending and the same-sex desire it elicits as threatening, at some level, to
the stability of a heterosexual code of desire and binary signification,
that threat is perhaps at least partly averted by the very fluidity of gender that enables it in the first place. In other words, if with Sor Juana
we imagine not only gender but also sex as a superficial inscription
that does not go beyond its performance or remit to an unconstructed
natural given, then we should not read Castaño's cross-dressed body
as that of a man in feminine drag but, rather, as something else: if not
exactly a woman, then nevertheless a perfectly legitimate wife.[35] This
suggestion does not so much foreclose the play's homoerotic subtext
as it pluralizes its erotic economy: the drama's mode of desire is not
exclusively homoerotic or heterosexual, but both.

One could argue that the comedy's requisite monogamous, heterosexual marriage closure effectively contains any subversion of gender
that Castaño's transvestism mobilizes. In the end, the original pairs
of lovers are recast: Leonor will wed Carlos, and Ana, Juan.[36] Pedro's
complete disavowal of his erotic desire for Castaño, at the moment
s/he sheds her womanly garments, would seem to support the containment and regulation of an ambivalent economy of desire.

> *Don Pedro*
> ¿Pues quién eres tú, portento,
> que por Leonor te he tenido?
>
> *Castaño*
> No soy sino el perro muerto
> de que se hicieron los guantes.

.   .   .   .

Don Pedro
¡Mataréte, vive el cielo!

Castaño
¿Por qué? Si cuando te di
palabra de casamiento,
que ahora estoy llano a cumplirte,
quedamos en un concierto
de que si por ti quedaba
no me harías mal. . . .

.   .   .   .

Don Pedro
(Tan corrido ¡vive el Cielo!
de lo que me ha sucedido
estoy, que ni a hablar acierto;
mas *disimular* importa,
que ya no tiene remedio
el caso). Yo doy por bien
la burla que se me ha hecho,
porque se case mi hermana
con don Juan.
(ll. 3305–8, 3311–17, 3345–53, italics mine)

[*Don Pedro*
Then who are you, beautiful,
whom I took for Leonor?

Castaño
I'm just the dead dog
from whom the gloves were made.

.   .   .   .

Don Pedro
By God, I'll kill you!

Castaño
Why? When I gave you
my word of marriage,
that I'm now eager to make good on,

we made an agreement
that if you were the one to call it off,
you wouldn't hurt me. . . .

. . . .

Don Pedro
(My God! I'm so embarrassed
by what has happened to me
that I can't even speak;
but it's important to *conceal*
my humiliation because I can do
nothing now.) I'll accept
the joke that's been played on me,
so long as my sister marries
Don Juan.]

But if the subversion of gender codes effected by Castaño's cross-dressing (and Pedro's desire for him/her) is neutralized or somehow disciplined by Pedro's threats of physical harm to Castaño when his/her "true" sexual identity is revealed and, more importantly, by the marriage closure required by the comic form, it is far more compelling to attend to the various means by which that containment fails, to the displacements and the ambivalences that are not entirely resolved when the final curtain falls.[37]

Although the threat of bodily punishment to Castaño ("Mataréte" [I'll kill you]) would seem to suggest Pedro's repulsion at his former desire for another male body, one could argue that the anxiety that the discovery of Castaño's on-again, off-again femininity elicits in him is but the reverse side of the same coin of erotic desire that prompted his marriage proposal in the first place. Desire and anxiety, as we have seen, always go hand in hand. What is more, the Hymen (and in this case triple marriage) closure, synonymous with the restoration of both honor and order, is possible only because Castaño's transvestism solved, momentarily, the gender imbalance in the play. The arithmetic is fairly straightforward: there are three galanes and only two damas. Castaño as (a second) Leonor provides, temporarily, the extra wife's body required so that the various overlapping triangles of desire

(Pedro-Leonor-Carlos, Juan-Ana-Carlos, and even Leonor-Carlos-Ana) can give way to binary symmetries (Leonor-Carlos, Ana-Juan, and, most importantly, Pedro–Castaño as Leonor). But, as Emilie Bergmann has compellingly argued, "*Los empeños de una casa* departs from the norm of *comedia* plots in which intellectual women are subdued through marriage.... Leonor's marriage to a man *she has chosen* is *both* a concession to comic convention—the only ending possible for a work belonging to such a public genre as theater—and a symbolic resolution to the problem of female autonomy." [38] The marriage reconfigurations exceed, then, the dominant heterosexual ideology. The drama ends, after all, with Castaño still partly in drag; the fact that at the end of the play Pedro remains unmarried confirms the ambiguity of the final Hymen closure. At one level, his bachelorhood can be understood as an almost formulaic "punishment" for his authorial transgression in having attempted to interrupt true comedia love by dramatizing a script of his own writing. More provocatively, however, Pedro's status as fifth wheel and his expressed need to "disimular" [conceal] suggests the irreconcilability of his desire (metonymically displaced from Leonor onto Castaño) with institutional sanction. Somewhat ironically, it is the galán destined for perpetual bachelorhood—and not one of the future husbands—who carries out the central reading of a "wife's body" in *Los empeños de una casa*. But—to return to the way in which Sor Juana rewrites and even parodies the traditional honor script—there is a crucial distinction between Pedro's misreadings and those of a Calderonian husband like Gutierre. Gutierre's misreading of his wife's body—which, I have suggested, inscribes Calderón's critique of inquisitorial practices—results in the play's final tragedy. It is, in fact, the grisliness of the tragedy that encodes the critique. By contrast, Pedro's misreading of the body that he comes closest to marrying—Castaño's—is an enabling condition for the casa to become *des-empeñada*.

Illegibility in—and also for—Sor Juana is not so much a source of epistemologic anxiety, then, as it is a kind of refuge, analogous in many respects with the refuge she sought to find in the convent ("sólo sé que aquí me vine"). She makes her imperfect wife's body subject, no longer object, of misreading, strategically appropriating somatic illegibility in order to empty it of its punitive content and charge it otherwise. Gender illegibility in particular is mobilized throughout Sor Juana's text as a mode of resistance, a subtle but striking *treta del débil* (trick of the weak) that empowers a body-text that resists, at all costs, being read as a perfecta casada.[39]

Castaño at Home: *American Terrains*

Throughout this chapter I have concerned myself with reading Castaño's transvestite, American body as that of an imperfect wife and with uncovering the instabilities and indeed the fluidity of gender and racial discourses on which such a reading is founded. But there are a number of other promising directions in which Castaño's body or, more generally, wives' bodies might lead us in a New World context. The trajectories I outline in the next several paragraphs are by no means exhaustive; I cite them only to provisionally mark an American terrain of and for the sorts of readings that *Perfect Wives, Other Women* engages. One obvious direction would be to follow Castaño's eastward trajectory from America to Spain, to reread, in other words, *La perfecta casada* and *El médico de su honra* not just before but in a sense after or alongside *Los empeños de una casa* and the particular histori cal — and colonial — context it inscribes. Such a reading would follow Mary Gaylord's valuable suggestion of "rereading canonical texts of what we have been used to calling Spain's Golden Age in the light of their historical two-world contexts." [40] An equally productive direction would be to consider possible analogies between colonialism and marriage, between "patrimony" and "matrimony," [41] or, more specifically, between the body of the wife and the body of the subordinated, colonial Other. This is precisely the direction proposed by James D. Fernández in his provocative "New World reading" of Cervantes's "El celoso extremeño" as "a complex investigation of the issues of freedom, subjection, seduction and resistance in matrimony and other relationships of subordination." [42]

A slightly different version of that same project might plot the intersection of the discourses of race and gender that is staged on Castaño's cross-dressed, Mexican body alongside other, more sinister such crossings. The work of Stephen Greenblatt, Louis Montrose, José Rabasa, and Margarita Zamora, among others, on the eroticization of New World landscapes or on the feminization and even hystericization of Amerindian bodies would be indispensable here, as would Jonathan Goldberg's work on the identification of Moors and natives as sodomites.[43] Representations of New World cannibalism but also of the "noble savage" (even projects as seemingly benign as Las Casas's) take on entirely different connotations in this light, none of them particularly favorable. As Juliana Schiesari convincingly argues, "domestication of the private sphere and imperialism abroad are cojoined in the early modern period by ideological practices that sought to restrict and dominate the various constructed others of European manhood: the feminine, the savage, the bestial." [44] There are, in fact, a number of suggestive and disturbing implications that come from reading alignments of this sort, the most glaring for us, perhaps, that in imperial Spain gendered constructions of New World Others served political and ideological purposes not vastly different from the uses to which gendered constructions of Old World Others had been submitted. Or, to frame the issue in terms more familiar to the argument of *Perfect Wives*, we might claim that the same sorts of transcodifications and displacements that obtain between the body of the wife and the body of a Morisco or converso Other in early modern Spain also obtain— if on different terms—between the body of the wife and the body of an American Other.

This being the case, a corollary project and yet another direction in which the cross-dressed Castaño might lead us would consist of examining the problem of containment, considered throughout this book with respect primarily to the bodies of wives and, indirectly, to those of converso or Morisco Others, regarding, instead, the bodies of New World Others. A good place to begin this sort of investigation would be early modern catechisms used for the conversion of natives, another textual site where subjectivity and surveillance suggestively — and problematically — intersect. The questions surrounding conversion and, specifically, the literalization of different types of conversion sacraments (marital, eucharistic, baptismal) posed in the first chapter of this study could thus be productively opened up to the practice of conversion in the New World, a practice that might be understood as the colonizing of an interior space, the disciplining of (different forms of) desire. Vicente Rafael's work on the process of conversion in the Philippines (and the manuals used for those ends) would be quite useful here; we might ask (evoking Mencía's "ya ni para sentir soy mía") whether the forms of appropriation that Rafael persuasively describes as inherent to the processes of both conversion and conquest might also be inherent to a certain understanding of marriage in the early modern period. He states: "Conversion, like conquest, can thus be a process of crossing over into the domain — territorial, emotional, religious or cultural — of someone else and claiming it as one's own. Such a claim can entail not only the annexation of the other's possessions but, equally significant, the restructuring of his or her desires as well." [45]

Still another alternative would be to position Castaño's (or Sor Juana's) transvestism not only alongside those of a Garatuza or el Tapado but also alongside that of a Catalina de Erauso, whose gender fictions did more than raise a few nervous eyebrows in both the Old World and the New. We might read the cross-dressing of the *monja alférez* not only as a challenge to operative gender norms, but also in terms of broader relations of power and resistance (colonial and otherwise). We might cull Sor Juana's text for similar instances.

A different but no less promising direction for future study would be to consider the material practice of marriage in the New World, particularly, the question of mixed marriages between Spanish men and native women, and the extent to which (and the reasons for which) these unions were institutionally sanctioned by state or church. We might profitably read the baroque caste taxonomies and pigmentocracies that burgeoned in colonial Spanish America against the limpieza de sangre statutes that were so heavy-handedly implemented on the other side of the Atlantic. Alternately, we might examine how those very statutes (and the socioeconomic anxieties that fueled them) crossed over from the Old World to the New, how the Jewish and Moorish "problems" were dealt with on American soil, and how the question of marriage was brought to bear on the matter. This brings us to a different version of a question that has haunted this project all along: the institutional presence of the Inquisition, but now in its American incarnation. Recent scholarship suggesting that the so-called Indian Inquisition was more active in prosecuting nonorthodox beliefs and practices than previously thought might lead us to reevaluate the terms of the relation *Perfect Wives* proposes between the body of the wife and the body of the racial Other.[46] Indeed, the very concept of racial Other would need to be carefully defined in a New World inquisitorial context (and not just in its possible relation to the othering of wives' bodies) since the ready supply of Amerindian bodies—and souls—that the Indian Inquisition examined and disciplined in no way implied that the bodies and souls of Spain's Old World Others (suspected crypto-Jews or crypto-Muslims) were not read for signs of accusatory difference in the Americas. On the contrary, they were, as vehemently as they had been in Spain itself.

Conclusion

"Como anillo al dedo"

If *Empeños de una casa* takes up, in its way, the story of the illegibility of the wife's body that *Perfect Wives, Other Women* recounts, it also tells a very different story. One could argue, in fact, that a reading of Sor Juana's play does not fit here "como anillo al dedo" [as a ring on a finger], to borrow Sancho Panza's words, that it does not perfect—complete—the readings of the textual wives of Luis de León and Calderón de la Barca. Neither conduct manual nor honor play, *Empeños* offers no prescriptions—textual or medical—for perfecting the wife's body but, rather, flaunts its seductive imperfections. Womanly perfection can only be conjugated by the verb "estar" ("estoy dama perfecta") in Sor Juana's text; like gender itself, it is contingent, accidental—a positioned form of "being." Illegibility in the play is not so much a source of anxiety (as in *La perfecta casada*) or a pretext for punishment (as in *El médico de su honra*) as it is a necessary condition for its plural erotic economies. What is more, the same illegibility that in Fray Luis and Calderón revolves around the question of adultery is deliberately transposed in Sor Juana's drama onto categories of gender and race. Perhaps most notably, it is difficult to locate in the play the inquisitorial subtexts that, I have argued, make *La perfecta casada* and *El médico de su honra* much more defiant and contestatory works than has previously been imagined. If *Empeños* contains traces of Sor Juana's past run-ins with institutional power in New Spain (or hints of future ones), those traces, those hints, are subtle at best.

But if the same tensions that make the wife's body such a compelling site for reading various forms of anxiety in early modern Spain are either absent from or figure very differently in colonial Mexico (or in Sor Juana's text), there is no question that Sor Juana is a worthy and even complicitous interlocutor to Fray Luis and Calderón. From its opening scene to its very last, *Los empeños de una casa* repeatedly reveals the inherent instabilities of the various sorts of binarisms that inhabit the honor code (male/female, blanca/morena, indeed, perfect wife/other woman) and, by extension, of any binarism that purports to demarcate Otherness (racial, religious, imperial, etc). This is perhaps nowhere better seen than in the play's closing moments: with Castaño still in drag asking Celia for her hand—suggesting a marriage between two women—only seconds after a marriage between two men has been abruptly called off under threat of violence. One might argue that it is here, in this final ambivalence, that *Los empeños de una casa* best "completes"—best reads—*La perfecta casada* and *El médico de su honra*. The endings of Fray Luis's treatise and Calderón's play are, as we have seen, equally complex and problematic. I would like to close *Perfect Wives* by reexamining these imperfect closings and, specifically, by tracking the movements of a hand that conspicuously crops up at the end of all three works.[1]

It should perhaps not surprise us to discover the presence of hands at the end of three texts that so crucially turn on the question of matrimony. In early modern Spain and America—as throughout Europe—the giving of the hand was considered an essential (and not accidental) component of the marriage ritual, as Covarrubias attests: "Darse las manos, es señal de amistad, y entre los desposados, cerimonia esencial" [The giving of hands is a sign of friendship, and between those who are to be wed, an essential ceremony].[2] The wife's hand given at the end of *La perfecta casada* is not the hand given in marriage per se, but the hand of Proverbs 31:31 that Fray Luis glosses in the treatise's final chapter: "Dadle del fruto de sus manos; y lóenla en las puertas de sus obras" [Give her a share in the fruit of her hands, and let her works tell her praises at the city gates]. It is, significantly, a hand that is given over to labor, that is valued for—and in a sense remunerated by—its own production value. Consistent with the economic subtext that informs the treatise, the perfect wife is praised for the fruit of her hands—her handiwork—and not that of her womb. Radically different in tenor if not perhaps in form, the giving of Leonor's hand to Gutierre in the final scene of *El médico de su honra* represents a disquieting ending to a disquieting play. But their marriage, sanctioned by the king, does not violate convention for an honor drama; on the contrary, the giving of Leonor's hand immediately following the macabre perfecting of Mencía's body reinvests honor with (or in) a wife's body that is sentenced to be read for symptoms of otherness. The marriage closure at the end of a comedia de enredos like *Los empeños de una casa* was not only expected, but anything less would have constituted an intolerable generic breach. The marriages of Leonor to Carlos and of Ana to Juan conform, on the surface, with the dramatic formula for restoring order (it, too, is "paso de la comedia") even as we are left with the suspicion that either of these women could easily meet Mencía's fate, that their bodies are somehow already marked by—or for—imperfection.

But where there is a first hand, very often there lurks a second. If the texts of Fray Luis, Calderón, and Sor Juana each end, as we have seen, with a giving of a hand, this gesture is haunted by another hand—the hand of an Other—that radically destabilizes the already problematic closure that the giving of the first hand enacts. If the first hand is the hand of the wife that will be banded with a ring as her body is officially pronounced of the same flesh as her husband, this second hand reinscribes her agency and points, defiantly, to the will of the wife—a will that is performatively constituted in civil and canon law by the very act of giving the hand. In her striking reading of early modern anatomies of the hand, Katherine Rowe suggests that "for early modern writers, following Aristotle by way of Galen, the location of agency in relation to the body is the chief intellectual tenor of representations of the hand."[3] This was standard fare in the early modern period; the hand—specifically, the hand's instrumentality ("instrumento de los instrumentos" [instrument of instruments], remarks Covarrubias)—both metaphorically and metonymically stood for agency. But the second hands that appear at the end of *La perfecta casada*, *El médico de su honra*, and *Los empeños de una casa* are as much marked hands as they are willful hands: bloody or bruised, indelibly signed by a constitutive violence that underwrites their agency.

In Fray Luis, this other hand is the hand of the Jewish widow Judith, who not only violates, as I suggested at the end of chapter 2, each and every one of the prescriptions and proscriptions the treatise offers its wifely readers, but appears in the text quite literally red-handed, her hands still warm with Holofernes' blood. The biblical text is unambiguous in localizing Judith's agency in her hand, even as it authorizes her crime by alluding to a divine instrumentality. "Praise God, who has not withdrawn his mercy from the house of Israel, but has shattered our enemies by my *hand* this very night. Then she took the head out of the pouch, showed it to them, and said, 'Here is the head of Holofernes. . . . The Lord struck him down by the *hand* of a woman." [4] The wife's labor becomes a murder, the "fruit of her hands" from the text of Proverbs 31 is either substituted by or, more likely, revealed as the decapitated head Judith holds out as trophy, the head in hand that crowns her own—and those of her ilk—as *perfectas casadas*. Similarly colored by violence, the second hand of *El médico de su honra* is the bloody handprint of the Jewish doctor Ludovico, the handprint that eerily marks the scene of murder and that Gutierre tries to appropriate as his medical coat of arms. (Early modern coats of arms for physicians in fact regularly depicted at least one hand and often two—physician-agent's and patient's—the former taking the pulse of the latter.) [5] And yet this hand painted by Ludovico in Mencía's blood speaks more eloquently than Mencía was ever allowed to do in life, pointing the finger at the inquisitorial science practiced on her wifely body. It is, ironically, in this final, postmortem indictment where the wife's will is most starkly exercised: in the critique of the honor code— both sexual and social—that the hand soaked in her blood silently utters.

This other hand of *Médico,* a text written in the perfected wife's blood, might be read as a disturbingly apt pretext for Sor Juana's 1694 renunciation, a text she pens in her own blood and signs "yo, la peor de todas," after having been tragically "perfected"—silenced—by her male confessors and by the church's institutional sanction. But this takes us in still another direction, one that is difficult to detect in *Empeños* or to anticipate in 1683. *Our* last hand, then—the other hand that closes *Empeños* and also *Perfect Wives*—is not a whole hand at all, but the finger Celia gives Castaño in the final lines of the play.

Castaño
Dime, Celia, algún requiebro
y mira si a mano tienes
una mano.

Celia
      No la tengo
que la dejé en la cocina;
pero ¿bastaráte un dedo?

Castaño
Daca, que es el dedo malo,
pues es él con quien encuentro.

[*Castaño*
Flatter me, Celia,
and see if you have
a hand that's handy.

Celia
I don't have one,
for I left it in the kitchen;
but would a finger be enough for you?

Castaño
Give it here, then, for it's the bad finger,
since it's the one (with which) I find.]

Celia's final gesture is ripe with meaning, particularly when her finger—or Sor Juana's hand behind it—is measured against the hands
of Fray Luis and Calderón. Celia first denies Castaño her hand with
the excuse that she has left it in the kitchen: her proper place as determined not only by the position of her body—as potential wife—but,
more crucially, by her class position—as domestic servant. She nimbly
substitutes one hand for another, capitalizing—via the pun—on the
confusion between her body (more specifically, the agency of her body
that is condensed in her hand) and the instrument of her labor: the
mano that minces food as handily as Celia and Castaño mince words.[6]

But more suggestive than Celia's denial of her own hand (and this too
has provocative implications; like Leonor—and perhaps more so—

she chooses the fate of her body, and decides for herself to whom she will or will not give her hand) is her offer of a finger in its place, a finger she knows to be riddled in excess even as she pronounces its insufficiency: "¿bastaráte un dedo?" [would a finger be enough for you?]. The term *dedo malo* (bad finger) had several meanings in the seventeenth century, all of which are present in Castaño's reply. Literally, it was a bruised or swollen finger that, despite a patient's best efforts to protect it, was especially prone to repeated injuries. "Dedo malo" was also said of a person with a less than sterling reputation, whose past offenses made him a handy scapegoat, a usual suspect for any wrongdoing.[7] But this bruised, suspect "bad finger," synecdoche for the hand in marriage Celia does *not* give, is also, of course, a phallic substitute that rehystericizes Castaño's transvestite body, carrying the drama's plays on gender to even further extremes. Covarrubias's definition of *higa*, a gesticulation of the hand that is roughly equivalent to giving the finger, is instructive.

> Es una manera de menosprecio que hazemos cerrando el puño y mostrando el dedo pulgar por entre el dedo índice y el medio; es disfraçada pulla. La higa antigua era tan solamente una semejança del miembro viril, estendiendo el dedo medio y encogiendo el índice y el auricular.
>
> [It is a form of derision we express by closing the fist and exposing the thumb between the index and middle fingers; it is a disguised affront. The ancient *higa* was nothing more than a semblance of the viril member, (formed by) extending the middle finger and bending the index and ring fingers.][8]

The grotesquely swollen dedo malo that Celia gives Castaño not only represents the most radical departure from the various hands given in marriage at the end of *Empeños,* then (or, for that matter *La perfecta casada* and *El médico de su honra*) but, like Sor Juana's own, it is a finger that will accommodate no ring, that resists being banded by any anillo al dedo, or confined in any *breve cárcel* (brief prison). It is a finger we might hold up against Sor Juana's final silence, a last sleight of hand that not only draws a very different sort of *rótulo al silencio* (caption on silence),[9] but beguilingly entangles the bodies of perfect wives and other women.

If Fray Luis, Calderón, and Sor Juana seem, at first blush, strange bedfellows, the perfect and imperfect wives' hands and bodies their texts entangle come together at a surprising number of sites. Fray Luis's take on the wife's body is in some respects the most complex of the three. *La perfecta casada* can be read not only as a conduct manual in the traditional sense, but also as a manual about interpretation that poignantly responds to the charges that kept Fray Luis imprisoned in the Inquisition's jails for five years. The wife becomes not just the subject (assuming the text is destined for a female audience, which is not necessarily the case, or at least not exclusively) and object of reading, but the site on which questions regarding both the possibilities and the dangers of reading in an inquisitorial context are posed and contested. But this posing—or this contesting—gives rise to a number of paradoxes. If Fray Luis attempts, on one hand, to discipline and contain the body of la casada according to repressive norms that would, in theory, transform it into that of a perfect wife, he resists, on the other hand, the very construct he elaborates. The numerous contradictions that beset and even adorn the textual body of *La perfecta casada* are perhaps the best proof of his lack of orthodoxy to the same principles his treatise seems to put forth. Those contradictions are for the most part manifested in the failure—both logical and rhetorical—of analogy throughout the text. If Fray Luis relies on analogy as a fundamental reading strategy that corresponds to an Aristotelian conception of the universe as a Great Chain of Being, analogy in *La perfecta casada* is troubled by an excess that undermines the ontologic semblance on which it is putatively grounded. But what is perhaps most seductive about Fray Luis's perfect wife is the way she gestures toward her imperfect incarnation in the Calderonian honor dramas. Adultery in Fray Luis is already understood not in terms of sexual transgressions of a marital promise, but rather as a disjunction between codes that threatens legibility, as a conflict between forms of seeming and being, between the accidental and the essential.

In Calderón, the imperfect and—according to her husband's reading—adulterous wife's body is contained, inquired, and finally textualized. Intersections between the wife's body and the Other's body become particularly charged in *El médico de su honra*, given the metaphoric substratum of disease, maculacy, and blood cleansing the play elaborates. Recasting the wife's body as an inquired body and the husband's surveillance as a kind of performative, self-fulfilling inquisition that only confirms its own questionable assumptions suggests that Calderón may have encoded in the play a critique of punitive reading practices that take themselves for authoritative, like those that informed limpieza de sangre statutes, for example. The play also dramatizes the extent to which signs of adultery always give way to an adultery of signs. One of the most compelling continuities between Fray Luis and Calderón can be located in the way in which their respective readings of wives' bodies privilege categories of Otherness over those of Sameness, or of the accidental over the essential, even, or particularly, at those instances where the opposite seems to be true. In Fray Luis this obtains primarily through the problematic status of analogy in the text. In Calderón, the literalization of the metaphor (like that of el médico de su honra) that ostensibly favors a conjunctive semiosis or a conjunctive conception of allegory (of the sort that is the basis of the later autos sacramentales) tends, instead, toward disjunctiveness, toward a semiotic adultery visible in the resistance to containment strategies, in the migration of visible signs, or in the importance of the category of the accidental in the play.

A reading of Sor Juana alongside Fray Luis and Calderón suggests the ways in which the pervasive intersections of race and gender discourses in early modern Spain—intersections generally founded on questions of Otherness and of illegibility—were translated to a New World context. Sor Juana's New World version of wifely illegibility might be seen as a radicalization—an Americanization—of the paradoxes of the Old. Indeed, her rewriting of the honor script as a cross-dressed comedia de enredos in *Los empeños de una casa* completely resemanticizes the illegibility of the wife's body, transposing it onto gender categories that are entwined with racial ones. The adultery of signs that exposes, in Calderón, the inherent failures of any program of interpretation that univocally seeks to wed truth with punishment serves other purposes in Sor Juana. The instabilities with which somatic reading is fraught are embraced in her work for the plural erotic registers they generate and for the constructed and even accidental nature of race and gender categories they reveal.

Among the issues raised by the kinds of continuities I trace between the readings of the wives' bodies that appear in the works of Fray Luis, Calderón, and Sor Juana is a questioning of received notions of literary and epistemic periodization. It is a commonplace of Hispanic Golden Age literary studies, for example, to advance Luis de León as supreme representative — cipher, even — of a sixteenth-century Spanish Renaissance ("la figura más excelsa y el más exacto *resumen* del Renacimiento hispano" [the most exalted and precise summary of the Hispanic Renaissance]), Calderón de la Barca of a seventeenth-century Spanish Baroque ("la *síntesis* más completa de nuestro siglo barroco" [the most complete synthesis of our baroque century]), and Sor Juana of a New World baroque ("la voz más viva, graciosa y entonada del barroco hispanoamericano" [the most lively, graceful, and harmonious voice of the Spanish American baroque]).[10] Fray Luis's ascribed sense of proportion and harmony are often cited in contrast to the metaphoric excesses and monstrous disproportions of Calderón, or to the New World "strangeness" of Sor Juana.[11] Indeed, it may be argued that Fray Luis and Calderón–Sor Juana could respectively be taken as synecdoches for what Foucault describes as a sixteenth-century analogic epistème, in which writing is conceived as the "prose of the world," and a seventeenth-century allegorical one, in which "words wander off on their own, without content, without resemblance."[12]

If the apparent neatness of such an alignment is formally seductive, however, it is a neatness we should distrust. Readings of the wife's body may seem like an odd place from which to address questions of historic, epistemic, or ideological shifts. But if the wife's body is read as a transcoder for other areas, a site on which both interpretive and cultural anxieties are projected, then perhaps the choice will not seem so farfetched. In fact, one reading of the anxieties surrounding somatic interpretation to which the wife's body gives rise might suggest that in Spain the shift from an "analogic" (or "classic") to an "allegoric" (or "baroque") mode of reading the world, a shift that Foucault situates roughly at the beginning of the seventeenth century, occurred (or was at least anticipated) somewhat earlier. This possibility clearly involves a rethinking of traditional histories that ascribe Spain a belated modernity vis-à-vis the rest of Europe. An even stronger reading of these problems might lead us to altogether abandon even the most

benign sense of temporality that informs periodization in order to in-
terrogate, instead, the cultural conditions within which this sort of
"baroque" distrust in semblance proliferated in Counter-Reformation
Spain, even in the presence of a Tridentine dogma that sought to monogamize the marriage between sign and meaning. The promiscuity of
that relation (what at different moments throughout this work I have
referred to as an adultery of signs) is not only the logical aftermath
of Reform, but also, paradoxically, a backlash of Tridentine efforts
to curb that same disjunctiveness.[13] It is also at least partly related—
particularly where the reading of bodies is concerned—to the institutional presence of the Inquisition in Spain. In this sense, it would be
possible to argue that the Spanish Inquisition helped produce the very
conditions—or the very anxieties—it sought to regulate: a threatening disjunction between an "orthodox" exterior and a "heretic" or
"nonorthodox" interior.[14]

But perhaps the crucial point to be made here—and the direction
in which all the "other hands" of Fray Luis, Calderón and Sor Juana
inevitably point—is that reading never takes place in a vacuum, that
attention to mechanisms of interpretation cannot pretend that practices of signification are divorced from cultural and political practices.
And it is this marriage, more so than the marriage between husband
and wife, that should concern us. Let me situate my own reading of
early modern wives' bodies within the theoretical moment in which
we, as early-twenty-first-century readers of Fray Luis, Calderón, and
Sor Juana find ourselves and gesture toward some of the larger questions that this kind of project engages, locating it at an intersection of
various critical practices, between formalist and nonformalist modes
of reading. If my project seems to entail a turn toward a latter-day for-
malism—particularly toward a belated deconstructive critical practice that privileges moments of textual illegibility and sites of semiotic
instability, that turn is not intended to foreclose but rather to render
flagrant other kinds of instabilities. In arguing for a reconsideration
of early modern readings of the wife's body in terms of questions of
interpretation, my intention has not been to decontextualize or de-
historicize readings of these texts or of the bodies they circumscribe.
On the contrary, if in their attention to and anxieties over issues of
reading and misreading these bodies raise questions over hermeneu-

tics, for instance, the interpretive tensions they mobilize extend well beyond formal categories. Not only does this sort of project remit to social, political, and cultural anxieties of sixteenth- and seventeenth-century Spain and America, but, what is more, it inscribes this kind of historicizing move as a constitutive and not just accidental theoretical premise. What makes sixteenth- and seventeenth-century Spain such fertile ground for this type of critical practice is that it represents a historical moment when confusions over seeming and being were not only overtly politicized, but potentially dangerous, in which codes of reading and mechanisms of signification were a matter of politics as well as of poetics, in which not just textual bodies but flesh and blood ones were quite literally read for signs of accusatory difference.

Notes

Preface

1 Sebastián de Covarrubias, *Tesoro de la lengua castellana o española* (1611), facsimile ed., ed. Martín de Riquer (Barcelona: Editorial Alta Fulla, 1943), 818. Translation mine. Clarification may be helpful concerning the use I make throughout this book of Covarrubias's *Tesoro*, a text that has become a kind of touchstone for studies of early modern Spain. I read Covarrubias's definitions here and elsewhere in this work not as a transparent window or privileged lens into early modern Spanish culture (the *Tesoro* is as politically and ideologically charged as any other text) but as a useful index of that culture and society, in spite of (if not perhaps because of) its being as compromised and as problematic as any other founding text of early modern European culture.

2 I explore that critique here in particular relation to limpieza de sangre statutes, but the argument could be more broadly made. The criticism of honor that the play encodes could be considered in relation to the continuation of war in the Netherlands, for example — a war with high human and material costs, fought largely in the name of honor, and one that Philip IV refused to abandon until an honorable peace treaty ("paz con honor") could be negotiated.

3 Thomas Laqueur, *Making Sex: Body and Gender from the Greeks to Freud* (Cambridge: Harvard University Press, 1990), 118. Laqueur writes: "The images through which bodies and pleasures were understood in the Renaissance are less a reflection of a particular level of scientific understanding, or even of a particular philosophic orientation, than they are the expression of a whole fabric or field of knowledge. Myriad discourses echo through the body." Laqueur's reading of the social, cultural, and even aesthetic constructedness of anatomy has been important for the sort of reading of the wife's body I undertake here: "Anatomy, and nature as we know it more generally, is obviously not pure fact, unadulterated by thought or convention, but rather a richly complicated construction based not only on observation, and on a variety of social and cultural

constraints on the practice of science, but on an aesthetics of representation as well" (164).

4 See Judith Butler, *Bodies That Matter: On the Discursive Limits of "Sex"* (New York: Routledge, 1993). In linking the question of the body's materiality with that of gender performativity, Butler suggests that "what constitutes the fixity of the body, its contours, its movements, will be fully material, but materiality will be rethought as the effect of power, as power's most productive effect." Among the stakes of such a reformulation (of bodily materiality) is "the recasting of the matter of bodies as the effect of a dynamic of power, such that the matter of bodies will be indissociable from the regulatory norms that govern their materialization and the signification of those material effects" (2).

5 Stallybrass and White's contention that "the body cannot be thought separately from the social formation, symbolic topography and the constitution of the subject" is crucial for my reading of the wife's body. "It is not that . . . any appeal to the body is a kind of mystification: it is rather that the body is actively produced by the junction and disjunction of symbolic domains and can never be legitimately evaluated 'in itself.'" Peter Stallybrass and Allon White, *The Politics and Poetics of Transgression* (Ithaca: Cornell University Press, 1986), 192.

Chapter 1   Visible Signs:
Reading the Wife's Body in Early Modern Spain

1 Juan de Quiñones, *Memorial de Juan de Quiñones dirigido a Fray Antonio de Sotomayor, inquisidor general, sobre el caso de Francisco de Andrada, sospechoso de pertenecer a la raza judía, discutiendo sobre los medios de conocer y perseguir a ella* (Madrid: Biblioteca Nacional, VE, box no. 16, 1632), cited in George Mariscal, *Contradictory Subjects: Quevedo, Cervantes, and Seventeenth-Century Spanish Culture* (Ithaca: Cornell University Press, 1991). Translation is my own in consultation with Mariscal's published English translation. Mariscal's reading of the passage is incisive: "The Jew is doubly marked, by both circumcision and menstruation, and it is through his body that the seemingly separate codes of race and sexuality collapse into each other" (43–44). If, as Mariscal suggests, the Jew's body becomes the meeting place of discourses of exclusion, I would argue that that conflation is perhaps best seen on the female, specifically, the wife's, body.

2 Another example of the attribution of menstruation to Jews (both male

and female) can be found in the 1630 *Discurso contra los judíos traducido de lengua portuguesa en castellano por el Padre Fray Diego Gavilán Vela:* "Otros dizen que el Biernes sancto todos los Iudios, y Iudias, tienen aquel día fluxo de sangre, y que por este respecto son casi todos de color pálido." Cited in Josette Riandère La Roche, "Du discours d'exclusion des juifs: Antijudaïsme ou antisémitisme?" in *Les problèmes de l'exclusion en Espagne, XVI–XVII siècles,* ed. Agustín Redondo (Paris: Sorbonne, 1983), 65 n. 37.

3   Natalie Zemon Davis, "Women on Top," in *Society and Culture in Early Modern France* (Stanford: Stanford University Press, 1975), 124–51.

4   I am indebted to Jacques Lezra for his invaluable suggestions for revising this chapter and in particular for helping me expound the relation between the categories of wife and woman with respect to emerging early modern discourses.

5   "El cuerpo social no era un agregado inorgánico de individuos, de átomos, sino de moléculas complejas: gremios, colegios, cofradías, ayuntamientos, corporaciones. . . . Los privilegios no recaían sobre el individuo en cuanto tal, sino en cuanto miembro de uno de estos organismos." [The social body was not an inorganic aggregate of individuals, of atoms, but of complex molecules: guilds, colleges, brotherhoods, municipalities, associations. . . . Privileges were granted not to the individual as such, but only to the member of one such organization.] Antonio Domínguez Ortiz, *Las clases privilegiadas en el antiguo régimen,* 3d ed. (Madrid: Istmo, 1985), 12. Mariscal suggests that "each of the ensembles described by Domínguez Ortiz functioned as a site upon which subjects were constituted, and in a real sense the concept of subjectivity as the intersection of multiple subject positions is impossible to understand without first understanding 'society' as a configuration of different group interests and investments." Mariscal, *Contradictory Subjects,* 36.

6   "Virtually all forms of subjectivity in this period depended on different degrees and kinds of 'maleness,' rather than on the historically more recent male/female binomial." Mariscal, *Contradictory Subjects,* 27.

7   Similarly, although my argument has benefited from recent studies and histories of early modern women that have sought to recover women's voices from the silences of history (I am thinking here of the work of Mary Elizabeth Perry, Margaret King, and many others), the readings that follow do not represent a comprehensive inquiry into the role of women as wives in sixteenth- and seventeenth-century Spain.

8   I am grateful to María Willstedt for her help with this translation.

9   Jesús de Bujanda, "Recent Historiography of the Spanish Inquisition,"

in *Cultural Encounters: The Impact of the Spanish Inquisition in Spain and the New World*, ed. Mary Elizabeth Perry and Anne J. Cruz (Berkeley: University of California Press, 1991), 227–28.

10 As Anne Cruz and Mary Elizabeth Perry convincingly argue, "the Spanish Inquisition thus became a major theater for cultural encounters among the many peoples throughout the Hispanic world." Perry and Cruz, *Cultural Encounters*, ix.

11 Nancy Armstrong and Leonard Tennenhouse, introduction to *The Ideology of Conduct: Essays on Literature and the History of Sexuality*, ed. Nancy Armstrong and Leonard Tennenhouse (New York: Methuen, 1987), 1.

12 Jacob Burckhardt, *The Civilization of the Renaissance in Italy*, trans. S. G. C. Middlemore (New York: Penguin Books, 1990).

13 The classic reference here is Joan Scott Kelly's "Did Women Have a Renaissance?" in *Women, History, and Theory: The Essays of Joan Kelly* (Chicago: University of Chicago Press, 1984), 19–50.

14 Stephen Jay Greenblatt, *Renaissance Self-Fashioning: From More to Shakespeare* (Chicago: University of Chicago Press, 1980); Thomas Green, "The Flexibility of the Self in Renaissance Literature," in *The Disciplines of Criticism: Essays in Literary Theory, Interpretation, and History*, ed. Peter Demetz, Thomas Greene, and Lowry Nelson Jr. (New Haven: Yale University Press, 1968), 241–264.

15 J. E. Hartzenbusch, " 'Prólogo' a las comedias de Calderón," cited in Américo Castro, "El concepto del honor en los siglos XVI y XVII," *De la edad conflictiva: Crisis de la cultura española en el siglo XVII*, 3d ed. (Madrid: Taurus, 1972), 322.

16 Gustavo Correa, "El doble aspecto de la honra en el teatro del siglo XVII," *Hispanic Review* 26 (1958): 99–107.

17 The most complete study of uxoricide plays in early modern Spain is Matthew Stroud's monograph, *Fatal Union: A Pluralistic Approach to the Spanish Wife-Murder Comedias* (Lewisburg: Bucknell University Press, 1990).

18 David A. Boruchoff, abstract for *Rhetoric and Redemption in Inquisitorial Spain: Intolerance and the Invention of the Novel* (forthcoming).

19 Theoretically informed Hispanism of the last ten to fifteen years—I am thinking here of the groundbreaking work carried out by Electa Arenal, Inés Azar, Emilie Bergmann, David Boruchoff, Israel Burshatin, María Mercedes Carrión, Anne Cruz, James Fernández, Mary Gaylord, Robert González Echevarría, Mary Gossy, Jacques Lezra, George Mariscal, Melveena McKendrick, Mary Elizabeth Perry, Ruth El Saffar, Elena Sánchez Ortega, Paul Julian Smith, Alison Weber, Diana de Armas Wilson, to

name but a few — has, in fact, made great strides in reading early modern Spanish and Spanish American literature in relation to questions about the body, or, more specifically, about the body in relation to alternate models of subjectivity, or institutional controls, or early modern discourses of race and gender, and so on, all of which come to bear on the study that follows. On the body of evidence in "El curioso impertinente" see my "La herida de Camila: La anatomía de la prueba en 'El curioso impertinente,' " in *En un lugar de la Mancha: Estudios cervantinos en honor de Manuel Durán*, ed. Georgina Dopico Black and Roberto González Echevarría (Salamanca: Ediciones Almar, 1999), 91–108.

20 R. Howard Bloch, *Medieval Misogyny and the Invention of Western Romantic Love* (Chicago: University of Chicago Press, 1991), 47. In chapter 2, I take up Bloch's definition of misogyny in greater detail.

21 On the legibility/illegibility of the hymen, see Mary Gossy's *The Untold Story: Women and Theory on Golden Age Texts* (Ann Arbor: University of Michigan Press, 1989).

22 Sebastián de Covarrubias, *Emblemas morales* (1610), facsimile ed., ed. Carmen Bravo-Villasante (Madrid: Fundación Universitaria Española, 1978), n.p.

23 Of course, even in the case of the "virgin," the lack of ambiguity is only apparent. Celestina's mending points to the inherent artificiality of *any* reading that seeks to hypostatize fixed meaning onto an unstable, plural sign (be it the body or the word).

24 Gossy, *Untold Story*, 45.

25 A project with a different focus than this one but still concerned with the anxieties surrounding the legibility or illegibility of the wife's body might frame these issues in relation to the noticeable absence of mothers in early modern Spanish literature in general and in the Golden Age comedia specifically. The absence of mothers in texts of the Spanish Golden Age has been a particularly thorny issue for Hispanists; although it has attracted a fair amount of critical attention over the years, the question of the missing mother remains largely unanswered. Ruth El Saffar provides several possible reasons for the surprising absence of mothers in the literature:

By the end of the sixteenth century, the figure of the mother virtually disappears from the Spanish stage and from the literary texts. The daughter appears, like Athena, to have emerged directly from the heads of their fathers. The mothers, for their part, seem to have been entirely swallowed up in the patriarchal social structure that prescribed for them the roles of silence and obedience. Part of the reason is that the role of mothers as defined by the period was one of self-giving, so that she in effect disappears into the lives of those whose nurturance and growth she provides. Should she stand out as a character, it would indicate something wrong with her, an excess of ego or self-assertion. In fact, it is only in those plays and stories in which the mother is "abnormally" ambitious or assertive that she appears at all. Another reason for the absence of mothers in plots of drama or fiction is one based on the realities of family life. Mothers in fact did not take an active part in arranging the important events in their children's lives. Mothers also tended to die early, making the father the figure of constancy in a family in which the husband may have been widowed several times. A deeper reason for the absence of representation of mothers has to do with the extreme degree to which they were repressed both externally and within the psyche. Plays by the seventeenth-century court playwright Calderón de la Barca underscore the support and protection awarded men who overcome the love of their wives to enforce marital codes of fidelity. In a series of wife-murder plays Calderón shows the male hero, having killed his wife out of fear of her interest in someone else, restored to the social order and honored by the king.

El Saffar, *Rapture Encaged: The Suppression of the Feminine in Western Culture* (London: Routledge, 1994), 67–68.

26 Severo Sarduy, for example, defines baroque artificiality in terms of a semantic substitution and a proliferation of signifiers: "El artificio barroco se manifiesta por medio de una sustitución que podríamos llamar al nivel del signo: el significante que corresponde al significado . . . ha sido escamoteado y sustituido por otro totalmente alejado semánticamente de él. . . . Otro mecanismo de artificialización del barroco es el que consiste en obliterar el significante de un significado dado pero no remplazándolo por otro, por distante que éste se encuentre del primero, sino por una cadena de significantes." [Baroque artifice manifests itself by means of a substitution at what we might term the level of the sign: the signifier that corresponds to the signified . . . vanishes and is substituted by another that is completely removed from it semantically. . . . Another mechanism of baroque artificialization is that which consists of obliterating the signifier of a given signified but not replacing it with another, distant as it may be from the first, but with a chain of signifiers.] Sarduy, *Barroco* (Buenos Aires: Editorial Sudamericana, 1974), 169–70. Translation mine.

27 Sebastián de Covarrubias, *Tesoro de la lengua castellana o española*, 45. Translation mine.

28 Given the biblical association of adultery and idolatry, on one hand

("vale idolatrar"), and cultural anxieties in sixteenth-century Spain about a kind of idolatry (crypto-Judaism or crypto-Islam) on the part of false conversos, on the other, it is not difficult to imagine that adultery could be charged — as I argue it is in the case of the honor plays — with semantic valences that not only exceed a marital context but that remit to preoccupations about limpieza de sangre. The semantic resonances and etymologic identity between adultery and adulteration support this argument, since the impure blood of cristianos nuevos was charged with adulterating and debasing the pure blood of cristianos viejos. From a semiotic perspective, idolatry is as problematic (or as disjunctive) as adultery. If adultery involves a missing signifier that then attracts other "incorrect signifiers" to take its place, idolatry can be conceived as a fetishism of the literal that points to the absence of an ultimate signified.

29 On the connection between adultery and idolatry, see John Freccero, "The Fig Tree and the Laurel: Petrarch's Poetics," in *Literary Theory/Renaissance Texts*, ed. Patricia Parker and David Quint (Baltimore: Johns Hopkins University Press, 1986), 20–32.

30 At some levels, this liminality is merely an extension of her body's illegibility with respect to adulterous transgressions, since marriage and adultery are easily alignable with categories of Same and Other.

31 A colorful summary of the workings of this sort of objectification can be found in the justification Don Quixote offers Sancho of how he has chosen Dulcinea for his dama: "¿Piensas tú que las Amarilis, las Filis, las Silvias, las Dianas, las Galateas, las Fílidas y otras tales de que los libros, los romances, las tiendas de los barberos, los teatros de las comedias están llenos, fueron verdaderamente damas de carne y hueso, y de aquellos que las celebran y celebraron? No, por cierto, sino que las más se las fingen, por dar subjeto a sus versos, y porque los tengan por enamorados y por hombres que tienen valor para serlo." [Do you think that the Amaryllises, the Phyllises, the Sylvias, the Dianas, the Galateas, and all the rest of which the books, the ballads, the barber shops, the comic theaters, are full, were genuinely ladies of flesh and blood and the mistresses of those who celebrated their charms? Certainly not. Most of them were invented to serve as subjects for verses and to enable the poets to prove themselves lovers or capable of being such.] Miguel de Cervantes *Don Quijote de la Mancha*, ed. Francisco Rico (Barcelona: Crítica, 1999, bk. 1, 25, 285. Translation is from Miguel de Cervantes, *Don Quixote*, trans. Walter Starkie (New York: Signet, 1964), bk. 1, 25, 249. For an insightful reading of the ways in which the figure of woman was constructed as an Other against which emerging forms of the male subject in early modern Spain could take shape, see Mariscal, *Contradictory Subjects*, 132.

32 The dialectic of Self and Other proves to be, as Luce Irigaray demonstrates, a radically false binary; they are, in the end, merely two sides of the same coin. Judith Butler eloquently and succinctly summarizes Irigaray's argument as follows: "But it is, of course, Irigaray who exposes the dialectic of Same and Other as a false binary, the illusion of a symmetrical difference which consolidates the metaphysical economy of phallogocentrism, the economy of the same. In her view, the Other as well as the Same are marked as masculine; the Other is but the negative elaboration of the masculine subject with the result that the female sex is unrepresentable—that is, it is the sex which, within the signifying economy, is not one." Butler, *Gender Trouble* (New York: Routledge, 1990), 103. See also Sherry B. Ortner, "Is Female to Male as Nature Is to Culture?" in *Women, Culture, and Society,* ed. Michelle Zimbalist Rosald and Louise Lamphere (Stanford: Stanford University Press, 1974), 67–87.

33 See Joan Wallach Scott, *Gender and the Politics of History* (New York: Columbia University Press, 1988): "Gender is a constitutive element of social relationships based upon perceived differences between the sexes, and gender is a primary way of signifying relationships of power. . . . Established as an objective set of references, concepts of gender structure perception and the concrete and symbolic organization of all social life. To the extent that these references establish distributions of power (differential control over or access to material and symbolic resources), gender becomes implicated in the conception and construction of power itself" (42–45).

34 Davis, "Women on Top," 127.

35 See James D. Fernández, "The Bonds of Patrimony: Cervantes and the New World," *PMLA* 109, 5 (1994): 977, for an incisive and provocative reading of Cervantes's "El celoso extremeño."

36 The passage continues: "Gender control, then, represents one of the most pervasive and complex of cultural mechanisms. During the Counter-Reformation, the Church and the State reinscribed misogyny by focusing on women's powers to lead men's souls to hell. While other minorities were condemned for their unorthodox beliefs and practices, only women as a group were viewed as inherently dangerous to men. Control of the female body was thus not only an economic strategy, but one of the most important means of ensuring men's salvation." Perry and Cruz, *Cultural Encounters,* xvii–xviii.

37 In her study of witch-hunting in the early modern period as a gender-specific violence directed against women, Anne Llewellyn Barstow attributes the relative scarcity of witch-hunts in Spain to the fact that the

Inquisition was "already sated with victims," contending that "Spanish women were seen by Spanish men as a part of their group, not as outsiders." Barstow writes:

I believe that Trevor-Roper was on the right track when he argued that the Spanish Inquisition did not instigate a witchcraze because it was already sated with victims, chiefly Jews and Muslims. I would like to combine his idea with Kamen's observations about the power of the Spanish family, however, and suggest that it was not simply crude satiation but a more subtle combination of forces based on gender roles. . . . Spanish men guaranteed their honor and their identity as Spaniards through the purity of their race and religion, a purity they traced through family blood ties and religious orthodoxy. Heretics, Jews, and Moors were therefore suspect on the grounds of religion, and the latter two on grounds of race as well. But Spanish women were seen by Spanish men as a part of their group, not as outsiders. As mothers, they were in fact the guarantors of group purity. I conclude that before they can become the targets of mass persecution, women *as a group* must be perceived as outsiders, as capable of turning against those who see themselves as insiders in a society. And this is precisely what did not occur in Spain. (93)

But if in Spain there does not occur the same kind of violence against women that can be found throughout Northern Europe, I would argue that a more symbolic sort of violence did occur—a violence that targets women as potential sources of contamination and corruption. My point, then, is not so much that women—and wives in particular—were deemed Other, but quite the contrary, that their real power—and their real threat—derives from the fact that they are a kind of Other within. See Barstow, *Witchcraze: A New History of the European Witch Hunts* (San Francisco: Pandora, 1994).

38 *Canons and Decrees of the Council of Trent,* trans. Rev. H. J. Schroeder (Rockford: Tan Books, 1978), 190. Italics mine.

39 Drawing on the passage of Cervantes's "El curioso impertinente" that I have cited as epigraph to this chapter, Bruce Wardropper has studied the honor question as both a legal and dramatic phenomenon precisely in terms of this type of literalization of the text of theology. He writes: "The honor problem arises, then, as a result of a belief in the *literalness* of the foundation of a sacrament [marriage and its attendant one-flesh doctrine]. . . . The harm perhaps would not have been excessive, would not have led to such disastrous results, if some of [the husbands] had not gone on to combine this belief with a too literal interpretation of Christ's injunction to cut off an offending hand or foot, and pluck out

an offending eye. A wife being her husband's limb, of his own flesh and blood, he had an obligation to amputate her if she gave offence." War-dropper, "Calderón's Comedy and His Serious Sense of Life," in *Hispanic Studies in Honor of Nicholson B. Adams,* ed. John Esten Keller (Chapel Hill: University of North Carolina Press, 1966), 85–86.

40 If, as Foucault has suggested, "the history of the order imposed on things" is "the history of the Same" and "the history of madness" is "the history of the Other," might it not be possible to conceive of marriage and adultery within such a framework, inasmuch as marriage is align-able with order and sameness and the threat of adultery is that of a certain madness ("loco amor"), not only perpetrated by an-Other, but that transforms the wife's body into something Other? See Michel Foucault, *The Order of Things: An Archaeology of the Human Sciences* (London: Tevistock Publications, 1970).

41 Pietro Redondi, *Galileo: Heretic,* trans. Raymond Rosenthal (Princeton: Princeton University Press, 1987), 208.

42 *Canons and Decrees of the Council of Trent,* 72.

43 Redondi, *Galileo,* 221. The possibility of consubstantiation that, pace Luther, would be applied to Lutheran eucharistic theology, had been opened by Ockham's revival of Democritan atomism. Ockham argued, against Aristotelian-Thomist metaphysics, in favor of an identification of quantity with substance. The implications of this identification were lethal to transubstantiation's philosophical foundations: if the consecrated bread retained its quantity (accidents such as color, odor, and weight), it would also retain its substance as bread. "Luther did not intend to stipulate a canonical theory on the disappearance of the substance of the bread and wine. His was the claim of returning to the Augustinian conception of the mystery, eliminating as 'sophistical subtlety' the controversy on transubstantiation in order to assume a simply sacramental vision of the real presence concomitant with perceptible phenomena." Ibid., 223.

44 Jaroslav Pelikan explains Reformed theologians' use of the word "sign": "Although the use of the term 'sign' for 'sacrament' pertained to the definition of sacrament as such, and specifically also to baptism, most of the debate about it arose over its adequacy in application to the Lord's Supper. It was a 'calumny,' Reformed teachers replied to their critics, to charge them with maintaining that there was 'no mystery' in the Supper, but only a 'bare sign'. . . . The bread and wine were, rather, 'visible signs, which represent the body and the blood to us and to which the name and title of body and blood is attributed.' Even 'represent' was not an adequate term; it would be more accurate to say that they 'present' the

body and the blood." Jaroslav Pelikan, *The Christian Tradition: A History of the Development of Doctrine. Vol. 4. Reformation of Church and Dogma (1300–1700).* (Chicago: University of Chicago Press, 1984), 192.

45 *Canons and Decrees of the Council of Trent,* 79. Italics mine.

46 As early as 1215, the Fourth Lateran Council had promulgated transubstantiation as dogma, arguing that "the body and blood [of Jesus Christ] are truly contained in the Sacrament of the Altar under the outward appearance of bread and wine, the bread having been transubstantiated into the body and the wine into the blood." Decrees of the Fourth Lateran Council, cited in Jaroslav Pelikan, *The Christian Tradition: A History of the Development of Doctrine. Vol. 3. The Growth of Medieval Theology, 600–1300.* (Chicago: University of Chicago Press, 1978), 203–4.

47 "St. Thomas had the intellectual audacity to affirm that which his predecessors—from Albert the Great to St. John of Damascus and Algero—had only timidly suggested: that Eucharistic phenomena are sensible phenomena separated from substance, accidents without a subject. Hence the quantity (extension) of the Consecrated Host is not sustained either by the material of the bread or by the surrounding air. It persists, miraculously, without substance. So too with all the other accidents that adhere to extension: the notorious 'color, odor, and taste.' These persist and act 'as if' they depend on a substance, but in reality they persist and act without substance." Redondi, *Galileo,* 213. Thomas specifically addresses the transubstantial miracle in questions 73 through 83 of the *Summa theologica:* "All the substance of the bread is transmuted into the body of Christ. . . . [T]herefore, this is not a formal conversion but a substantial one. Nor does it belong to the species of natural mutations; but, with its own definition, it is called transubstantiation." Thomas Aquinas, *Summa theologica,* ed. Thomas Gilby (Garden City: Doubleday, 1969), 375.a4.

48 Covarrubias's definition of *hostia* includes a relatively faithful rendering of the Thomistic argument: "En la Yglesia Católica llamamos hostia a la forma que el sacerdote consagra en la missa, en la qual, después de dichas las palabras de la consagración por el celebrante, la sustancia de pan material se convierte en la sustancia del cuerpo de Nuestro Redentor Jesu Christo, quedando tan solamente los accidentes de cantidad, color y sabor, sin sugeto, por un modo misterioso e inefable, el qual, ni los sentidos pueden percibirle ni la razón alcançarle, pero todo lo suple la fe para confirmar el coraçon sencillo y christiano." [In the Catholic Church we call 'host' the form that the priest consecrates in Mass, where, after the words of the consecration are pronounced by the celebrant, the substance of the material bread becomes the substance of the body of

Our Redeemer Jesus Christ, with only the accidents of quantity, color, and taste remaining, without subject, by some mysterious and ineffable means, which neither the senses can perceive nor the mind comprehend, but all of which faith supplies for the confirmation of the simple and Christian heart.] Covarrubias, *Tesoro*, 702. That the particulars of the Tridentine debate over transubstantiation were conceived not as isolated theological questions but, rather, as issues that formed part of a broader cultural currency can be adduced in part from the level of detail and the very specific (theologic) language contained in the definition.

49 Fray Luis de León, *De los nombres de Cristo*, ed. Federico de Onís (Madrid: Espasa-Calpe, 1949), 2:219, italics mine. Translation is taken from Luis de León, *The Names of Christ*, trans. Manuel Durán and William Kluback (New York: Paulist Press, 1984).

50 The Council of Trent's Twenty-Fourth Session reaffirmed the sacramentality of marriage, the Church's authority in enforcing (and hence being able to dispense) prohibition of marriage by reason of consanguinity, and, significantly, the indissolubility of marriage even by reason of adultery:

Canon 7. If anyone says that the Church errs in that she taught and teaches that in accordance with evangelical and apostolic doctrine the bond of matrimony *cannot be dissolved* by reason of adultery on the part of one of the parties, and that both, or even the innocent party who gave no occasion for adultery, cannot contract another marriage during the lifetime of the other, and that he is guilty of adultery who, having put away the adulteress, shall marry another, and she also who, having put away the adulterer, shall marry another, let him be anathema. (*Canons and Decrees of the Council of Trent*, 182)

Insofar as Trent established the indissolubility of marriage and the prohibition of remarriage during the life of an adulterous spouse, the honor play's prescription of murder in the case of adultery might be seen as a way around this. In other words, while canon law bans the dissolution of adulterous marriages, civil law allows a form of it.

51 Luther had argued that marriage, although instituted by God and blessed by Christ, was not a sacrament because it was universally valid among Christians and non-Christians alike. The Tridentine institutionalization of the sacramentality of marriage against Luther's claims to the contrary was, to a great degree, politically motivated. The church did not want to give up control over one of the mechanisms (perhaps the most effective) whereby it actively legislated in affairs of state. See Roland H. Bainton, *The Reformation in the Sixteenth Century* (Boston: Beacon Press, 1956):

Luther had no mind to make [marriage] merely a civil contract, but it is not a sacrament in the strict sense of the term and for that reason is not a monopoly of the Church. This assertion undercut one of the devices whereby the Church in the Middle Ages had exercised control over lay life. Unions were prohibited up to the seventh degree of physical relationship and also on account of spiritual relationship incurred through standing sponsor at baptism. Except, however, in the case of close blood ties the prohibitions could be relaxed by the authority of the Church. Since the royal houses of Europe were interrelated, scarcely any marriage could be contracted without ecclesiastical investigation and dispensation for an appropriate fee. When then marriage was declared not to be a sacrament at all, the state stepped in where the Church went out and the prohibited degrees were gradually dropped. (47)

See also Joan Lockwood O'Donovan, *Theology of Law and Authority in the English Reformation* (Atlanta: Scholars Press, 1991), 47.

52   Peter Stallybrass and Allon White, *The Politics and Poetics of Transgression* (Ithaca: Cornell University Press, 1986), 191. Stallybrass and White go on to suggest that disgust "always bears the imprint of desire." In Spain, that desire for the excluded low will be manifested, in part, through the sort of conflation I argue for here: between the bodies of the cultural Others and the body of the wife, the "legitimate" object of Christian, male desire. See also Judith Butler on the relation between the subject and its repudiated "outside": "This zone of uninhabitability will constitute the defining limit of the subject's domain; it will constitute that site of dreaded identification against which — and by virtue of which — the domain of the subject will circumscribe its own claim to autonomy and to life. In this sense, then, the subject is constituted through the force of exclusion and abjection, one which produces a constitutive outside to the subject, an abjected outside, which is, after all, 'inside' the subject as its own founding repudiation." Butler, *Bodies That Matter: On the Discursive Limits of "Sex"* (New York: Routledge, 1993), 3.

53   Albert A. Sicroff, "The Spanish Obsession," *Midstream* (spring 1957): 70. Italics mine.

54   Alfonso el Sabio, *Antología* (Mexico: Porrúa, 1982), 147, italics mine. Translation mine.

55   Covarrubias, *Tesoro,* 720.

56   In the case of the wife, this impurity was seen as a function of her nonvirginal (and thereby nonlegible) status. Vives's account of virginity, for example, includes an ideal of absolute incorruption that has problematic implications for the wife: "Llamo virginidad a la integridad de la mente

que se extiende hasta el cuerpo, *entereza total, exenta de toda corrupción y contagio*" [I call virginity the integrity of the mind that extends to the body, *total integrity, exempt from all corruption and contagion*]. Juan Luis Vives, *Obras completas* (Madrid: Aguilar, 1949), 1006, italics mine. The virgin is equated not only with purity and integrity, but with exemption from contagion; the wife's body becomes, by extension, a site of corruption and decay. Paradoxically, in the case of Jews and Moors, excessive cleanliness was seen as a mark of impurity, providing an example of the extent to which the literal understanding of a term can be constructed as somehow opposite its figural understanding within a particular context.

57 Augustín Redondo, "Le discourse d'exclusion des 'déviants' tenu par l'Inquisition à l'époque de Charles Quint," in *Les problèmes de l'exclusion en Espagne, XVI–XVII siècles*, ed. Redondo (Paris: Sorbonne, 1983), 30.

58 Biblioteca Nacional de España, ms. 9653, 182, cited in Mercedes García Arenal, *Los Moriscos* (Granada: Universidad de Granada, 1996), 44.

59 Covarrubias, *Tesoro*, 38.

60 Jacques Lezra, *Unspeakable Subjects: The Genealogy of the Event in Early Modern Europe* (Stanford: Stanford University Press, 1997).

61 Covarrubias, *Tesoro*, 33.

62 The *acaso* is also inscribed in the allegorical "Loa" that precedes the drama, in which personifications of "Mérito" [Merit], "Diligencia" [Diligence], "Fortuna" [Fortune] and "Acaso" [Chance/Accident] argue over which of the four is most favored by "Dicha" [Fate.] Speaking in its own defense, Acaso argues:

> Del Acaso, una sentencia
> dice que se debe hacer
> mucho caso, pues el ser
> pende de la contingencia.
> Y aun lo prueba la evidencia,
> pues no se puede dar paso
> sin que intervenga el Acaso;
> y no hacer de él caso, fuera
> grave error: pues en cualquiera
> caso, hace el Acaso al caso
>
> [To Chance, an aphorism says
> one should pay
> great attention, since being
> itself hangs on contingency.
> And this is proved by evidence

for one cannot take a step
without Chance intervening;
and to ignore Chance, would be
a grave error: since, in any
case, it is Chance that makes the case.]

Sor Juana Inés de la Cruz, *Los empeños de una casa*, in *Obras completas*, ed. Francisco Monterde (Mexico: Porrúa, 1989). Translation mine.

Chapter 2 "Pasos de un peregrino":
Luis de León Reads the Perfect Wife

1 Y al cavo del dicho proçesso ay una sentencia diffinitiva dada e pronunçiada en auto publico contra el dicho Fernan Sanchez Daviguelo. Por la cual el susodicho fue declarado por hereje apostata y a ser muerto como tal, e fue mandado desenterrar y sacar sus guesos del lugar sagrado donde estubiesen, y en detestaçion del dicho crimen quemarlos publicamente e sus bienes fuern [*sic*] confiscados a la camara e fisco de su Majestad. La pronunciacion y data della en la dicha ciudad el dicho dia viernes veinte e nueve dias del mes de junio de mill e quatroçientos e noventa e dos haziendose auto publico en ensalçamiento de nuestra Sta. fe catolica en la plaça de la yglesia mayor de la dicha ciudad. Por la qual dicha sentencia pareze la dicha Elvira Sanchez fue declarada por hereje apostata y aver caydo e incurrido en sentencia de excomunion mayor y en perdimiento de todos sus bienes . . . y mandaron desenterrar su cuerpo e guesos y quemarlos publicamente.

[And at the end of this process a definitive sentence was given and pronounced in a public auto-da-fé against the aforementioned Fernan Sanchez Daviguelo. In which the suspect was declared guilty of apostate heresy and condemned to death. It was also ordered that his remains be disinterred and removed from the sacred ground where they had lain, that they be burned publicly in abhorrence of the said crime, and that his property be confiscated by the royal chamber and exchequer. The pronouncement and its date in that city and on that Friday, 29 June 1492, was made in an auto-da-fé in exaltation of our Holy Catholic faith in the plaza of the main church in that city. By that sentence it seems that the aforementioned Elvira Sanchez was declared guilty of apostate heresy and fell under and was sentenced to excommunication and the loss of all of her property . . . and they ordered that her body and bones be disinterred and burned publicly].

Proceso inquisitorial de Fray Luis de León, ed. Angel Alcalá (Salamanca: Junta de Castilla y León, Consejería de Cultura y Turismo, 1991), 679–80. Translations are my own. See also Fray Luis de León, *Escritos desde la cárcel: Autógrafos del primer proceso inquisitorial*, ed. José Barrientos García (Madrid: Ediciones Escurialenses, 1991). On the historical "synchronicity" of 1492, see María Rosa Menocal, *Shards of Love: Exile and the Origins of the Lyric* (Durham: Duke University Press, 1994).

2   "I dize mas como la dicha Elvira Sanchez su suegra, muger del dicho Hernan Sanchez Villanueva Aviuelo, pasando por la calle la Tora que llevavan los judios en proçesion a pedir agua se avia fincado de rrodillas y la abia adorado e mandadole a ella y a otras sus criadas que la adorasen y se humillasen y que la dicha testigo le abia dicho que por que se avian de humillar pues era de judios, y que la dicha Elvia Sanchez respondiera que porque era mayor que nuestra ley y della avia salido la nuestra." [And she further says how the aforementioned Elvira Sanchez, her mother-in-law and the wife of the said Hernan Sanchez Villanueva Aviuelo, had fallen to her knees when she passed on the street the Torah which the Jews were carrying in a procession in order to ask for water, how she had blessed it, and how her mother-in-law had ordered her and her other female servants to bless it and to humble themselves. The said witness also recounts that she had asked her why they had to kneel down, since it belonged to the Jews, and that the said Elvira Sanchez must have responded that because it was older than our law and that from it had come our law.] *Proceso inquisitorial de Fray Luis de León*, 679. Translation mine.

3   Marcelino Menéndez Pelayo writes: "Si yo os dijese que fuera de las canciones de San Juan de la Cruz, que no parecen ya de hombre sino de ángel, no hay lírico castellano que se compare con él, aún me parecería haberos dicho poco" [If I were to tell you that, apart from the songs of San Juan de la Cruz (St. John of the Cross), which seem to be written by an angel rather than a man, there is no Castilian lyric poet that can compare with him, it would still seem to me that I had told you little]. Cited in Juan Luis Alborg, *Historia de la literatura española* (Madrid: Gredos, 1986) 1:821. Translation mine. Similarly, Angel C. Vega qualifies Fray Luis as the greatest lyric poet in the world.

4   In the dedication to the third book of *De los nombres de Cristo*, Fray Luis makes mention of—and responds to—the criticism that *La perfecta casada* elicited: "Y porque juntamente con estos libros (*De los nombres de Cristo*) publiqué una declaración del capítulo último de los Proverbios, que intitulé *La perfecta casada*, no ha faltado quien diga que no era de mi persona ni de mi profesión decirles a las mugeres casadas lo que deven hazer" [The first edition also added the text of another book of mine,

my comments to the Book of Proverbs, a book that bears the title *The Perfect Wife*. This also has been criticized: Some readers think I am not qualified, because of my calling and because of the fact that I am not married, to tell married women how they should act and behave]. Luis de León, *De los nombres de Cristo*, ed. Federico de Onís (Madrid: Espasa-Calpe, 1940), bk. 3, pp. 6–7. English translation is from Luis de León, *The Names of Christ*, trans. Manuel Durán and William Kluback (New York: Paulist Press, 1984), 265. Subsequent English quotations from *De los nombres de Cristo* are adapted from the translation of Durán and Kluback and are cited parenthetically by page number in the main body of the text.

5 Manuel Durán, *Luis de León* (Boston: Twayne, 1971), 100.

6 Aubrey F. G. Bell, *Luis de León: A Study of the Spanish Renaissance* (Oxford: Clarendon Press, 1925), 262. Translation mine.

7 Joaquín Antonio Peñalosa, Introduction to Fray Luis de León, *La perfecta casada.* (Mexico: Porrúa, 1985): xvii–xviii.

8 Colin P. Thompson, *The Strife of Tongues* (New York: Cambridge University Press, 1988), 229.

9 J. A. Jones, "The Sweet Harmony of Luis de León's *La perfecta casada*," *Bulletin of Hispanic Studies* 62, 3 (1985): 263.

10 In the introduction to the third book of *De los nombres de Cristo*, Fray Luis responds to those who accused him of overstepping the bounds of his "oficio" by writing a manual for wives by noting that the treatise is, first and foremost, exegetical in nature, and, as a result, entirely "proper" to his role: "Resta agora decir algo a los que dicen que no fue de mi cualidad ni de mi hábito escribir del oficio de la casada; que no lo dijeran, si consideraran primero que es oficio del sabio antes que hable mirar bien lo que dice. Porque pudieran fácilmente advertir que el Espíritu Santo no tiene por ajeno de su autoridad escribirles a los casados su oficio, y que yo en aquel libro lo que hago solamente es poner las mismas palabras que Dios escribe, y declarar lo que por ellas les dice, que es propio oficio mío, a quien por título particular incumbe el declarar las Escrituras." [Something more should be added here: To those who objected my discussing the role of the perfect married woman, claiming that this subject should be off limits to a monk, my answer is simple. The Holy Spirit has dealt with such a subject in the Bible, and my role when writing my book was simply to point out what the Bible has said about such matters. This role, as a theologian, is proper and normal to me and my training does prepare me for it.] de León, *De los nombres de Cristo*, bk. 3, p. 12. Translation from Durán and Kluback, 268.

11 Quotations of *La perfecta casada* are from Luis de León, *La perfecta ca-*

sada, ed. Mercedes Etreros (Madrid: Taurus, 1987), and are subsequently cited parenthetically in the text by page number. English translations, unless otherwise indicated, are amended from Luis de León, *The Perfect Wife*, trans. Alice Philena Hubbard (Denton: College Press, Texas State College for Women, 1943) and are also cited parenthetically by page number. If no page number is indicated, translation is mine.

12 The acrostic takes on particular significance in light of cabalistic teaching (with which Fray Luis was undoubtedly familiar) whereby the whole of creation is encoded in the twenty-two letters of the Hebrew alphabet.

13 Covarrubias's definition of *afeite* registers the extent to which *La perfecta casada* was considered the authoritative text on matters of cosmetic: "Es una mentira muy conocida y una hipocresía mal dissimulada; véase fray Luis de León en la Perfecta casada, contra los afeites" [It means a very well-known lie and a poorly dissembled piece of hypocrisy; see Fray Luis de León's commentary against *afeites* in *La perfecta casada*]. Sebastián de Covarrubias, *Tesoro de la lengua castellana o española*, 46.

14 I cite by way of example one of the numerous "aprovaciones" that preface Quevedo's *Buscón:* "se ha hallado que no tiene cosa contra nuestra santa Fe Catholica. . , Por tanto por tenor de los presentes, de nuestra cierta sciencia, y por la Real Autoridad que usamos en esta parte, damos licencia y facultad al dicho Roberto Duport . . . pueda imprimir y vender, y hazer imprimir y vender el susodicho libro, y todos los cuerpos que del quisiere." [it has been found that it contains nothing against our holy Catholic faith. . . . Therefore, by the accord of those present, of our certain science, and by the Royal Authority that we exert in this matter, we grant license and power to the said Roberto Duport. . . . He may print and sell, and have printed and sold the aforementioned book, and all the bodies (copies) of it that he may wish.] Francisco de Quevedo, *Vida del Buscón llamado Don Pablos*, ed. Fernando Lázaro Carreter (Barcelona: Editorial Juventud, 1968), 33–34. Translation mine.

15 Alexander A. Parker, for example, describes *La perfecta casada* as "a treatise in praise of women, which had been a favourite topic in the literary tradition of Courtly Love. In the numerous works treating of this subject, woman had, of course, been idealized as a sort of goddess, and was not a creature of flesh and blood with a real life to live in the material world. In *La perfecta casada*, however, she is, as the title indicates, a married woman, and at once the idealized feminist literature is brought down to the plane of social duties and moral obligations." Parker, *The Philosophy of Love in Spanish Literature, 1480–1680* (Edinburgh: Edinburgh University Press, 1985), 111. Melveena McKendrick suggests that Fray Luis's text is "one of the most noble defences of woman in sixteenth-century

Spain," in which she is represented not as "the idealized, unattainable creation of the imagination of courtly lovers and neo-Platonic theorists [but as] a real person with a valuable social function." McKendrick, *Woman and Society in the Spanish Drama of the Golden Age: A Study of the 'mujer varon'* (London: Cambridge University Press, 1974), 10.

16 Fray Luis explains the relation between husband and wife in terms of debt and repayment: "Y demás desto, decir Salomón que la buena casada paga bien y no mal a su marido, es avisarle a él que, pues ha de ser paga, lo merezca el primero tratándola honrada y amorosamente. Porque aunque es verdad que la naturaleza y estado pone obligación en la casada, como decimos, de mirar por su casa y de alegrar y descuidar continuamente a su marido . . . no por eso han de pensar ellos que tienen licencia para serles leones y para hacerlas esclavas" (99). [Over and above this, when Solomon declares that the good wife shall repay her husband with good and not evil, it is to warn him, that since it is to be paid, he should first earn it, by treating his wife honourably and lovingly. For while it is true that her nature and estate impose upon the married woman, as we said, the obligation to look after her husband's home, and to gladden and soothe him unfailingly . . . let not husbands think they are privileged on this account to be as lions unto their wives, and to make them into slaves (24).] There is a second passage that goes so far as to justify wifely disobedience in specific circumstances: "Y cuando quisiere ser aun escaso en [dar limosna] el marido, la mujer, si es en lo demás cual aquí la pintamos, no debe por eso cerrar las entrañas a la limosna. . . . Porque si el marido no quiere, está obligado a querer, y su mujer, *si no le obedece* en su mal antojo, confórmase con la voluntad que él debe tener de razón" (121, italics mine). [But granted that in the matter of almsgiving a husband should still want to be grudging, a wife, if she is in every other particular perfect as we here represent her, will not consider it her duty, on her husband's account, to shut away her loving kindness from such charities. . . . The reason is clear: if a husband is unwilling to be charitable, nevertheless it is his duty to be willing, and his wife, *by not obeying him* in his wrong notion, conforms herself to the good will which he ought reasonably to have (45).]

17 Bloch argues that "such essentialist definitions of gender are dangerous not only because they are wrong or undifferentiated but, once again, because historically they have worked to eliminate the subject from history. . . . [W]hat is called for is not the repression of the topic but its critique." R. Howard Bloch, *Medieval Misogyny and the Invention of Western Romantic Love* (Chicago: University of Chicago Press, 1991), 6.

18 Ibid., 60.

19 See, for example, Elias L. Rivers, *Fray Luis de León: The Original Poems* (London: Grant and Cutler, 1983).

20 Translation by Colin Thompson, *Strife of Tongues*, 76.

21 Whether or not Fray Luis intended his frontispiece — which would become a kind of signature — as an affront to the Inquisition is perhaps not as important as the fact that it was thus read. Fray Luis's Latin exposition to the *Book of Job* of 1580 (the first text he published following his release) was, in fact, denounced to the Valladolid Inquisition on 20 October 1580 for being disrespectful and even insulting toward the Holy Office: "El provincial de la Orden de Santo Francisco desta provincia, fray Nicolás Ramos, a enbiado a este sancto officio el libro que a conpuesto fray Luis de León con la calificación que él dél hizo, que embiamos con ésta a v.s. para que nos mande lo que en él debamos hazer; y *en la enblema del libro berá v.s. quan desacatado es para el sancto officio.* Que el libro por andar muy común no lo enbiamos." [The Provincial of the Order of St. Francis of this Province, Fray Nicolás Ramos, has sent this Holy Office the book written by Fray Luis de León and his opinion of it, which we enclose . . . so that you can tell us what we should do. *You will see from the book's emblem how insulting it is to the Holy Office.* Since the book is easily obtainable, we have not sent it.] Cited in Thompson, *Strife of Tongues*, 74, italics mine.

22 "Acusación del fiscal a Fray Luis de León. — Valladolid, 5 de mayo de 1572," BN, Ms. 12747, fols. 147–48, cited in de León, *Escritos desde la cárcel*, 435–36. This and subsequent translations of passages from Fray Luis's *Escritos* are my own.

23 "Respuesta de Fray Luis de León a la acusación del fiscal, presentada ante los licenciados Diego González y Realiego en la audiencia de la mañana — Valladolid, 10 de mayo, 1572." Cited in ibid., 74, italics mine.

24 Hubbard's translation has been modified in favor of a more literal translation of the Spanish text.

25 The insufficiency of the Vulgate translation is raised at various moments throughout the treatise; in a later passage relegating the wife to the interior of the house, for example, Fray Luis once again corrects the translator's inaccuracy by remitting to the "original" (i.e., Hebrew): "Adonde lo que decimos *que tengan cuidado de sus casas,* el original dice así: *y que sean guardas de su casa*" (158) [And where we say 'having a care of the house,' the original says that they are to be the guardians of their homes (73)].

26 "Respuesta de Fray Luis de León al interrogatorio de la primera audiencia — Valladolid, 18 de abril, 1572." Cited in de León, *Escritos desde la cárcel*, 61.

27 Fray Luis had defended literal readings, such as those practiced by the "maestros hebreos," in words that invoked the authority of Augustine.

> Iten me acuerdo que en las mismas congregaciones, diziendo el maestro Leon que *de los dottores hebreos* el no tomaria mas de las declaracion de los vocablos de su lengua, dixo alli un maestro, y no me acuerdo con certindad qual dellos fue, mas de que me parecio bien lo que dixo, y fue: que tambien se podia tomar de los dichos dottores cosas que tocasen a declaracion de la tierra sancta y de sus lugares o *de las costumbres de aquella gente, y tambien quando diesen algun sentido literal a algun paso de la Escrittura,* que fuese de verdadera y sana dottrina, y no contradixese a los sanctos; que no se avia de desechar por ser dellos, porque la verdad es buena qualquier que sea el que la dize, como lo enseña Sancto Augustin."

> [Likewise, I remember that in the same congregations, when the teacher León was saying that he would not take more *from the Hebrew authorities* than the explanation of the words of their language, a teacher then said, and I do not remember with certainty which one of them he was, but I liked what he said, which was: that one could also take from the aforementioned authorities things that may concern the explanation of the Holy Land and its regions or *the customs of those peoples, and also when they give some literal meaning of some passage of Scripture,* that might be of true and sound doctrine, and not contradict the Saints; that one had not to dismiss such things for coming from them, because, as St. Augustine teaches, truth is good no matter who says it.]

> Ibid., 62, italics mine. Translations are my own.

28 Luis de León, *Cantar de los cantares de Salomón,* ed. José Manuel Blecua (Madrid: Gredos, 1994), 47–48. Translation mine.

29 Fray Luis indirectly remits, in this way, to the exegetical debates that were current in early modern Spain. His allusion to a pedagogical function in the literal sense of Scripture could be seen, for example, as complying with the anonymous but well-known verses (first cited by Nicholas of Lyra in the fourteenth century) that expanded Origen's threefold exegetical method to a four-leveled enterprise:

> Littera gesta docet, quid credas allegoria,
> Moralis quid agas, quo tendas anagogia.

> [The letter teaches events, allegory what you should believe,
> Morality teaches what you should do, anagogy what mark you
>   should be aiming for.]

His earlier allusion (cited in the prologue to the *Cantar de los cantares*) to the "corteza" of letters could be seen, in contrast, as subscribing to the Augustinian exegetical tradition that was much more popular in Spain and that tended to conceive of interpretation as two-leveled: the exterior/literal ("corteza") and the interior/figural ("meollo"). English translation of anonymous Latin verses cited in Henri de Lubac, *Medieval Exegesis*, vol. 1 (Grand Rapids: Eerdmans, 1998), 1.

30 The allusion to "palabras desnudas" in Fray Luis's prologue to his translation of the *Cantar* suggests the same type of somatization (and, arguably, feminization) of the word evidenced by the "palabras preñadas" passage. The problem, however, is that as a *figure* for literalness, nakedness itself is already a trope, and thus becomes (for the body of the word) an impossible condition.

31 "En las [Sagradas Letras], como en una tienda común y como en un mercado público y general, para el uso y provecho general de todos los hombres, pone la piedad y Sabiduría divina copiosamente todo aquello que es necesario y conviene a cada un estado" (76) [In the Scriptures, as in a general store, or a public market, for the common use and profit of all men, the Divine compassion and wisdom places in abundance all that is necessary and befitting to each state (4)].

32 de León, *De los nombres de Cristo*, bk. 1, p. 11. Translation from Durán and Kluback, 38.

33 See the third book of *De los nombres de Cristo* for a long defense of the vernacular:

> Assí que, no piensen, porque veen romance, que es de poca estima lo que se dize; mas al revés, viendo lo que se dize, juzguen que puede ser de mucha estima lo que se escrive en romance y no desprecien por la lengua las cosas. . . . Mas dirán que no lo dizen sino por las cosas mismas, que, siendo tan graves, piden lengua que no sea vulgar, para que la gravedad del dezir se conforme con la gravedad de las cosas. A lo cual se responde que una cosa es la forma del dezir, y otra la lengua en que lo que se escrive se dize. En la forma del dezir la razón pide que las palabras y las cosas que se dizen por ellas sean conformes . . . mas en lo que toca a la lengua, no ay differencia, ni son unas lenguas para dezir unas cosas, sino en todas ay lugar para todas.
>
> [Let us now reverse the situation: Our readers should not despise a text because it is written in Castilian, thinking the contents and ideas dealt with in it must be of little importance. Rather, seeing that the matters dealt with in such a Spanish text are indeed lofty and sublime, they should then hold in higher esteem the language that expresses them. . . . Some

will then claim that lofty ideas should always be expressed in a lofty language, not a modern one. We should answer them that style and language are two different things. With respect to style it is true that words and sentences should be adapted to the thoughts they try to convey . . . but with respect to languages there is no basic difference among them, there are no languages that should be held in reserve and used only for certain subjects. Each and every language is capable of expressing the whole range of human knowledge.]

Ibid., bk. 3, pp. 7–8. Translation Durán and Kluback, 266.

34 See Henry Charles Lea, *Chapters from the Religious History of Spain Connected with the Inquisition* (Philadelphia: Lea Brothers, 1890): "It was in the vernacular Bibles, however, that the greatest danger was felt to lie. . . . Even works of devotion, books of hours and the like are forbidden in the Index of 1559 because they contain fragments and passages of Scripture. In the general rules prefixed to the Index of 1583 there is a sweeping prohibition of vernacular Bibles and all portions thereof; and the strict interpretation designed for this is seen in the exceptions made of texts quoted in Catholic books and the fragments contained in the canon of Mass, provided they do not stand alone but are embodied in sermons or explications" (53).

35 The phrase "the order of things" is, of course, the title of the English translation of Michel Foucault's *Les mots, les choses*. I adopt it here in its Foucauldian sense.

36 Aubrey F. G. Bell criticizes Fray Luis's style in *La perfecta casada* for this very reason: "If any fault is to be found with Luis de León's style it would be that it is occasionally rhetorical and sometimes too rich. This abundance sprang from an abundance of matter and thought, as though one sentence and simile came boiling and bubbling over another." Bell's supporting footnote is particularly significant for a reading of the workings of analogic semblance in the treatise: "He is not afraid of superlatives. . . . The hallmark of his style is the frequency of the connecting particles. . . . Of a succession of sixty-seven sentences in *La Perfecta Casada*, § iii, twenty-four begin with y, sixteen with porque, four with que, four with pues, two with mas, and one each with pero, entendiendo que, por lo cual, por manera que, lo cual, allende de que, mayormente que, and ansi que." Bell, *Luis de León*, 263.

37 For a classic account of the history of this concept, see Arthur Lovejoy, *The Great Chain of Being: A Study of the History of an Idea* (Cambridge: Harvard University Press, 1936). Manuel Durán has commented on the presence of the Great Chain of Being in the intellectual foundations of

Fray Luis's thought: "A physical world made up of four elements, a Great
Chain of Being that culminates in Man (himself a microcosm, the humors
in his body being but a 'translation' of the four elements), and finally
points upwards towards God, the whole surrounded by the crystal sphere
of the heavens, which in turn produce a music, a harmony (this is an idea
inspired perhaps by the teachings of that elusive and mysterious Greek
philosopher Pythagoras . . .), this is the universe in which Luis de León
grew up and wrote his poems." Durán, *Luis de León*, 41.

38 J. A. Jones has explored how a worldview based on the concept of universal harmony specifically informs the notion of "woman" in *La perfecta casada:* "That this view of the inherent order and harmony of life
and creation was not merely a topical Renaissance notion incorporated
into the writing of his obrecillas as a pleasurable indulgence, but a concept central to his life and the world and to all of his work will, I hope,
be illustrated in this study of *La perfecta casada* in which we encounter
the concept of harmony expressed not in the abstract, introspective and
philosophical context of the major poems but in a very concrete, practical situation in life, namely, that of the married woman." Jones, "Sweet
Harmony", 260.

39 Fray Luis's interest in language as a means of reaching the Divinity can
be gleaned from his earliest sermons. In a sermon based on a reading
of Ecclesiastes 27:2, prepared for a panegyric to St. Augustine on his
feast day and probably dating from the late 1550s, Fray Luis examines
the workings of linguistic similitudes and its theologic dimensions: "Et
quamvis res omnes aliae aliis sint similes, tamen nescio quo pacto fit, ut
quo alia res melior praestantiorque est, & quo magis bonitate, dignitate,
splendore distat a caeteris, eo illius similitudo, atque imago aliqua extet
in pluribus." [And although all things are similar to one another, nevertheless by some means it happens that the better and the more excellent
a thing is, and the further it is distant from the rest in goodness, dignity
and splendour, the more its likeness and image exists in many things.]
Colin Thompson explains the passage as follows: "Metaphors, he argues,
are possible only because in God's creation each thing is related to every
other thing through common divine origin. There is therefore a relationship between any two things in the created order which exists before
they are expressed in words, and indeed makes such expressions possible. Fray Luis means that metaphorical language is more than a poetic
device. It is possible only because the universe was created by God and
it becomes the literary representation of the nature of that creation."
Thompson, *Strife of Tongues*, 8–9.

40 See John Freccero, "The Fig Tree and the Laurel: Petrarch's Poetics,"

in *Literary Theory/Renaissance Texts*, ed. Patricia Parker and David Quint (Baltimore: Johns Hopkins University Press, 1986), 20–32. Freccero writes: "The ultimate end of desire is God, in whom the soul finds its satisfaction. The ultimate end of signification is a principle of intelligibility in terms of which all things may be understood. God the Word is at once the end of all desire and the ultimate meaning of all discourse. . . . The theology of the Word binds together language and desire by ordering both to God" (22). Marcia Colish similarly points to a kind of semiotic theology at work in Augustine: "In his discussion of Christ as the Interior Teacher, Augustine thus presents a theory of words as signs in the knowledge of God which specifies their status as true, though partial, representations of their objects, and which also clarifies their functions in conveying knowledge to two different kinds of subjects, believers and non-believers." Colish, *The Mirror of Language: A Study in the Medieval Theory of Knowledge* (Lincoln: University of Nebraska Press, 1983), 57.

41 The passage inscribes a striking paradox with respect to the materiality or immateriality of words. The almost organic relation that obtains between words and things ("de donde nace" [from which it is born]) suggests that names are not, in fact, immaterial beings ("seres espirituales"), but are imbued in corporeality. Fray Luis deftly sidesteps the apparent contradiction by delineating two species of names, "unos que están en el alma y otros que suenan en la boca" de León, *De los nombres de Cristo*, bk. 1, p. 31 [those which are in the soul and those which are in our lips (45)], the former spiritual in nature, the latter bodily. It is precisely through the physicality of words (at the level of the figure of the letter) that a Cratylism of the sort Fray Luis describes can survive — by paradoxically succumbing to — the accidents that befall "things."

42 "No se guarda esto siempre en las lenguas; es grande verdad. Pero si queremos dezir la verdad, en la primera lengua de todas casi siempre se guarda. . . . [E]n la Sagrada Escriptura, se guarda siempre en todos aquellos nombres que Dios puso a alguno, o por su inspiración se pusieron a otros." [The truth is that this is not always realized in language. Yet if we want to tell the truth in the first of all languages, Hebrew, it is almost always observed. . . . In the Bible this is preserved in all those names which God gave to someone or which through his inspiration were given to others.] de León, *De los nombres de Cristo*, bk. 1, p. 33. Translation from Durán and Kluback, 46–47.

43 In his use (and even abuse) of analogy as a means of achieving the universal "eslavonamiento" that brings man to God, Fray Luis could be seen as an heir of St. Thomas. On Thomas's use of analogy, Colish writes: "For Thomas, then, analogical knowledge of God is one species within the

general category of conceptual signs of God. Like all signs of God, analogies refer to a reality Whose nature is already known in part by faith. Analogy is more serviceable than are straightforward names of God in displaying the doctrine of the Trinity because it can signify relationships as well as things and because it can elucidate the relationships between things that are both similar and different." Colish, *Mirror of Language*, 127.

44 Foucault cites Descartes's *Regulae* as a prime example of this type of mistrust in similitudes: "It is a frequent habit when we discover several resemblances between two things, to attribute to both equally, even on points in which they are in reality different, that which we have recognized to be true of only one of them." Foucault, *The Order of Things: An Archaeology of the Human Sciences* (London: Tevistock Publications, 1970), 47. The danger of analogy, as Descartes would understand it, resides in the creation of false homologies due to a tendency toward overextension or overcompensation of analogic identity. This is, in a sense, the very danger to which *La perfecta casada* paradoxically succumbs.

45 Citing the almost identical paradox of invoking virile women for humanist defenses of gynocracies, Constance Jordan writes: "The women who illustrate feminine excellence are noted for acting courageously and intelligently — in short, a manner specified as virile. These women logically prove the worth of their sex by denying it: a strange form of defense. While it questions sexual stereotypes, that some women can do men's work, it also seems to confirm gender-related values, that everything female is inferior." Jordan, "Feminism and the Humanists: The Case of Sir Thomas Elyot's Defence of Good Women," in *Rewriting the Renaissance: The Discourses of Sexual Difference in Early Modern Europe*, ed. Margaret Ferguson, Maureen Quilligan, and Nancy J. Vickers (Chicago: University of Chicago Press, 1986), 252. See also Constance Jordan, *Renaissance Feminism: Literary Texts and Political Models* (Ithaca: Cornell University Press, 1990).

46 Hubbard's translation has been modified to render the passage more in keeping with the language of the Spanish text.

47 Covarrubias's entry for *ramera* is equally suggestive: "Ramera. Es lo mesmo que cerca de los latinos meretrix. Estas vivían fuera de los muros de las ciudades, y a ellos arrimavan unas choçuelas a modo de hornillos o bovedillas, por lo qual las llamaron fornicarias. Estas *salían algunas vezes a los caminos reales,* no lejos de los molinos del trigo y otras vezes de los del azeyte, y sobre unas estacas armavan sus choçuelas y las cubrían con ramas, de donde se dixeron rameras." [*Ramera* is the same as the Latin *meretrix* (harlot). They lived outside the city walls, and against

these they would place dwellings that looked like little bowls or domes, on account of which they called them fornicators. They would *appear at times on the high roads,* not far from the wheat mills and sometimes near the oil mills, and they would put their dwellings on stakes and cover them with *ramas* (branches), which is why they were called *rameras*.] Covarrubias, *Tesoro,* 895, italics mine. The etymological genealogy Covarrubias provides for the term "ramera" points to a contiguity between a woman's body (and the uses to which she and others submit it) and her house, a relation that is crucial to *La perfecta casada*'s reading of the body of la perfecta casa-da. This contiguity can quite easily be conceived, where the ramera is concerned, in terms of the dress or ornament that covers the body (Fray Luis's "bordados" [handwrought trimmings], "encrespos" [crisping pins], and "afeites" [cosmetics]) or the covering that dresses the house (Covarrubias's "ramas"), both of which identify and even denominate the woman in question as a whore. That the pilgrim is, according to the *Tesoro,* attired in "vestido propio" [proper clothing] by which he is instantly recognized is, in this context, anything but coincidental; like the ornamented prostitute, he too is visually marked by his dress. Both figures are, in this sense, legible from the outside. The fact that rameras wandered the "caminos reales" [high roads] in search of potential clients is not irrelevant to Fray Luis's text, particularly since marriage is described as a camino real on which the casada wanders in search of wifely perfection.

48 Jacques Lezra's careful reading of this passage in terms of the relation between Sinn and Form (and as a theological version of the sort of materiality of the word that informs Freud's Wolf Man, for example) has been invaluable for my own reading. Lezra writes: "The fluidity of Fray Luis' example is an appropriate way of indicating to what extent Sinn and Form seem to have come together here. But this coming-together is not a material one, but rather based on the hypostatized relation of accident to essence. This relation is invariable and ideal, and it has no better proof than the correspondence of the letter (as figure) to the (material) accidents of what it names." Lezra, "Icarus Reading: Trope, Trauma, and Event in Shakespeare, Cervantes, and Descartes" (Ph.D. diss., Yale University, 1990), 40.

49 The issue of whether figures of letters can be castrated largely depends on the materiality ascribed the letter and its possible relations to the materiality of bodies. See Lezra's reading of Lacan in his "Icarus Reading."

50 On Ave/Eva, see, for example, Henry Kraus, "Eve and Mary: Conflicting Images of Medieval Women," in *Feminism and Art History,* ed. Norma Broude and Mary D. Garrard (New York: Harper and Row, 1982), 79–

99. Peter Damian's verses, cited by Kraus, are a good example of the way that Mary's holiness (Ave) was conceived as a sort of antidote to Eva's sinfulness: "That angel that greets you with 'Ave' / Reverses sinful Eva's name / Lead us back, O holy Virgin, / Whence the falling sinner came" (84).

51 Such a reading might, for example, cast Fray Luis as romero (recalling his offer that opens the text to guide Doña María on the road of matrimony "como suelen los que han . . . *peregrinado* por lugares extraños" [76] [as those who have . . . gone on *pilgrimage* through strange places (3)] and the casada (ornamented in the trappings of excess) as the ramera who seduces him. Alternately, this sort of reading might trace the monstrous transformations the casada undergoes at the hands of Fray Luis, satisfying first the exigencies of one term and then the other. Traveling on the camino real of marriage, she herself is, after all, also a sort of pilgrim, whose body becomes prostituted by the very text that reads her.

52 López Pinciano's *Philosophía antigüa poética* registers the "impropriety" of this pilgrim language, which opposes the alleged stability of "lenguaje propio" [proper language]:

> Y esto baste del vocablo propio. Vamos al peregrino que es su contrario. Vocablo peregrino se dize al que es fuera de vso, el qual, o es desvsado o peregrino de todo. . . . Passa el vocablo y se muda en otro, o según su cuerpo, o según su alma—llamo el cuerpo las letras y sylabas de que es compuesto, y digo alma a su significación.

> [And this is enough concerning the word that is proper. Let us turn to the pilgrim, which is its opposite. Pilgrim is said of a word that is out of use, or that is antiquated or completely strange. . . . The word passes and changes into another, either in body or in spirit. (I call the body the letters and syllables of which it is composed, and the spirit, its signification.)]

> Alonso López Pinciano, *Philosophía antigüa poética*, ed. Alfredo Carballo Picazo (Madrid: Consejo Superior de Investigaciones Científicas, 1953), 126–32. Translation mine. See Mary Gaylord's remarkable reading of López Pinciano's poetics in Gaylord, "The Whole Body of Fable with All of Its Members: Cervantes, Pinciano, Freud," in *Quixotic Desire: Psychoanalytic Perspectives on Cervantes*, ed. Ruth El Saffar and Diana de Armas Wilson (Ithaca: Cornell University Press, 1993), 117–34; and Gaylord, "El lenguaje de la conquista y la conquista del lenguaje en las poéticas españolas del Siglo de Oro," in *Actas del IX Congreso de la Asociación Internacional de Hispanistas*, ed. Sebastián Neumeister et al. (Frankfurt am Main: Vervuert, 1989), 1:469–75.

53 Hubbard's translation has been modified to render the passage more in keeping with the language of the Spanish text.

54 Fray Luis succumbs, in this sense, to the same inevitability of metaphor that Derrida describes in "White Mythology" with specific reference to the text of philosophy, arguing that philosophical discourse cannot avoid metaphor, particularly in those instances when it most vehemently asserts its literalness. See Jacques Derrida, "La mythologie blanche" in *Marges de la philosophie*, (Paris: Editions de Minuit, 1972), 247–324. What is more, operating within the dynamics of a system that equates the straight path with literalness and the curved path with figurative-ness, the path away from metaphor leads, inevitably, back to metaphor (perhaps of a more pernicious sort), since straight steps on a winding road lead (quite literally, in this case) off the beaten path. The seemingly irresolvable conflict between a straight linearity and a curvilinearity that muddles the pilgrim's steps can also be aligned quite neatly within the binary opposition male/female that is already current in Aristotle's *Metaphysics* and that is explicitly tied to aestheticized readings of the male and female bodies (as respectively straight and curvaceous). While the effort at enderezamiento would seem to place Fray Luis on the masculine side of the polemic, his deviant pilgrimage into an empirical world of feminine detail ("experiencia . . . ajena a mi profesión"), on one hand, and the inevitable sense of detour (the very nature of gloss) that pervades — and in a sense organizes — his text, on the other, places him on the side of the feminine. Even more suggestive, in this context, is the analogic principle of identity established between the pilgrim (at home) and Fray Luis in their respective capacities as guides; the empirical grounding of the pilgrim's authority would seem to require a deviant crossing of gender lines on Fray Luis's part, if he were to follow in the precarious footsteps of his own analogy ("Y como . . . así yo"). Such a crossing is qualified, however, by the textual mediation that justifies his self-appointment, based on an unmentioned relation of supplementarity between "sagradas letras" and "experiencia pasada." If Fray Luis will take the place of woman, it is of a woman dressed not only in the prostitute's garb but, moreover, in the (made-up) words and letters of the texts that would undress her.

55 Mary Elizabeth Perry, *Gender and Disorder in Early Modern Seville* (Princeton: Princeton University Press, 1990), 48. Italics mine. Perry goes on argue: "A nineteenth-century historian suggested that respectable matrons wore the distinctive head-covering out of sympathy with stigmatized prostitutes, hoping to mitigate the harshness of restrictions on them. Another possible explanation is that yellow head-coverings

did not really become symbols of prostitution because prostitutes did not comply with the rule. It is also possible that non-prostitute women wanted to appear daring, or that they wanted to rebel against dress restrictions. Realizing their inability to define themselves if they simply conformed to official definitions of good women, they may have seized the power to define themselves through appearance. Officials did not try to explain this blurring of categories for women but simply decreed that prostitutes must henceforth distinguish themselves by adding a tinsel ornament to their head-covering" (48–49).

56 Tertullian, *The Apparel of Women*, trans. J. Arbesmann et al., in *Disciplinary, Moral, and Ascetical Works* (New York: Fathers of the Church, 1959), 146.

57 The uncontained woman—casada or ramera—was in fact deemed a serious threat in early modern Spain. As Perry notes: "Wandering women free from enclosure in marriage or convent worried many who saw them as the most potent symbol of disorder. One response, fired by impatience with women who did not conform to prescriptions for enclosure, called for establishing a workhouse to confine the many 'lost' and vagabond women who wandered about Seville." Perry, *Gender and Disorder*, 69.

58 *La perfecta casada*'s conflation (and condemnation) of a "woman in public" with a "public woman" clearly evokes the biblical figure of the roaming harlot of Proverbs 7. In addition, enclosure is explicitly tied in the text to the idea of covering the body: "Como es de los hombres el hablar y salir a luz, así dellas el *encerrarse y encubrirse*" (158, italics mine) [As it pertains to men to go out, and to engage in discussions, so it behooves women to *seek seclusion and to conceal themselves* (74)]. Although Fray Luis's concern for shrouding is consonant with a conception of female sexuality as a monstrous lure that requires veiling to prevent contamination, it is decidedly at odds with the pervasive subtext of adultery that equates covering with the adulterous, ontologic deception of cosmetic.

59 It is not coincidental that the casada outside the casa is compared by Fray Luis to a fish out of water; the scene not only dramatizes the disjunctive *translatio* of catachresis but can be read as the logical supplement (the verbal cognate as well as the material leftover) to the example of catachresis provided by Augustine in *De doctrina christiana: a piscina* emptied of its *piscis*. Augustine writes: "Who does not use the word piscina [basin, pool, pond tank, or other large container of water] for something which neither contains fish nor was constructed for the use of fish, when the word itself is derived from piscis [fish]? This trope is called catachresis." See St. Augustine of Hippo, *De doctrina christiana: On Christian Doctrine,*

trans. D. W. Robertson (New York: Macmillan, 1958), bk. 3, chap. 29, p. 103. Neither is it accidental that Freud uses the twisting of the feet of Chinese women as an example of the "double attitude [acceptance and denial] of fetishists" regarding the castration of women. To cite Freud: "In very subtle cases the fetish itself has become the vehicle both of denying and of asseverating the fact of castration. . . . Naturally a fetish of this kind constructed out of two opposing ideas is capable of great tenacity. Sometimes the double attitude shows itself in what the fetishist—either actually or in phantasy—does with the fetish. It is not the whole story to say that he worships it; very often he treats it in a way which is plainly equivalent to castrating it. . . . Another variety of this [double attitude], which might be regarded as a race-psychological parallel to fetishism, is the Chinese custom of first mutilating a woman's foot and then revering it. The Chinese man seems to want to thank the woman for having submitted to castration." Freud, *Sexuality and the Psychology of Love,* ed. Philip Rieff (New York: Macmillan, 1963), 219. Although problematic, it is nonetheless tempting to consider Fray Luis's analogy between the fish out of water and the lame casada as a linchpin of sorts that permits a reading of Freud's fetishism in terms of Augustine's catachresis. Both the fetish (in its Freudian reading) and catachresis (in its Augustinian one) serve as substitutes, after all, for something perceived as missing, whether the woman's (specifically, the mother's) phallus or the proper word.

60 To the extent that Fray Luis's house(d)wife is lame of foot, she evokes an oedipal narrative that is legible throughout the text; carried to its furthest extremes, the containment of the wife's body within the interior of the house engenders incest.

61 As Patricia Parker convincingly argues, "A woman must stay within a private place—the home—because her body contains a private place, a place or 'enclosure' that adultery would break into, and make a 'common' rather than a particular property. . . . The wandering woman—out of her place, become a 'harlot,' and 'full of words'—must be kept in her place, like her counterpart within the body, that 'mother' which is curiously 'mooveable' and which in the language of contemporary gynecology causes problems and inversion when it strays from its proper place." P. Parker, *Literary Fat Ladies: Rhetoric, Gender, Property* (London: Methuen, 1987), 105–6. On the house-body relation, see also Peter Stallybrass, "Patriarchal Territories: The Body Enclosed," in *Rewriting the Renaissance: The Discourses of Sexual Difference in Early Modern Europe,* ed. Margaret Ferguson, Maureen Quilligan, and Nancy J. Vickers (Chicago: University of Chicago Press, 1986), 123–42; and Mary S.

Gossy, *The Untold Story: Women and Theory in Golden Age Texts* (Ann Arbor: University of Michigan Press, 1989). Gossy's argument is particularly suggestive for my reading here: "Architecturally, a window is the element of a building that is least decidable. It is neither inside nor outside the building and (whether glazed or not) it can be transparent, a place for looking out and in. Unlike a door, though, it limits the transit of human bodies between the inside and the outside; the senses may use it as a vehicle for perception, but the body itself does not pass through it except in extraordinary, rule-breaking circumstances (burglary, escape, suicide). . . . For these reasons, the window becomes an architectural locus of desire, and the *celosía* is made to function as a hymen in that locus" (106).

62 Fray Luis goes so far as to exclude honesty from the virtues of the perfecta casada on the grounds that it is (or should be) her very essence: "El ser honesta una mujer no se cuenta ni debe contar entre las partes de que esta perfección se compone, sino antes es como el subjeto sobre el cual todo este edificio se funda, y para decirlo enteramente en una palabra, es como el ser y la substancia de la casada. Porque sino tiene esto, no es ya mujer, sino alevosa ramera y vilísimo cieno, y basura la más hedionda de todas y la más despreciada" (90). [Fidelity in a wife does not count, nor should it count, among those qualities of which this perfection consists, rather is it like the foundation on which the entire superstructure is upbuilded. In a word, faithfulness is like the very marrow and innate being of a perfect wife. For if a wife is without honour, she is not a wife, but a treacherous harlot, the vilest mire, a reeking refuse-heap, and of all beings the most despicable (16).]

63 The analogy Fray Luis establishes between the father's sleep and the casada's elides an important distinction. Whereas the patriarch's sin is solely one of omission ("mientras el padre . . . duerme" [while the father . . . slumbered]) since it is the enemy that exerts subjective agency over the act of "sembrar cizaña" [to sow (discord)], the sleeping wife's sin becomes a more serious one of commission as well, since through her neglect—her inagency ("con su descuido y sueño" [with her slackness . sloth])—she assumes grammatical agency over the intrusion that ults in her house's devastation ("así ella . . . meterá" [the wife . . . ill make room]). If, through her body's contiguity with her house, the casada is object of forceful violation, she is also, in this sense, assigned culpability as a transgressive subject.
    Stallybrass, "Patriarchal Territories," 127.

5 There is a curious passage in *La perfecta casada* that legitimizes woman's silence precisely in terms of the contiguity that operates between house

and body. The body in question, however, is not that of a woman at all but of a tortoise:

Cuenta Plutarco, que Fidias, escultor noble, hizo a los elienses una imagen de Venus que afirmaba los pies sobre una tortuga, que es animal mudo y que nunca desampara su concha; dando a entender que las mujeres, por la misma manera, han de guardar siempre la casa y el silencio. (155)

[Plutarch relates that Phidias, that noble sculptor, made for the inhabitants of Elis an image of Venus with her feet set upon a tortoise, an animal which has no voice, and which never comes out of its shell, thus giving us to understand that women, following their example, must always remain at home, and must always practise silence. (70–71)]

If it may be argued, as Fray Luis seems to do here, that the turtle is an apt icon for woman's enclosure because its "house" is inextricably connected with its body, it is also possible to read that metonymy in the opposite direction. Rather than rendering the (turtle's) body immobile, then, the condition (of having one's house on one's back) invests the house with a mobility that in some respects makes the turtle the most errant animal of all.

66   On the equation between being a writer and being a woman, see Bloch, *Medieval Misogyny*.

67   Makeup (in its relation to the material cost of perpetrating ontological transgressions) first surfaces "out of place," for example, in an argument against costliness in a casada (95). It reappears, a few pages later, in the midst of an indictment of "el sueño de la mañana" (113–14). The charge against morning sleep is dismissed, however, as a lesser evil in comparison with the illicit rituals of cosmetic.

68   The danger of feminine beauty, as Fray Luis understands it, is not only that it awakens the desire of an improper Other, but that this improper desire in turn awakens the woman's desire for *being* an object of desire: "Y no sólo es esta belleza peligrosa, porque atrae a sí y enciende en su cobdicia los corazones de los que la miran, sino también porque despierta a las que la tienen a que gusten de ser cobdiciadas" (170) [Beauty of this sort is not only fraught with peril because it draws the hearts of all beholders to itself, and inflames them with desire, but also because in women gifted with beauty is awakened a craving for being desired (84)].

69   From at least as early as Plato, identical lexical borrowings figure in admonishments of an emasculated, densely metaphorical style in rhetoric (particularly in its "effeminate," Asiatic manifestation) and of the excessive use of coloring in painting. Quintilian's almost axiomatic distinction

between the masculine eloquence of the virile orator and an "effeminate," "prostituted" Ciceronian style is a case in point, as is the imagery of a cheap, wanton coloring corrupting the (phallic) efficacy of the line that characterizes the sixteenth-century *disegno-colore* quarrel in Italy and, subsequently, the rest of Europe. The fine line that separates acceptable ornament ("vestido sancto" [holy dress]) from a visually threatening, overwhelming excess ("aquella *artillería* toda" [all that *artillery*]) is no different whether it is employed in the domain of language, the painted image, or the wife's body. In all three cases, coloring is chastized on moral grounds for its excess, for blinding the unwary spectator ("¿a quién ha de cegar?" [whom does this *blind?*]), for luring the vision away from that which is essential — the sujeto — and turning it, instead, toward the contingent — the accidente. On the association between Ciceronian rhetoric and feminine coloring, see Jacqueline Lichtenstein, *La couleur éloquente: Rhétorique et peinture à l'age classique* (Paris: Flammarion, 1989), particularly the chapter titled "Des limites du discours à l'éloquence de l'image."

The excesses of coloring in makeup that *La perfecta casada* condemns on charges of adulteration and falsification become analogous, in this sense, to the excesses and abuses of color in both painting and rhetoric. The charge of ontological frivolity leveled against that which "comes second" is, on a broader level, an indictment of figural representation in general. And yet, it is fairly obvious that Fray Luis does not practice what he preaches. On the contrary, *La perfecta casada* is everywhere dependent on categories of the visual and the figurative; there is no dearth of irony in the fact that its founding metaphor is one of painting and, moreover, of painting an anatomically and tropologically (given the allusion to "colors" and "parts") correct "virtuosa casada, con todas sus colores y partes" [virtuous wife with all her colors and parts]. What the alignment of these respective colors reveals is one of the central contradictions of all those that so seductively mar the face of *La perfecta casada*. In the act of denigrating makeup's "rosy, pale, blonde, and golden" as adulterous aberrations, Fray Luis explicitly enlists the colors of both painting and rhetoric. The very denomination of makeup as "adultery, harlotry, a never-ceasing wrongdoing" can be read as an example of the aberrant rhetorical trope of catachresis, inasmuch as it divorces these terms from their "proper" contexts, and grafts them, instead, onto categories of ontological fidelity, legibility, and subjectivity.

The contradiction with respect to color that Fray Luis's text registers is, in many ways, anticipated by St. Augustine. In *De doctrina christiana*, the founding text of Christian liturgical interpretation that explicitly addresses the question of ambiguity in reading, Augustine's examples of grand rhetorical style (a style "adorned with verbal ornaments" and "forceful with emptions of the spirit" are none other than Cyprian's and Ambrose's exhortations against "women who color, or discolor, their features with paint" (Augustine, *De doctrina christiana*, 150, 157, respectively). The choice of passages seems almost ironic, inasmuch as they condemn, at a thematic level, the very same ornaments and colors for which they serve as example at a formal level. For a thoughtful study of the Christian transformation and "antifeminization" of Stoic cosmetic theology, see Marcia Colish, "Cosmetic Theology: The Transformation of a Stoic Theme," in *Assays: Critical Approaches to Medieval and Renaissance Texts* (Pittsburgh: University of Pittsburgh Press, 1981), 3–14.

70 It would not be difficult to conceive of the husband as a foil of sorts for the reader's position, given the citational nature of Fray Luis's text (and especially the censures of makeup as adultery). The reader reads an-Other text as she reads Fray Luis's, just as the husband reads an-Other's body when he gazes on the face of his made-up wife.

71 Hubbard's translation has been modified slightly.

72 See Bloch's incisive reading of patristic attacks on cosmetics: "That which is secondary, artificial, and thus assimilated to woman is considered to participate in a supervenient and extraneous rival Creation that in the thought of the fathers can only distract man's attention from God's original 'plastic skill.' " Bloch, *Medieval Misogyny*, 41.

73 Tertullian, for example, who is also cited by Fray Luis, makes almost the identical argument:

"No habéis de exceder de lo que el aderezo simple y limpio se debe, de lo que agrada al Señor porque sin duda le ofenden las que se untan con unciones de afeite el rostro, las que manchan con arrebol sus mejillas, las que con hollín alcoholan los ojos; porque sin dubda les desagrada lo que Dios hace, y arguyen en sí mismas de falta a la obra divina; reprehenden al Artífice que a todos nos hizo. Reprehéndenle pues le enmienden, pues le añaden. Que estas añadiduras tómanlas del contrario de Dios, esto es, del demonio, porque ¿quién otro será maestro de mudar la figura del cuerpo sino el que transformó en malicia la imagen del alma? El sin duda es el que compuso este artificio para en nosotros poner en Dios las manos en cierta manera. Lo con que se nasce, obra de Dios es, luego lo que se finge y artiza, obra será del demonio." (141)

[We must not go beyond what is desired by those who strive for natural and demure neatness. We must not go beyond what is pleasing to God. For, surely, those women sin against God who anoint their faces with creams, stain their cheeks with rouge, or lengthen their eyebrows with antimony. Obviously, they are not satisfied with the creative skill of God; in their own person, without doubt, they censure and criticize the Maker of all things! Surely they are finding fault when they try to perfect and add to His work, taking these their additions, of course, from a rival artist. This rival artist is the Devil. For, who else would teach how to change the body but he who by wickedness transformed the spirit of man? It is he, no doubt, who prepared ingenious devices of this sort that in your own persons it may be proved that to a certain degree you do violence to God. Whatever is born, that is the work of God. Obviously, then, anything else that is added must be the work of the Devil.] Tertullian, *Apparel of Women*, 135–36. (This passage is not in Hubbard's translation.)

74 The passage that Fray Luis cites from (and attributes to) Tertullian reads as follows: " 'Salid, salid aderezadas con los afeites y con los trajes vistosos de los Apóstoles. Poneos el blanco de la sencillez, el colorado de la honestidad; alcoholad con la vergüenza los ojos, y con el espíritu modesto y callado. En las orejas poned como arracadas las palabras de Dios. Añadad a vuestros cuellos el yugo de Cristo. . . . Vestid seda de bondad, holanda de santidad, púrpura de castidad y pureza, que afeitadas desta manera, será vuestro enamorado el Señor.' " [Go forth to meet those angels, adorned with the cosmetics and ornaments of the Prophets and Apostles. Let your whiteness flow from simplicity, let modesty be the cause of your rosy complexion; paint your eyes with demureness, your mouth with silence; hang on your ears the words of God, bind on your neck the yoke of Christ. . . . Dress yourselves in the silk of probity, the fine linen of holiness, and the purple of chastity. Decked out in this manner, you will have God Himself for your lover.] Ibid., 149.

75 Fray Luis's solution for the paradox of the mujer de valor is that there is some extrawomanly agency operating through her: "Porque cosa de tan poco ser como es esto que llamamos mujer, nunca ni emprende ni alcanza cosa de valor ni de ser, si no es porque la inclina y la alienta alguna fuerza de increíble virtud que o el cielo ha puesto en ella, o algún don de Dios singular. Que pues vence su natural, y sale de madre como río" (87). [For so insignificant a thing as this which we call woman never undertakes or succeeds in carrying out anything essentially worthwhile unless she be drawn to it, and stimulated, and encouraged by some force of incredible resoluteness which either God, or some singular gift of God, has placed within her soul. Since she conquers her very nature, and, like a river overflowing its banks, breaks all bounds (14).]

76 See Perry, *Gender and Disorder*.

77 Jacqueline Lichtenstein writes:

> Feminine, indecent, unnamable, and illicit, makeup gives itself over to
> the gaze in the dissolution of speech. The beauties of coloring are those
> of the Medusa. And this Medusa of abundant and terrifying hair occurs
> in painting with the features of a woman who has often been represented
> by painters as holding the head of a man by his hair: the figure of Judith.
> We should not be surprised that the story of Judith had such success from
> the time of the Renaissance. Whatever her other meanings—and we do
> not pretend to any scientific or iconographic truth—Judith seems also
> an allegory of makeup, an allegory of painting in its essence and in its
> effects. . . . After all, . . . Holofernes died from having been seduced by
> the gleaming finery of femininity, from having desired the opposite sex
> in its brilliance and having met it in its reality.

Lichtenstein, "Making-up Representation: The Risks of Femininity," in
Misogyny, Misandry, and Misanthropy, ed. R. Howard Bloch and Frances
Ferguson (Berkeley: University of California Press, 1989), 85. Lichten-
stein goes on to demonstrate how in works on rhetoric from the Counter-
Reformation, the figure of Judith (notably, framed in the act of cutting
off Holofernes' head) was used to allegorize eloquence.

78 See Freud on Judith and Holofernes in *The Taboo of Virginity* and *Sexu-
ality and the Psychology of Love,* both in *Standard Edition of the Com-
plete Psychological Works of Sigmund Freud,* trans. James Strachey and
Anna Freud (London: Hogarth Press, 1953). See also the chapter titled
"Judith, Holofernes, and the Phallic Woman," in Mary Jacobus, *Reading
Woman: Essays in Feminist Criticism* (New York: Columbia University
Press, 1986), 110–36.

Chapter 3   The Perfected Wife: Signs of Adultery and the Adultery of Signs in Calderón's *El médico de su honra*

1 Pedro Calderón de la Barca, *El médico de su honra,* ed. D. W. Cruickshank (Madrid: Castalia, 1989), 209, l. 2833. References to this edition
are parenthetically cited by page and line number within the text. English translations unless otherwise noted, are from *The Surgeon of His
Honour,* trans. Roy Campbell (Madison: University of Wisconsin Press,
1960).

2 I refer to the two other plays that together with *El médico de su honra*
form a sort of Calderonian honor trilogy, specifically, to *El pintor de su
deshonra,* in which Serafina's perfect body cannot be painted by her hus-

band until it has been deemed imperfect and is then only painted in blood, and to *A secreto agravio, secreta venganza*, in which Leonor's "adulterous" body serves to reify the male bond between her husband and Don Juan. Pedro Calderón de la Barca, *Obras completas*, ed. Angel Valbuena Prat (Madrid: Aguilar, 1952).

3   See Bruce Wardropper, "The Dramatization of Figurative Language in the Spanish Theatre," *Yale French Studies* 47 (1982): 189–98. Wardropper has rightly suggested that horses in Calderón generally represent an embodied lust. Horses of lust, he writes, "are a mappa mundi of the four elements, with the attributes of creatures proper to each one: the horses fly like birds, dart like fish, flash like comets, and display the brute force of wild beasts. They are often introduced at the beginning of a play . . . to convey a sense of the 'unbridled' passion of the rider they have just unseated, who must, so to speak, roll into the plot propelled by the force of his own lust" (194). The description is fitting for Enrique, whose "lustful" motives toward Mencía will lead to such disastrous ends. Enrique himself suggests that where jealousy is concerned, the horse serves as an extension of himself: "Y no fue, sino que al ver / tu casa, montes de celos / se le pusieron delante / porque tropezase en ellos; que aun un bruto se desboca / con celos" (135) [To see your house here raised such rugged mountains / Of jealousy in front of him, that he / Stumbled over them; for even brutes / Go mad with jealousy, and bolt with rage (10)]. Beyond this, the horse that unseats Enrique fits into an economy of lustful desire, in which horses and wives are the tokens of exchange. When Gutierre gives him a horse at his departure, the prince comments: "el me ganó la dama y yo le gané el caballo" (97, ll. 493–94) [He wins my lady, and I gain his horse (15)].

4   Questions over the "facticity" of the husbands' punishment and its incompatibility with Christian morality has dominated the critical field since the early nineteenth century when the study of honor in Spanish Golden Age drama began. Frank P. Casa summarizes the prevailing position as follows: "Alexander Parker, Albert Sloman and P. N. Dunn in subsequent works have followed [Edward] Wilson's lead and have firmly established: (1) that far from applauding or even tolerating the bloody deed, Calderón condemns the perversion of Christian morality that the honor system implies; (2) that the king's acceptance of Gutierre's action rather than indicating the approval of society is a manner of reenforcing the barbarity by having an equally cruel man approve of it." Casa, "Crime and Responsibility in *El médico de su honra*," in *Homenaje a William L. Fichter: Estudios sobre el teatro antiguo hispánico y otros ensayos*, ed. A. David Kossoff and José Amor y Vázquez (Madrid: Cas-

talia, 1971), 128. Casa goes on to agree with the first of these conclusions, while disagreeing with the second, arguing instead that "the king's assent to the murder of Mencía is then nothing but a tacit surrender of his exclusive right to render justice in his kingdom and a recognition of his inability to rule, pre-figuring therefore his eventual and total loss of power" (136).

5 Américo Castro, *De la edad conflictiva: Crisis de la cultura española en el siglo XVII* (Madrid: Taurus, 1961), 45. Translation mine.

6 See Melveena McKendrick, "Honour/Vengeance in the Comedia: A Case of Mimetic Transference?" *Modern Language Review* 79, 2 (1984): 313–35. "If in real life the merest suspicion of *mala sangre* [bad blood] excluded a man from the preferment he sought, on stage, the merest suspicion of a stain on, or threat to, his wife's virtue robbed him of his honour." McKendrick goes on to suggest that "the relation between life and drama where honor was concerned, was a close one, but it was not a direct one." She departs somewhat from the arguments of Castro and van Beysterveldt, suggesting that what the husbands are complaining against in their diatribes against honor is "their thraldom to the conception of the individual as a creature that lives by and for his social identity, a conception to which they themselves subscribe" (330–33).

7 *Recopilación de las leyes destos reynos hecha por mandado de la Magestad Catholica del Rey Don Philippe segundo, nuestro Señor,* generally referred to as *Nueva recopilación* (Alcalá de Henares, 1569), in Melveena McKendrick, *Woman and Society in the Spanish Drama of the Golden Age* (London: Cambridge University Press, 1974), 15. English translation mine. Needless to say, the *Recopilación* is silent on the issue of a husband's adultery. The only stipulation on the husband is that he not kill one (wife or lover) without also killing the other: "assi que no pueda matar al uno i dexar al otro" [thus, he cannot kill one and leave the other]. This is an issue in *El médico de su honra,* in which Enrique's royal blood shields him from Gutierre's revenge.

8 See C. A. Jones, "*Honor* in Spanish Golden-Age Drama," *Bulletin of Hispanic Studies* 35 (1958): 199–210. "In my opinion the code of honour in the Spanish drama of the Golden Age is a convention which, although not entirely divorced from reality or morals, is closely concerned with neither of these things, and a defence of the code of honour, or an attack on it, should not refer to the conditions of real life, nor to any contemporary moral opinions, without bearing in mind that it is bound up with the popular entertainment of the time" (206).

9 Sánchez Ortega writes: "La figura del 'marido calderoniano,' de la sangrienta reacción meridional es un arquetipo literario universal. ¿Qué

puede decir sobre el tema el historiador? ¿Estamos ante un tópico o se trata de una realidad? Echemos un vistazo al Registro del Sello del Archivo General de Simancas. Los maridos que se han acogido al perdón real por haber dado muerte a la esposa infiel mientras el interesado se marchaba a la guerra a Granada son casos tan frecuentes que no cabe lugar a dudas. El 'marido calderoniano' era una realidad social que probablemente no desapareció en los siglos XVI y XVII, aunque—como todas las epidemias—tuviera sus períodos álgidos y sus crisis." [The figure of the "Calderonian husband," of the bloody meridional reaction, is a universal literary archetype. What can the historian say on the subject? Are we faced with a topos or a historical reality? Let's take a look at the Registry of the General Archives of Simancas. Husbands who have taken refuge in royal pardon for having put to death their unfaithful wife while the interested party goes off to the war in Granada are so common that there can be no doubt about it. The "Calderonian husband" was a social reality that probably did not disappear during the sixteenth and seventeenth centuries, although—like all epidemics—it would have its decisive moments and crises.] Sánchez Ortega, "La mujer en el Antiguo Régimen: Tipos históricos y arquetipos literarios," in *Nuevas perspectivas sobre la mujer: Actas de las primeras jornadas de investigación interdisciplinaria* (Madrid: Seminario de Estudios de la Mujer de la Universidad Autónoma de Madrid, 1982), 1:120. Translation mine.

10   Whether or not husbands killed wives, the Inquisition's preoccupations for limpieza included sexual purity; the association, then, between honor and limpieza need not be as "transferential" as McKendrick suggests, since adulterous wives were in fact tried by the inquisition for their infidelity: "A juzgar por los pleitos inquisitoriales y civiles, las relaciones sexuales fuera del matrimonio eran mucho más frecuentes de lo que pudiera pensarse en una sociedad que había hecho de la virginidad femenina uno de los elementos del honor, tanto popular como de las clases elevadas. Ante el tribunal del Santo Oficio o de las Chancillerías vemos desfilar con frecuencia a mujeres casadas y solteras que han mantenido relaciones 'ilícitas'—como las denominan en los textos—, es decir, al margen de la pauta oficial marcada por la sociedad." [Judging by the inquisitorial and civil cases, extramarital sexual relations were much more frequent than one would think in a society that had made feminine virginity one of the elements of honor for both the common people and the higher classes. Filing past the tribunal of the Holy Office or that of the Chancelleries we often see married and single women who have maintained "illicit" relations (as they are called in the texts), which is to say,

relations outside the official guidelines established by society.] Ibid., 119. Translation mine.

11 Ruth El Saffar writes: "Cervantes's work shows in many places how the marriage structure, based on a model of dominance and submission, produces in the one called to assert his control a terror and anxiety that only makes of this would-be paradise a torment. . . . Calderón, in an even more powerful way, probes the terror that possesses the one whose gender role requires that he dominate and subdue another." El Saffar, "The 'I' of the Beholder: Self and Other in Some Spanish Golden Age Texts," *Hispania* 75, 4 (1992): 866.

12 Lope's extraordinary *El castigo sin venganza* is one of the rare exceptions to this tenet. There, a wife's adultery is not only consummated but represented, through a sort of mirror trick, on the space of the stage.

13 See José Antonio Maravall, *La cultura del barroco: Análisis de una estructura histórica* (Barcelona: Ariel, 1975). Maravall's study of the baroque is posited on a totalizing concept of dominant ideology; it should be noted, however, that he also points to the ways in which the "restored tradition" was open to question.

14 Valerie Traub's insightful reading of strategies of containment at work in *Hamlet, Othello,* and *The Winter's Tale* has been indispensable for my own reading of these tactics in *El médico de su honra.* According to Traub, "Male anxiety toward female erotic power is channeled into a strategy of containment; the erotic threat of the female body is psychically contained by means of a metaphoric and dramatic transformation of women into jewels, statues, and corpses. Indeed, together, the plays seem motivated toward this end: to give women speech only to silence them; to make women move only to still them; to represent their bodies on stage only to enclose them; to infuse their bodies with warmth only to coldly 'encorpse' them. What is crucial about these plays, however, is not so much the eventual status of women as reified objects . . . but the *process* by which the drama renders them as such, the *transformation* that occurs as the motive and telos of dramatic action." Traub, *Desire and Anxiety: Circulations of Sexuality in Shakespearean Drama* (New York: Routledge, 1992), 26.

15 See Georg Wilhelm Friedrich Hegel, *Aesthetics,* trans. T. M. Knox (Oxford: Clarendon Press, 1975), 558–62.

16 Peter Stallybrass, "Patriarchal Territories: The Body Enclosed," in *Rewriting the Renaissance: The Discourses of Sexual Difference in Early Modern Europe,* ed. Margaret Ferguson, Maureen Quilligan, and Nancy J. Vickers (Chicago: University of Chicago Press, 1986), 125.

17 If Mencía's words reinforce the implicit analogy between the house and
the female body, they may also suggest an extension of that analogy (an
extension in some senses legitimized by the one-flesh doctrine's literalization in the honor plays) to include the body of the husband, whose
integrity is at least figuratively penetrated by the entrance of an-Other
man within the house. Gutierre's reaction to a transgressive entrance
into his house is perhaps best understood in terms of this kind of substitutability (particularly between "casa" and "esposa"): "Suspiros al cielo
doy / que mis sentimientos lleven, / si es que a mi casa se atreven, /
por ver que en ella no estoy" (139, ll. 1337–40) [But I send bitter sighs to
God above / That anyone, perceiving I am absent, / Should dare to set
a foot inside my house (38)].

18 Translation mine.

19 The transfer is dangerous in a more immediate sense. If (short of mystic
rapture) the ascetic desire to liberate the soul is obtainable only by means
of the body's death, transferring the locus of the soul's imprisonment
onto the Other's body implies also transferring the unspoken death wish
that the language of incarceration inscribes, a sort of "muero porque no
mueres" [I die because you do not].

20 Traub, *Desire and Anxiety*, 28. See also Abbe Blum, " 'Strike all that look
upon with marble': Monumentalizing Women in Shakespeare's Plays,"
in *The Renaissance Englishwoman in Print: Counterbalancing the Canon*,
ed. Anne M. Haselkorn and Betty S. Travitsky (Amherst: University of
Massachusetts Press, 1990), 99–118. Perhaps nowhere in Calderón is this
kind of "monumentalizing" strategy of containment as crucial, or problematic, as in *El pintor de su deshonra*.

21 The body—specifically, the wife's body—as container thus becomes a
threat to a unified male subjectivity since, as Traub suggests, "in the act
of orgasm, male experience of the female body is not so much that of
an object to be penetrated and possessed, but of an enclosure into which
the male subject merges, dissolves, and in the early modern pun, dies."
Traub, *Desire and Anxiety*, 27. In other words, if masculine penetration
of the female body (whether the literal penetration of sexual intercourse
or the figural penetration that places both Gutierre's soul and his honor
within Mencía's body) reifies phallogocentric power, the pleasure that
derives from that act (the orgasm that ostensibly ensues) tends, instead,
toward its dissemination, its virtual erasure. Insofar as orgasmic release
is imagined as a merging of the male Self with(in) the female Other, the
figuration of the female body as container can provoke a male anxiety
of indifferentiation.

22 Her phrasing is suggestive in another sense; while the ablative "con" in

"romper con el silencio" [breaking (with) the silence] is perhaps best read as implying concomitance (and a certain identity) between the ruptures of silence and of desire's icy prison, the preposition also lends itself to a reading that assigns silence a certain instrumentality in that break, suggesting perhaps, that as a strategy of control, verbal containment is not only doomed to failure, but inevitably participates in its own downfall.

23 See Roberto González Echevarría on the literalization of metaphor as more metaphorical than metaphor itself in his insightful reading of *La Celestina*. González Echevarría, *Celestina's Brood: Continuities of the Baroque in Spanish and Latin American Literatures* (Durham: Duke University Press, 1993). See also Susanne Wofford's brilliant reading of performatives on the Shakespearean stage, "*To You I Give Myself, For I Am Yours:* Erotic Performance and Theatrical Performatives in *As You Like It*," in *Shakespeare Reread: The Texts in New Contexts*, ed. Russ McDonald (Ithaca: Cornell University Press, 1994), 147–69.

24 In her study on performativity in *Don Juan*, Shoshana Felman revises the Aristotelian conception of tragedy along just these lines to suggest that tragedy is engendered not in the imitation of action, but rather in its linguistic inscription. Felman's proposition is suggestive for *El médico de su honra:* "The source of the tragic consists . . . in the encounter between act and language. Might we not once again modify Aristotle's definition with a Nietzschean annotation, noting that the essence of tragedy might be not the act, but rather the speech act, that in any case the tragic act *par excellence* turns out to be not murder but a speech performance?" Felman, *The Literary Speech Act: Don Juan with J. L. Austin, or Seduction in Two Languages*, trans. Catherine Porter (Ithaca: Cornell University Press, 1983), 96.

25 The irony is that insofar as performativity is roughly alignable with (linguistic) reification, it also becomes alignable with the (reificatory) containment strategies it repudiates, disclosing, in the seeming paradox, the extent to which such strategies are inherently destined to fail. That marriage, too, can be similarly aligned with both containment (of erotic desire) and linguistic performativeness ("with these *words*, I thee wed") is not without equally rich yet troubling implications.

26 Translation mine.

27 But if the possibility of conceiving linguistic dissemination in terms of aerial contamination corresponds to the work's medical subtext, the idea of responding to "agravios" (presumably against wifely honor) by pairing "quejas" with "desengaños" seems to invoke a legal framework also present in the drama and points, moreover, to the implicit figure of arbitrating judge who will weigh one against the other. At various moments

throughout the play, King Pedro is called on to fill this role, living up to his epithet of "Justiciero" (147). For reasons that are all too clear, however, Mencía chooses to argue her case of agravio outside official judicial channels. Her "courtroom" is not the "alcázar's" [fortress's] royal chambers but a bedchamber, at one level, at another, the theater itself. The implication, then, is that here the position of judge must either remain at least provisionally unoccupied or else be filled outside the text by the body of the dramatic spectator.

28   The relation is further complicated by Gutierre's own call on the wind as agent of violence, substituting in his version Mencía's body for the word's.

> *Gutierre*
> No me espanto, bien mío;
> que el aire que mató la luz, tan frío
> corre, que es un aliento
> respirando del céfiro violento,
> y que no sólo advierte
> muerte a las luces, a las vidas muerte,
> y pudieras dormida
> a sus soplos perder también la vida.
>
> . . . .
>
> ¿No has visto ardiente llama
> perder la luz al aire que la hiere,
> y que a este tiempo de otra luz inflama
> la pavesa? Una vive y otra muere
> a sólo un soplo. Así, desta manera,
> la lengua de los vientos lisonjera
> matarle la luz pudo, y darme luz a mí
> (169–70, ll. 1993–2000, 2003–09, italics mine)

> [*Gutierre*
>   I do not wonder
> That it blew out the lamp, my love, so chilly
> It blows — it seems a breath from the fierce, wild
> West wind that bodes not death to candles only —
> But human lives! And you, while sleeping here,
> Might even catch your death from it yourself.
>
> . . . .
>
> Have you not seen a burning flame blown out
> By a strong gust that at the same time kindles
> A flame in a dull cinder? At one breath

A flame dies and another flame is born.
So, likewise, with one flick of its fawning
A flattering tongue the wind can, in one thrice,
Deprive you of your flickering light and give
Some lustre to myself. (55)]

The complementarity both Gutierre and Mencía had earlier ascribed their loving conjugal relation now becomes fatally charged: "una vive y otra muere" [A flame dies and another flame is born]. The image Gutierre invokes of a "tongue of wind" is potent, particularly since it is a tongue that kills not only lights but lives.

29   In a reading of a passage from Mallarmé, Felman suggests that acts are constituted as acts only in relation to language: "The act, Mallarmé suggests here, is that which *leaves traces*. Now there are no traces without language: the act is legible as such (that is, as effect, as reality effect) only within a context in which it is *inscribed*." Felman, *Literary Speech Act*, 93.

30   López Pinciano's definition of honor as a question of its public legibility is suggestive in this context: "La honra, dice el Philósopho, es juycio de la estimación de la persona bienhechora; quiérolo dezir de otra manera, acaso seré mejor entendido. La honra es una estimación, la qual estimación se manifiesta con hechos; de manera que no es honrado vno, sino es que con alguna obra lo sea. Hónrase vn hombre con darle assiento honrado, con darle de comer de la riqueza pública, o con darle vn hábito de cauallero, o con darle vna borla de doctor y con otras cosas semejantes." [According to the Philosopher Aristotle, honor is a judgment of the esteem of a beneficent person. I would like to say it another way; perhaps I will be better understood. Honor is an estimation that is manifest through deeds, so that one is not honorable unless it is by means of some act. A man is honored by giving him a seat of honor, by feeding him with public riches, or by presenting him with knightly vestments, or by awarding him a doctor's tassel, and by other similar things.] Alonso López Pinciano, *Philosophía antigüa poética*, ed. Alfredo Carballo Picazo (Madrid: Consejo Superior de Investigaciones Científicas, 1953), 110.

31   Perhaps the most candid assessment in the play of the public/private binarism as it concerns the question of honor appears, significantly, neither in Mencía's mouth nor in Gutierre's (they are guardians of words), but rather in Leonor's. In her legal case before the king about the "publicidad" with which Gutierre repeatedly entered her house (and, by metaphoric extension, her body), licensed, significantly, by his unfulfilled

word of future marriage ("Diome palabra que sería mi esposo" [105, l. 649] [He gave his word that he would be my husband (20)]), Leonor points to the ambivalence—and even the hypocrisy—of the honor code's strictures: "Mas la publicidad a tanto pasa, / y tanto esta opinión se ha dilatado, / que en secreto quisiera más perdella, / que con público escándalo tenella" (106, ll. 661–64) [For now the public voice is so much feared / And so great is one's terror of opinion / That most would sooner lose their fame in secret / Than keep it pure in face of public scandal (20)]. Her situation suggests how even in its more pedestrian form (as gossip) linguistic dissemination can have ruinous consequences; her dishonor is, after all, strictly a function of "dilation." But Leonor seems to forget at times the importance of linguistic containment, to the extent that Pedro must remind her not to argue her "caso de honor" publicly.

What is more, Leonor's curse at the close of the first act, is a striking example of the almost infectious quality of performativity.

> ¡Muerta quedo! ¡Plegue a Dios,
> ingrato, aleve y cruel,
> falso, engañador, fingido,
> sin fe, sin Dios y sin ley,
> que como inocente pierdo
> mi honor, venganza me dé
> el cielo! ¡El mismo dolor
> sientas, que siento, y a ver
> llegues, bañado en tu sangre,
> deshonras tuyas, porque
> mueras con las mismas armas
> que matas, amén, amén!
> ¡Ay de mí!, mi honor perdí.
> ¡Ay de mí!, mi muerte hallé.
> (121, ll. 1007–20)

> [Oh, I could die! false, feigning, hateful,
> Unfeeling, treacherous, ungrateful,
> Oh, lawless, Godless, void of faith!
> May God bear witness, to your shame,
> That, innocent, I lost my name
> Because of you! May Heaven scathe
> You with my vengeance: may the same
> Suffering that I feel, the shame
> That so unjustly I have borne,

Make you and yours a thing of scorn!
Your forehead may your wife adorn
And drag your honour in the mud!
My grief be yours, and may the same
Weapons with which you slew me, slay you!
May the same jealousies repay you,
And of your anguish make a game!
May you be cursed the same as I!
Amen! Since I have lost my name
There's nothing for me but to die! (28)]

Here, the performative force of Leonor's curse attaches to statements
she intends as constative. Thus, her qualifying her loss of honor as
"mi muerte hallé" [There's nothing for me but to die!] can be read as
being anachronically (given the perfect tense she uses) premonitory. The
"muerte" she has found (or will find) is not, as she suspects, having lost
Gutierre as husband, but, ironically, the royal sentence to marry him at
the play's end.

32 Covarrubias's entry for *bíbora* [snake] explicitly inscribes an image of
an "imperfect wife": "Escriven della que concibe por la boca, y que en
el mesmo acto corta la cabeça al macho, apretando los dientes, o por el
gusto que recibe o por el desgusto que teme recebir después al parir de los
vivoreznos, los quales siendo en número muchos, los postreros que han
tomado más cuerpo y fuerça, malsufridos y cansados de esperar, rompen
el pecho de la madre.... Con toda su ponçoña se haze de su mesma carne
antídoto y remedio para contra ella, y contra algunas enfermedades....
Es comparada a ella la muger que en lugar de regalar y acariciar a su
marido le mata.... A la muger que es brava de condición dezimos que
es una bívora. Ay algunas emblemas y hieroglyficos de la bívora." [It is
written that it (the female viper) conceives through the mouth and that
in the very act it cuts off the head of the male by clasping its teeth, either
because of the pleasure that it receives or because of the displeasure it
fears to receive after the birth of the baby vipers, these being great in
number. The last ones born, which are larger and stronger, and impatient
and tired of waiting, break through the chest of the mother.... With all
its venom, an antidote and remedy are made from its own flesh for use
against it and against some maladies.... Comparable to it is the woman
who, instead of indulging and cherishing her husband, kills him....
Of the woman who is ill-tempered, we say that she is a viper. There are
some emblems and hieroglyphs of the viper.] Sebastián de Covarrubias,
Tesoro de la lengua castellana o española, 218.

33 Pedro Calderón de la Barca, *The Surgeon of Honour*, trans. Gwynne Edwards, in *Plays: One* (London: Methuen Drama, 1991), 42.

34 If Gutierre is the most rigorous role-player in *El médico de su honra*, he is by no means the only one. Indeed, almost every one of the play's characters participates in the metatheatricality so typical of Calderon, adopting and discarding disguises throughout the drama. The persistent preoccupation with disguises and recognition suggests the extent to which identity is conceived as a spectacle in the play, rendering the soy quien soy even more problematic. This obtains at all social levels, from the king down to Coquín. If, on one hand, Pedro commands tremendous ontological authority in his role as king, for example, it is, on the other, an authority that is precariously grounded, given that in his desire for panoptic knowledge and in the flexibility of the Self that his disguises represent (as a means, precisely, to secure that knowledge), the king finds an unexpected double in the marginal figure of Coquín. The gracioso's total relativization of the soy quien soy formula into "soy quien vuestra majestad quisiere" (108, ll. 712–13) [I am whomever your Majestry wants me to be (translation mine)] explicitly underscores the disjunctiveness of the formula and is not unlike the surrender of the Self that Pedro resorts to, adopting disguises as a means of diagnosing his kingdom. Coquín's body, it must be remembered, is, like Mencía's, also under scrutiny, submitted to an "examinación de cosquillas" [tickling examination] by the king. The threat of bodily punishment (specifically, losing his teeth) hangs over the gracioso for almost the entire work. The possibility of conceiving of him as a sort of double for the king might suggest the extent to which the king's authority is precarious at best.

35 Translation mine.

36 José Antonio Maravall, *Teatro y literatura en la sociedad barroca* (Madrid: Seminarios y Ediciones, 1972), 100.

37 Pedro Calderón de la Barca, *Life Is a Dream*, trans. Edwin Honig (New York: Hill, 1970), 9.

38 Covarrubias, *Tesoro*, 459.

39 A seventeenth-century inquisitor whose professional memoires are recorded in "Las cosas que se han de observar y practicar en las Ynqqnes, con algunos cassos particulares y extraordinarios que me parecen dignos de notar por ejemplares, para quando suceda caso semejante" [The things that should be observed and practiced in the inquisitions, with some peculiar and extraordinary cases that seemed worthy of noting down as exemplary, for when a similar case occurs (again)] writes of various cases of clerics accused of being alumbrados who justified carnal

contact with women by means of this type of logic: "Como de cierto
clérigo tenido en buena reputación, que últimamente dio en defender
que el dormir con una muger, y tener ósculos y otros tocamientos deso-
nestos, no sólo no era peccado pero meritorio, porque no passando más
adelante, antes davan una higa al demonio, como el que *potuit transgredi
et non est transgressus*" [Like a certain priest of good reputation who recently argued that sleeping with a woman, and engaging in kissing and
other indecent touching not only was not a sin, but was praiseworthy
because, by not going any further, they were scorning the devil, like
one who "was capable of transgressing but did not"]. MS 831, Biblioteca Nacional de Madrid, cited in Louis Condillac and Robert Jammes,
"Amours et sexualité a travers les mémoires d'un inquisiteur du XVIIe
siècle," in *Amours légitimes, amours illégitimes en Espagne, XVIe–XVIIe
siècles*, ed. Augustín Redondo (Paris: Sorbonne, 1985), 192.

40 The full passage reads as follows:

> Pruebas de honor son peligrosas pruebas;
> pero con todo quiero
> escribir el papel, pues considero,
> y no con necio engaño,
> que es de dos daños éste el menor daño,
> si hay menor en los daños que recibo.
> (189, 2408–13)

> [Trials of honour are most perilous.
> But I will write this letter, since I think
> That it would be the lesser of two evils
> If he remained, than if he went away—
> That is, if there is such a thing as "lesser"
> Amongst these evils that I bear each day. (67)]

41 See Covarrubias's etymology of *cetro:* "La mesma significación tiene
vara (*latine virga*)" [*vara* (rod) has the same meaning (in Latin, *virga*)].
Covarrubias, *Tesoro*, 413. The entry for *vara* ("*latine virga, quasi verga*,"
p. 993) in turn remits to the entry for *verga:* "*Membrum virile*" (1002).
Vara also has an explicitly theatrical meaning that is particularly suitable to the honor plays' endings: "*virgula divina*, cuando en la comedia o
tragedia estavan las cosas tan rebueltas que era necessario entreviniesse
algún dios que con esta vara los aquietasse, declarando algún misterio
y cosa que hasta allí les era encubierto" [*virgula divina* ("divine rod"),
when things in a tragedy or comedy were in such disorder, that it was
necessary for some god to intervene who pacified them with this *vara*,

expounding some mystery and something that up until then had been concealed (994)].

42 Although Pedro is tenacious in his testing, his methodology is not infallible, as his doomed examination of his brother (with Gutierre in hiding) confirms.

43 Translation mine.

44 On theologic hermeneutics and its relation to a teleology of truth, see Felman, *Literary Speech Act.*

45 Covarrubias, *Tesoro,* 575, 885, and 738, respectively.

46 The interplay of the three might be schematically represented as follows:

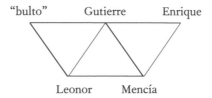

47 This shifting is perhaps not unlike that which Lacan points to as crucial for understanding the two scenes of reading in Poe's "The Purloined Letter." If the analogy were to be extended, perhaps the relevant question would be *what* in *El médico de su honra* would replace the "letter" as the signifier that acts as catalyst for the various positions that individual subjects assume in the narrative episodes. One possible answer is "honor," which functions in the honor plays in much the same way as Lacan suggests the "letre volée/volante" does in Poe's story, that is, as something to be stolen, as symbol of a lack (and even of castration, although Lacan does not explicitly use the term): "the signifier is . . . by nature symbol only of an absence." Lacan, *The Seminar of Jacques Lacan,* ed. Jacques-Alain Miller (New York: W.W. Norton, 1988), 54. In "Le facteur de la verité," Derrida has taken Lacan to task for what he perceives to be a sort of "phallogocentrism" on his part in attributing to this absence the status of a transcendental signified: "le sens de la nouvelle, le vouloir-dire de la lettre volée . . . est découvert. Découverte d'un vouloir dire (la vérité) herméneutique, le déchiffrement (celui de Dupin, celui du Séminaire) arrive lui-même à destination" [The sense of the tale, the meaning of the purloined letter . . . is uncovered. The deciphering (Dupin's, the Seminar's), uncovered via a meaning (the truth), as a hermeneutic process, itself arrives at its destination]. Derrida, *La carte postale: De Socrate à Freud et au-delà* (Paris: Flammarion, 1980), 472. Translation from Derrida, *The Post Card: From Socrates to Freud and Beyond,* trans. Alan Bass (Chicago: University of Chicago Press,

1987), 444. Derrida's critique could likewise be applied to the vouloir-dire honor since honor, as it is constructed and defined in these plays, is by nature a phallogocentric concept. The fact that criticism of these plays has, for the most part, hinged on honor as the central issue affirms its reified status.

48 It is by no means coincidental in this context that some of the most fervid inquisitors were themselves of converso origin.

49 Almost the identical structure of the double triangle of desire that appears in *El médico de su honra* can be articulated for *A secreto agravio*, but with an important difference. There, the third position of the triangle wherein the husband plays the adulterous spouse is occupied not by another woman, but, provocatively, by another man (in this case the long-lost friend, Don Juan, who returns from the dead in much the same way as Don Luis does), suggesting a reading of the play in terms of a homosocial continuum. There are numerous instances in the drama that suggest not only an overinvestment in the Lope-Juan relation (that mirrors the overinvestment in the relation between husband and wife and in the literalness of the one-flesh doctrine), but moreover, where Don Juan almost literally takes the place of a marital partner (even in the dramatization of the two shall become doctrine). Fittingly, the play ends not with the remarriage of Don Lope (there is no "other woman" with whom he could contract matrimony) but rather with his reinduction into the exclusively male space of war/public history, a space from which women are categorically excluded.

50 Covarrubias, *Tesoro*, 553.

51 The state of seventeenth-century optics confirms the nonmimetic visual exchange, particularly in the case of a convex surface such as the dagger's: "ay algunos [espejos] que hazen los rostros disformes, unas vezes muy anchos y otras largos y angostos, lo qual consiste en la forma en que está labrado y en la hoja de detrás . . . los que son hechos a manera de globos [convexos], buelven las figuras lo de abaxo arriba." [There are some (mirrors) which deform faces, sometimes making them very wide and other times, long and narrow. This depends on the way in which it is made and on the back sheet (of glass). . . . Mirrors which are made in the manner of (convex) spheres turn the images upside down.] Covarrubias, *Tesoro*, 554.

52 Calderón's choice of reigning monarch for the play could be attributable, at least in part, to the historical record, specifically, to the infante Enrique's murder of his brother, King Pedro el Cruel.

53 This is by no means the last appearance of the dagger in the play. Gutierre picks it up again, once Enrique drops it. "Muera Mencía, su sangre /

bañe el pecho donde asiste; / y pues aqueste puñal / hoy segunda vez me rinde / el infante, con él muera" (184, 2305–09) [Let Mencía die / and wash with her own blood / The breast that it inhabits! By this dagger / Confided, by the Prince, a second time / To my possession, let her perish now! (64)]. Despite Gutierre's words here, he does not kill Mencía with the prince's dagger. The dagger is, nonetheless, instrumental to the murder: with it Gutierre "hires" Ludovico at knifepoint to effect the fatal cure. "Señor, / de mi casa me sacasteis / esta noche; pero apenas / me tuvisteis en la calle, / cuando un puñal me pusisteis / al pecho, sin que cobarde / vuestro intento resistiese" (196, ll. 2542–48) [My lord, out of my house / Tonight you came and fetched me: but then hardly, / Hardly had we descended to the street, when you, / Thrusting a dagger to my chest (whose threat / I was too terrified to disobey) (71)].

54 Covarrubias, *Tesoro*, 245.

55 See Exodus 12:5–13: "Your lamb shall be without blemish. . . . And [the whole assembly of the congregation of Israel] shall take the blood and strike it on the two side posts and on the upper door post of the houses, wherein they shall eat it. . . . And the blood shall be to you for a token upon the houses where ye are; and when I see the blood I shall pass over you, and the plague shall not be upon you to destroy you, when I smite the land of Egypt."

56 This English quotation is from the translation by Gwynne Edwards, p. 96.

57 See Elisabeth Bronfen, *Over Her Dead Body: Death, Femininity, and the Aesthetic* (New York: Routledge, 1992).

58 The acts of covering and uncovering are suggestive not only of Gutierre's revenge, which must be public in order to remain private ("Este fue el más fuerte medio / para que mi afrenta acabe / disimulada" [199, ll. 2606–08] [This is the subtlest means by which the cause/ Of death can be dissembled" (73)]) but, more compellingly, in relation to the uncovering of Mencía's wounds: "Y así contando la muerte, / y diciendo que fue lance / forzoso hacer la sangría, / ninguno podrá probarme / lo contrario, si es posible / que una venda se desate" (199, ll. 2612–17) [And so, when I recount her death, and say / That bleeding was found necessary, none / Can prove the contrary, nor yet allege / The leech's bandage did not come undone (73)].

59 Covarrubias, *Tesoro*, 543.

60 Bruce Wardropper, "Calderón's Comedy and His Serious Sense of Life," in *Hispanic Studies in Honor of Nicholas B. Adams*, ed. John Esten Keller (Chapel Hill: University of North Carolina Press, 1966), 184.

61 What is more, if in accordance with seventeenth-century medical knowl-

edge the prescription of a sangría responds to the play's insistence on purification, that purification is only possible because bloodletting was likened to menstruation. Sangrías for men in particular were intended to purify them of intoxicating excess in the same way that menstrual flow was thought to purify women. Although menstruation was imagined to cleanse the body of pollutants, the menstruating woman was conceived as a threat, a source of impurity and contamination. Both secular law and medical practice of early modern Spain reaffirm the Judaic law that called for isolating the menstruating wife.

62 Given the subtext of blood, even menstrual blood, in the final act of the play, it is noteworthy that one of the entries in Covarrubias's definition of *falta* remits explicitly to menstruation: "Falta. Lo mesmo que en latín dezimos *defectus*, de do puede traer origen; o del verbo *fallo, fallis*. Poner falta en alguna cosa es dar a entender que no está caval. . . . Falta en la muger preñada, los meses que ha tenido faltos de su regla." [*Falta*. The same as when in Latin we say *defectus* (failure), from which it could derive; or from the verb *fallo, fallis* (to fail). *Poner falta en alguna cosa* (To mark a lack in something) is to make it understood that it is not perfect. *Faltas*, with regard to a pregnant woman, are the months that she has missed her period.] Covarrubias, *Tesoro*, 583.

63 See José Ruano de la Haza's reading of the honor dramas as "tragedias mixtas" [mixed tragedies], in which the anagnorisis that occurs in the play does not take place onstage, but rather in the audience. Ruano de la Haza, "Hacia una nueva definición de la tragedia calderoniana," *Bulletin of the Comediantes* 35, 2 (1983): 165–80.

Chapter 4   The Imperfect Wife:
Sor Juana's *Empeños*

1 Sor Juana Inés de la Cruz, *Obras completas*, ed. Francisco Monterde (Mexico: Porrúa, 1989), pp. 318–19. Translation by John Charles.

2 In 356, the patriarch Athanasius of Alexandria wrote to the emperor Constantius in regard to the virgins of the Church of Alexandria: "The Son of God, our Lord and Saviour Jesus Christ, having become man for our sakes . . . in addition to all His other benefits bestowed this also upon us, that we should possess upon earth, in the state of virginity, a picture of the holiness of the angels. Accordingly, such as have attained this virtue, the Catholic Church has been accustomed to call the brides of Christ." Athanasius, *Apologia ad Constantium* 33.49: *Patrologia Greca* 25:640B. Cited in Peter Brown, *The Body and Society:*

Men, Women, and Sexual Renunciation in Early Christianity (New York: Columbia University Press, 1988), 259. See especially Brown's chapter 13, titled " 'Daughters of Jerusalem': The Ascetic Life of Women in the Fourth Century."

3   The rhetoric of the ceremony is quite fascinating in this respect. The officiating priest would call forth the future nun: "Come, bride of Christ and receive the crown that God has prepared for you from time immemorial." The novice responded, "The angel of the Lord who guards my body accompanies me. I have renounced the kingdom of this world and the vanities of the century out of love for my lord, Jesus Christ, whom I saw, whom I loved, in whom I believed and whom I made the object of my predilection. I am his servant and will wait upon him like a slave." She would then receive a ring of fidelity as token of her marriage to God, proclaiming, "The Lord has dressed me in a gown sewn of gold and has adorned me with precious and countless jewels." I have compiled the account of Sor Juana's profession ceremony from the following sources: Anita Arroyo, *Razón y pasión de Sor Juana* (Mexico: Porrúa, 1952); Marié-Cécile Benassy-Berling, *Humanismo y religión en Sor Juana Inés de la Cruz* (Mexico: Universidad Nacional Autónoma de México, 1983); Padre Diego Calleja, *Vida de Sor Juana*, ed. E. Abreu Gómez (Mexico: Antigua Librería Robredo, 1936); Clara Campoamor, *Sor Juana Inés de la Cruz* (Madrid: Ediciones Júcar, 1984); Juan M. Galaviz, *Juana Inés de la Cruz* (Madrid: Ediciones Quorum, 1992); Julio Jiménez Rueda, *Sor Juana Inés de la Cruz en su época* (Mexico: Porrúa, 1951); Josefina Muriel, *Conventos de monjas en la Nueva España* (Mexico: Editorial Santiago, 1946); Muriel, *Los recogimientos de mujeres* (Mexico: Universidad Nacional Autónoma de México, 1974); Muriel, *Las mujeres de Hispanoamérica: Epoca colonial* (Madrid: Editorial MAPFRE, 1992); Elizabeth Wallace, *Sor Juana Inés de la Cruz: Poetisa de corte y convento* (Mexico: Ediciones Xochitl, 1944).

4   See Electa Arenal's study of Sor Juana and other nuns of the period, "The Convent as Catalyst for Autonomy," in *Women in Hispanic Literature: Icons and Fallen Idols*, ed. Beth Miller (Berkeley: University of California Press, 1983): 147–83. See also an expanded study of some of the same issues in Electa Arenal and Stacy Schlau, *Untold Sisters: Hispanic Nuns in Their Own Works* (Albuquerque: University of New Mexico Press, 1989).

5   *Respuesta a Sor Filotea*, in de la Cruz, *Obras completas*, 831. English translation is from Sor Juana Inés de la Cruz, *A Sor Juana Anthology*, trans. Alan Trueblood (Cambridge: Harvard University Press, 1988), 212. If it could be argued that the *Respuesta* in some senses conforms to the generic requirements of the conventual autobiography, a better case can be made that it exceeds — and perhaps redefines — the limits of the genre.

6 The problems with readings of this sort is that they have generally tended
   to cast Leonor's character strictly as a dramatized Sor Juana. On one
   hand, and as Stephanie Merrim has demonstrated, it is equally plausible
   to consider *both* Leonor and Ana as two halves (the dark and light hero-
   ines) of Sor Juana. On the other hand, if Leonor (or Leonor and Ana) do
   share certain biographical specifics with Sor Juana (primarily their intelligence), there is no reason to overliteralize the connection. See Merrim,
   "*Mores Geometricae:* The 'Womanscript' in the Theater of Sor Juana Inés
   de la Cruz," in *Feminist Perspectives on Sor Juana,* ed. Stephanie Merrim
   (Detroit: Wayne State University Press, 1991), 94–123.

7 Stephanie Jed insightfully examines the label "Tenth Muse" that was
   applied to Sor Juana and suggests that it was implicated in the European politics of constructing the "New World" as a museum. Specifically, she points to how various discourses and institutions that invoked
   the Tenth Muse epithet "were united by the common 'museal' project of
   ruling new lands and peoples and making them 'vendible.' " Jed, "The
   Tenth Muse: Gender, Rationality, and the Marketing of Knowledge," in
   Women, "Race," and Writing in the Early Modern Period, ed. Margo Hendricks and Patricia Parker (New York: Routledge, 1994), 195. "A woman
   of genius" is the title of Margaret Sayers Peden's bilingual edition of the
   Respuesta: Sor Juana Inés de la Cruz, *A Woman of Genius: The Intellectual Autobiography of Sor Juana Inés de la Cruz,* trans. Margaret Sayers
   Peden (Salisbury, Conn.: Lime Rock Press, 1982).

8 Ludwig Pfandl, *Sor Juana Inés de la Cruz, la décima musa de México: Su
   vida, su poesía, su psique,* ed. Francisco de la Maza (Mexico: Instituto
   de Investigaciones Estéticas de la Universidad Nacional Autónoma de
   México, 1963), 13.

9 Emilie Bergmann, "Sor Juana Inés de la Cruz: Dreaming in a Double
   Voice," in *Women, Culture, and Politics in Latin America,* ed. Emilie Bergmann, Janet Greenberg, Gwen Kirkpatrick et al. (Berkeley: University
   of California Press, 1990), 157.

10 Octavio Paz, *Sor Juana Inés de la Cruz, o Las trampas de la fe* (Mexico:
   Fondo de Cultura Económica, 1982), 157–58. English translation from
   Octavio Paz, *Sor Juana, or The Traps of Faith,* trans. Margaret Sayers
   Peden (Cambridge: Belknap Press, 1988), 110–11.

11 Frederick Luciani wisely cautions against taking too literally the biographical details inscribed either in the *Respuesta* or in the poems (and
   the same argument could of course be made for *Empeños*), without attending to their rhetoricity or their intertextuality. He writes: "Indeed,
   biographers from Father Calleja to Octavio Paz have erred in reading
   the brief anecdotal passages in the *Reply* as if they were precious bits

of real life incrusted in the letter's dense rhetorical matrix, bits of life whose historical veracity is indisputable, and which give us immediate access to the 'real' Juana Inés. What biographers have failed to consider is the possibility that these anecdotes may be grounded as much in other texts as in life." Luciani, "Octavio Paz on Sor Juana Inés de la Cruz: The Metaphor Incarnate," *Latin American Literary Review* 15, 30 (1987): 11–12.

12 *Respuesta a Sor Filotea*, in de la Cruz, *Obras completas*. Translation from Sor Juana Inés de la Cruz, *A Sor Juana Anthology*, trans. Alan Trueblood, 211.

13 Paz writes: "El proceso de masculinización se confunde con el de apren-dizaje; para saber, hay que ser hombre o parecerlo. La idea de disfrazarse de hombre, cortarse el pelo y, en fin, neutralizar su sexualidad bajo el hábito monjil, son sublimaciones o más bien, traducciones de su deseo: quiere apoderarse de los valores masculinos porque quiere ser como un hombre. . . . El estado religioso fue la neutralización de su sexualidad corporal y la liberación y transmutación de su libido." [The movement toward the masculine is mingled with the process of apprenticeship: in order to learn, one must be a man, or be like a man. Disguising herself as a man, cutting her hair, and, finally, neutralizing her sexuality beneath a nun's habits are sublimations or, better, translations of her wish: she wants to possess masculine values because she wants to be like a man. . . . The religious state was the neutralization of her bodily sexuality and the liberation and transmutation of her libido.] Paz, *Sor Juana Inés de la Cruz*, 159. Translation is from Sayers Peden, p. 112.

14 It can also be argued, as Aída Beaupied has convincingly done, that Sor Juana's *Narciso* inscribes an androgynous figuration of the divinity. See Beaupied, "Narciso hermético: Sor Juana Inés de la Cruz y José Lezama Lima" (Ph.D. diss., Yale University, 1988).

15 Sor Juana Inés de la Cruz, "Romance 48: Respondiendo a un caballero del Perú, que le envío unos barros diciéndole que se volviese hom-bre," in *Obras completas*, 63. English translation from Sor Juana Inés de la Cruz, *Poems*, trans. Margaret Sayers Peden (Binghamton: Bilingual Press, 1985), 21–23.

16 Salmacis is the nymph with whom Hermaphroditus joined, becoming, in the process, double-sexed. The pool in which the transsexualization took place also became known as Salmacis.

17 Paz, *Sor Juana Inés de la Cruz*, 290–92. Translation from Paz, Sor Juana Inés de la Cruz, 221.

18 See Bruce Wardropper, "Calderón's Comedy and His Serious Sense of

Life," in *Hispanic Studies in Honor of Nicholson B. Adams,* ed. John Esten Keller (Chapel Hill: University of North Carolina Press, 1966), 179–93.

19 See María M. Crocetti's splendid reading of the glass cupboard in *La dama duende* as hymen. Crocetti, *"La dama duende:* Spatial and Hymeneal Dialectics," in *The Perception of Women in Spanish Theater of the Golden Age,* ed. Anita K. Stoll and Dawn L. Smith (Lewisburg: Bucknell University Press, 1991), 51–66.

20 Sor Juana Inés de la Cruz, *Los empeños de una casa,* ed. Celsa Carmen García Valdés (Barcelona: Promociones y Publicaciones Universitarias, 1989). References to this edition are cited parenthetically by line number throughout the text. English translations are my own in consultation with Sor Juana Inés de la Cruz, *The House of Trials,* trans. David Pasto (New York: Peter Lang, 1997).

21 Lope de Vega, *Arte nuevo de hacer comedias en este tiempo* (Madrid: Viuda de A. Martín, 1621). On cross-dressing on the early modern Spanish stage, see the fundamental studies by Melveena McKendrick, *Woman and Society in the Spanish Drama of the Golden Age: A Study of the 'mujer varonil'* (London: Cambridge University Press, 1974); Carmen Bravo Villasante, *La mujer vestida de hombre en el teatro español, siglos XVI–XVII* (Madrid: Sociedad General Española de Librería, 1976); and Jean Canavaggio, "Los disfrazados de mujer en la comedia," in *La mujer en el teatro y la novela del siglo XVII: Actas del II Coloquio del Grupo de Estudios sobre Teatro Español* (Toulousse-Le Mirail: Université de Toulousse-Le Mirail, 1979), 133–45.

22 Sandra Messinger Cypess puts the number of Spanish Golden Age plays in which men cross-dress as women at around thirty, in comparison with more than two hundred plays in which women dress as men. See Messinger Cypess, "Re/Velados en *Los empeños de una casa," Hispamérica* 64/65 (1993): 177–85.

23 Mary Elizabeth Perry, *Gender and Disorder in Early Modern Seville* (Princeton: Princeton University Press, 1990), 132.

24 Cited in Perry, *Gender and Disorder,* 127. See also Carmelo Viñas Mey, *El problema de la tierra en la España de los siglos XVI y XVII* (Madrid: Consejo Superior de Investigaciones Científicas, 1941), 47.

25 Among the charges leveled against the theater was the virtual effeminization of its male audience:

The committee of three theologians set up by Philip II in 1598 to investigate the effects of the public theatres came up with arguments that were, in the light of Spain's military and economic problems at the time, even more forceful. First they invoked the authority of the Church fathers and classical commentators in support of the time-honored and still familiar argument that the theatre perpetrates evil and immorality by reminding the present of past wickedness, by encouraging evil thoughts with love intrigues (a prime target) and by corrupting the innocent by putting ideas into their heads, offering them examples of how to deceive husbands, suborn servants and so on. . . . Pressing the point even further, they argued that the playhouses diverted men from military pursuits, making them effeminate and soft, and unfit for work and war.

Melveena McKendrick, *Theatre in Spain, 1490–1700* (Cambridge: Cambridge University Press, 1989), 202. See also Emilio Cotarelo y Mori, *Bibliografía de las controversias sobre la licitud del teatro en España* (Madrid, 1904); Edward M. Wilson, "Nuevos documentos sobre las controversias teatrales, 1650–1681," *Actas del Segundo Congreso Internacional de Hispanistas*, ed. Jaime Sánchez Romeralo y Norbert Poulussen (Nijmegen: Asociación Internacional de Hispanistas, 1967), 155–70; J. C. J. Metford, "The Enemies of the Theatre in the Golden Age," *Bulletin of Hispanic Studies* 28 (1951): 76–92; and J.-M. Díez-Borque, *Sociedad y teatro en la España de Lope de Vega* (Barcelona: A. Bosch, 1978).

26 An edict of February 1600 reversed a 1596 decree banning actresses from theatrical representation: "The Council had clearly been convinced that it was better for women to appear on stage than for boys to dress up and act as women; it is unlikely that much notice had been taken of the 1596 decree anyway in the two and a bit years the theatre had been open between 1596 and 1600. The edict went on to impose restrictions on actresses—no masculine dress, no extravagant dressing outside the theatre, *no unmarried women*—which were in the course of the seventeenth century to become as familiar as they were ineffective." McKendrick, *Theatre in Spain*, 203, italics mine.

27 J. de J. Núñez y Domínguez, *Vidas mexicanas* (Mexico: Editorial Xochitl, 1945), 23. See also Julio Jiménez Rueda, *Herjías y supersticiones en la Nueva España: Los heterodoxos en México* (Mexico: Imprenta Universitaria, 1946).

28 Irving A. Leonard, *Baroque Times in Old Mexico* (Ann Arbor: University of Michigan Press, 1959), 161–62. See also J. de J. Núñez y Domínguez, "Don Antonio de Benavides, el incógnito *Tapado*," in *Vidas mexicanas*, 27. Núñez writes, "Don Antonio de Benavides, alias *el Tapado*, fue un aventurero que se hizo pasar por marqués de San Vicente y llegó a México con falsos nombramientos reales como Visitador de la Nueva

España; descubierto y procesado, se le ahorcó el 12 de julio de 1684"
[Don Antonio de Benavides, alias *el Tapado,* was an adventurer who
passed himself off as the Marquis of San Vicente and arrived in Mexico
with a false royal commission as Inspector of New Spain; found out and
prosecuted, he was hanged on July 12, 1684].

29 Sor Juana Inés de la Cruz, "Romance 25: Con ocasión de celebrar el
primer año que cumplió el hijo del señor virrey, le pide a su excelencia
indulto para un reo," in *Obras completas,* 35–36. Translation mine. The
poem continues:

> A Herodes en este día
> pidió una mujer, por premio,
> que al Sagrado Precursor
> cortase el divino cuello:
>
> fue la petición del odio,
> de la venganza el deseo,
> y ejecutó la crueldad
> de la malicia el precepto.
>
> Vos sois Príncipe Cristiano,
> y yo, por mi estado, debo
> pediros lo más benigno,
> y Vos no usar lo sangriento.
>
> [On this very day, a woman
> asked Herod, as a favor,
> to cut the divine neck
> of the Blessed Precursor:
>
> it was an entreaty to hatred,
> a desire for vengeance,
> and cruelty executed
> the precept of malice.
>
> You are a Christian Prince,
> and I, in my state, ought to
> ask of you what is most benign,
> and You, not practice what is bloody.]

30 Judith Butler, *Bodies That Matter: On the Discursive Limits of "Sex"* (New
York: Routledge, 1993), 125, italics mine. Butler writes: "I want to underscore that there is no necessary relation between drag and subversion.

... At best, it seems, drag is a site of a certain ambivalence, one which reflects the more general situation of being implicated in the regimes of power by which one is constituted and, hence, of being implicated in the very regimes of power that one opposes."

31 Covarrubias, *Tesoro*, 145.

32 Valerie Traub succinctly summarizes the various sides of the polemic as follows:

Whereas formalist critics often ignore the impact of the boy actor on the text's signification, historical critics such as Jardine and Orgel conversely emphasize the extent to which early modern theatrical practice enabled what is increasingly called a "transvestite" theater. In this, they follow the lead of the anti-theatricalists in conflating the material reality of the boy actor with the play's action. Indeed, the concept of a "transvestite theater" *per se* seems to confuse mimetically not only the reality of the play with the world of the theater, but also the phenomena of transvestism and male homoeroticism. . . . The material conditions of the early modern theater offered a *de facto* homoerotic basis upon which to build structures of desire, which were then, through theatrical representation, made available not only to male but to female audience members.

Traub, *Desire and Anxiety: Circulations of Sexuality in Shakespearean Drama* (New York: Routledge, 1992), 121–22.

33 Jean Howard's argument that "a man, and especially a boy, who theatricalizes the self as female, invites playing the woman's part in sexual congress" is suggestive in light of the marriage proposal Castaño elicits from Pedro. Howard, "Cross-Dressing, the Theater, and Gender Struggle in Early Modern England," in *Crossing the Stage: Controversies on Cross-Dressing*, ed. Leslie Ferris (New York: Routledge, 1993), 25.

34 Traub, *Desire and Anxiety: Circulations of Sexuality in Shakespearean Drama*, 118.

35 One might argue that Sor Juana anticipates Judith Butler in underscoring the artificiality not just of gender but of the very notion of sex itself. Butler writes: "If the immutable character of sex is contested, perhaps this construct called 'sex' is as culturally constructed as gender; indeed, perhaps it was always already gender with the consequence that the distinction between sex and gender turns out to be no distinction at all . . . [G]ender is not to culture as sex is to nature; gender is also the discursive/cultural means by which 'sexed nature' or a 'natural sex' is produced and established as 'prediscursive,' prior to culture, a politically neutral surface *on which* culture acts." Butler, *Gender Trouble* (New York: Routledge, 1990), 7.

36 One of the most disturbing aspects of the Calderonian honor dramas consists precisely of the widowed husband's remarriage as the final curtain drops. The terms on which he offers his hand suggests that the cycle of suspicion-inquisition-murder will be reenacted on the body of his wife. The reconciliation between Ana and Juan at the end of *Los empeños de una casa* is equally disturbing. This is not only because it pairs Ana with a husband whom she no longer loves, but, moreover, because the action of the play has effectively provided Juan with the evidence necessary to become, once the marriage is consummated, a suspicious honor husband, a Gutierre in his own right. In a soliloquy early in act 3, Juan's words are reminiscent of any number of honor-drama husbands:

> Con la llave del jardín,
> que dejó en mi poder Celia
> para ir a lograr mis dichas,
> quiero averiguar mis penas.
> ¡Qué mal dije averiguar,
> pues a la que es evidencia
> no se puede llamar duda!
> Pluguiera a Dios estuvieran
> mis celos y mis agravios
> en estado de sospechas.
> Mas ¿cómo me atrevo, cuando
> es contra mi honor mi ofensa,
> sin ser cierta mi venganza
> a hacer mi deshonra cierta?
> (ll. 2234–47)

> [With the key to the garden
> that Celia left in my possession
> in order to obtain my happiness,
> I wish to investigate my anxieties.
> How I misspoke by saying "investigate,"
> for that which is evidence
> cannot be called doubt!
> I wish to God that
> my jealousy and injuries
> were mere suspicions.
> But how can I dare
> to assure my disgrace,
> when the offense is against my honor
> and vengeance still uncertain?]

Clearly Ana's transgression is nowhere as serious as it would have been had she and Juan already been married; but given her history with Juan, there is little question that once married, the slightest cast of doubt on her honor will warrant her murder.

37   Roberto González Echevarría's lucid reading of monstrosity in *La vida es sueño* has been instrumental to my thinking on irresolution despite the marriage closure in *Los empeños de una casa*. Gónzalez Echevarría writes: "In the end, Basilio is dethroned, but he survives the crisis; Segismundo is crowned king while still being dressed in pelts; and Rosaura, although having consented to marry Astolfo, continues to be dressed as a woman but wearing man's weapons. . . . The end of the play is neither tragic nor comic. There is, instead, a clash among the various theatrical codes: the marriages, as in comedy, may bespeak a certain order, as do Segismundo's concluding words, but visually the monsters continue to be monsters, and the most important feature of these monsters is their visible appearance, which reveals their 'deformity.' " González Echevarría, *Celestina's Brood: Continuities of the Baroque in Spanish and Latin American Literatures* (Durham: Duke University Press, 1993), 95.

38   Bergmann, "Sor Juana Inés de la Cruz," 153, italics mine.

39   By treta del débil, I refer to the sort of gesture of subtle resistance that Josefina Ludmer has outlined in her provocative reading of Sor Juana's *Respuesta* (cited in chapter 2 above). See Ludmer, "Tretas del débil," in *La sartén por el mango: Encuentro de escritoras latinoamericanas*, ed. Patricia Elena González and Elena Ortega (Río Piedras: Huracán, 1984), 47–54.

40   Mary Gaylord, "Pulling Strings with Master Peter's Puppets: Fiction and History in *Don Quixote*," *Cervantes: Bulletin of the Cervantes Society of America* 18, 2 (1998): 122. Gaylord goes on to define her project in the following terms: "Beyond the work of recovering direct references to New World people, places and events, I have been seeking to understand how the dramatically new perspective afforded by a particular set of historical events and by awareness of a previously unimagined geography alters the agendas, the content and even the forms of literary production in the sixteenth- and seventeenth-century Hispanic world. In this undertaking, the greatest challenge and the most compelling interest attach to those works which, like Cervantes's masterpiece, we have grown accustomed to thinking of as quintessentially *Old World* writings." This project has also been elaborated by Gaylord in previous articles. See especially "El lenguaje de la conquista y la conquista del lenguaje en las poéticas del siglo de oro," *Actas del IX Congreso de la Asociación Internacional de Hispanistas*, ed. Sebastián Neumeister et al. (Frankfurt am Main: Vervuert,

1989), 1: 469–75; "Spain's Renaissance Conquests and the Retroping of Identity," *Journal of Hispanic Philology* 16 (1992): 126–36; "The True History of Early Modern Writing in Spanish: An American Perspective," *Modern Language Quarterly* 57 (1996): 213–25; "*Don Quixote* and the National Citizenship of Masterpieces," in *Field Work: Sites for Literary and Cultural Studies*, ed. Marjorie Garber, Paul B. Franklin, and Rebecca L. Walkowitz (London: Routledge, 1996), 97–105.

41 I borrow the wordplay—and indeed the deeper relation it discloses—from the title of James D. Fernández's brilliant reading of "El celoso extremeño," "The Bonds of Patrimony: Cervantes and the New World," *PMLA* 109, 5 (1994): 969–81.

42 Ibid., 972.

43 See Stephen Jay Greenblatt, *Marvelous Possessions: The Wonder of the New World* (Chicago: University of Chicago Press, 1991); Louis Montrose, "The Work of Gender and Sexuality in the Elizabethan Discourse of Discovery," in *Discourses of Sexuality: From Aristotle to AIDS*, ed. Domna C. Stanton (Ann Arbor: University of Michigan Press, 1992), 138–84; José Rabasa, *Inventing America: Spanish Historiography and the Formation of Eurocentrism* (Norman: University of Oklahoma Press, 1993); Margarita Zamora, *Reading Columbus* (Berkeley: University of California Press, 1993); Jonathan Goldberg, *Sodometries: Renaissance Texts, Modern Sexualities* (Stanford: Stanford University Press, 1992).

44 Juliana Schiesari, "The Face of Domestication: Physiognomy, Gender Politics, and Humanism's Others," in *Women, "Race," and Writing in the Early Modern Period*, ed. Margo Hendricks and Patricia Parker (London: Routledge, 1994), 70.

45 Vicente Rafael, *Contracting Colonialism: Translation and Christian Conversion in Tagalog Society under Early Spanish Rule* (Ithaca: Cornell University Press, 1988), ix.

46 For a valuable summary of recent work on the Mexican Inquisition in particular, see Richard E. Greenleaf, "History of the Mexican Inquisition: Evolution of Interpretations and Methodologies," in *Cultural Encounters: The Impact of the Inquisition in Spain and the New World*, ed. Mary Elizabeth Perry and Anne J. Cruz (Berkeley: University of California Press, 1991), 248–76. See also Solange Alberro's extraordinary study of the Mexican Inquisition in the early modern period. Alberro, *La actividad del Santo Oficio de la Inquisición en Nueva España* (Mexico: Instituto Nacional de Antropología e Historia, 1981).

Conclusion: "Como anillo al dedo"

1   See Jacques Lezra's remarkable reading of Cervantes's hand in *Unspeakable Subjects: The Genealogy of the Event in Early Modern Europe* (Stanford: Stanford University Press, 1997).

2   Sebastián de Covarrubias, *Tesoro de la lengua castellana o española* (1611), facsimile ed., ed. Martín de Riquer (Barcelona: Editorial Alta Fulla, 1943), 786.

3   Katherine Rowe, " 'God's handy worke': Divine Complicity and the Anatomist's Touch," in *The Body in Parts: Fantasies of Corporeality in Early Modern Europe*, ed. David Hillman and Carla Mazzio (New York: Routledge, 1997), 285–309.

4   Judith 14: 14–15. Italics mine.

5   See Rowe, " 'God's handy worke.' "

6   The *Diccionario de Autoridades* defines *mano* as "instrumento de madera, hierro u otro metal, que sirve para moler o desmenuzar alguna cosa" [wooden, steel, or metal instrument that is used to grind or mince something]. Cited in Sor Juana Inés de la Cruz, *Los empeños de una casa*, ed. Celsa Carmen García Valdés (Barcelona: Promociones y Publicaciones Universitarias, 1989), 270. Translation mine.

7   The *Diccionario de Autoridades* offers the following definition: "el dedo malo: frase vulgar que se dice de aquel que ya ha caído en desgracia, y por eso se le atribuye todo lo mal hecho: a imitación del dedo que padece uñero, golpe o herida, que por más que el paciente procure reservarle, todo tropieza en él, para aumentar su dolor" [bad finger: vulgar phrase said of someone who has fallen into disgrace and for that reason is charged of all wrongdoings: in imitation of the finger that has an ingrown nail, or is bruised or hurt, which, no matter how much the patient tries to protect, everything strikes, to worsen its pain]. Cited in *Empeños*, 270. Translation mine.

8   Covarrubias, *Tesoro*, 689.

9   In her *Respuesta*, Sor Juana negotiates the double bind that Sor Filotea's letter has placed her in—a double bind between a prescribed silence and the need to reply to the accusations against her—by giving her silence a voice, by inscribing a brief caption on it. She writes: "pero como [el silencio] es cosa negativa, aunque explica mucho con el énfasis de no explicar, es necesario ponerle algún breve rótulo para que se entienda lo que se pretende que el silencio diga. . . ." [because since silence is a negative thing, although it explains a great deal precisely by not explaining, it is necessary to inscribe a brief caption upon it, so that what it is

intended that silence speak might be understood. . . .] *Respuesta a Sor Filotea* in de la Cruz, *Obras completas,* 828.

10   The characterizations of Fray Luis and Calderón are taken from Juan Luis Alborg, *Historia de la literatura española* (Madrid: Gredos, 1986), 1:803 and 2:663, respectively. The description of Sor Juana is from Enrique Anderson Imbert and Eugenio Florit, eds., *Literatura hispanoamericana: Antología e introducción histórica* (Orlando: Holt, Rinehart, and Winston, 1970), 1:161.

11   On Sor Juana's "strangeness," see Octavio Paz, *Sor Juana Inés de la Cruz, o Las trampas de la fe* (Mexico: Fondo de Cultura Económica, 1982).

12   Foucault writes: "At the beginning of the seventeenth century, during the period that has been termed, rightly or wrongly, the Baroque, thought ceases to move in the element of resemblance. Similitude is no longer the form of knowledge but the occasion of error, the danger to which one exposes oneself when one does not examine the obscure region of confusions." Foucault, *The Order of Things: An Archaeology of the Human Sciences* (London: Tevistock Publications, 1970), 47.

13   A different version of this same project might explore the means by which the disjunctive semiotics we associate with the baroque could be understood in terms of an adultery of signs. I do not mean to suggest by this that previously signs were monogamous, so to speak (clearly it is not their nature) but, rather, that in the period typically known as the baroque (roughly the seventeenth century, in Spain and Spanish America) the signifier-signified relation not only is understood as contractual—and even sacramental, after Trent—but moreover, that the disjunctiveness of that relation becomes increasingly threatening and, as a result, increasingly charged.

14   As Hans Gumbrecht suggests,

Quite expectedly for us, the Spanish Inquisition ended up producing as an effect what had been presupposed as its cause and legitimation. . . . What makes the Inquisition singular in the early modern context—and what perhaps provoked its recourse to physical repression and extermination—was the new experience of an endlessness of interpretation. The initial insistence of the accused on their orthodoxy was no longer sufficient to dilute the inquisitors' suspicions; this was why they quite regularly proceeded to extracting "confessions" under conditions of torture. But, as modern subjects, the Inquisitors distrusted the "evidence" they produced under conditions of torture, thereby making a formal confirmation of such testimony, some days after the torturing, a legal requirement. Quite naturally, the defendants used to recant. This led to renewed torture—and opened up the unending chain of acts of interpretation which could ultimately only be cut short through the auto de fe.

Gumbrecht, "Sign-Concepts in European Everyday Culture between Renaissance and Early Nineteenth Century," Unpublished, 11–13. One possible outcome of this type of claim is to return to the controversies surrounding 1492 and raise the question of how the expulsions and forced conversion program officially initiated that year might have contributed not only to this sort of epistemologic ungrounding but also to the pervading sense of desengaño often invoked to distinguish a Spanish from a broader European baroque. By effectively eradicating "visible" difference (forcing it underground) and inscribing, instead, an at best questionable Sameness suspected of harboring a secretly legible difference, expulsion shifted Otherness from a religious issue to a racial one, redefining it as a problem of reading and misreading bodies.

Bibliography

Alberro, Solange. *La Actividad del Santo Oficio de la Inquisición en Nueva España*. Mexico: Instituto Nacional de Antropología e Historia, 1981.

Alborg, Juan Luis. *Historia de la literatura española*. Madrid: Gredos, 1986.

Alfaro Torre, Paloma, Antonia María Ortiz Ballesteros, and Martín Muelas Herraiz, eds. *Fray Luis de León y su época: Bibliografía y documentos*. Cuenca: Universidad de Castilla–La Mancha, 1992.

Alfonso el Sabio. *Antología*. Mexico: Porrúa, 1982.

Alvarez Aranguren, Lucio. *La gramática española del siglo XVI y Fray Luis de León*. Madrid: Servicio de Publicaciones de la Junta de Comunidades de Castilla–La Mancha, 1990.

Alvarez Turienzo, Saturnino, ed. *Fray Luis de León: El fraile, el humanista, el teólogo*. Madrid: Ediciones Escurialenses, 1992.

———. *Escritos sobre Fray Luis de León*. Salamanca: Ediciones de la Diputación de Salamanca, 1993.

Anderson Imbert, Enrique, and Eugenio Florit, eds. *Literatura hispano-americana: Antología e introducción histórica*. Vol. 1. Orlando: Holt, Rinehart, and Winston, 1970.

Aquinas, St. Thomas. *Summa theologica*. Ed. Thomas Gilby. Garden City: Doubleday, 1969.

Arenal, Electa. "The Convent as Catalyst for Autonomy." In *Women in Hispanic Literature: Icons and Fallen Idols*, ed. Beth Miller, 147–83. Berkeley: University of California Press, 1983.

Arenal, Electa, and Stacy Schlau. *Untold Sisters: Hispanic Nuns in Their Own Works*. Albuquerque: University of New Mexico Press, 1989.

Aristotle. *Poetics*. Trans. Ingram Bywater. New York: Garland, 1980.

Armstrong, Nancy, and Leonard Tennenhouse. Introduction to *The Ideology of Culture: Essays on Literature and the History of Sexuality*, ed. Nancy Armstrong and Leonard Tennenhouse. New York: Methuen, 1987.

Arroyo, Anita. *Razón y pasión de Sor Juana*. Mexico: Porrúa, 1952.

Augustine of Hippo, St. *De doctrina christiana: On Christian Doctrine*. Trans. D. W. Robertson. New York: Macmillan, 1958.

———. *The Confessions of Saint Augustine*. Trans. Rex Warner. New York: Mentor, 1963.

Austin, J. L. *How to Do Things with Words*. Cambridge: Harvard University Press, 1962.

Avicenna. *Canon of Medicine*. Trans. O. Cameron Gruner. London: Luzac, 1930.

Bainton, Roland H. *The Reformation in the Sixteenth Century*. Boston: Beacon Press, 1956.

Bakhtin, Mikhail. *Rabelais and His World*. Trans. Hélène Iswolsky. Bloomington: Indiana University Press, 1984.

Barstow, Anne Llewellyn. *Witchcraze: A New History of the European Witch Hunts*. San Francisco: Pandora, 1994.

Barthes, Roland. *Roland Barthes par Roland Barthes*. Paris: Seuil, 1975.

Beaupied, Aída. "Narciso hermético: Sor Juana Inés de la Cruz y José Lezama Lima." Ph.D. diss., Yale University, 1988.

Bell, Aubrey F. G. *Luis de León: A Study of the Spanish Renaissance*. Oxford: Clarendon Press, 1925.

Benassy-Berling, Marié-Cécile. *Humanismo y religión en Sor Juana Inés de la Cruz*. Mexico: Universidad Nacional Autónoma de México, 1983.

Bergmann, Emilie. "Sor Juana Inés de la Cruz: Dreaming in a Double Voice." In *Women, Culture, and Politics in Latin America*, ed. Emilie Bergmann, Janet Greenberg, Gwen Kirkpatrick et al., 151–72. Berkeley: University of California Press, 1990.

Bergmann, Emilie, Janet Greenberg, Gwen Kirkpatrick et al., eds. *Women, Culture, and Politics in Latin America*. Berkeley: University of California Press, 1990.

Bilinkoff, Jodi. *The Avila of Saint Teresa: Religious Reform in a Sixteenth-Century City*. Ithaca: Cornell University Press, 1989.

Bloch, R. Howard. "Medieval Misogyny." In *Misogyny, Misandry, and Misanthropy*, ed. R. Howard Bloch and Frances Ferguson, 1–24. Berkeley: University of California Press, 1989.

———. *Medieval Misogyny and the Invention of Western Romantic Love*. Chicago: University of Chicago Press, 1991.

Blum, Abbe. " 'Strike all that look upon with mar[b]le': Monumentalizing Women in Shakespeare's Plays." In *The Renaissance Englishwoman in Print: Counterbalancing the Canon*, ed. Anne M. Haselkorn and Betty S. Travitsky, 99–118. Amherst: University of Massachusetts Press, 1990.

Boruchoff, David A. Abstract for *Rhetoric and Redemption in Inquisitorial Spain: Intolerance and the Invention of the Novel*. Forthcoming.

Bravo Villasante, Carmen. *La mujer vestida de hombre en el teatro español, siglos XVI–XVII*. Madrid: Sociedad General Española de Librería, 1976.

Bressan, Luigi. *Il Canone Tridentino sul divorzio per adulterio e l'interpretazione degli autori.* Rome: Universita Gregoriana Editrice, 1973.

Bronfen, Elisabeth. *Over Her Dead Body: Death, Femininity, and the Aesthetic.* New York: Routledge, 1992.

Brown, Peter. *The Body and Society: Men, Women, and Sexual Renunciation in Early Christianity.* New York: Columbia University Press, 1988.

Bujanda, Jesús de. "Recent Historiography of the Spanish Inquisition." In *Cultural Encounters: The Impact of the Spanish Inquisition in Spain and the New World,* ed. Anne J. Cruz and Mary Elizabeth Perry, 221–47. Berkeley: University of California Press, 1991.

Bullough, Vern L. "Medieval Medical and Scientific Views of Women." *Viator* 4 (1973): 485–501.

Burckhardt, Jacob. *The Civilization of the Renaissance in Italy.* Trans. S. G. C. Middlemore. New York: Penguin Books, 1990.

Butler, Judith. *Gender Trouble.* New York: Routledge, 1990.

———. *Bodies That Matter: On the Discursive Limits of "Sex".* New York: Routledge, 1993.

Calderón de la Barca, Pedro. *Obras completas.* Ed. Angel Valbuena Prat. Madrid: Aguilar, 1952.

——— *The Surgeon of His Honour.* Trans. Roy Campbell. Madison: University of Wisconsin Press, 1960.

———. *Life Is a Dream.* Trans. Edwin Honig. New York: Hill, 1970.

———. *El médico de su honra.* Ed. D. W. Cruickshank. Madrid: Castalia, 1989.

———. *The Surgeon of Honour.* Trans. Gwynne Edwards. In *Plays: One.* London: Methuen Drama, 1991.

Calleja, Padre Diego. *Vida de Sor Juana.* Ed. E. Abreu Gómez. Mexico: Antigua Librería Robredo, 1936.

Caminero, Juventino. *La razón filológica en la obra de Fray Luis de León.* Kassel: Publicaciones de la Universidad de Deusto, 1990.

Campoamor, Clara. *Sor Juana Inés de la Cruz.* Madrid: Ediciones Júcar, 1984.

Canavaggio, Jean. "Los disfrazados de mujer en la comedia." In *La mujer en el teatro y la novela del siglo XVII: Actas del II Coloquio del Grupo de Estudios sobre Teatro Español,* 133–45. Toulousse-Le Mirail: Université de Toulousse-Le Mirail, 1979.

Canons and Decrees of the Council of Trent. Ed. H. J. Schroeder. Rockford: Tan Books, 1978.

Casa, Frank P. "Crime and Responsibility in *El médico de su honra.*" In *Homenaje a William L. Fichter: Estudios sobre el teatro antiguo hispánico y otros ensayos,* ed. A. David Kossoff and José Amor y Vázquez, 127–37. Madrid: Castalia, 1971.

Cascardi, Anthony. *The Limits of Illusion: A Critical Study of Calderón.* Cambridge: Cambridge University Press, 1984.

Castro, Américo. *De la edad conflictiva: Crisis de la cultura española en el siglo XVII.* Madrid: Taurus, 1961.

Cervantes, Miguel de. *Obras completas.* Ed. Angel Valbuena Prat. Madrid: Aguilar, 1980.

———. *Don Quijote de la Mancha.* Ed. Francisco Rico. Barcelona: Crítica, 1999.

———. *Don Quixote.* Trans. J. M. Cohen. New York: Penguin, 1950.

Chartier, Roger. *The Order of Books.* Trans. Lydia C. Cochrane. Stanford: Stanford University Press, 1994.

Cixous, Hélène. "The Laugh of the Medusa." Trans. Keith Cohen and Paula Cohen. In *New French Feminisms: An Anthology,* ed. Elaine Marks and Isabelle de Courtivron, 245–64. New York: Schocken Books, 1981.

Colish, Marcia. "Cosmetic Theology: The Transformation of a Stoic Theme." In *Assays: Critical Approaches to Medieval and Renaissance Texts,* 3–14. Pittsburgh: University of Pittsburgh Press, 1981.

———. *The Mirror of Language: A Study in the Medieval Theory of Knowledge.* Lincoln: University of Nebraska Press, 1983.

Condillac, Louis, and Robert Jammes. "Amours et sexualité a travers les mémoires d'un inquisiteur du XVIIe siècle." In *Amours légitimes, amours illégitimes en Espagne, XVIe–XVIIe siècles,* ed. Augustín Redondo, 183–94. Paris: Sorbonne, 1985.

Correa, Gustavo. "El doble aspecto de la honra en el teatro del siglo XVII." *Hispanic Review* 26 (1958): 99–107.

Cotarelo y Mori, Emilio. *Bibliografía de las controversias sobre la licitud del teatro en España.* Madrid, 1904.

Covarrubias, Sebastián de. *Emblemas morales.* 1610. Facsimile ed. Ed. Carmen Bravo-Villasante. Madrid: Fundación Universitaria Española, 1978.

———. *Tesoro de la lengua castellana o española.* 1611. Ed. Martín de Riquer. Barcelona: Editorial Alta Fulla, 1943.

Crocetti, María M. *"La dama duende:* Spatial and Hymeneal Dialectics." In *The Perception of Women in Spanish Theater of the Golden Age,* ed. Anita K. Stoll and Dawn L. Smith, 51–66. Lewisburg: Bucknell University Press, 1991.

Cruz, Anne J. *"Homo ex machina?:* Male Bonding in Calderón's *A secreto agravio, secreta venganʒa." Forum for Modern Language Studies* 25, 2 (1989): 154–66.

————. "Studying Gender in the Spanish Golden Age." In *Cultural and Historical Grounding for Hispanic and Luso-Brazilian Feminist Literary Criticism,* ed. Hernán Vidal, 193–221. Minneapolis: Institute for the Study of Ideologies and Literature, 1989.

Cruz, Anne J., and Mary Elizabeth Perry, eds. *Cultural Encounters: The Impact of the Inquisition in Spain and the New World.* Berkeley: University of California Press, 1991.

————. *Culture and Control in Counter-Reformation Spain.* Minneapolis: University of Minnesota Press, 1992.

Curtius, Ernst Robert. "Corporal Metaphors." In *European Literature and the Latin Middle Ages,* trans. Willard R. Trask, 136–38. Princeton: Princeton University Press, 1973.

Cvitanovik, Dinko, ed. *La idea del cuerpo en las letras españolas, siglos XIII a XVII.* Bahía Blanca: Instituto de Humanidades Universidad Nacional del Sur, 1973.

Davis, Natalie Zemon. *Society and Culture in Early Modern France.* Stanford: Stanford University Press, 1975.

de Arfe y Villafañe, Juan. *De varia conmensuración para la escultura y architectura.* Sevilla: Andrea Pesioni, 1585.

de Jesús, Teresa. *Obras completas.* Ed. Efrén de la Madre de Dios and Otger Steggink. Madrid: Biblioteca de Autores Cristianos, 1962.

————. *Libro de la vida.* Ed. Dámaso Chicharro. Madrid: Cátedra, 1979.

de la Cruz, Sor Juana Inés. *A Woman of Genius: The Intellectual Autobiography of Sor Juana Inés de la Cruz.* Trans. Margaret Sayers Peden. Salisbury, Conn.: Lime Rock Press, 1982.

————. *Poems.* Trans. Margaret Sayers Peden. Binghamton: Bilingual Press, 1985.

————. *A Sor Juana Anthology.* Trans. Alan Trueblood. Cambridge: Harvard University Press, 1988.

————. *Los empeños de una casa.* Ed. Celsa Carmen García Valdés. Barcelona: Promociones y Publicaciones Universitarias, 1989.

————. *Obras completas.* Ed. Francisco Monterde. Mexico: Porrúa, 1989.

————. *The House of Trials.* Trans. David Pasto. New York: Peter Lang, 1997.

de León, Fray Luis. *The Perfect Wife.* Trans. Alice Philena Hubbard. Denton: College Press, Texas State College for Women, 1943.

————. *De los nombres de Cristo.* Ed. Federico de Onís. Madrid: Espasa-Calpe, 1949.

————. *Obras completas.* Madrid: Biblioteca de Autores Cristianos, 1959.

————. *The Names of Christ.* Trans. Manuel Durán and William Kluback. New York: Paulist Press, 1984.

————. *Poesía*. Ed. Manuel Durán and Michael Atlee. Madrid: Cátedra, 1984.

————. *La perfecta casada*. Ed. Joaquín Antonio Peñalosa. Mexico: Porrúa, 1985.

————. *La perfecta casada*. Ed. Mercedes Etreros. Madrid: Taurus, 1987.

————. *Escritos desde la cárcel: Autógrafos del primer proceso inquisitorial*. Ed. José Barrientos García. Madrid: Ediciones Escurialenses, 1991.

————. *Cantar de los cantares de Salomón*. Ed. José Manuel Blecua. Madrid: Gredos, 1994.

de Man, Paul. *Allegories of Reading: Figural Language in Rousseau, Nietzsche, Rilke, and Proust*. New Haven: Yale University Press, 1982.

————. "Autobiography as De-Facement." In *The Rhetoric of Romanticism*, 67–81. New York: Columbia University Press, 1984.

Derrida, Jacques. *Éperons: Les Styles de Nietzsche / Spurs: Nietzsche's Styles*. Trans. Barbara Harlow. Chicago: University of Chicago Press, 1979.

————. *La carte postale: De Socrate à Freud et au-delà*. Paris: Flammarion, 1980.

————. *Marges de la philosophie*. Paris: Editions de Minuit, 1972.

————. *The Post Card: From Socrates to Freud and Beyond*. Trans. Alan Bass. Chicago: University of Chicago Press, 1987.

Díez-Borque, José María. *Sociedad y teatro en la España de Lope de Vega*. Barcelona: A. Bosch, 1978.

Domínguez Ortiz, Antonio. *Las clases privilegiadas en el antiguo régimen*. 3d ed. Madrid: Istmo, 1985.

Dopico Black, Georgina. "La herida de Camila: La anatomía de la prueba en 'El curioso impertinente.'" In *En un lugar de la Mancha: Estudios cervantinos en honor de Manuel Durán*, ed. Georgina Dopico Black and Roberto González Echevarría, 91–108. Salamanca: Ediciones Almar, 1999.

Dunn, Peter. "Honour and the Christian Background in Calderón." In *Critical Essays on the Theatre of Calderón*, ed. Bruce Wardropper, 24–60. New York: New York University Press, 1965.

Durán, Manuel. *Luis de León*. Boston: Twayne, 1971.

El Saffar, Ruth. *Beyond Fiction: The Recovery of the Feminine in the Novels of Cervantes*. Berkeley: University of California Press, 1984.

————. "The 'I' of the Beholder: Self and Other in Some Spanish Golden Age Texts." *Hispania* 75, 4 (1992): 862–74.

————. *Rapture Encaged: The Suppression of the Feminine in Western Culture*. London: Routledge, 1994.

El Saffar, Ruth, and Diana de Armas Wilson, eds. *Quixotic Desire: Psycho-*

analytic Perspectives on Cervantes. Ithaca: Cornell University Press, 1993.

Elliott, J. H. *Spain and Its World, 1500–1700*. New Haven: Yale University Press, 1989.

Epstein, Rabbi Dr. I., ed. *The Babylonian Talmud: Seder Mo'Ed*. London: Sancino Press, 1938.

Feher, Michael, Ramona Naddaff, and Nadia Tazi, eds. *Fragments for a History of the Human Body: Part One*. Cambridge: MIT Press, 1989.

Felman, Shoshana. *The Literary Speech Act: Don Juan with J. L. Austin, or Seduction in Two Languages*. Trans. Catherine Porter. Ithaca: Cornell University Press, 1983.

Ferguson, Margaret, Maureen Quilligan, and Nancy J. Vickers, eds. *Rewriting the Renaissance: The Discourses of Sexual Difference in Early Modern Europe*. Chicago: University of Chicago Press, 1986.

Fernández, James D. "La *Vida* de Teresa de Jesús y la salvación del discurso." *Modern Language Notes* 105, 2 (1990): 283–302.

———. "The Bonds of Patrimony: Cervantes and the New World." *PMLA* 109, 5 (1994): 977–93.

Fernández Alvarez, Manuel. *Fray Luis de León: La poda floreciente, 1591–1991*. Madrid: Espasa-Calpe, 1991.

Foucault, Michel. *The Order of Things: An Archaeology of the Human Sciences*. London: Tevistock Publications, 1970.

———. *The Birth of the Clinic*. Trans. A. M. Sheridan Smith. New York: Pantheon Books, 1973.

———. *The History of Sexuality*. Vol. 1, *An Introduction*. Trans. Robert Hurley. New York: Vintage Books, 1978.

———. *The History of Sexuality*. Vol. 2, *The Use of Pleasure*. Trans. Robert Hurley. New York: Vintage Books, 1985.

———. *The History of Sexuality*. Vol. 3, *The Care of the Self*. Trans. Robert Hurley. New York: Vintage Books, 1986.

———. "What Is an Author?" In *Textual Strategies: Perspectives in Post-Structural Criticism*, ed. Josué V. Harari, 141–160. Ithaca: Cornell University Press, 1994.

Freccero, John. "The Fig Tree and the Laurel: Petrarch's Poetics." In *Literary Theory/Renaissance Texts*, ed. Patricia Parker and David Quint, 20–32. Baltimore: Johns Hopkins University Press, 1986.

Freud, Sigmund. *Standard Edition of the Complete Psychological Works of Sigmund Freud*. Trans. James Strachey and Anna Freud. London: Hogarth Press, 1953.

———. *Sexuality and the Psychology of Love*. Ed. Philip Rieff. New York: Macmillan, 1963.

Galaviz, Juan M. *Juana Inés de la Cruz*. Madrid: Ediciones Quorum, 1992.

Galen. *Galeni opera omnia*. Leipzig: C. Knobloch, 1964.

Gallop, Jane. *Thinking through the Body*. New York: Columbia University Press, 1988.

Gavilán Vela, Diego, trans. *Discurso contra los judíos traducido de lengua portuguesa en castellano*. 1630.

García Arenal, Mercedes. *Los moriscos*. Granada: Universidad de Granada, 1996.

Gaylord, Mary. "El lenguaje de la conquista y la conquista del lenguaje en las poéticas españolas del Siglo de Oro." In *Actas del IX Congreso de la Asociación Internacional de Hispanistas*, ed. Sebastián Neumeister et al., 1:469–75. Frankfurt am Main: Vervuert, 1989.

———. "Spain's Renaissance Conquests and the Retroping of Identity." *Journal of Hispanic Philology* 16 (1992): 126–36.

———. "The Whole Body of Fable with All of Its Members: Cervantes, Pinciano, Freud." In *Quixotic Desire: Psychoanalytic Perspectives on Cervantes*, ed. Ruth El Saffar and Diana de Armas Wilson, 117–34. Ithaca: Cornell University Press, 1993.

———. "*Don Quixote* and the National Citizenship of Masterpieces." In *Field Work: Sites for Literary and Cultural Studies*, ed. Marjorie Garber, Paul B. Franklin, and Rebecca L. Walkowitz, 97–105. London: Routledge, 1996.

———. "The True History of Early Modern Writing in Spanish: An American Perspective." *Modern Language Quarterly* 57 (1996): 213–25.

———. "Pulling Strings with Master Peter's Puppets: Fiction and History in *Don Quixote*." *Cervantes: Bulletin of the Cervantes Society of America* 18, 2 (1998): 117–47.

Ginzburg, Carlo. *The Cheese and the Worms: The Cosmos of a Sixteenth-Century Miller*. Trans. John and Anne Tedeschi. New York: Dorsett Press, 1989.

Girard, René. *Deceit, Desire, and the Novel*. Trans. Yvonne Freccero. Baltimore: Johns Hopkins University Press, 1981.

Godzich, Wlad, and Nicholas Spaddaccini, eds. *Literature among Discourses: The Spanish Golden Age*. Minneapolis: University of Minnesota Press, 1986.

Golderg, Jonathan. *Sodometries: Renaissance Texts, Modern Sexualities*. Stanford: Stanford University Press, 1992.

González Echevarría, Roberto. "On Cipión's Life and Adventures: Cervantes and the Picaresque." *Diacritics* 10, 3 (fall 1980): 15–26.

———. "Humanism and Rhetoric in *Comentarios reales* and *El Carnero*." In *In Retrospect: Essays on Latin American Literature*, ed. Elizabeth S. and

Timothy J. Rogers, 8–23. York, S.C.: Spanish Literature Publications, 1987.

————. *Celestina's Brood: Continuities of the Baroque in Spanish and Latin American Literatures.* Durham: Duke University Press, 1993.

Gossy, Mary S. *The Untold Story: Women and Theory in Golden Age Texts.* Ann Arbor: University of Michigan Press, 1989.

Granjel, Luis S. *La medicina española del siglo XVII.* Salamanca: Ediciones Universidad de Salamanca, 1978.

Greenblatt, Stephen Jay. *Renaissance Self-Fashioning: From More to Shakespeare.* Chicago: University of Chicago Press, 1980.

————. *Marvelous Possessions: The Wonder of the New World.* Chicago: University of Chicago Press, 1991.

Greene, Thomas. "The Flexibility of the Self in Renaissance Literature." In *The Disciplines of Criticism: Essays in Literary Theory, Interpretation, and History,* ed. Peter Demetz, Thomas Greene, and Lowry Nelson Jr., 241–64. New Haven: Yale University Press, 1968.

Greenleaf, Richard E. "History of the Mexican Inquisition: Evolution of Interpretations and Methodologies." In *Cultural Encounters: The Impact of the Inquisition in Spain and the New World,* ed. Anne J. Cruz and Mary Elizabeth Perry, 248–76. Berkeley: University of California Press, 1991.

Gumbrecht, Hans Ulrich. "Sign-Concepts in European Everyday Culture between Renaissance and Early Nineteenth Century." Unpublished.

Habib Arkin, Alexander. *La influencia de la exégesis hebrea en los comentarios de Fray Luis de León.* Madrid: Instituto Benito Arias Montano, 1966.

Hegel, Georg Wilhelm Friedrich. *Aesthetics.* Oxford: Clarendon Press, 1975.

Hendricks, Margo, and Patricia Parker, eds. *Women, "Race," and Writing in the Early Modern Period.* New York: Routledge, 1994.

Hesse, Everett. "A Psychological Approach to *El médico de su honra.*" *Romanistisches Jahrbuch* 28 (1977): 326–40.

Hippocrates. *On Intercourse and Pregnancy.* Trans. T. U. H. Ellinger. New York, 1952.

Honig, Edwin. *Calderón and the Seizures of Honor.* Cambridge: Cambridge University Press, 1972.

Howard, Jean. "Cross-Dressing, the Theater, and Gender Struggle in Early Modern England." In *Crossing the Stage: Controversies on Cross-Dressing,* ed. Leslie Ferris, 20–46. New York: Routledge, 1993.

Huarte de San Juan, Juan. *Examen de ingenios para las ciencias.* Ed. Esteban Torres. Madrid: Editora Nacional, 1976.

Jacobus, Mary. "Judith, Holofernes, and the Phallic Woman." In *Reading*

Woman: Essays in Feminist Criticism, 110–36. New York: Columbia University Press, 1986.

Jacobus, Mary, Evelyn Fox Keller, and Sally Shuttleworth, eds. *Body/ Politics: Women and the Discourses of Science*. New York: Routledge, 1990.

Jed, Stephanie. "The Tenth Muse: Gender, Rationality, and the Marketing of Knowledge." In *Women, "Race," and Writing in the Early Modern Period*, ed. Margo Hendricks and Patricia Parker, 195–208. New York: Routledge, 1994.

Jiménez Rueda, Julio. *Herejías y supersticiones en la Nueva España: Los heterodoxos en México*. Mexico: Imprenta Universitaria, 1946.

———. *Sor Juana Inés de la Cruz en su época*. Mexico: Porrúa, 1951.

Jones, C. A. "*Honor* in Spanish Golden-Age Drama." *BHS* 35 (1958): 199–210.

Jones, J. A. "The Sweet Harmony of Luis de León's *La perfecta casada*." *Bulletin of Hispanic Studies* 62, 3 (1985): 259–69.

Jordan, Constance. "Feminism and the Humanists: The Case of Sir Thomas Elyot's Defence of Good Women." In *Rewriting the Renaissance: The Discourses of Sexual Difference in Early Modern Europe*, ed. Margaret Ferguson, Maureen Quilligan, and Nancy J. Vickers, 248–58. Chicago: University of Chicago Press, 1986.

———. *Renaissance Feminism: Literary Texts and Political Models*. Ithaca: Cornell University Press, 1990.

Kamen, Henry. *Inquisition and Society in Spain*. Bloomington: Indiana University Press, 1985.

Kelly, Joan. "Did Women Have a Renaissance?" In *Women, History, and Theory: The Essays of Joan Kelly*, Chicago: University of Chicago Press, 1984, 19–50.

Kraus, Henry. "Eve and Mary: Conflicting Images of Medieval Women." In *Feminism and Art History*, ed. Norma Broude and Mary D. Garrard, 79–99. New York: Harper and Row, 1982.

Lacan, Jacques. *Ecrits: A Selection*. Trans. Alan Sheridan. New York: W. W. Norton, 1977.

———. *The Seminar of Jacques Lacan*. Ed. Jacques-Alain Miller. New York: W. W. Norton, 1988.

Laqueur, Thomas. *Making Sex: Body and Gender from the Greeks to Freud*. Cambridge: Harvard University Press, 1990.

Lea, Henry Charles. *Chapters from the Religious History of Spain Connected with the Inquisition*. Philadelphia: Lea Brothers, 1890.

Le Goff, Jacques. "Corps et idéologie dans l'Occident médiéval: La révolution corporelle." *L'imaginaire médiévale: Essais.* Paris: Gallimard, 1985.

Leonard, Irving A. *Baroque Times in Old Mexico.* Ann Arbor: University of Michigan Press, 1959.

Lezra, Jacques. "Icarus Reading: Trope, Trauma, and Event in Shakespeare, Cervantes, and Descartes." Ph.D. diss., Yale University, 1990.

—————. *Unspeakable Subjects: The Genealogy of the Event in Early Modern Europe.* Stanford: Stanford University Press, 1997.

Lichtenstein, Jacqueline. *La couleur éloquente: Rhétorique et peinture à l'age classique.* Paris: Flammarion, 1989.

—————. "Making Up Representation: The Risks of Femininity." In *Misogyny, Misandry, and Misanthropy,* ed. R. Howard Bloch and Frances Ferguson, 77–87. Berkeley: University of California Press, 1989.

Lockwood O'Donovan, Joan. *Theology of Law and Authority in the English Reformation.* Atlanta: Scholars Press, 1991.

Lope de Vega y Carpio, Félix. *Arte nuevo de hacer comedias en en este tiempo.* Madrid: Viuda de A. Martín, 1621.

—————. *Obras completas.* Madrid: Turner, 1993–97.

López Pinciano, Alonso. *Philosophía antigüa poética.* Ed. Alfredo Carballo Picazo. Madrid: Consejo Superior de Investigaciones Científicas, 1953.

Lovejoy, Arthur. *The Great Chain of Being: A Study of the History of an Idea.* Cambridge: Harvard University Press, 1936.

Lubac, Henri de. *Medieval Exegesis.* Vol. 1. Grand Rapids: Eerdmans, 1998.

Luciani, Frederick. "Octavio Paz on Sor Juana Inés de la Cruz: The Metaphor Incarnate." *Latin American Literary Review* 15, 30 (1987): 6–25.

Ludmer, Josefina. "Tretas del débil." In *La sartén por el mango: Encuentro de escritoras latinoamericanas,* ed. Patricia Elena González and Eliana Ortega, 47–54. Río Piedras: Huracán, 1984.

Maclean, Ian. *The Renaissance Notion of Woman: A Study in the Fortunes of Scholasticism and Medical Science in European Intellectual Life.* Cambridge: Cambridge University Press, 1990.

Maravall, José Antonio. *Teatro y literatura en la sociedad barroca.* Madrid: Seminarios y Ediciones, 1972.

—————. *La cultura del barroco: Análisis de una estructura histórica.* Barcelona: Ariel, 1975.

Mariscal, George. *Contradictory Subjects: Quevedo, Cervantes, and Seventeenth-Century Spanish Culture.* Ithaca: Cornell University Press, 1991.

Mazzotta, Giuseppe. *Dante: Poet of the Desert.* Princeton: Princeton University Press, 1979.

McKendrick, Melveena. *Woman and Society in the Spanish Drama of the Golden Age: A Study of the 'mujer varonil'*. London: Cambridge University Press, 1974.

―――. "Honour/Vengeance in the Comedia: A Case of Mimetic Transference?" *Modern Language Review* 79, 2 (1984): 313–35.

―――. *Theatre in Spain, 1490–1700*. Cambridge: Cambridge University Press, 1989.

Menocal, María Rosa. *Shards of Love: Exile and the Origins of the Lyric*. Durham: Duke University Press, 1994.

Merrim, Stephanie. "*Mores Geometricae:* The 'Womanscript' in the Theater of Sor Juana Inés de la Cruz." In *Feminist Perspectives on Sor Juana*, ed. Stephanie Merrim, 94–123. Detroit: Wayne State University Press, 1991.

Messinger Cypess, Sandra. "Re/Velados en *Los empeños de una casa*." *Hispamérica* 64/65 (1993): 177–85.

Metford, J. C. J. "The Enemies of the Theatre in the Golden Age." *Bulletin of Hispanic Studies* 28 (1951): 76–92.

Montrose, Louis. "The Work of Gender and Sexuality in the Elizabethan Discourse of Discovery." In *Discourses of Sexuality: From Aristotle to AIDS*, ed. Domna C. Stanton, 138–84. Ann Arbor: University of Michigan Press, 1992.

Muriel, Josefina. *Conventos de monjas en la Nueva España*. Mexico: Editorial Santiago, 1946.

―――. *Los recogimientos de mujeres*. Mexico: Universidad Nacional Autónoma de México, 1974.

―――. *Las mujeres de Hispanoamérica: Epoca colonial*. Madrid: Editorial MAPFRE, 1992.

Núñez y Domínguez, J. de J. *Vidas mexicanas*. Mexico: Editorial Xochitl, 1945.

Ortner, Sherry B. "Is Female to Male as Nature Is to Culture?" In *Women, Culture, and Society*, ed. Michelle Zimbalist Rosald and Louise Lamphere, 67–87. Stanford: Stanford University Press, 1974.

Parker, Alexander A. *The Philosophy of Love in Spanish Literature, 1480–1680*. Edinburgh: Edinburgh University Press, 1985.

Parker, Patricia. *Literary Fat Ladies: Rhetoric, Gender, Property*. London: Methuen, 1987.

―――. "Metaphor and Catachresis." In *The Ends of Rhetoric: History, Theory, Practice*, ed. John Bender and David Wellbery, 60–73. Stanford: Stanford University Press, 1990.

Paz, Octavio. *Sor Juana Inés de la Cruz, o Las trampas de la fe*. Mexico: Fondo de Cultura Económica, 1982.

―――――. *Sor Juana, or The Traps of Faith*. Trans. Margaret Sayers Peden. Cambridge: Belknap Press, 1988.

Pelikan, Jaroslav. 1978. *The Christian Tradition: A History of the Development of Doctrine*. Vol. 3, *The Growth of Medieval Theology, 600–1300*. Chicago: University of Chicago Press.

―――――. *The Christian Tradition: A History of the Development of Doctrine*. Vol. 4, *Reformation of Church and Dogma, 1300–1700*. Chicago: University of Chicago Press, 1984.

Peñalosa, Joaquín Antonio. Introduction to Fray Luis de León, *La perfecta casada*. (Mexico: Porrúa, 1985): xvii–xviii.

Perry, Mary Elizabeth. *Gender and Disorder in Early Modern Seville*. Princeton: Princeton University Press, 1990.

Perry, Mary Elizabeth, and Anne J. Cruz. *Cultural Encounters: The Impact of the Spanish Inquisition in Spain and the New World*. Berkeley: University of California Press, 1991.

Pfandl, Ludwig. *Sor Juana Inés de la Cruz, la décima musa de México: Su vida, su poesía, su psique*. Ed. Francisco de la Maza. Mexico: Instituto de Investigaciones Estéticas de la Universidad Nacional Autónoma de México, 1963.

Plath, Sylvia. *The Collected Poems*. New York: Harper, 1995.

Power, David. *The Sacrifice We Offer: The Tridentine Dogma and Its Reinterpretation*. New York: Crossroad, 1987.

Proceso inquisitorial de Fray Luis de León. Ed. Angel Alcalá. Salamanca: Junta de Castilla y León; Consejería de Cultura y Turismo, 1991.

Quevedo, Francisco de. *Vida del Buscón llamado Don Pablos*. Ed. Fernando Lázaro Carreter. Barcelona: Editorial Juventud, 1968.

―――――. *Poesía original completa*. Ed. José Manuel Blecua. Barcelona: Planeta, 1981.

Quiñones, Juan de. *Memorial de Juan de Quiñones dirigido a Fray Antonio de Sotomayor, inquisidor general, sobre el caso de Francisco de Andrada, sospechoso de pertenecer a la raza judía, discutiendo sobre los medios de conocer y distinguir a ella*. Madrid: Biblioteca Nacional, VE, box no. 16, 1632.

Quintilian. *Institutiones oratoriae*. Ed. James J. Murphy. Carbondale: Southern Illinois University Press, 1987.

Rabasa, José. *Inventing America: Spanish Historiography and the Formation of Eurocentrism*. Norman: University of Oklahoma Press, 1993.

Rafael, Vicente. *Contracting Colonialism: Translation and Christian Conversion in Tagalog Society under Early Spanish Rule*. Ithaca: Cornell University Press, 1988.

Recopilación de las leyes destos reynos hecha por mandado de la Magestad

Catholica del Rey Don Philippe segundo, nuestro Señor. Alcalá de Henares, 1569.

Redondi, Pietro. *Galileo: Heretic.* Trans. Raymond Rosenthal. Princeton: Princeton University Press, 1987.

Redondo, Augustín. "Le discours d'exclusion des 'déviants' tenu par l'Inquisition à l'époque de Charles Quint." In *Les problèmes de l'exclusion en Espagne, XVI–XVII siècles,* ed. Augustín Redondo. Paris: Sorbonne, 1983.

Redondo, Augustín, ed. *Les problèmes de l'exclusion en Espagne, XVI–XVII siècles.* Paris: Sorbonne, 1983.

————. *Amours légitimes, Amours illégitimes en Espagne, XVIe–XVIIe siècles.* Paris: Sorbonne, 1985.

————. *Le corps comme métaphore dans l'Espagne des XVIe et XVIIe siècles.* Paris: Sorbonne, 1992.

————. *Le corps dans la société espagnole des XVIe et XVIIe siècles.* Paris: Sorbonne, 1992.

————. *Les représentations de l'autre dans l'espace ibérique et ibéro-américaine.* Paris: Sorbonne, 1993.

Riandère La Roche, Josette. "Du discours d'exclusion des juifs: Anti-judaïsme ou antisémitisme?" In *Les problèmes de l'exclusion en Espagne, XVI–XVII siècles,* ed. Augustín Redondo. Paris: Sorbonne, 1983.

Rivers, Elias L. *Fray Luis de León: The Original Poems.* London: Grant and Cutler, 1983.

Rojas, Fernando de. *La Celestina: Tragicomedia de Calisto y Melibea.* Ed. Dorothy S. Severin. Madrid: Alianza Editorial, 1988.

Rose, Mary Beth, ed. *Women in the Middle Ages and the Renaissance: Literary and Historical Perspectives.* Syracuse: Syracuse University Press, 1986.

Rowe, Katherine. " 'God's handy worke': Divine Complicity and the Anatomist's Touch." In *The Body in Parts: Fantasies of Corporeality in Early Modern Europe,* ed. David Hillman and Carla Mazzio, 285–309. New York: Routledge, 1997.

Ruano de la Haza, José. "Hacia una nueva definición de la tragedia calderoniana." *Bulletin of the Comediantes* 35, 2 (1983): 165–80.

Sabuco de Nantes Barrera, Oliva. *Nueva filosofía de la naturaleza del hombre no conocida ni alcançada de los grandes filósofos antiguos, la cual mejora la vida y salud humana.* Madrid: Librería de los Sucesores de Hernando, 1922.

Sánchez Ortega, Elena. "La mujer en el Antiguo Régimen: Tipos históricos y arquetipos literarios." In *Nuevas perspectivas sobre la mujer: Actas de las primeras jornadas de investigación interdisciplinaria,* 1: 107–26.

Madrid: Seminario de Estudios de la Mujer de la Universidad Autónoma de Madrid, 1982.

Sarduy, Severo. *Barroco*. Buenos Aires: Editorial Sudamericana, 1974.

Scarry, Elaine. *The Body in Pain: The Making and Unmaking of the World*. New York: Oxford University Press, 1985.

————. *Literature and the Body: Essays on Populations and Persons*. Baltimore: Johns Hopkins University Press, 1988.

Schiesari, Juliana. "The Face of Domestication: Physiognomy, Gender Politics, and Humanism's Others." In *Women, "Race," and Writing in the Early Modern Period*, ed. Margo Hendricks and Patricia Parker, 55–72. London: Routledge, 1994.

Severin, Dorothy. *Tragicomedy and Novelistic Discourse in Celestina*. Cambridge: Cambridge University Press, 1989.

Shakespeare, William. *The Riverside Shakespeare*. Ed. Harry Levin et al. Boston: Houghton Mifflin, 1974.

Shergold, N. D., and J. E. Varey, eds. *Teatros y comedias en Madrid, 1698–1699: Estudio y documentos*. London: Tamesis Books, 1979.

Sicroff, Albert A. "The Spanish Obsession." *Midstream*. (spring 1957): 63–76.

Smith, Paul Julian. *Writing in the Margins: Spanish Literature of the Golden Age*. Oxford: Clarendon Press, 1988.

————. *The Body Hispanic: Gender and Sexuality in Spanish and Spanish American Literature*. Oxford: Clarendon Press, 1989.

Soufas, Teresa S. "Calderón's Melancholy Wife-Murderers." *Hispanic Review* 52 (1984): 181–203.

Stallybrass, Peter. "Patriarchal Territories: The Body Enclosed." In *Rewriting the Renaissance: The Discourses of Sexual Difference in Early Modern Europe*, ed. Margaret Ferguson, Maureen Quilligan, and Nancy J. Vickers, 123–42. Chicago: University of Chicago Press, 1986.

Stallybrass, Peter, and Allon White. *The Politics and Poetics of Transgression*. Ithaca: Cornell University Press, 1986.

Stoll, Anita K., and Dawn L. Smith, eds. *The Perception of Women in Spanish Theater of the Golden Age*. Lewisburg: Bucknell University Press, 1991.

Stroud, Matthew. *Fatal Union: A Pluralistic Approach to the Spanish Wife-Murder Comedias*. Lewisburg: Bucknell University Press, 1990.

Suleiman, Susan Rubin, ed. *The Female Body in Western Culture: Contemporary Perspectives*. Cambridge: Harvard University Press, 1986.

Tanner, Tony. *Adultery in the Novel: Contract and Transgression*. Baltimore: Johns Hopkins University Press, 1979.

Tertullian. *The Apparel of Women*. Trans. J. Arbesmann et al. In *Disci-*

plinary, Moral, and Ascetical Works, New York: Fathers of the Church, 1959.

Thompson, Colin P. *The Strife of Tongues.* New York: Cambridge University Press, 1988.

Traub, Valerie. *Desire and Anxiety: Circulations of Sexuality in Shakespearean Drama.* New York: Routledge, 1992.

Viñas Mey, Carmelo. *El problema de la tierra en la España de los siglos XVI y XVII.* Madrid: Consejo Superior de Investigaciones Científicas, 1941.

Vincent, Bernard. "Un espace d'exclusion: La prison inquisitoriale au XVIe siècle." In *Les problèmes de l'exclusion en Espagne, XVI–XVII siècles.* Ed. Augustín Redondo. Paris: Sorbonne, 1983.

Vives, Juan Luis. *Obras completas.* Madrid: Aguilar, 1949.

Walker Bynum, Caroline. *Fragmentation and Redemption: Essays on Gender and the Human Body in Medieval Religion.* New York: Zone Books, 1991.

Wallace, Elizabeth. *Sor Juana Inés de la Cruz: Poetisa de corte y convento.* Mexico: Ediciones Xochitl, 1944.

Wallach Scott, Joan. *Gender and the Politics of History.* New York: Columbia University Press, 1988.

Wardropper, Bruce. "Calderón's Comedy and His Serious Sense of Life." In *Hispanic Studies in Honor of Nicholson B. Adams,* ed. John Esten Keller, 179–93. Chapel Hill: University of North Carolina Press, 1966.

———. "The Dramatization of Figurative Language in the Spanish Theatre." *Yale French Studies* 47 (1982): 189–98.

Weber, Alison. *Teresa of Avila and the Rhetoric of Femininity.* Princeton: Princeton University Press, 1990.

Wilson, Edward M. "Nuevos documentos sobre las controversias teatrales, 1650–1681." In *Actas del Segundo Congreso Internacional de Hispanistas,* ed. Jaime Sánchez Romeralo and Norbert Poulussen, 155–70. Nijmegen: Asociación Internacional de Hispanistas, 1967.

Wofford, Susanne L. "*To You I Give Myself, For I Am Yours:* Erotic Performance and Theatrical Performatives in *As You Like It.*" In *Shakespeare Reread: The Texts in New Contexts,* ed. Russ McDonald, 147–69. Ithaca: Cornell University Press, 1994.

Zamora, Margarita. *Reading Columbus.* Berkeley: University of California Press, 1993.

Index

Accident: "accidents without subject" (Thomist theory of transubstantiation), 34–35, 83, 227 n.47; in Calderón, 46, 109–112, 118, 124, 158, 182, 212; and circumcision, 43; in conduct literature, 20, 47; Covarrubias on, 45, 228 n.48; as female agency, 44–45, 47; in Fray Luis, xiii, 46, 80, 82–84, 97, 211–212, 241 n.41, 243 n.48; in honor plays, 47; and makeup, 250 n.69; scholastic understanding of, 45; in Sor Juana, 46–47, 182, 188, 205, 212; and transubstantiation, 34–35, 45, 226 n.43, 228 n.48

Adultery, 11, 31, 96, 247 n.61; in Calderón, 4, 111; in Cervantes, 23; cosmetic adultery (*see* Makeup: cosmetic adultery); Covarrubias on, 28–29; difficulties of reading, 27–29, 42, 52, 82, 97, 113, 116–117, 120, 147–155, 179, 205, 211–212; in Fray Luis, 56, 58, 93, 96, 211; and honor code, 4, 42; and honor plays, 16–17, 19, 115, 228 n.50; of husband, 145, 255 n.7, 267 n.49; and idolatry, 28–29, 222–223 n.28, 223 n.29; in Lope de Vega, 23, 257 n.12; as penetration of husband's body, 115, 135, 197, 258 n.17; punishment for, 19, 27, 38, 114 (*see also* Wife: wife-murder in

honor plays); as threat to blood purity, 115, 223 n.28

Alfonso X, el Sabio, 40–41, 88, 114

Alumbrados, 141, 264 n.39

Ambrose, Saint, 98, 102, 251 n.69

Amerindians, x, 8, 38–39, 202, 204. *See also* Other, body of

Analogy: in Calderón, 132, 148, 150, 258 n.17; Thomas Aquinas and, 76, 241–242 n.43; *See also* León, Fray Luis de: and analogy

Arcipreste de Hita (Juan Ruiz), 14, 84

Arenal, Electa, 169, 220 n.19

Aristotle, 29, 34, 46, 52, 207, 211, 245 n.54, 259 n.24, 261 n.30

Armstrong, Nancy, and Leonard Tennenhouse, 13

Augustine, Saint, xiii, 46, 52, 76, 246–247 n.59, 250–251 n.69; in Fray Luis, 237 n.27, 238 n.29, 240 n.39; and sign theory, 72, 81, 241 n.40

Bainton, Roland H., 228–229 n.51

Baptismal sacrament, x, 8, 38–40, 43–44, 202

Baroque, 35, 74, 213–214, 257 n.13, 281 n.12, 282 n.14; and Calderón, 139, 213; and sign theory, 27, 31, 222 n.26, 281 n.13; and Sor Juana, 46, 171, 179, 186, 193, 213

Georgina Dopico Black is Associate Professor in the
Department of Spanish and Portuguese at New York
University. She edited, with Roberto González Echevarría,
En un lugar de la Mancha: Estudios cervantinos
en honor de Manuel Durán, published by
Ediciones Almar in 1999.

Library of Congress Cataloging-in-Publication Data

Dopico Black, Georgina.
Perfect wives, other women : adultery and Inquisition in early
modern Spain / Georgina Dopico Black.
p. cm.
Includes bibliographical references and index.
ISBN 0-8223-2650-7 (cloth : alk. paper) —
ISBN 0-8223-2642-6 (pbk. : alk. paper)
1. Adultery—Spain—History. 2. Wives—Spain—History.
3. Inquisition—Spain—History. I. Title.
HO806 .D66 2001
306.73'6'0946—dc21   00-057814